SCHOOL IMPROVEMENT PROGRAMS

A Handbook for Educational Leaders

SCHOOL IMPROVEMENT PROGRAMS

A Handbook for Educational Leaders

James H. Block

Susan Toft Everson

Thomas R. Guskey

New York • Toronto • London • Auckland • Sydney

Copyright ©1995 by Scholastic Inc.

No part of this publication may be reproduced in whole or in part, or stored in a retrieval system, or transmitted in any form or by any means, electronic, mechanical, photocopying, recording, or otherwise, without permission of the publisher. For information regarding permission, write to Scholastic Inc., 555 Broadway, New York, NY 10012.

ISBN 0-590-49501-1

12 11 10 9 8 7 6 5 4 3 2 1   1 2 3 4 5/9

Printed in the U.S.A.

Library of Congress Cataloging-in-Publication Data

School improvement programs: a handbook for educational leaders /
   [edited by] James H. Block, Susan Toft Everson, Thomas R. Guskey.
    p.   cm.
   Includes bibliographical references (p.) and index.
   ISBN 0-590-49501-1
    1. School improvement programs—United States. 2. School management and organization—United States. 3. Educational innovations—United States. I. Block, James H. II. Everson, Susan Toft. III. Guskey, Thomas R.
LB2822.S36   1994
371.2'00973—dc20   93-37824
                                                                          CIP

Designed by Joan Gazdik Gillner
Production by Editorial Service and Publications Management

To All Children:

Ours Drive Us Forward

BILLY

CHRISTOPHER

COURTNEY

JENNIFER

MICHAEL

CONTENTS

Preface xi

Acknowledgements xvii

Contributors xix

PART I:
INTRODUCTION TO SCHOOL IMPROVEMENT PROGRAMS 1

   Chapter 1 — School Improvement:
   A Program Perspective.
      James H. Block, *University of California, Santa Barbara* 3

PART II:
A MENU OF SCHOOL IMPROVEMENT PROGRAMS 19

   LEARNING INNOVATIONS 23

   Chapter 2 — Cooperative Learning.
      David W. Johnson and Roger T. Johnson,
      University of Minnesota 25

   Chapter 3 — Critical Thinking.
      Robert J. Marzano, *Mid-continent Regional*
      Educational Laboratory, Denver 57

   Chapter 4 — Interactive Learning
   and Hypermedia Technology.
      Robert Bortnick, *Elk Grove (IL) School District 59* 77

   Chapter 5 — Mastery Learning.
      Thomas R. Guskey, *University of Kentucky* 91

   TEACHING INNOVATIONS 109

   Chapter 6 — Assessment as a School
   Improvement "Innovation"?
      Richard J. Stiggins, *Assessment Training Institute* 111

Chapter 7 — Direct Instruction to Accelerate Cognitive Growth.
Douglas Carnine, Bonnie Grossen, and Jerry Silbert, *University of Oregon* 129

Chapter 8 — Instructional Alignment.
S. Alan Cohen, *University of San Francisco* 153

Chapter 9 — Mastery Teaching.
Madeline Hunter, *University of California, Los Angeles* 181

Chapter 10 — Peer Coaching: Quality Through Collaborative Work.
Pam Robbins, *Private Educational Consultant* 205

Chapter 11 — Teaching for Literacy.
Peter Winograd, Connie Bridge, *University of Kentucky* 229

Chapter 12 — Writing Across the Curriculum.
Carol Dixon, Harold Horn, *University of California, Santa Barbara* 247

SCHOOLING INNOVATIONS 265

Chapter 13 — Learning from Accelerated Schools.
Henry M. Levin, *Stanford University* 267

Chapter 14 — Early Childhood Education.
David P. Weikart, *High/Scope Research Foundation* 289

Chapter 15 — Effective Schools: The Evolving Research and Practices.
Lawrence W. Lezotte, *Effective Schools Products* 313

Chapter 16 — Invitational Education.
William W. Purkey, *University of North Carolina, Greensboro* ...343

Chapter 17 — Outcome-based Education: From Instructional Reform to Paradigm Restructuring.
William G. Spady, *The High Success Network* 367

Chapter 18 — The Quality School.
William Glasser, *Institute for Reality Therapy* 399

Chapter 19 — The School Development Program.
James P. Comer, *Yale University* 415

PART III:
SELECTING AND INTEGRATING
SCHOOL IMPROVEMENT PROGRAMS 431

Chapter 20 — Selecting School Improvement Programs.
Susan Toft Everson, *Mid-continent Regional Educational Laboratory* 433

Chapter 21 — Integrating School Improvement Programs.
Thomas R. Guskey, *University of Kentucky* 453

Collected References 473

Author Index 497

Subject Index 503

PREFACE

The idea for this volume sprang from two events in the mid 1980s. One was the 1984 publication of Benjamin S. Bloom's seminal article "The search for methods of group instruction as effective as one-to-one tutoring" in the professional journal *Educational Leadership*. The other was the 1986 publication of the American Educational Research Association's third edition of the influential *Handbook of Research on Teaching* (Wittrock, 1986).

The first event signaled to us how far educational research had come over the last decade in addressing matters of schooling practice. In this article, Bloom reviewed some of the major practical concepts and techniques that educational researchers had proposed might make a difference in student learning and then estimated how much difference each variable typically made when used. Interestingly, those ideas and practices that made the most difference in student learning were ones directly under educator control—curriculum building, teaching, and testing. Moreover, many of these ideas and practices seemed combinable with others to make even more pronounced differences in the future. So—Bloom challenged educators to combine them so as to realize in virtually all students, under ordinary group-based classroom conditions, the learning we have historically realized for only our best students, under special tutorial conditions. He alluded to this challenge as solving the *two-sigma problem* in student learning.

Each of the editors eagerly accepted Bloom's challenge, and in our national and international staff development work, we concentrated on helping educators solve the *two-sigma problem* with their schooling. We worked to help them understand those powerful research-based concepts and techniques that they controlled and integrate them into their school and classroom lives. We eagerly awaited, too, the latest findings on these and even newer research-based concepts and practices so that we might target our staff development work still closer to meeting Bloom's challenge.

But the second event temporarily dashed our hopes. Though thirteen years had passed between publication of the *Second Handbook* and the *Third* and though a variety of research-based schooling, curriculum-building, teaching, and testing innovations had been developed in the interim, most of these innovations went unmentioned. Even the best-known of these innovations, such as mastery learning and cooperative learning, received scant treatment. And lesser-known but hugely popular and influential innovations such as Madeline Hunter's mastery teaching and William Glasser's quality schooling received only a handful or two of citations in over one thousand double-columned pages of text!

Since all three of the editors were deeply convinced by their staff development experience that greater progress in linking research to practice had been made than the substance of the *Third Handbook* acknowledged and since we believed that greater progress needed to be made yet, we began to assemble a volume that would showcase certain research-based school improvement innovations that the *Handbook* had overlooked. At the admonition of many of the original developers of these innovations, such as Albert Mamary of the outcome-based education movement, we strived for a volume that would *compliment* the strengths of each innovation and yet recognize their difference in respective strengths. We also wanted a volume that would suggest how these differences might be *complemented*.

Preface

This book that has emerged is intended to help school leaders understand and use major research-based school improvement programs. We present here some of the best of these innovative programs and provide some first steps, some heuristics, for selecting and integrating certain of them into your own particular school improvement gestalt.

The book is divided into three parts. Part I attempts to do for the concept of school improvement *programs* what other works have already done for the concept of school improvement *processes* (Fullan & Stiegelbauer, 1991; Goodlad, 1984). That is, this part rationalizes your study of programs as fundamental tools of school improvement and change. Remember that to some colleagues, your serious consideration of any program will seem a leadership act not of rationality but of irrationality instead. Indeed, these colleagues may even insinuate that you must be a little bit crazy. Part I should give you some ammunition to respond that you are crazy like a fox!

Part II describes some major school improvement programs, innovations selected on the basis of our 70+ years of combined experience in working with savvy school leaders such as yourself. We had been concerned that the founders of these programs never had a common forum for presenting their particular innovation in their own terms. So we asked each founder or a founder-identified spokesperson to describe:

1. What his or her innovation is;
2. How it works;
3. How well it works;
4. Where it is headed.

PREFACE

We figured that each founder/spokesperson would provide kinds of intentions, insights, data, and directions about his or her innovation that only a loving parent might possess. We also figured that each might write about his or her innovation with a passion that other writers might not possess. While such passion might, in some cases, border on what some readers might consider mere self-promotion, we were willing to take this risk.

Our resulting menu consists of the following school improvement programs and would have included others (e.g., learning styles) had their busy founders/spokespersons not had other writing commitments. We have judged and classfied the programs as to whether each primarily focuses on changing schools by affecting how school leaders perceive learners and their learning, teachers and their teaching, or schools and their schooling. We have then presented the programs within each category in alphabetical order.

LEARNING	TEACHING	SCHOOLING
COOPERATIVE LEARNING	ASSESSMENT	ACCELERATED SCHOOLS
CRITICAL THINKING	DIRECT INSTRUCTION	EARLY CHILDHOOD EDUCATION
INTERACTIVE LEARNING	INSTRUCTIONAL ALIGNMENT	EFFECTIVE SCHOOLS
MASTERY LEARNING	MASTERY TEACHING	INVITATIONAL EDUCATION
	PEER COACHING	OUTCOME BASED EDUCATION
	TEACHING FOR LITERACY	QUALITY SCHOOLS
	WRITING ACROSS CURRICULUM	SCHOOL DEVELOPMENT PROGRAM

Part III provides help in selecting and integrating some of the programs from this menu. For purposes of selection, the initial chapter of this section develops some general guidelines for managing planned change. It then develops a planned change decision-making process against which the potential of each of our program entrees can be assessed. These guidelines and this process are drawn from the experience of one of the editors as a staff developer for a leading federal educational research and development laboratory—the Mid-continent Regional Educational Laboratory—deeply concerned with matters of translating theory and research into practice. Since the guidelines and the process are firmly grounded in research on and experience with planned school improvement and change, they should help in making more informed choices about each program's value for your particular schooling situation.

As shall be seen at the end of this chapter, each of our menu entrees emphasizes some aspects of the schooling process and de-emphasizes or ignores others. No one program is, therefore, likely to serve all your school improvement needs, and several programs may need to be integrated to meet your desires. So, for purposes of integration, the next chapter in Part III will provide some heuristics for linking the concepts and techniques of one program to those of other ones and some sample applications of these heuristics. These heuristics and applications are drawn from the experience of another of the editors as a leader in staff development nationally and internationally. Admittedly, the heuristics are still rough and, hence, the applications will seem somewhat unrefined. Still, they should help stimulate you to think about how various programs might supplement and complement one another and to generate a school improvement plan whose whole is more than the sum of its individual programmatic parts.

PREFACE

We hope you, the school leader, find this organization helpful. The stakes in school improvement and change are higher than ever before, especially for our kids. If this book can help just a few school leaders like yourself to understand, to select, and to integrate some of our menu of research-based learning-teaching-schooling programs as part of your school improvement gestalt, then the volume will have served its purpose.

J.H.B.
Santa Barbara, CA

ACKNOWLEDGEMENTS

The microcomputer was supposed to revolutionize book writing and publishing. Well, it has in that authors are now more dependent than ever on a whole host of people. We are no exception.

First, we would like to thank the technical support people at the University of California, Santa Barbara, Department of Education for their gracious giving of time and expertise. We had some twenty different manuscripts that had to be converted from their authors' hardware and software to our own. Barbara Hamill and Alan Moses accomplished these conversions with efficiency and with good-humored jibes about the senior author's penchant for outdated technology.

Second, we would like to acknowledge the administrative support people at UCSB. Priscilla Drum, Department Chair, has graciously allowed the senior author access to technical and secretarial staff at a time of severe budgetary constraints. Jeanne Chambers, Department Management Service Office, has equally graciously made sure that that access was reasonable and fair.

Third, we would like to recognize our collegial support staff at UCSB and at McREL/Kansas City. At McRel, Sandy Berger was instrumental in providing substantive feedback to the authors as the volume unfolded, and Diane Wilber and Rosalie Alagna were kind enough to package that feedback and pass it on. Even though the Laboratory was in the process of consolidating and moving, Sandy, Diane, and Rosalie never let their anxieties add to our own. At UCSB, Ken Hazelip was central in providing substantive and bibliographic assistance to the authors; Dr. Laura Wilde, Dr. Min Bista, and Tim Quiroz provided additional substantive and editorial assistance and were kind enough to read and critique each manuscript as part of a hands-on class in school reform.

Finally, we would like to praise the secretarial support staff here at UCSB. Elaine Nicklanovich allowed the frequent intrusions of the senior author into her office to use her pencil sharpener; she helped with some bibliographic work, too. Robin Stark lent her wit and experience to word processing early in the project and at the project's close; in between, she left to complete a more important project of her own—a baby boy. Jovita Huerta was instrumental in word processing at the project's close; her friendship and demeanor calmed more than one troubled water in the sea of word processing. Lastly, Hildegard Lagerquist was the project's soul and spirit from beginning to end. Hildy kept track of the day-to-day details of book organization and production and, more than once, helped the senior author keep track of himself, too. Often, toward the project's end, she would stay after hours, keeping her husband waiting for dinner. We thank you, Hildy, for your time, expertise, loyalty, and dedication. The latter traits, especially, betoken the special human touch and dignity you have brought to a taxing effort.

Thanks again to all of you!

CONTRIBUTORS

BLOCK, JAMES H., Professor, Department of Education, University of California, Santa Barbara, Santa Barbara, CA 93106

BORTNICK, ROBERT M., Associate Superintendent, Elk Grove School District #59, 2123 South Arlington Heights Road, Arlington Heights, IL 60005

BRIDGE, CONNIE, Professor and Associate Dean for Educational Reform and Research, College of Education, University of Kentucky, Lexington, KY 40506

CARNINE, DOUGLAS, Professor, School of Education, University of Oregon, 805 Lincoln Street, Eugene, OR 97401

COHEN, S. ALAN, Professor, College of Education, University of San Francisco, Ignation Heights, 2130 Fulton Street, San Francisco, CA 94117

COMER, JAMES P., Maurice Falk Professor of Child Psychiatry, Yale Child Study Center, 230 S. Frontage Road, P.O. Box 207900, New Haven, CT 06520–7900.

DIXON, CAROL N., Senior Lecturer, Graduate School of Education, University of California, Santa Barbara, Santa Barbara, CA 93106

EVERSON, SUSAN TOFT, Director of School Improvement Services, Mid-continent Regional Educational Laboratory, 3100 Broadway, Suite 209, Kansas City, MO 64111

GLASSER, WILLIAM, President, The Institute for Reality Therapy, 7301 Medical Center Drive, Canoga Park, CA 93107

GROSSEN, BONNIE, Research Associate, School of Education, University of Oregon, 805 Lincoln Street, Eugene, OR 97401

GUSKEY, THOMAS R., Professor, College of Education, University of Kentucky, Lexington, KY 40506

HORN, HAROLD, Fellow, South Coast Writing Project, Graduate School of Education, University of California, Santa Barbara, Santa Barbara, CA 93106

Contributors

HUNTER, MADELINE M., Senior Lecturer Emeritus, School of Education, University of California, Los Angeles, Moore Hall 228-B, 405 Hilgard Avenue, Los Angeles, CA 90024

JOHNSON, DAVID W., School of Education, University of Minnesota, 202 Pattee Hall, 150 Pillsbury Drive S. E., Minneapolis, MN 55455

JOHNSON, ROGER T., School of Education, University of Minnesota, 202 Pattee Hall, 150 Pillsbury Drive S. E., Minneapolis, MN 55455

LEVIN, HENRY M., Professor and Director, Accelerated Schools Project, Stanford University, 402 CERAS, Stanford, CA 94305

LEZOTTE, LAWRENCE W., Senior Vice President, Effective Schools Products, 2199 Jolly Road, Suite 160, Okemos, MI 48864

MARZANO, ROBERT J., Director of Research, Mid-continent Regional Educational Laboratory, 2550 S. Parker Rd., Suite 500, Aurora, CO 80014

PURKEY, WILLIAM W., Professor, School of Education, University of North Carolina, Greensboro, Greensboro, NC 27412

ROBBINS, PAM, Private Educational Consultant, 2371 Stonehouse Drive, Napa, CA 94558

SILBERT, JERRY, Research Associate, School of Education, University of Oregon, 805 Lincoln Street, Eugene, OR 97401

SPADY, WILLIAM G., Director, The High Success Network, Inc., P. O. Box 1630, Eagle, CO 81631

STIGGINS, RICHARD J., Assessment Training Institute, 215 S.W. Washington Street, Portland, OR 97204

WEIKART, DAVID P., President, High/Scope Educational Research Foundation, 600 North River Street, Ypsilanti, MI 48198

WINOGRAD, PETER, Professor, College of Education, University of Kentucky, Lexington, KY 40506

PART I

Introduction to School Improvement Programs

School Improvement: A Program Perspective

James H. Block
University of California, Santa Barbara

Coursing across American public schools are some innovative school improvement programs. What is important about these programs is not their popularity, for the mass appearance and then disappearance of popular innovations are common in American educational history (Cuban, 1990; Warren, 1990). No, what is important is these innovations' bold style and substance.

These programs are *core* (Thompson, 1967). That is, each assumes that public schools were established to perform some basic societal function, namely, to provide free, universal, and quality mass education. So each program concentrates on reforming/restructuring public schooling's essential technologies—curriculum building, teaching, and/or testing—for performing that core function.

These programs are *big*. Each offers optimistic beliefs about learners, teachers, and schools—beliefs about all students' capacities to learn well, fast, and/or confidently; beliefs about all teachers' capacities to teach excellently, quickly, and/or humanely; and beliefs about all schools' capacities to educate effectively, efficiently, and/or invitingly. Each offers, too, an amalgam of ideas and techniques for realizing these beliefs, an amalgam that forms a scaffolding for the conduct of a particular school's curriculum-building, teaching, or testing affairs. This scaffolding is specific enough to suggest some general school reform/restructuring tasks, yet general enough to allow school leaders to accomplish these tasks in their own specific ways.

These programs are *research-based*. While these bases may not meet the methodological criteria of some researchers (e.g., Guskey, 1992), they do meet the action criteria of practitioners—they are useful and seem to make a difference. School leaders know that each program has been implemented by colleagues under actual school conditions. They further know that these colleagues have generated some kind of locally validated evidence that the program worked.

These programs are *institutionalized* (Miles, 1983). In a discipline often more concerned with passing bandwagons, these programs have become ingrained in the schooling woodwork. Most have a decade or more of work behind them dealing with development, dissemination, and implementation. Most also have local, regional, and national networks of practitioners and researchers who continue to elaborate each program's beliefs and techniques.

WHY NOW?

There was a time, not so long ago, when *core, big, research-based*, and *institutionalized* improvement programs were, of course, not a major concern for many public school leaders.

Leaders were supposed to focus instead on smaller units of change than the entire school, especially on certain individuals. They were also supposed to be turning their attention from the problems of improvement to the possibilities of public school replacement, especially those proffered by private schools or the business community. They were supposed to look, too, beyond specific programs to generic processes for their school improvement salvation.

Why, then, should these programs hold such a prominent place in the thinking of some of America's savviest school leaders today? My experience with the programs of mastery learning and outcome-based education (see Block, Efthim, & Burns, 1989) suggests that four historical factors shaped these leaders' thinking:

1. *problems* at the public schooling's core;
2. *policymakers'* attempts to tamper with this core;
3. *professionals'* reactions to this tampering; and
4. *possibilities* for professionals to act as policymakers themselves.

CORE TECHNOLOGY PROBLEMS

Like others (Murphy, 1990; Passow, 1990), I believe that current interest in certain school improvement programs is more than some knee-jerk reaction to another galvanizing event in recent educational history (e.g., release of *A Nation at Risk* [1983]). It is, rather, a reaction to chronic, largely unresolved problems in public schooling that has been building from the late fifties.

Elsewhere I have recounted four of these problems (Block, Efthim, & Burns, 1989). Two have bedeviled public school leaders in the student learning arena—the promotion of more *excellence* and more *equity*. School leaders have still largely been unable to promote excellence without sacrificing equity or equity without sacrificing excellence. The other two problems have bedeviled them in the student teaching arena—the promotion of greater *economy* and greater *excitement*. School leaders have still largely been unable to promote economy without sacrificing excitement or excitement without sacrificing economy.

The significance of these chronic teaching-learning problems lay, I contend, not so much in their technical aspects, though there were clearly issues of substance (i.e., "know what") and form (i.e., "know how") involved, but rather in their moral ones (cf. Sergiovanni, 1992). By the 1980s, these problems were widely perceived to have undermined the moral legitimacy of American public schools. In essence, they exposed basic flaws at the institution's core, flaws that fed public concerns as to whether schools should be trusted and funded any longer to teach this or any future generation of American youngsters.

STATE-LEVEL POLICYMAKERS

I suspect that even obvious core problems during the eighties might have been finessed by America's public school leaders of the nineties. After all, Americans had been historically rather forgiving with their public schools' teaching-learning shortfalls. Most still viewed their public schools from a local perspective as an asset whose overall community value should offset even serious flaws.

But as the moral legitimacy of the public school was called into question, the institution itself became vulnerable to nonlocal meddling in local affairs. National pressure groups of all stripes and colors began to invite other American social institutions to press public schools to either put up or shut up in matters of mass teaching and learning. Business, together with federal, state, and local legislative, judicial, and executive institutions, was especially courted. Some groups even went so far as to suggest that if public schools could not be pressed to put up, they should be shut down. For these groups, various forms of private, not public, schools represented the future of schooling across the nation.

Central in this meddling process was a new breed of educational specialists—educational evaluators and public policy analysts (Haveman, 1987)—whose training reflected a special concern for moral matters of values. Unparalleled federal interventions into public schooling during the late fifties through the early seventies had provided these specialists a field day to sharpen their valuing skills. And, by and large, the specialists did not like what they saw. Local variation in the implementation and effectiveness of national programs from one setting to the next seemed too great (Berman & McLaughlin, 1978). So not content with simply sinking local implementations that perhaps should have been sunk, these specialists began to try shaping more standardized replacements. In short, they began to attempt to help make federal educational public policy rather than to just evaluate it.

Fortunately, these late seventies and early eighties federal-level educational public policymakers still seemed sensitive to the widespread belief that schooling was ultimately a local affair. So even their suggested federal interventions tended to leave the core technologies of local schooling largely unscathed. Indeed, most of these specialists' suggested public policy pronouncements about local school improvement seemed more concerned with *circumscribing* the school inputs and learner outputs of the teaching-learning process than with *prescribing* the process itself.

But in the early eighties as these federal-level policymakers began a hasty retreat from even framing the schooling process (Boyd, 1990), their state-level counterparts began to step into the breech. Styling their statehouses as being more conversant with local educational matters than the White House, they began to tread where their federal counterparts largely had not and to meddle more with the local schooling process itself. Notably, they began to become more and more prescriptive about the core of schooling itself, especially its curriculum-building/teaching/learning technologies.

Elsewhere, Thomas Guskey and I (Guskey & Block, 1991) have chronicled one example of this growing prescriptiveness from the state of Missouri (see Honig, 1990, for another example from California). There, about 1980, state educational policymakers began a decade-long incursion into their public schools' core affairs.

Dissatisfied that Missouri's schools were not consistently delivering the free, universal, and quality public education that all students deserved, the State Board of Education began the ball rolling by prodding the state Department of Elementary and Secondary Education (DESE) to reform/restructure schools statewide. DESE responded by suggesting a generic prescription for improved teaching within the state — an Instructional Management System — followed by some name brand teaching/learning options — the school improvement programs of Curriculum Alignment, Instructional Alignment, Mastery Learning, and Cooperative Learning. State legislators then kept the ball rolling by passing a 1985 Excellence in Education Act that gave DESE legal mandates for making additional generic and name brand prescriptions in the areas of curriculum building and testing. Out of these mandates came the *Missouri Core Competencies and Key Skills* curriculum guides and the *Missouri Mastery and Achievement Tests*, early stabs at implementing statewide the school improvement programs of Outcome-based Education and Assessment.

While these intrusions were perceived by state-level policymakers as being relatively benign (indeed, DESE officials were careful to stress that this state-level package of curriculum building, teaching, and testing reforms should be thought of as only a skeleton for local reform), many local educational authorities nevertheless felt state-level havoc being wreaked at their local-level schooling doors. And even when this skeleton proved to be helpful and successful for a large number of local districts and schools, still a number of Missouri school leaders took pains to keep it in the closet. What some leaders called a miracle in cities like Springfield and Jefferson City was more like a mirage in cities like St. Louis and Kansas City.

PROFESSIONALS

In some ways, I could stop here in describing how certain *core, big, research-based,* and *institutionalized* school improvement programs have worked their way into the thinking of many public school leaders. Effectively, what these state-level prescriptions for local educational reform did was to hold public school practitioners' feet still closer to the moral fire of educational "accountability." And there is no question in my mind that some current interest in these innovations simply stems from certain school leaders' cynical attempts to get state educational policymakers off their backs. Indeed, each of this volume's contributors can probably cite examples of their program being seized as window dressing by these leaders and pushed down from the principal's or central office as a panacea with little concern for teacher interpretation and buy-in. And like other top-down innovations that fail to allow local tailoring (McLaughlin, 1976), such program applications have invariably struggled and given their program developers and supporters more than one professional black eye.

To stop here, though, would be to shortchange those savvy public school leaders who had more fundamental reasons for using certain of these school improvement programs. State-level public policymakers' meddling in local classroom practitioners' teaching-learning affairs during the eighties generated, I contend, a collective practitioner identity crisis (cf. Smith, Dwyer, Prunty, & Kleine, 1987, on the link between school change and professional identity) because while federal policymakers' mandates could be largely ignored because they rarely touched the core of practitioners' work, state policymakers' mandates increasingly could not.

So, what were simple issues of moral accountability for the policymakers became complex issues of professional vulnerability for practitioners. Teachers and other certified classroom personnel began to re-experience an old schism between doing the kind of work that others wanted done and doing the kinds they wanted to do. Scholars (e.g., Schlechty, 1976) refer to this schism as acting like a bureaucrat or a professional (see Sirotnik, 1985, for some acting characteristics). I prefer to call it acting like a public employee or a professional.

Now, while many classroom practitioners essentially resolved this schism by choosing one identity over the other, a growing number refused to react in such an either/or fashion. Indeed, these latter staff members began to proact in a bold, new, both/and manner. Recognizing that their profession was on the line, these practitioners mobilized to reclaim moral control over the conduct of their classrooms' core affairs. In essence, these classroom professionals began to style themselves not just as educational public policy brokers but as policymakers instead. They realized that if state-level officials can form public educational policy through core *mandates*, then so can professionals form policy through their core *actions*.

POSSIBILITIES

Certain savvy school leaders, I propose, sensed this growing yearning among some of their teaching staff for more professional control over the emergent school reform/restructuring public policy agenda. These leaders recognized that their policy-making-oriented, classroom-level professionals wanted to be *publicly accountable* and, hence, better public employees. The staff members were already paying closer attention to the issues foremost in the minds of state-level policymakers, especially issues of quality schooling for all. Moreover, they were realizing that their current core ideas and techniques provided quality schooling for only the few and were already turning to alternative ideas and techniques for reforming/restructuring the core. Common core/integrated curriculum ideas and techniques (e.g., critical thinking, writing across the curriculum, teaching for literacy) now made more sense to them than tracked/disintegrated ones. So did teaching ideas and techniques that favored the many (e.g., cooperative learning and mastery learning/teaching; direct and aligned instruction; accelerated, effective, and developed schools; early childhood and outcome-based education) rather than the few. Testing techniques that develop talent (e.g., authentic, performance-based assessment) made more sense than those that simply select it, too.

These school leaders also recognized that their policy-making-oriented, classroom-level professionals wanted to be more *self-determined* (Deci, 1980) and, hence, better practitioners, too. Part of becoming more self-determined involved becoming more *skillful* and hence more "response-able" with regard to core matters. Part also involved becoming more *willful* and hence more "responsible," too. So their staff members were already searching hard for additional valid and reliable ideas and techniques of curriculum building, teaching, and testing, especially ones that would empower them in the process. They seemed especially drawn to intrinsically motivating ideas and techniques (e.g., interactive and invitational learning, peer coaching, and quality schooling), for such ideas and techniques made teaching seem more fun and less work. These concepts and practices challenged their current skill levels; made them curious about core theory, research, and practice; offered real or perceived chances for control of core development and delivery; and/or provided an element of fantasy to their professional existence (see Malone and Lepper, 1986). They also offered numerous opportunities for collegial discussion, deliberation, and collaboration (Joyce, Weil, & Showers, 1992).

Accordingly, these savvy school leaders chose specific school improvement programs for voluntary adoption consideration to further prime their respective staffs' *classroom professional as public policymaker* stirrings. While on the surface, many of these programs seemed to have little in common, underneath each shared features that seemed to encourage the possibility of more of their staff members thinking of themselves as being *publicly accountable, yet professionally self-determined practitioners, too.*

Earlier, I noted some of these shared features. I highlighted that these specific school improvement programs are *core, big, research-based,* and *institutionalized.*

Core programs are obviously important from the perspective of the classroom professional as policymaker. If policymakers distrust public school professionals to be accountable around the core, and if professionals feel vulnerable because of this mistrust, then obviously more professional focus on reforming/restructuring the core seems warranted. Such focus sends messages to policymakers that the public professionals who should care, do care about schooling matters of concern to their constituency and themselves. In an era when the mind-sets of professionals and policymakers seem so different (Shavelson, 1988), such messages are critical to establishing what I have elsewhere called political alignment (Block, 1991). In essence, they say that professionals and policymakers are on similar schooling wavelengths and ready to talk and to act in common terms about the public good.

Whereas core programs allow classroom professionals to address policymakers' concerns with issues of public accountability, big programs allow them to address professional self-determination issues of willfulness. Big programs are morally, technically, and intrinsically motivating.

These programs' optimistic beliefs about learners, teachers, and schools offer hope. Day in and day out, their classroom users are reminded that there are differences to be made in all students and that they can make them. Such hope has invariably led to a climate in which change is routinely expected, regardless of the school's surroundings. Such climate, in turn, has generated a spirit for school reform/restructuring that animates professionals toward collective thought, feeling, and action for the school's good even when outside or inside realities make such reform/restructuring appear to be hopeless.

These programs' variety, coupled with their scaffold-like nature, also provides choices, especially ones about various curriculum, teaching, and testing concepts and techniques. Such choices have challenged their classroom users to stretch professionally. When these stretches have worked, the practitioners usually have felt more in control of their careers and have often exercised that control in new directions by stretching again. And when the stretches have not worked, the practitioners have usually been curious as to why and to how to stretch in the future.

While big programs address professional self-determination concerns of willfulness, research-based ones tackle concerns of skillfulness. Each program offers a set of ideas and techniques and local, regional, or national mentors that have all been tested in the crucible of practice. So each offers both distinct, workable possibilities and people for providing professional staff development. This development can usually take place at a variety of schooling sectors—elementary, secondary, or tertiary; of schooling levels—classroom, school, district, or state; of teaching expertise—novices or veterans; and of subject matter specialization—single or multiple subjects.

Lastly, institutionalizable programs speak to issues of public accountability and self-determination over time. Such programs demand users who are skillful and committed professionals, people who will do more than simply graze on a set of ideas and techniques and who will continue to use them in the absence of mandates or even key personnel. The development of such professionals, especially committed ones, requires a long-term, systematic commitment to change. While one-shot approaches to professional development, and even scatter-shot ones, may suffice for purposes of innovation, repeated-shot, targeted approaches such as coaching are required for purposes of institutionalization.

SUMMARY

This chapter has addressed the question of why certain innovative programs of school improvement, such as the menu that follows in Part II, are now so prominent in the current school reform/restructuring landscape. I have proposed that these programs possess a certain style and substance for responding to a set of issues that has been bubbling in American education since at least the 1950s and that came to a head in the 1980s.

As for their style and substance, I have suggested that these programs possess four essential characteristics. They are *core* in that they focus on one or more of the basic technologies of schooling—curriculum building, teaching, and/or testing—so that public schools can continue to perform their basic societal function of providing free, universal, and quality mass education. They are *big* in that they are optimistic in their beliefs about all students' capacities to learn, all teachers' capacities to teach, and all schools' capacities to educate and in that they provide a generous scaffolding of ideas and techniques for realizing these beliefs. They are *research-based* in that they have been used and seemed to make a difference under actual school conditions. And they are *institutionalized* in that they offer both time-tested processes and practitioners for their development, dissemination, and implementation.

As for the issues to which these programs respond, I have contended that they are a response to a string of historical factors. One was some chronic problems that by the 1980s were widely perceived as challenging the moral legitimacy of public schools. These mass teaching-learning problems had exposed serious flaws at our public schools' core and occasioned serious public concern as to whether local schools should be trusted and funded to educate America's youth.

Two was first federal and then state-level educational public policymakers' attempts to tamper with this core. Whereas the feds tried to move circumscriptively to clean up this core mess, their state-level counterparts were bolder and moved more prescriptively. Working under the moral mantle of educational accountability, these policymakers began to meddle at the technical core of local public school practice itself, especially classroom curriculum building, teaching, and testing affairs.

Three was the local classroom professionals' reactions to all this tampering. This meddling raised public school classroom practitioners' vulnerabilities and provoked an identity conflict between acting like a public employee or like a professional. While some school staff members resolved this conflict by becoming either better public employees or better professionals, a growing number seemed to want to become both. These latter staff members yearned to become better classroom professionals as public policymakers themselves and to seize more professional control over the emergent school reform/restructuring agenda.

Four was the possibilities that savvy school leaders saw in *core, big, research-based,* and *institutionalized* school improvement programs to further prime their staffs' *classroom professional as policymaker stirrings*. At the center of these stirrings was a concern for building a profession that was publicly accountable, yet self-determined, too. These leaders recognized that:

- *core* programs allow classroom professionals to address issues of public accountability;
- *big* and *research-based* programs allow them to address issues of professional self-determination; and
- *institutionalized* programs allow them to address issues of public accountability and professional self-determination over time.

The *professional as public policymaker* movement, which is just gathering steam among teachers and teacher organizations across this country, takes various forms, most notably, site-based management and teacher empowerment. Grudging recognition of this movement on the part of administrators and administrator organizations is just gathering steam, too.

Yet the curriculum building/teaching/learning problems in American public schooling are chronic; they cry out for many more school leaders to take moral and technical hold of schooling's core and to reverse the rot. Just as other savvy leaders have helped their own staffs to make educational public policy by their actions, so can you by your own.

I invite you to use the remainder of this volume to study, select, and integrate some of the innovative school improvement programs that follow for your building's use. Use them to help staff ask whether your building has addressed such chronic problems as excellence and equity in student learning and economy and excitement in teaching. Use them to help staff consider how current curriculum building, teaching, and testing ideas and practices might be adapted or replaced so as to better address these problems in the future. Use them to acquaint staff with the utility of contemporary educational research for discovering even better practices. And use them to remind staff that authentic school improvement must be, in the words of Larry Lezotte, a long-term journey, not a short-term event.

In so using our menu of school improvement programs, you will honor other colleagues on your staff dedicated to becoming more publicly accountable, yet professionally self-determined. You will honor yourself, too, and your dedication to America's public schools as a bastion of free and quality schooling for all.

PART II

A Menu of School Improvement Programs

In this section of the book a number of well-known educators describe school and classroom innovations for which they are advocates. We want to be clear about the process used to select the innovations included in the book and to emphasize that our selections are by no means all-encompassing. Our hope is that these innovations and the framework we build around them in Parts I and III provide a base and a structure upon which educators can build their plans for change. That base and structure can easily be enriched by continual additions of new innovations. In our selection of innovations, we attended to the issues of substance, quality, and impact; we urge the readers to do the same as they encounter and consider new ideas for implementation.

Some time ago during a conversation, the three authors realized that because of our experience working with school people, we disagreed with the notion that schools remain the same and that change is rare. In our work in schools and districts, we have been amazed by the energy, time, and money administrators and teachers devote to staff development, school improvement, and planning. Often there was a frenzy of activity at the local level. Further, we noticed that in locations across the country many of the same ideas and activities were getting attention. However, as you will read in our own chapters, we also saw frustrated "implementers." Presenters suggested that their "innovations" should receive the main emphasis in schools and that every other idea should and could fit under that emphasis. Unfortunately, a process to make that happen had not been clearly articulated. Through our discussion, the authors came to believe that a framework was missing for understanding the nature of innovation, using an informed decision-making process to select innovations, and for applying a strategy to integrate innovative ideas. And so the idea for this book emerged. We decided that we would collect descriptions of the most popular research-based innovations and to describe a framework to help people implement those innovations wisely.

To identify and select the chapters in this section, we used a modified "delphi" process. Individually, the three of us listed the research-and-development-based school improvement innovations we thought should be included in the volume because of their familiarity in schools. As mentioned before, we attended to issues of quality, substance, and impact. Then we compared our lists and developed a master list, which we showed to knowledgeable school people (e.g., assistant superintendents for curriculum, staff development directors, principals, teachers) for their review. We ended up with a list of twenty-one innovations. We then used the same selection method to identify authors for each chapter. We invited each author to write a description of the innovation for which he or she in known. The twenty-one invitations we sent resulted in the eighteen chapters included in this section. In most cases the authors who declined (e.g., Howard Gardner) were committed to other work at the time. Obviously, additions to this section would enhance it; school people would have a larger selection from which to choose ideas for implementation that meet their needs. Without seeming redundant, we again want to encourage additions; and we envision a companion volume, a loose-leaf binder to which documents describing new innovations may be added over time. The framework we present in this book is not limited to use with the following chapters, although we focus our attention on them.

In order to help readers apply the framework to the chapters in this section, we have coded each innovation by identifying the area(s) of schooling or the "Big Variables" for which they are primarily known. Everson's chapter describes these "Big Variables" in greater detail and presents a matrix to match them to each innovation. Based on the matrix, we have encoded each innovation in the upper right-hand corner of its introductory text.

We have also adopted another convention by sorting our school improvement program innovations according to their emphasis on learning, teaching, or schooling. Learning-oriented innovations tend to emphasize some "Big Variables," and teaching-oriented or schooling-oriented innovations tend to emphasize others. So, as Guskey's final chapter in this volume demonstrates, learning-oriented school improvement innovations will often need to be integrated with teaching- and schooling-oriented ones so as to influence the particular combination of "Big Variables" in which you, the school leader, is interested.

LEARNING INNOVATIONS

- INSTRUCTION ORGANIZATION/ MANAGEMENT (CLASSROOM)
- ORGANIZATION/ MANAGEMENT (SCHOOL)

Cooperative Learning

David W. Johnson and Roger T. Johnson
University of Minnesota

Two are better than one, because they have a good reward for toil. For if they fall, one will lift up his fellow; but woe to him who is alone when he falls and has not another to lift him up. . . . And though a man might prevail against one who is alone, two will withstand him. A threefold cord is not quickly broken.

Ecclesiastes 4:9–12

Cooperative learning is an old idea (Johnson, Johnson, & Holubec, 1993). The Talmud clearly states that in order to learn you must have a learning partner. In the first century, Quintilian argued that students could benefit from teaching one another. The Roman philosopher Seneca advocated cooperative learning through such statements as "Qui Docet Discet" (when you teach, you learn twice). John Amos Comenius (1592–1679) believed that students would benefit both by teaching and being taught by other students. In the late 1700s, Joseph Lancaster and Andrew Bell made extensive use of cooperative learning groups in England.

The cooperative learning idea was brought to the United States in 1806 when a Lancastrian school was opened in New York City. The idea was further emphasized within the Common School Movement in the early 1800s. In the last three decades of the nineteenth century, Colonel Francis Parker especially brought to his advocacy of cooperative learning in the public schools an enthusiasm, idealism, practicality, and intense devotion to freedom, democracy, and individuality. When he was superintendent of the public schools in Quincy, Massachusetts (1875–1880), more than 30,000 visitors a year, on average, came to observe his democratic use of cooperative learning procedures.

Parker's advocacy of cooperation among students dominated U.S. education through the turn of the century. Following Parker, John Dewey promoted the use of cooperative learning groups as part of his famous project method in instruction. In the late 1930s, however, interpersonal competition began to be emphasized in schools, followed by individualistic learning in the late 1960s. So only now, after forty years of exploring competitive and individualistic learning—and after numerous research studies demonstrating the efficacy of cooperative learning—is the idea of returning to the traditional American use of cooperative learning gaining currency.

To understand cooperative learning as a research-based school practice, it is first necessary to understand what cooperation is. And in order to use cooperative learning in the classroom, it is necessary to understand the essential elements that differentiate cooperative learning from traditional classroom grouping and a well-implemented cooperative lesson from a poorly implemented one.

Numerous operationalizations of cooperative learning have been developed, ranging from direct/concrete to more conceptual approaches. Cooperative learning's beauty is that what is good for students is even better for faculty. Cooperative learning is part of a basic change in organizational structure from a competitive-individualistic, "mass manufacturing" model of organizing to a high-performance, team-based organizational structure. Cooperative procedures can be used throughout the school and school district as well as in the classroom.

STUDENT-STUDENT INTERACTION

Achievement is a we *thing, not a* me *thing, always the product of many heads and hands.*

John Atkinson

In every classroom, no matter what the subject area, teachers may structure lessons so that students:

1. Engage in a win-lose struggle to see who is best.
2. Work independently on their own learning goals at their own pace and in their own space to achieve a preset criterion of excellence.
3. Work cooperatively in small groups, ensuring that all members master the assigned material.

These are three ways student-student interaction may be structured in school classes: competitively, individualistically, and cooperatively.

When students are required to *compete* with each other for grades, they work against each other to achieve a goal that only one or a few students can attain. There is a negative interdependence among goal achievements; students perceive that they can obtain their goals if and only if the other students in the class fail to obtain their goals (Deutsch, 1962; Johnson, Johnson, &

Holubec, 1993). Students are graded on a norm-referenced basis that requires them to work better, faster, and more accurately than their peers. In doing so, they strive to best their classmates, deprive others of success (my winning means that you lose), celebrate classmates' failures (your failure makes it easier for me to win), view resources such as grades as limited (only a few of us will get A's), recognize their negatively linked fate (the more you gain, the less for me; the more I gain, the less for you), and believe that the more competent and hard-working individuals become the "haves" and the less competent and less deserving individuals become the "have nots" (only the strong prosper).

When students are required to work *individualistically*, they work by themselves to accomplish learning goals unrelated to those of the other students. Students' goal achievements are independent; students perceive that the achievement of their learning goals is unrelated to what other students do (Deutsch, 1962; Johnson, Johnson, & Holubec, 1993). Individual goals are assigned, and students' efforts are evaluated on a criterion-referenced basis. Each student has his or her own set of materials and works at his or her own speed, ignoring the other students in the class. Students are expected and encouraged to focus on their strict self-interest (how well can I do), value only their own efforts and success (if I study hard, I may get a high grade), and ignore as irrelevant the success or failure of others (whether my classmates study or not does not affect me).

Cooperation is working together to accomplish shared goals. Within cooperative activities individuals seek outcomes that are beneficial to themselves *and* all other group members. Cooperative learning is the instructional use of small groups so that students work together to maximize their own and each other's learning. In *cooperative learning situations* there is a positive interdependence among students' goal attainments; students perceive that they can reach their learning goals if and only if the other students in the learning group also reach their goals (Deutsch, 1962; Johnson, Johnson, & Holubec, 1993). Class members are split into small groups after receiving instruction from the teacher. They then work through the assignment until all group members have successfully understood and completed it.

Cooperative efforts result in participants striving for mutual benefit so that all group members benefit from each other's efforts (your success benefits me and my success benefits you), recognizing that all group members share a common fate (we all sink or swim together here), realizing that one's performance is mutually caused by oneself and one's colleagues (we cannot do it without you), and feeling proud and jointly celebrating when a group member is recognized for achievement (You got an A! That's terrific!).

In summary, students' learning goals may be structured to promote competitive, individualistic, or cooperative efforts. In the ideal classroom, all students would learn how to work collaboratively with others, compete for fun and enjoyment, and work autonomously on their own. The teacher decides which goal structure to implement within each lesson. Unfortunately, most teachers decide to use the competitive structure. They least utilize the most powerful and important of the three — cooperative learning. And even when teachers think they are using cooperative learning they are often simply placing students in groups. There is more to cooperative learning than simply grouping students; there are essential components of cooperation that must be carefully implemented so cooperative learning actually takes place.

Basic Elements of Cooperative Learning

United we stand, divided we fall.
                    Watchword of the American Revolution

Simply placing students in groups and telling them to work together does not mean that they know how to cooperate or that they will do so even if they know. There are many ways group efforts can go wrong (Johnson & Johnson, 1989a). Less able members sometimes "leave it to George" to complete the group's tasks, thus creating a *free-rider* effect whereby group members expend decreasing amounts of effort and just go through the motions of teamwork. At the same time, the more able group members may expend less effort to avoid the *sucker effect* of doing all the work. High ability group members may be deferred to and may take over the important leadership roles in ways that benefit them at the expense of the other group members (the *rich-get-richer* effect). In a learning group, for example, the more able group members may give all the explanations of what is being learned. Since the amount of time spent explaining correlates highly with the amount learned, the more able members learn a great deal while the less able members flounder as a captive audience. The time spent listening in group brainstorming can reduce the amount of time any individual has to state his or her ideas. Group efforts can be characterized by self-induced helplessness, diffusion of responsibility and social loafing, ganging up against a task, reactance, dysfunctional divisions of labor ("I'm the thinkist, and you're the typist"), inappropriate dependence on authority, destructive conflict, and other patterns of behavior that debilitate group performance.

Many teachers believe that they are implementing cooperative learning when in fact they are missing its essence. In order for a lesson to be cooperative, five basic elements must be carefully structured (Johnson, Johnson, & Holubec, 1993).

The first element of a cooperative lesson is *positive interdependence*. Students must believe that they are linked with others in such a way that one cannot succeed unless the other members of the group succeed (and vice versa); that is, they "sink or swim together."

In a math class, for example, a teacher assigns her students a set of math problems. Students are placed in groups of three. The instructional task is for students to solve each story problem correctly and understand the correct strategy for doing so. The teacher creates positive goal interdependence by requiring group members to agree on the answer and the strategies for solving each problem. Positive role interdependence is structured by assigning each student a role. The reader reads the problems aloud to the group. The checker makes sure that all members can explain how to solve each problem correctly. The encourager in a friendly way encourages all members of the group to participate in the discussion, sharing their ideas and feelings. Resource interdependence is created by giving each group one copy of the problems to be solved. All students work the problems on scratch paper and share their insights with each other. Positive reward interdependence is structured by giving each group five points if all members score above 90 percent on the test given at the end of the unit.

The most important type of positive interdependence is goal interdependence. All cooperative learning starts with a mutually shared group goal.

The second element of a cooperative lesson is *face-to-face promotive interaction* where students help, encourage, and support each other's efforts to learn. Students promote each other's learning by explaining how to solve problems, discussing the nature of the concepts and strategies being learned, teaching their knowledge, and explaining the connections between present and past learning. In the math lesson, the teacher must provide the time, knee-to-knee seating arrangements, and encouragement for students to exchange ideas and help each other learn.

The third element is *individual accountability*, where the performance of each student is assessed and the results given back to the group and the individual. It is important that group members know who needs more assistance in completing the assignment and that they cannot "hitchhike" on the work of others. Common ways of structuring individual accountability include giving each student a test and randomly selecting one student's test results to represent the efforts of the entire group.

The fourth element of a cooperative lesson is *social skills*. Groups cannot function effectively if students do not have and use the needed leadership, decision-making, trust-building, communication, and conflict-management skills. These skills have to be taught just as purposefully and precisely as academic skills. Many students have never worked cooperatively in learning situations and therefore lack the needed social skills. In the math lesson, the teacher emphasizes the skill of "checking to make sure everyone understands." The teacher defines the skill as the phrases and the accompanying nonverbal behaviors to be used by the checker. The group roles are rotated each day. When the teacher sees students engaging in the skill, she praises the group and/or records the instance on an observation sheet. Procedures and strategies for teaching students social skills may be found in Johnson (1991, 1993), Johnson and F. Johnson (1994), and Johnson, Johnson, & Holubec (1993).

Finally, the fifth element of a cooperative lesson is *group processing*. At the end of the math period, the groups process their functioning by answering two questions: What is something each member did that was helpful for the group? and What is something each member could do to make the group even better tomorrow? Such processing enables learning groups to focus on group maintenance, facilitates the learning of social skills, ensures that members receive feedback on their participation, and reminds students to practice the small-group skills required to work cooperatively. Some of the keys to successful processing are allowing sufficient time for it to take place, making it specific rather than vague, varying the format, maintaining student involvement in processing, reminding students to use their social skills while they process, and ensuring that clear expectations of the purpose of processing have been communicated. Often each group is required to turn in a summary of their processing that is signed by all group members.

TYPES OF COOPERATIVE LEARNING GROUPS

These problems are endemic to all institutions of education, regardless of level. Children sit for twelve years in classrooms where the implicit goal is to listen to the teacher and memorize the information in order to regurgitate it on a test. Little or no attention is paid to the learning process, even though much research exists documenting that real understanding is a case of active restructuring on the part of the learner. Restructuring occurs through engagement in problem posing as well as problem solving, inference making and investigation, resolving of contradictions, and reflecting. These processes all mandate far more active learners, as well as a

different model of education than the one subscribed to at present by most institutions. Rather than being powerless and dependent on the institution, learners need to be empowered to think and learn for themselves. Thus, learning needs to be conceived of as something a learner does, not something that is done to a learner.
                                                    Catherine Fosnot (1989)

Students often feel helpless and discouraged, especially when they are facing a difficult class or when they have just entered school. Giving them cooperative learning partners provides hope and opportunity. One of the most important aspects of school life is empowering students by organizing them into cooperative teams. It is social support from and accountability to valued peers that motivate committed efforts to achieve and succeed. Cooperative learning groups empower their members by making them feel strong, capable, and committed. If classrooms are to be places where students care about each other and are committed to each other's success in academic endeavors, a cooperative structure must exist.

A cooperative structure consists of the integrated use of three types of cooperative learning groups. Cooperative learning groups may be used to teach specific content (formal cooperative learning groups), to ensure active cognitive processing of information during direct teaching (informal cooperative learning groups), and to provide students with long-term support and assistance for academic progress (cooperative base groups). Any assignment in any curriculum for students of any age may be done cooperatively. When used in combination, cooperative formal, informal, and base groups provide an overall structure for school learning.

FORMAL COOPERATIVE LEARNING GROUPS

Formal cooperative learning groups may last for one class period or for several weeks to complete specific tasks and assignments (such as solving a set of problems, completing a curriculum unit, writing a report or theme, conducting an experiment, or reading a story, play, chapter, or book). Any course requirement or assignment may be reformulated to be cooperative. In formal cooperative learning groups the teacher:

1. Specifies the objectives for the lesson (one academic and one social skill).
2. Makes a series of decisions about how to structure the learning groups (what size groups, how students are assigned to groups, what roles to assign, how to arrange materials, and how to arrange the room).
3. Teaches the academic concepts, principles, and strategies that the students are to master and apply and explains the task to be completed and the criteria for success, the positive interdependence, the individual accountability, the expected student behaviors, and the criteria for success.
4. Monitors the functioning of the learning groups and intervenes to teach collaborative skills and to provide assistance in academic learning when it is needed.
5. Evaluates student performance against the preset criteria for excellence and ensures that groups process how effectively members worked together.

An example of the use of formal cooperative learning groups may be found in science experiments. Students are given the instructional tasks of timing how long a candle burns in a quart jar and generating a number of answers to the question "How many factors make a difference in how long the candle burns in the jar?" Students are assigned to heterogeneous pairs. Each pair is given one candle and one quart jar (resource interdependence). The positive goal interdependence is for pairs to decide on one answer that both members can explain. The social skills the teacher expects to see are encouraging each other's participation and elaborating on what students are learning by relating it to previous lessons. Students light their candle, place the quart jar over it, and time how long the candle burns. The teacher moves from group to group monitoring the interaction between pair members. The pairs' results are announced. Then the pairs' hypotheses about the factors influencing how long the candles burn are written on the board. The pairs then repeat the experiment in ways that test which of the suggested factors do in fact make a difference in how long the candle burns. The next day students individually take a quiz on the factors affecting the time a candle burns in a quart jar (individual accountability), and their scores are totaled to determine a joint score that, if high enough, earns them bonus points (reward interdependence). They spend some time discussing the helpful actions of each member and what they could do to be even more effective in the future (group processing).

Science experiments are only one of the many ways formal cooperative learning may be used. Cooperative learning is appropriate for any instructional task. Formal cooperative learning should be used whenever the learning goals are highly important, the task is complex or conceptual, problem solving is required, divergent thinking or creativity is desired, a high quality of performance is expected, higher-level reasoning strategies and critical thinking are needed, long-term retention is desired, or the social development of students is one of the major instructional goals (Johnson & Johnson, 1989).

INFORMAL COOPERATIVE LEARNING GROUPS

Informal cooperative learning groups are temporary ad-hoc groups that last anywhere from a few minutes to one class period. During a lecture, demonstration, or film these groups can be used to focus student attention on the material to be learned, set a mood conducive to learning, help set expectations as to what will be covered in a class session, ensure that students cognitively process the material being taught, and provide closure to an instructional session. During direct teaching the instructional challenge for the teacher is to ensure that students do the intellectual work of organizing material and of explaining, summarizing, and integrating it into existing conceptual structures. Informal cooperative learning groups are often organized so that students engage in three-to-five-minute *focused discussions* before and after a lecture and three-to-five-minute *turn-to-your-partner* discussions interspersed throughout a lecture. In this way, the main problem of lectures can be countered: "The information passes from the notes of the professor to the notes of the student without passing through the mind of either one."

COOPERATIVE BASE GROUPS

Cooperative base groups are long-term heterogeneous cooperative learning groups with stable membership. The purposes of the base group are to give the support, help, and encouragement each member needs to make academic progress (attend class, complete all assignments, learn) and to develop cognitively and socially in healthy ways. Base groups meet daily (or whenever the class meets). They are permanent (lasting from one to several years) and provide the long-term caring peer relationships necessary to influence members consistently to work hard in school.

They formally meet to discuss the academic progress of each member, provide help to each other, and verify that each member is completing assignments and progressing satisfactorily through the academic program. Base groups may also be responsible for letting absent group members know what went on in class. Informally, members interact every day within and between classes, discussing assignments and helping each other with homework. The use of base groups tends to improve attendance, personalize the work required and the school experience, and improve the quality and quantity of learning. The larger the class or school and the more complex and difficult the subject matter, the more important it is to have base groups.

APPROACHES TO COOPERATIVE LEARNING

It is only when we develop others that we permanently succeed.
                                   Harvey S. Firestone, Firestone Tires

Approaches to implementing cooperative learning may be placed on a continuum, with conceptual applications at one end and direct applications at the other. *Conceptual applications* are based on an interaction among theory, research, and practice (Cohen, 1986; Johnson, Johnson, & Holubec, 1993). Teachers are taught a general conceptual model of cooperative learning (based on the essential elements of positive interdependence, face-to-face interaction, individual accountability, social skills, and group processing—the "essential elements approach"), which they use to tailor cooperative learning specifically for their circumstances, students, and needs. Using the five basic elements of cooperation, faculty can analyze their current curricula, students, and instructional goals and design cooperative learning experiences specifically for their instructional goals and the ages, abilities, and backgrounds of their students. Becoming competent in implementing the basic elements is a requirement for obtaining real expertise in cooperative learning. In essence, teachers are taught an expert system of implementing cooperative learning that they use to create a unique adaptation to their specific circumstances, students, and needs. The resulting expertise is based on a metacognitive understanding of cooperative learning.

Conceptual applications may be contrasted with *direct applications* that consist of packaged lessons, curricula, and strategies that are used in a lock-step manner. The direct approach can be divided into three subcategories. Teachers can adopt a strategy (such as groups-of-four in intermediate math) that is aimed at using cooperative learning in a specific subject area for students of a certain age ("strategy approach"), they can adopt a curriculum package that is aimed at a specific subject area and grade level ("curriculum package approach"), or they can replicate a lesson they observed ("lesson approach"). In essence, faculty are trained to use a specific cooperative activity, lesson, strategy, or curriculum package in a Step 1, Step 2, Step 3 manner without any real understanding of cooperation. The curriculum package approach is represented by the work at Johns Hopkins (Slavin, Leavey, & Madden, 1982). Some of the most powerful strategy approaches include the "jigsaw method" developed by Elliot Aronson and his colleagues (Aronson, 1978), the "coop/coop strategy" developed by Spencer Kagan (Kagan, 1988), and the "group project method" developed by the Sharans (Sharan & Sharan, 1976).

While the two types of applications are not contradictory, there are differences for the transfer of training from the workshop to the classroom and for the long-term implementation and survival of cooperative learning. In terms of transfer of training, conceptual applications are theory-based, while direct applications are materials- and procedures-based. The conceptual approach trains teachers to be engineers who adapt cooperative ideas to their specific circumstances, students, and needs. Direct approaches train teachers to be technicians who use the cooperative learning curriculum or strategy without understanding how it works. Engineering cooperative learning so that it works within their specific situations results in teachers being personally committed to cooperative learning, while technically conducting a cooperative learning lesson in a lock-step manner does not.

The conceptual approach, moreover, promotes research that tests theory that generalizes to many different situations. Direct approaches promote evaluation studies that are in essence case studies demonstrating how well the curriculum or strategy was implemented in a specific instance, but the results do not generalize to other situations and implementations. Conceptual approaches are also dynamic in that they are changed and modified on the basis of new research and refinements of the theory. Direct approaches are static in that they remain fixed no matter how the knowledge about cooperative learning changes.

In terms of long-term implementation and survival, when teachers gain expertise in cooperative learning through conceptual understanding, they become independent of outside experts and can generate new lessons and strategies as the need arises. They can also transfer their use of cooperative learning to create more cooperative collegial relationships, staff meetings, relationships with parents, and committees. They become important figures in the staff development process as they train their colleagues to use cooperative learning. Teachers trained in the direct approaches stay dependent on outside experts, cannot generate new lessons or strategies on their own, cannot transfer cooperation from the classroom to the school, and cannot train their peers (except in a direct way). Finally, the conceptual approach requires ongoing support and assistance in gaining expertise in cooperative learning. Direct approaches do not.

While we have been hard on direct approaches to cooperative learning, we still think they have value, if they are appropriately contextualized within a long-term implementation emphasizing conceptual understanding of the essential elements of well-structured cooperative lessons. Without the conceptual context, direct approaches are, in the long run, inadequate at best and counterproductive at worst. Simply presenting a theoretical framework, on the other hand, is also inadequate. A carefully crafted training program requires a combination of a clear conceptual understanding of the essential elements of cooperative learning, concrete examples of lessons and strategies, and continued implementation in classrooms and schools.

WHAT DO WE KNOW ABOUT COOPERATIVE EFFORTS?

Everyone has to work together; if we can't get everybody working toward common goals, nothing is going to happen.
Harold K. Sperlich, President, Chrysler Corporation

Learning together to complete assignments can have profound effects on students and faculty. A great deal of research has been conducted comparing the relative effects of cooperative, competitive, and individualistic efforts on instructional outcomes

(Johnson & Johnson, 1989a). These research studies began in the late 1800s when Triplett in the United States, Turner in England, and Mayer in Germany conducted a series of studies on the factors associated with competitive performance. In the 1940s Morton Deutsch, building on the theorizing of Kurt Lewin, proposed a theory of cooperation and competition that has served as the primary foundation on which subsequent research and discussion of cooperative learning have been based. Our own theorizing and research are directly based on Deutsch's work.

During the past ninety years over 550 experimental and 100 correlational studies have been conducted by a wide variety of researchers in different decades, with subjects of different ages, in different subject areas, and in different settings (see Johnson & Johnson, 1989a for a complete listing and review of these studies). Over the past twenty-five years, the authors themselves have conducted over eighty-five studies to refine our understanding of how cooperation works. We know far more about the efficacy of cooperative learning than we know about lecturing, departmentalization, the use of technology, or almost any other facet of education.

With the amount of research evidence available on cooperative efforts, it is surprising and even alarming that classroom practice is so oriented toward individualistic and competitive learning. It is time to reduce the discrepancy between what research indicates is effective and what students, teachers, and administrators actually do. Building on the theorizing of Lewin and Deutsch, we propose that the type of interdependence structured among students determines how they interact with each other, which, in turn, largely determines instructional outcomes. Structuring situations cooperatively results in promotive interaction, structuring situations competitively results in oppositional interaction, and structuring situations individualistically results in no interaction among students. These interaction patterns affect numerous variables, which may be subsumed within the three broad and interrelated outcomes of achievement effort exerted, quality of relationships among participants, and participants' psychological adjustment and social competence (see Figure 2.1) (Johnson & Johnson, 1989a).

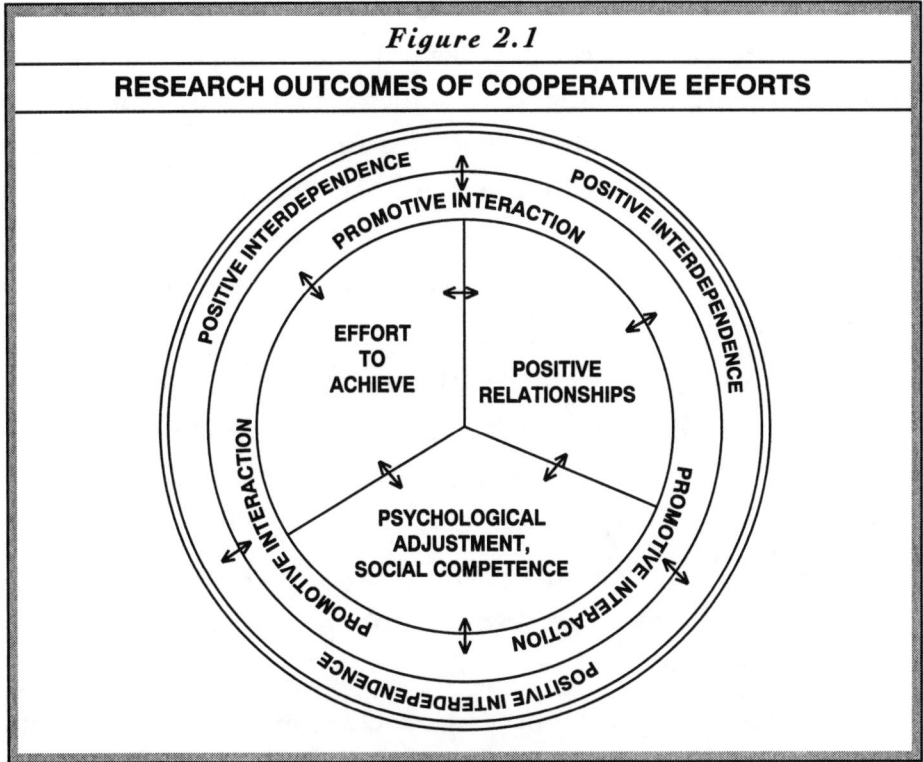

Figure 2.1
RESEARCH OUTCOMES OF COOPERATIVE EFFORTS

INTERACTION PATTERNS

Two heads are better than one.

Heywood

Students can obstruct as well as facilitate each other's learning. Or they can ignore each other. The way students interact depends on how teachers structure interdependence in the learning situation. Positive interdependence results in students promoting each other's learning and achievement. *Promotive interaction* may be defined as individuals encouraging and facilitating each other's efforts to achieve, complete tasks, and produce in order to reach the group's goals. While positive interdependence in and of itself may have some effect on outcomes, it is the face-to-face promotive interaction among individuals fostered by the positive interdependence that most powerfully influences efforts to achieve, caring and committed relationships, and psychological adjustment and social competence. Students focus on increasing their own achievement *and* on increasing the achievement of their groupmates.

Promotive interaction is characterized by individuals (Johnson & Johnson, 1989):

1. Providing each other with efficient and effective help.
2. Exchanging needed resources such as information and materials and processing information more efficiently and effectively.
3. Providing each other with feedback in order to improve the subsequent performance of their assigned tasks and responsibilities.
4. Challenging each other's conclusions and reasoning in order to promote higher-quality decision making and greater insight into the problems being considered.
5. Advocating the exertion of effort to achieve mutual goals.
6. Influencing each other's efforts to achieve the group's goals.
7. Acting in trusting and trustworthy ways.
8. Being motivated to strive for mutual benefit.

9. Having a moderate level of arousal characterized by low anxiety and stress.

Negative interdependence typically results in students opposing and obstructing each other's learning. *Oppositional interaction* occurs as students discourage and obstruct each other's efforts to achieve. Students focus on increasing their own achievement *and* on preventing any classmate from achieving more than they do. *No interaction* exists when students work independently without any interaction or interchange with each other. Students focus only on increasing their own achievement and ignore as irrelevant the efforts of others.

OUTCOMES

A faithful friend is a strong defense, and he that hath found him, hath found a treasure.
                                                            Ecclesiastes 6:14

Over 375 studies have been conducted over the past ninety years to answer the question of how successful competitive, individualistic, and cooperative efforts are in promoting productivity and achievement (Johnson & Johnson, 1989a). Since research participants have varied as to economic class, age, sex, and cultural background; since a wide variety of research tasks and measures of the dependent variables have been used; and since the research has been conducted by many different researchers with markedly different orientations working in different settings and in different decades, the overall body of research on social interdependence has considerable generalizability.

Three basic findings seem to emerge.

1. *Working together to achieve a common goal produces higher achievement and greater productivity than does working alone.*

This finding is so well confirmed by so much research

that it stands as one of the strongest principles of social and organizational psychology. Cooperative learning, furthermore, results in more higher-level reasoning, more frequent generation of new ideas and solutions (i.e., process gain), and greater transfer of what is learned within one situation to another (i.e., group to individual transfer) than does competitive or individualistic learning. The more conceptual the task, the more problem solving required; the more desirable higher-level reasoning and critical thinking, the more creativity required; and the greater the application of what is being learned to the real world, the greater the superiority of cooperative over competitive and individualistic efforts.

In the studies mentioned above, some cooperative learning procedures contained a mixture of cooperative, competitive, and individualistic efforts while others were "pure." The original Jigsaw procedure (Aronson, 1978), for example, is a combination of resource interdependence (cooperative) and individual reward structure (individualistic). Teams-Games-Tournaments (DeVries & Edwards, 1974) and Student-Teams-Achievement-Divisions (Slavin, 1980) are mixtures of cooperation and intergroup competition. Team-Assisted-Instruction (Slavin, Leavey, & Madden, 1982) is a mixture of individualistic and cooperative learning. When the results of "pure" and "mixed" operationalizations of cooperative learning were compared, the "pure" operationalizations produced higher achievement (see Johnson & Johnson, 1989a for details).

2. *Individuals care more about each other and are more committed to each other's success and well-being when they work together to*

get the job done than when they compete to see who is best or work independently.

This finding is true when individuals are homogeneous, and it is also true when individuals differ in intellectual ability, handicapping conditions, ethnic membership, social class, and gender. When individuals are heterogeneous, cooperating on a task results in more realistic and positive views of each other. As relationships become more positive, absenteeism and turnover of membership decreases, member commitment to organizational goals increases, feelings of personal responsibility to the organization increase, willingness to take on difficult tasks increases, motivation and persistence in working toward goal achievement increase, satisfaction and morale increase, willingness to endure pain and frustration on behalf of the organization increases, willingness to defend the organization against external criticism or attack increases, willingness to listen to and be influenced by colleagues increases, commitment to each other's professional growth and success increases, and productivity increases (Johnson & Johnson, 1989).

3. *Working cooperatively with peers and valuing cooperation result in greater psychological health and higher self-esteem than does competing with peers or working independently.*

Personal ego-strength, self-confidence, independence, and autonomy are all promoted by being involved in cooperative efforts with caring people who are committed to each other's success and well-being and who respect each other as separate and unique individuals. When individuals work together to complete assignments, they interact (mastering social skills and competencies), they promote each other's success (gaining self-worth), and they form personal as well as professional relationships (creating the basis for healthy social development). Individuals' psychological adjustment and health tend to increase when schools are dominated by cooperative efforts. The more individuals work cooperatively with others and see themselves as worthwhile and as having value, the greater their productivity and acceptance and support of others and the more autonomous and independent they tend to be. Cooperative experiences are not a luxury. They are an absolute necessity for the healthy development of individuals who can function independently.

There are bidirectional relationships among efforts to achieve, quality of relationships, and psychological health (Johnson & Johnson, 1989a). Each influences the others. First, caring and committed friendships come from a sense of mutual accomplishment, mutual pride in joint work, and the bonding that results from joint efforts. The more students care about each other, on the other hand, the harder they will work to achieve mutual learning goals. Second, joint efforts to achieve mutual goals promote higher self-esteem, self-efficacy, personal control, and confidence in their competencies. The psychologically healthier individuals are, on the other hand, the better able they are to work with others to achieve mutual goals. Third, psychological health is built on the internalization of the caring and respect received from loved ones. Friendships are developmental advantages that promote self-esteem, self-efficacy, and general psychological adjustment. The healthier people are psychologically (i.e., free of psychological pathology such as depression, paranoia, anxiety, fear of failure, repressed anger, hopelessness, and meaninglessness), on the other hand, the more caring and committed their relationships.

Since each outcome can induce the others, they are likely to be found together. They are a package, with each outcome a door into all three. And together they induce positive interdependence and promotive interaction.

THE COOPERATIVE SCHOOL

Take care of each other. Share your energies with the group. No one must feel alone, cut off, for that is when you do not make it.
Willi Unsoeld, Renowned Mountain Climber

Cooperative learning is more than an instructional procedure. It is a basic shift in organizational structure that extends from the classroom through the superintendent's office. For decades, business and industrial organizations have functioned as "mass manufacturing" organizations that divided work into small component parts performed by individuals who worked separately from and, in many cases, in competition with peers. Personnel were considered to be interchangeable parts in the organizational machine. Such an organizational structure no longer seems effective, and many companies are turning to the high productivity generated by teams.

Most schools have also been structured as mass manufacturing organizations. Teachers work alone, in their own rooms, with their own sets of students, and with their own sets of curriculum materials. Students could be assigned to any teacher because teachers were interchangeable parts in the education machine, and, conversely, teachers could be given any student to teach.

Schools need to change from a mass-manufacturing, competitive/individualistic organizational structure to a "high performance," cooperative, team-based organizational structure. The new organizational structure is generally known as "the cooperative school" (Johnson & Johnson, 1994).

In a cooperative school, students work primarily in cooperative learning groups, teachers and building staff work in cooperative teams, and district administrators work in cooperative teams. The organizational structures of the classroom, school, and district are then congruent. Each level of cooperative teams supports and enhances the other levels.

A cooperative school structure begins in the classroom. Teachers typically cannot promote isolation and competition among students all day and be collaborative with colleagues. What is promoted in the instructional situations tends to dominate relationships among staff members. Teachers who spend up to six hours a day telling students "Do not copy," "I want to see what you can do, not your neighbor," "Let's see who is best," and "Who is the winner?" will in turn tend to approach their colleagues with the attitudes of "Don't copy from me" and "Who is the winner in implementing this new teaching strategy?" When teachers spend most of their day structuring learning situations cooperatively and carefully creating positive interdependence, face-to-face promotive interaction, individual accountability, social skills, and group processing, they will in turn approach their colleagues with cooperative attitudes. In addition, by structuring cooperative learning and teaching students how to work effectively within cooperative teams, teachers themselves learn the skills and attitudes required to work cooperatively with their colleagues.

The second level in creating a cooperative school is to form collegial support groups, task forces, and ad hoc decision-making groups within the school. Just as the heart of the classroom is cooperative learning, the heart of the school is the collegial support group.

Collegial support groups are small cooperative groups whose purpose is to increase teachers' instructional expertise and success. The focus is on improving instruction in general and on increasing members' expertise in using cooperative learning in specific. Collegial support groups meet once a week for about one hour. The principal is a member of each collegial support group, moving from one meeting to another as time allows. A school governing council consists of the principal and one member of each collegial support group. Information shared in this meeting is passed on to each collegial support group. Most decisions are made in this group.

In addition, there are school task forces made up of one member of each collegial support group. Each task force focuses on a different issue. The task forces meet periodically to achieve specific tasks. Information about each task force is passed back to the collegial support group. A full faculty meeting is held once a month and whenever special issues needing active participation of all faculty arise.

The third level in creating a cooperative school is to implement administrative cooperative teams within the district. The superintendent should organize the district administrators into cooperative teams similarly to the way teachers organize students into cooperative learning groups. All administrators should be involved in cooperative teams that meet regularly and work on meaningful tasks. If administrators compete to see who is the best administrator in the district, they are unlikely to be able to promote cooperation among staff members of the school. The more the district and school personnel work in cooperative teams, the easier it will be for teachers to use cooperative learning, and vice versa.

FUTURE OF COOPERATIVE LEARNING

Educational practices come and go, but for several reasons cooperative learning will always be with us. First, the amount and consistency of research demonstrating the effectiveness of cooperative efforts are staggering. The fact that cooperative efforts promote greater productivity, more positive relationships, and greater psychological health than do competitive or individualistic efforts places cooperation in a class by itself. Any teacher who does *not* use cooperative learning cannot be considered fully competent. In schools where practice follows what we know about effective teaching, cooperative learning becomes the foundation of education.

Second, as the diversity of students in U.S. schools increases, cooperative learning is required to ensure that creative energy results rather than prejudice and ethnocentrism. Demographers predict that by 2020 minorities will comprise nearly half the total number of students. Such diversity provides opportunities and problems. Students need to learn about and take pride in their cultural and ethnic heritage, understand and appreciate the cultural and ethnic heritage of others, develop a superordinate identity as Americans, and internalize the democratic values expressed in our Constitution and Bill of Rights. In order to ensure that our heterogeneity is a source of creativity, energy, entrepreneurism, and sophistication, cooperative learning is required.

Third, changes in family and community structure have reduced the social support and quality of relationships experienced by many children. Caring, committed, supportive relationships are an absolute necessity for healthy social, cognitive, and physical development and psychological health. For many children, school has become the primary place where they are involved with peers and adults. Cooperative learning is essential for developing the caring relationships, social competencies, and coping skills children need to grow and develop in healthy ways and deal with the adversity in their lives. To manage stress and deal with adversity, the coping skills and social competencies resulting from working cooperatively with others give students in cooperative classrooms a developmental advantage.

Fourth, understanding interdependence is a requirement for citizenship in the world community. Because of technological, economic, ecological, and political interdependence, the solution to most problems cannot be achieved by one individual or country alone. The major problems faced by individuals (e.g., contamination of the environment, warming of the atmosphere, world hunger, international terrorism, nuclear war) are increasingly ones that cannot be solved by actions taken only at the national level. The internationalization of problems has increased so that there are no clear lines between domestic and international problems. The international affairs of one country are the internal affairs of other nations, and vice versa. Cooperation, therefore, must be established among disparate peoples and nations. Cooperative learning simultaneously models interdependence and provides students with the experiences they need to understand the nature of cooperation. Students who have had twelve to twenty years of cooperative learning will be better able to understand and manage interdependent systems than will students who have had twelve to twenty years of competitive and individualistic learning.

Fifth, business and industry are changing from mass-manufacturing to team-based/high-performance organizational structures in which work is done by self-managing teams. To prepare students to work in modern organizations, schools need to make similar changes in their organizational structure and have students primarily learn in cooperative learning groups, teachers work in collegial support groups focused on improving instruction, and administrators work in collegial support groups aimed at increasing the school district's productivity and effectiveness. Cooperative learning is the heart of modernizing the organizational structure of schools and school districts.

Sixth, cooperative learning is easily integrated with, and in some cases is a requirement for, other instructional practices such as mastery learning, effective elements of instruction, whole language, and critical thinking. Cooperative learning provides a foundation on which many other educational practices that require student-student interaction rest.

The widespread adoption of cooperative learning may be slowed, however, for several reasons. For one thing, the research data could be ignored, and educational practice could be separated from what we know is effective and ineffective. For another, the training of teachers could be done in ways that trivialize cooperative learning. Cooperative learning could be presented as a few gimmicky lessons and canned techniques in quick, superficial training sessions. With inadequate training, teachers could be dissatisfied with cooperative learning, stop using it, and resist using it again. Cooperative learning, though, is in fact a complex set of teaching practices that take at least one lifetime to master. Our training program for teachers usually takes three years, and even then teachers are expected to continue for the rest of their career refining their expertise in using cooperative learning and adapting it to the changing nature of their students and teaching situation.

Still another barrier may be that cooperative learning could be poorly implemented. Traditional classroom grouping—which does not emphasize positive interdependence, promotive interaction, individual accountability, social skills, and group processing—may be erroneously called cooperative learning.

Finally, the continual refinement of cooperative learning procedures depends on an active research program investigating the internal dynamics of cooperative groups. With increased understanding of what makes cooperation work, teaching procedures can be refined to make cooperative lessons even more effective. Without continuing research, cooperative learning will never reach its full potential.

SUMMARY AND CONCLUSIONS

Cooperative learning is the instructional use of small groups so that students work together to maximize their own and each other's learning. The effectiveness of cooperative efforts depends on how well positive interdependence, face-to-face promotive interaction, individual accountability, interpersonal and small group skills, and group processing are structured within the learning situation. These five essential elements may be structured within the learning situation, within the classroom, within the school, and within the school district.

In a cooperative school, students work primarily in cooperative learning groups and teachers and building staff work in cooperative teams, as do the district administrators. The heart of the cooperative school is cooperative learning. Cooperative learning groups may be used to teach specific content (formal cooperative learning groups), to ensure active cognitive processing of information during a lecture (informal cooperative learning groups), and to provide long-term support and assistance for academic progress (cooperative base groups).

In the classroom, teachers may use two general approaches to creating cooperative learning procedures: conceptual and direct. Long-term change in teaching practices depends on teachers understanding conceptually what cooperation is as well as their being able to conduct cooperative learning lessons. In the school, staff members work in collegial support groups especially to increase teachers' instructional expertise and success, in task forces to plan and implement solutions to school-wide problems, and in ad hoc decision-making groups to involve all staff members in important school decisions.

Cooperative learning is not a fad rising in popularity and then fading into obscurity. Cooperative learning is here to stay for such reasons as the breadth and consistency of the research supporting it, its success in providing a constructive context within which hetereogeneity is valued and differences are respected, the changes in family and community structure and the resulting need for schools to promote caring and committed relationships among students, the changes in world interdependence requiring citizens to understand and manage cooperative systems, the changes in business and industry requiring school graduates to be experienced in working in teams, and the ease with which it can be integrated with other instructional practices.

There are, however, obstacles to widespread use of cooperative learning. The evidence concerning effective teaching practices can be ignored, superficial training that lacks long-term follow-up in the classroom can trivialize cooperative learning, teachers can use cooperative learning practices poorly, and ongoing research programs can falter. Each of these obstacles must be avoided by thoughtful educators.

3

- CURRICULUM
- INSTRUCTION

Critical Thinking

Robert J. Marzano
Mid-continent Regional Educational Laboratory, Denver

There have been many calls for enhanced critical thinking within U.S. education. For example, the National Science Board Commission on Precollege Education in Mathematics, Science, and Technology (1983), the Commission on the Humanities (1980), the College Board (1983), the Panel on the General Professional Education of the Physician and College Preparation for Medicine (1984), the National Education Association (Futrell, 1987), and the American Federation of Teachers (1985) have all strongly advocated the enhancement of critical thinking to meet the challenges of a rapidly changing society. Most, if not all, of these calls have been fueled by current reports (e.g., Applebee, Langer, & Mullis, 1986a & b; Dossey, et al., 1988) that U.S. students, while improving in basic information processing skills, have consistently performed poorly in the more complex critical thinking skills such as solving non-routine problems and analyzing the strength and nature of persuasive discourse.

A common interpretation of the calls for enhanced critical thinking is to focus on enhancing students' reasoning ability—their ability to solve problems, analyze information, make decisions, and the like. But, as intuitively appealing as this approach is, critical thinking theorists such as Richard Paul (1990) and Bob Ennis (1987a, 1988b, 1989) warn that such an emphasis is shortsighted. They point out that there is more to critical thinking than reasoning, as is evidenced by the fact that such nefarious historical figures as Adolf Hitler were quite facile at solving problems. Rather, Paul and Ennis assert that critical thinking should ultimately improve the human condition. That is, inherent in the critical thinking concept is a type of thinking that is altruistic—thinking that is devoted to unselfish concern for others.

This notion that critical thinking involves more than a highly developed ability to reason can be traced back to ancient Greece. For example, Socrates is credited with the precept that "the unexamined life is not worth living." Golden, Berquist, and Coleman (1976) note that: "To Plato, truth was the only reality in life" (p.20). Indeed, the search for truth via the rigorous use of conscious thought was the driving force behind the work of Plato, Socrates, and Aristotle.

One might say, then, that there are at least two perspectives on critical thinking. One focuses on developing specific rational competencies that can be used in accomplishing a variety of cognitive goals. The other includes the development of these rational competencies along with a commitment to enhancing the human condition. Paul (1990) captures this distinction in his constructs of *weak sense* and *strong sense* critical thinking.

Weak sense critical thinking, according to Paul, involves reasoning about complex issues (e.g., decision making and problem solving) within the context of an egocentric or ethnocentric world view. In contrast, strong sense critical thinking involves reasoning about issues from a position detached from these biases.

Key to understanding Paul's distinction between weak sense and strong sense critical thinking is an understanding of egocentric and ethnocentric thinking. Egocentric thinking, as the name implies, is constrained by or totally contained within the parameters of one's ego identity. Piaget (1976) has listed some of the defining characteristics of egocentric thought. He notes that the egocentric thinker exhibits the following tendencies:

- confident in his own ideas . . ., naturally . . . [untroubled] about the reasons and motives which have guided his reasoning process (pp. 137–138)
- . . . being ignorant of his own ego, takes his own point of view to be absolute (p. 197)
- simply believes . . . without trying to find the truth (p. 203)
- assimilates everything he hears to his own point of view (p. 208)
- . . . does not try to prove whether such and such of his idea does or does not correspond to reality (p. 247)

Whereas most educators associate Piaget's work with children only, Paul (1990, p. 114) notes that the thinking of adults is frequently egocentric and that many adults are ignorant of the effects of their ego in their thinking and behavior.

Additionally, Paul notes that egocentric thinking invariably leads to ethnocentric thinking—reasoning within the parameters of societal beliefs and assumptions. He argues that over time the egocentric mind includes without question or scrutiny the world view of its immediate culture. This acceptance will characteristically include a "we/they" perspective—everything we believe is correct; everything they believe that is in contrast is incorrect. Indeed, the *Random House Dictionary of the English Language* (Flexner & Houck, 1987) defines "egoism" as the opposite of "altruism."

The inherent danger (and power) in ethnocentric thought is that it is infrequently challenged. Since ethnocentric thinking exists in the very environment that has created it, there is little or no chance of contradictory information being encountered or seriously considered. In effect, ethnocentric assumptions are to the ethnocentric thinker as water is to fish. They constitute a transparent filter through which she or he processes all information and all experience.

Weak sense critical thinking, then, fosters reasoning skills and abilities but does not address the world view within which those skills and abilities operate. Strong sense critical thinking assumes the development of reasoning skills and abilities and seeks to transform egocentric and ethnocentric world views to altruistic counterparts.

THE ROLE OF WEAK SENSE CRITICAL THINKING IN THE CURRICULUM

Although weak sense critical thinking is not the final goal of a critical thinking program, the mental competencies associated with weak sense critical thinking are prerequisites for strong sense critical thought. At its core, fostering weak sense critical thinking involves teaching and reinforcing various dispositions, skills, and abilities. For example, Ennis and his colleagues (Kennedy, Fisher, & Ennis, 1991) list thirteen critical thinking dispositions and twelve critical thinking skills. Whereas these dispositions are more attitudinal and affective in nature, the skills are more cognitive. Paul, et al. (1989) also makes such distinctions.

If one carefully studies the complete lists of Ennis and Paul, a great deal of overlap and some contradictions can be found. Regardless of these contradictions, the work of both men is extremely useful for educators attempting to develop programs or practices that enhance weak sense critical thinking. Figure 3.1 page 62 is a list of critical thinking dispositions and skills drawn from the work of both theorists.

Fostering weak sense critical thinking, then, involves such dispositions and skills as those in Figure 3.1. However, using these mental competencies requires specific types of tasks. That is, to enhance weak sense critical thinking, teachers must involve students in tasks that call for the use of its characteristic dispositions and skills. Such tasks tend to be: (1) partially specified, (2) multidimensional, (3) student directed, and (4) long term.

PARTIALLY SPECIFIED

Specification refers to the extent to which the final product of a task is predetermined. To illustrate, there are some tasks for which the outcomes are totally determined or fully specified. Consider, for example, answering questions of the multiple choice, true/false, fill-in-the-blank, matching, or short answer variety. The outcomes of each of these tasks are *fully specified* in terms of structure and content; hence, while engaged in them students have little, if any, chance of utilizing such critical thinking dispositions as suspending judgment or such skills as developing criteria for evaluation or clarifying issues and claims. A *partially specified* task would require students to specify the format and content of the final product, thus allowing for use of a variety of dispositions and skills from Figure 3.1.

Figure 3.1
DISPOSITIONS AND SKILLS OF WEAK SENSE CRITICAL THINKING

Dispositions:
- Being sensitive to the feelings, level of knowledge, and sophistication of others
- Seeking precision
- Taking a position (and changing a position) when the information warrants
- Looking for alternatives
- Taking into account the total situation
- Seeking reasons
- Suspending judgment and restraining impulsivity
- Exercising fair-mindedness and reciprocity
- Exploring thoughts underlying feelings and feelings underlying thoughts
- Seeking accuracy
- Trying to be well informed

Skills:
- Focusing on a question
- Analyzing arguments
- Judging the credibility of sources
- Observing and judging observation reports
- Deducing and judging deduction
- Generalizing
- Inferring explanatory conclusions
- Making and judging value judgments
- Refining terms and strategies
- Identifying assumptions
- Identifying and correcting errors in reasoning
- Distinguishing facts from opinions
- Using critical vocabulary
- Clarifying issues and claims
- Developing criteria for evaluation
- Making interdisciplinary connections
- Distinguishing relevant from irrelevant information
- Comparing and contrasting ideals with actual practice
- Exploring implications and consequences
- Noting significant similarities and differences

For example, the task of writing and producing a play is partially specified. During its execution a group of students would have to determine the content of the play, how it will be staged, who will perform specific parts, and so on. These activities would require the use of dispositions such as being sensitive to the feelings and level of knowledge of others and skills such as observing and clarifying issues.

MULTIDIMENSIONAL

Closely related to the characteristic of partial specification is multidimensionality. Multidimensional refers to the variety of mental operations that are used within a task and the variety of ways the task can be completed. Ideally, for effective use of the dispositions and skills of critical thinking, students must be engaged in tasks that require a wide variety of cognitive operations and that can be solved in multiple ways.

A small set of multidimensional tasks particularly suited to the classroom has been identified (Marzano, 1991a; Marzano, et al., 1992). Each of these tasks plus a brief description of the task's general purpose follow:

Task	General Purpose
decision making:	making an informed selection among seemingly equal alternatives
investigation:	developing an explanation for some past event or a scenario for some future event and then supporting the explanation or scenario
problem solving:	developing, testing, and evaluating a method or product for overcoming an obstacle or constraint
experimental inquiry:	generating, testing, and evaluating

	the effectiveness of hypotheses generated to explain a physical or psychological phenomenon and then using those hypotheses to predict future events
invention:	developing a unique product or process that fulfills some articulated need

To illustrate the variety of cognitive operations as well as possible solutions inherent in these tasks. Consider each task's component parts. These parts are listed in Figure 3.2.

As Figure 3.2 illustrates, each task is highly complex cognitively, requiring a variety of interdependent mental operations. For example, while engaged in decision making, a learner must select an issue about which to make a decision, weigh the importance of various alternatives, judge the extent to which alternatives possess identified characteristics, and so on. Figure 3.2 also illustrates that options are available within almost every step of every task. For example, while performing the task of invention the learner has options as to the situation or need to attend to, the purpose of the invention, the standards used to judge the invention, and so on.

STUDENT DIRECTED

Student directed refers to the extent to which students construct and direct the execution of the task. Ideally, students are allowed to specify all components of the task. Student directedness within decision making (see Figure 3.2), for example, means that the student, rather than a teacher, specifies the alternatives to be considered, the criteria to be used to assess the alternatives, the extent to which the alternatives possess the criteria, and the final selection.

Figure 3.2
COMMON CLASSROOM MULTIDIMENSIONAL TASKS

Decision-making Tasks:
  a) identifying the alternatives to be considered
  b) identifying the criteria used to assess the alternatives and their relative importance
  c) identifying the extent to which each alternative fulfills each criterion
  d) making a selection of alternatives

Investigation:
  a) generating an initial question to be answered and determining the significance of the question
  b) identifying the criteria or standards with which to evaluate the final product
  c) identifying and using primary and secondary sources
  d) drawing a conclusion from the information gathered and articulating the relationships between the information and the conclusion
  e) identifying the extent to which the final explanation/scenario meets the stated criteria/standards

Problem-solving Tasks:
  a) identifying the important factors affecting the problem situation along with the characteristics of the desired outcome and the constraints or obstacles in the way of achieving the desired outcome
  b) identifying the standards or criteria for a successful solution
  c) identifying the possible alternative ways of overcoming the obstacle or the constraint
  d) selecting and trying out an alternative
  e) identifying the extent to which the selected alternative produces a solution that meets the stated standards/criteria
  f) if other alternatives were tried, articulating the reasoning behind the order of their selection and the extent to which each meets the stated standards/criteria

Experimental Inquiry Tasks:
  a) explaining a phenomenon initially observed
  b) identifying the facts or principles behind the explanation
  c) making a prediction based on the facts and principles underlying the explanation
  d) setting up and carrying out an activity or experiment to test the prediction
  e) evaluating the results of the activity/experiment in terms of facts and principles that have been articulated
  f) making another prediction of future events based on the combined information from the original explanation and results of the activity

Invention Tasks:
  a) identifying a situation to improve on or an unmet need
  b) identifying a purpose for the invention
  c) identifying specific standards or criteria that the invention will meet
  d) developing a rough model, sketch, or outline of the product
  e) developing the product
  f) continually revising and polishing the product until it reaches a level of completeness consistent with the criteria/standards that were articulated

Student directedness also refers to the freedom and opportunity to identify the manner in which the outcomes or final products of the task will be reported. This means that students have choices other than the characteristic written or oral essay and report (Durst & Newell, 1989). All of the methods listed below are valid ways of reporting the results of the tasks described in Figure 3.2, ways, parenthetically, that often allow students to capture the process of their effort as well as the products.

- a videotape
- a newscast
- a graphic organizer with an explanation
- a slide show
- a dramatic presentation
- a demonstration

This list can be expanded even further if students are allowed and encouraged to develop *artifacts* along with their tasks. Artifacts are physical or artistic products (e.g., a song, poem, mural, sculpture) that represent some aesthetic or symbolic by-product associated with a task. For example, within a decision-making task about which action would have been best taken by the United States in Iraq, a student might develop a sketch as a supplement for her written report. Whereas the written report would be used to communicate the process used within the decision-making task and the conclusions drawn from it, the artifact (the sketch) would be used to communicate a specific effect associated with the conclusions drawn by the letter.

LONG TERM

Long term refers to the length of time necessary to complete a task. It seems intuitively obvious, and now empirically established, that to utilize many of the critical-thinking dispositions and skills in Figure 3.1 requires that tasks extend over prolonged periods of time, even years (Jaques, 1985). Obviously, a learner cannot easily analyze arguments, infer explanatory conclusions, or clarify issues and claims in a contracted interval of time.

There are limits, though, to the longevity of the tasks students can engage in within a regular classroom setting. Specifically, classroom tasks certainly could not extend beyond a quarter or a semester, since these are the intervals within which courses are traditionally offered. So, in practice, long-term classroom tasks would probably span no more than one to three weeks. This is typically the range of time covered within most "units" of instruction.

SUMMARY

In summary, to foster the dispositions and skills associated with weak sense critical thinking, students must be engaged in tasks that are partially specified, multidimensional, student directed, and long term in nature. This means that teachers would consistently present students with activities like those in Figure 3.3. These tasks illustrate how decision making, investigating, problem solving, experimental inquiry, and invention might be presented to students within a unit on weather.

As students engage in these tasks, the teacher would attempt to reinforce the dispositions and skills of critical thinking listed in Figure 3.1. For example, while students engaged in the invention task, the teacher might ask them to pay particular attention to seeking precision as they made their final edits on their design for a house that utilizes weather. Or the teacher might ask students

Figure 3.3
TASKS FOR A UNIT OF STUDY ON WEATHER/CLIMATE

DECISION MAKING

It is your job to select a place to live within the continental United States that has a climate that is the most conducive to the development (intellectual, emotional, and physical) of those who live there. Make your selection and report on:
  a) the alternatives you considered
  b) the criteria you used, the weights applied to each, and the reasoning behind your selection of criteria and their weights
  c) your selection

INVESTIGATION

You are a member of a weather forecasting team whose job it is to predict the weather as accurately as possible for our city over the next year. Make your prediction on a monthly basis and report on:
  a) the resource you used
  b) the standards you set for your predictions
  c) the conclusions you came to and how you came to them
  d) the extent to which your forecast met your standards

EXPERIMENTAL INQUIRY

It is a common belief that climate affects the morale of those who experience it. Make a prediction based on this principle and test that prediction. Report on:
  a) the information on which you based your prediction
  b) how you tested your prediction
  c) the results of your test
  d) the conclusion you came to in light of your original prediction

PROBLEM SOLVING

You are a group of engineers charged with developing a way of keeping the temperature of the Denver metro area within the range of +50 degrees to +75 degrees Fahrenheit. However, the range of temperature in Denver is −25 degrees to +98 degrees Fahrenheit within a single year. Report on:
  a) your plan of action
  b) those things you would have to invent that do not exist
  c) those resources you would need
  d) those things you would have to eliminate that currently exist

INVENTION

Your job is to design a house that does not just protect against weather but also utilizes as many different types of weather as possible (e.g., instead of protecting against rain, how could you use rain?). After you have designed your system, report on:
  a) your initial design
  b) the changes you made in your initial ideas
  c) the information you had to gather
  d) the new things you would have to create to implement your design
  e) the final edits you made while polishing your design

to pay particular attention to considering a variety of alternatives as they constructed a decision about a place within the continental United States most conducive to the intellectual, emotional, and physical development of its inhabitants.

Certainly there is no single way of fostering weak sense critical thinking. Indeed, the description above incorporates a variety of approaches and practices. However, there is a growing body of research to support the effectiveness of specific programs that are designed to enhance critical thinking (for a review of the research of critical thinking programs and practices, see Marzano, 1991b; Nickerson, Perkins, & Smith, 1985; Resnick, 1987). For example, Matthew Lipman's *Philosophy for Children* (Lipman, 1974, 1978, 1980) has been studied extensively (see Chance, 1986; Lipman, 1985) and has shown increased student performance on general aptitude as well as tests of logical reasoning. Similarly, the popular programs *Future Problem Solving* (Crabbe, 1982; Torrance, 1986) and *Odyssey of the Mind* (Gourley, 1981) are estimated to involve 150,000 students each year. Some 77 percent of 166 experimental studies that used a problem-solving orientation like those in *Future Problem Solving* and *Odyssey of the Mind* reported significant academic gains (Torrance, 1986). Wales's (1979; Wales & Stager, 1977) research in decision-making and investigation tasks has demonstrated, too, their long-term positive effects on academic performance.

Still, it will be difficult to fully implement weak sense critical thinking in U.S. education because the current system does not support the types of tasks that are involved nor associated critical thinking dispositions and skills. Currently, standard classroom tasks are usually highly (if not totally) specified, unidimensional, teacher directed, and short term in nature (Doyle, 1983; Fisher & Hiebert, 1988).

THE ROLE OF STRONG SENSE CRITICAL THINKING IN THE CURRICULUM

If fostering the dispositions and skills of weak sense critical thinking will be difficult in U.S. education, fostering strong sense critical thinking may be impossible. One barrier to the implementation of such thinking is the fact that there are no K-12 educational programs designed to enhance it. In fact, there are not even many clear-cut recommendations about how to foster strong sense critical thinking. Paul (1990), however, does imply that fostering the following intellectual virtues will help.

a) Intellectual Humility: Awareness of the limits of one's knowledge, including sensitivity to circumstances in which one's native egocentrism is likely to function self-deceptively; sensitivity to bias and prejudice in and limitations of one's viewpoint.

b) Intellectual Courage: The willingness to face and assess fairly ideas, beliefs, or viewpoints to which we have not given a serious hearing, regardless of our strong negative reactions to them.

c) Intellectual Empathy: Recognizing the need to imaginatively put oneself in the place of others to genuinely understand them.

d) Intellectual Good Faith (Integrity): Recognition of the need to be true to one's own thinking, to be consistent in the intellectual standards one applies, to hold oneself to the same rigorous standards of evidence and proof to which one holds one's antagonists.

e) Intellectual Perseverance: Willingness to pursue intellectual insights and truths despite difficulties, obstacles, and frustrations.

f) Faith in Reason: Confidence that in the long run one's own higher interests and those of humankind at large will be served best by giving the freest play to reason, by encouraging people to come to their own conclusions, and by developing their own rational faculties.

g) Intellectual Sense of Justice: Willingness to entertain all viewpoints sympathetically and to assess them with the same intellectual standards, without reference to one's own feelings or vested interests or to the feelings or vested interests of one's friends, community, or nation (p. 54).

Presumably, these virtues can be reinforced as students engage in discussion and introspection about controversial topics of import to them. For example, in a social studies class, students might discuss and analyze the Gulf War and/or the following crisis. This would necessarily include an objective examination of both sides of the issue. Students would try to identify the motives and values behind President Bush's/President Clinton's position and develop a line of reasoning that would support it. Concomitantly, students would identify the motives and values behind Saddam Hussein's position and develop a line of reasoning to support his actions. While this ideological discussion occurs students would practice the intellectual virtues with guidance and direction from the teacher as situations arose.

A second (and probably more serious) barrier to the implementation of strong sense critical thinking is that programs and practices that are specifically designed to effect strong sense critical thinking would be considered much too "radical" to be accepted within the current culture of education.

Specifically, there are a number of programs and practices that are part of what might loosely be called "the human potential movement." These are specifically designed to produce the necessary shift from an ethnocentric to an altruistic world view (for a review, see Meichenbaum, 1977; Watzlawick, Weakland, & Fisch, 1974; Zeig & Munion, 1990). They do so by a systematic and apparently fairly effective analysis of the underlying assumptions that hold an egocentric/ethnocentric world view in place (see Hartke, 1980; Knight, 1983).

The very theory from which such programs operate, however, explains the perception that they are radical. Specifically, they operate on the premise that an awareness of one's paradigm creates an ability to think and behave without the bias inherent in any given paradigm.

The concept of paradigm was popularized by Thomas Kuhn and his influential book *The Structure of Scientific Revolutions* (1962). For Kuhn, a paradigm is a mental perspective or "mental set" one takes while engaged in scientific inquiry. As it relates to everyday functioning, Lincoln and Guba (1985) define a paradigm as a systematic set of beliefs that help one make sense of the world, i.e., a way of interpreting the world. Smith (1982) also views paradigms as interpretational structures used to organize experience. He refers to a paradigm as a "theory of the world in our heads." He states:

> What we have in our heads is a theory of what the world is like, a theory that is the basis of all our perception and understanding of the world, the root of all learning, the source of all hopes and fears, motives and expectancies, reasoning and creativity. And this theory is all we have. If we can make sense of the world at all, it is by interpreting our interactions with the world in the light of our theory. The theory is our shield against bewilderment (p. 57).

Although the concept of paradigm was popularized by Kuhn, Hegel (in Schwartz & Ogilvy, 1979) was the first to appreciate that a paradigm can be both enabling and constraining. More recently, Patton (1980) has noted that

> A paradigm is a world view, a general perspective, a way of breaking down the complexity of the real world. As such, paradigms are deeply embedded in the socialization of adherents and practitioners; paradigms tell them what is important, legitimate, and reasonable. Paradigms are also normative, telling the practitioner what to do without the necessity of long existential or epistemological considerations. But it is this aspect of paradigms that constitutes both their strength and their weakness—their strength in that it makes action possible, their weakness in that the very reason for action is hidden in the unquestioned assumptions of the paradigm (p. 203).

A paradigm, then, both enables and inhibits perception. It provides a framework with which stimuli can be organized in meaningful ways, but because of its inherent assumptions, it limits what can be perceived. Some schools of anthropology and sociology consider the dominant paradigm within a society synonymous with the culture of that society. Specifically, the view of the ideational school of anthropology is that culture is a function of what is shared in the community members' minds. As Sathe (1983) notes: "Culture is a set of important understandings (often unstated) that members of a community share in common" (p. 6).

Combining the notions of culture as paradigm and paradigm as an organizing and limiting set of assumptions, one might say that culture represents a set of parameters that circumscribe the thinking and consequent behavior of the members of a given society. In short, culture appears to be a "box" within which individuals operate. On the positive side, this box constitutes a set of guiding principles on which individuals can rely to make decisions about how to operate. For example, Sathe (1983) states: "Culture affects the decision-making process because shared beliefs and values give organizational members a consistent set of basic assumptions and preferences" (p. 11). However, just as the culture of a society enables, so does it delimit by creating blinders to realities that are outside of the culture. Sathe (1983) refers to this as the development of "cultural blind spots." Ethnocentric thinking, then, involves thinking within the box created by the culture in which one lives. To think outside of this box (i.e., to think critically in the strong sense) requires an objectivity about one's culture, and it is this detachment that will be violently (sometimes metaphorically and sometimes literally) opposed by those who cannot perceive of a valid perspective outside of their own.

As a chilling example of a society's resistance to challenging its own paradigm, Paul cites former president Reagan's almost unquestioned claim that one country, the USSR, was the "focus of all evil in the world," an "evil empire." Paul notes that the fact that

> a one-dimensional explanation of this sort can still not only catch the public's fancy but seem intelligible to many national leaders, not to mention some intellectuals, testifies in my view to the primitive state of much of our thinking about nontechnical, nontechnological human problems (p. 91).

Paul goes so far as to assert that the thinking underlying President Reagan's evil empire speech is akin to the thinking exhibited by the UNESCO children interviewed by Piaget:

Michael M. (9 years, 6 months old): Have you heard of such people as foreigners? *Yes, the French, the Americans, the Russians, the English* . . . Quite right. Are there differences between all these people? *Oh yes, they don't speak the same language.* And what else? *I don't know.* What do you think of the French, for instance? Do you like them or not? Try and tell me as much as possible. *The French are very serious, they don't worry about anything, an' it's dirty there.* And what do you think of the Russians? *They're bad, they're always wanting to make war* (in Paul, 1990, p. 91).

In summary, ethnocentric thought may so dominate our current culture that there is little tolerance for strong sense critical thinking—for an ability to perceive the world from a perspective other than one's own. In fact, there is open hostility by at least one powerful organization to any attempt to expose U.S. students to world views other than our own. Specifically, the Citizens for Excellence in Education (CEE) seem to consider the use of public dollars to expose students to alternative world views as contradictory to God's plan that the U.S. should be the vehicle to bring the world to a fundamental Christian perspective. Specifically, Robert Simonds, (1985) President of CEE, states that:

> History will record either one of two things about this generation and this present national emergency.
>
> "A handful of socialist manipulators stole the American dream of a Biblically based form of government, without firing a shot, while the church slept," or
>
> "At just the precise 'point of no return', the American republic's form of Constitutional government was saved from total annihilation by a small band of courageous Bible-believing Christians who raised up 'God's

standards' before the American church and the nation's people. With little help and much courage, Christians turned the nation back to its foundations in the Christian principles of liberty, freedom and morality and a 'Christian world view' for society to enjoy and prosper in. The nation's youth were saved and re-established as her most precious asset for the future. The church was a sleeping spiritual giant that was aroused to action by a special few, committed to the restoration of America's greatness" (Simonds, 1985, p. 2).

Although unbeknownst to most educators, CEE and like-minded organizations have been highly successful in banning the teaching of strong sense critical thinking at the school and district levels across the country (see Jenkinson, 1988a & b).

Critical thinking, particularly in the strong sense, just may be vital to the existence of a pluralistic society. However, because it brings into question the predominant ethnocentric world view, critical thinking may require a battle if it is to be taught and reinforced in the public schools. My contention is that this is a battle that critical thinking educators will have little option but to wage. In the words of practitioners, we may have to walk our talk to model critical thinking for our students and our colleagues.

- CURRICULUM
- FACILITIES
- INSTRUCTION
- MOTIVATION

Interactive Learning and Hypermedia Technology

Robert Bortnick
Elk Grove (IL) School District 59

A growing number of school leaders both here and abroad believe that the notion of interactive learning holds a key to educational improvement and change for the new millennium. Such learning actively involves students in activities that require their response, activities that can and often do lead to further inquiry.

These same leaders also believe that new educational technologies, ones just emerging on the horizon, can significantly expand the amount and kind of interactive possibilities available in modern schools and classrooms. The leaders do not confuse interactive learning with simply the incorporation of multimedia in their schools. For example, the adding of visual imagery, often through the use of television (e.g. Channel One), will result in multimedia. But as captivating as TV is, it still is a largely passive media. So these leaders use imagery medias that require viewer interaction. Such multimedias are part of a larger hypermedia learning environment.

Hypermedia learning environments are ones in which the learner is constantly involved in a trail of inquiry. This trail of inquiry need not be linear or restricted to a single media, visual or otherwise. Nor need it be limited to a single technology. Today computers can be linked to video and audio sources to provide an interactive multimedia environment. Such an environment allows possibilities far beyond the common lecture and textbook environment. The static black-and-white print limits of the standard textbook can be expanded to full-color animated text and illustrations that can in turn respond to inquiry. A response may change some aspect of the illustration or link some aspect of it to background information, video clips, or sounds. A word or phrase that is activated can be pronounced or a definition can appear for the reader.

Hypermedia learning environments provide teachers and students with the power to manipulate and control richer learning activities than ever imagined. Students, in particular, are offered opportunities to explore, convey, and create knowledge as never before using an array of educational technologies that, when combined, have the power of the computer, the resources of large databases, and the audio and visual impact of television. With hypermedia, we are able to visit any place on earth, at any time in history. We can hear about it, see it, explore it. Moreover, we can explore these situations from a myriad of perspectives and learning paths responsive to our individual interests, purposes, knowledge, and whim.

This chapter will explore interactive learning, an important goal of education, since Socrates engaged his students in questioning at the other end of the log. The chapter begins by noting some emerging hypermedia technologies that make interactive learning increasingly possible and affordable for all students. Examples follow of how state-of-the-art hypermedia software achieves interactive learning. The chapter closes with a review of the research literature that supports hypermedia approaches to interactive learning.

HYPERMEDIA TECHNOLOGIES

Several new extensive, durable, and cost-effective technologies have been developed that lend themselves to hypermedia applications. Two emerging technologies in point are CD-ROM (Compact Disc—Read Only Memory) and videodisc.

CD-ROM provides extensive possibilities for storage of numbers, words, and audio data. Approximately 150,000 pages of text, a 100-volume encyclopedia, or 1,500 floppies can be stored on one compact disc, discs much like those found in any record store. The Beethoven Ninth Symphony CD-ROM (Voyager, 1990) is an example. In addition to a high quality sound reproduction of the symphony itself, this disc contains extensive information about its composer, an analysis of the music, and a summary of the history of music. This combination of sound and information makes the disc a complete source on Beethoven and one of his important works.

Whereas the CD-ROM stores numbers, words, and music in a compact and comprehensive form, videodisc stores video and audio data. Each disc stores 54,000 frames of pictures and accompanying sound tracks. A single side standardly contains half an hour of running video with stereo sound. One sound track may be in one language and another in a second language or some other audio format. For example, the original movie *High Noon* sound track may be on one track and a reviewer's critique on the other.

When CD-ROM and videodisc technologies are combined

with computers, the result is a powerful "on-line" archive of high quality audio, visuals, and data. The random access capability of these technologies allows their users to proceed quickly and accurately to desired information, typically through search procedures based on a key word or frame number. The users need not search the information in sequence in the way that one looks through a series of folders in a file cabinet. So users can rapidly and flexibly retrieve a response to a single inquiry or different responses for a wide range of different inquiries.

A third technology is on the horizon that is even more intriguing than CD-ROM and videodisc from a hypermedia perspective (Greenberger, 1990). This technology, of which CDI (Compact Disc Interactive) is the current example, combines into one delivery system the best qualities of video from videodisc and the massive storage of data and sound from CDs. Such advanced systems would permit a more efficient and cost-effective means of accessing large amounts of audio, visual, and numerical data with one CDI player and without the purchase of a VCR, a videodisc, and a CD player.

EXAMPLE APPLICATIONS

We have examined briefly the new technologies available for developing hypermedia learning environments. Now let us look closer at some examples of these technologies in action. Three projects in education are especially illustrative of hypermedia's exciting potential to promote interactive education. Each project creates learning environments that are interactive, that support exploration, and that use multimedia to enhance meaning. Each has the potential of allowing feedback, communicating ideas, and being integrated with visual and audio materials. Each provides students with tools to organize information in new ways, get feedback on their organization, and play with information in a "what if" manner.

SHAKESPEARE PROJECT

One project in hypermedia education that is drawing national attention is Roy Friedlander's Shakespeare Project at Stanford University. In response to the realization that "in class all we have to guide us is the printed text and no matter how rich and suggestive this text may be it does not help us imagine the real experience of theater—communal, sensual, illusion, and fleeting as a dream" (Friedlander, 1988, p.18), Friedlander and his colleagues have built a hypermedia simulation of Shakespearean theater. This simulation enables students to imagine the full sensory experience of a theater production, an experience just short of actual production. Using videodiscs combined with a set of computer programs called "On Stage," students can, for example:

- "Attend" rehearsals with directors and performers
- "Discuss" a play's key issues with interviewed actors
- View and instantly compare several intriguingly different versions of a particular scene
- Design their own "versions" of a crucial scene on a computerized digital stage
- Peruse an "archive" of hundreds of historical photographs documenting a rich array of sets, costumes, and props
- Browse through an "electronic" wardrobe and prop room, choosing costumes that suit their own interpretation of a play
- Create their own "case study" of a character's motivation and psychology

- Skip through the expanse of a play almost instantaneously, making comparisons that reveal the large, embracing structure of the complete play
- "Read" a staged performance with the ease and freedom with which we now read a text—stopping, starting, viewing, reviewing, and selecting segments for detailed study

Collectively, these multimedia activities create an interactive learning environment in which students watch scenes, take notes, write hypermedia essays, or design stages and scenes allowing various interpretations. The activities, in turn, are coupled with structured tutorials as well as opportunities to freely browse through libraries of still images. At every turn in participating in the activities, the tutorials, and the browsing, students can save any elements or combinations in an electronic notebook. This allows them to either create projects or prepare class demonstrations. For example, the student may choose to compare interpretations of different actors as they play a given character and thereby provide clear demonstrations of performers' choices and how these choices affect the final meaning of the work itself. A comparison of, say, Olivier's *Hamlet* to Mel Gibson's might be made.

POINT OF VIEW

A second program in hypermedia education drawing national attention is Point of View (Scholastic, 1990). This is also an interactive multimedia program with links ready for the integration of voice and video.

A time line of U.S. history constitutes Point of View's basic feature. Each point on this line can be activated to provide additional information. All the elements important to a good social studies program, including political, economic, geographical, and historical information, are included.

While Point of View illustrates the large data storage capability of the computer in an interactive format, the program does much more. First, it provides teachers and students with a number of powerful avenues to explore the information. The program has the capabilities to make charts, maps, and multimedia documentaries. The mapping and charting features, for example, provide some twenty categories of data for exploration, and while not all of the categories have complete data, information can be added to existing categories and new categories can be created. Students could examine, say, population trends, making maps of different areas of the country in terms of rural or urban population trends. Several maps could be opened simultaneously to allow comparisons between different areas of the nation on any of a number of variables. Mapped data could then be dynamically followed, examined, and compared across various time periods. For example, one could compare the rural population of the Northwest in the late 1800s with that of the early 1900s or of today. The chart of the Northwest states' rural population in the 1820s would be automatically recalculated when the time line control was moved to the 1920s.

Besides allowing teachers and students to explore the information built into the program's basic database, Point of View also allows them to add or explore new information. For example, essays developed on word processors elsewhere can be imported and combined with ones developed within the program itself to produce a history report complete with graphs, charts, maps, and texts. The report might also include other imports, too, such as new data, pictures, sounds (e.g., a political address), and even videodisc clips.

WRITER'S NETWORK

A third hypermedia educational program just now beginning to attract national attention is Writer's Network (Ideal Learning, 1990). This program is a network software package that provides support for both teachers and students for the entire writing process.

In the prewriting phase, students have note-taking and outliner utilities to help them collect, organize, and synthesize information. Students are given tools to assist them in moving seamlessly from drafting a paper on a word processor (e.g., MacWrite) to publishing it using a desk-top publishing program (e.g., PageMaker). Thus, they can easily enhance their writing with sounds, illustrations, graphics, and page layout features. Moreover, they have access to an extensive analytic tool kit of revising and editing aids during the drafting process, including readability, length, and verb tense analyses as well as a homonym checker. They also have an electronic bulletin board upon which they can collaborate, participate in cooperative learning activities, and develop editing skills through peer editing.

In the final writing stage, students "send" their papers to the teacher electronically. The teacher then uses a host of tools for analyzing them, including common-error analysis and fragment/run-on sentence identification. Other tools allow the teacher to comment through direct annotations on the students' papers. In particular, the teacher can access a holistic scoring mask to provide concrete, objective feedback in terms of the critical traits of good writing. These traits come from holistic analysis techniques adopted by the National Assessment of Educational Progress program and are widely used in statewide assessment programs such as the one in Illinois. And, since the newer computers have voice digitization capabilities, the recording and storing of voice annotations are becoming feasible. Thus, teachers and students could give feedback on papers with voice notes that can be retrieved by the student.

Writer's Network maintains, manages, and can research and analyze all of the information resulting from the teacher's commentary. The teacher can examine student growth from a baseline composition to the present assignment on a number of dimensions. Since this information is electronically available for students and classes, the teacher can easily diagnose needs and direct instruction in the most beneficial manner.

IMPORTANT LINES OF RESEARCH

So far we have seen at least three technologies that lend themselves to building hypermedia learning environments. We have also seen three examples of hypermedia learning environments being used to promote interactive learning in areas from the arts and humanities to the social sciences.

But school leaders have been disappointed before by new high technologies that promised more than they delivered. Is this the case for hypermedia? Well, the answer is a qualified no. The research to date has been promising on the use of hypermedia environments in promoting interactive learning. But there is still research to be done.

The most direct line of research in support of the use of hypermedia environments to promote interactive learning comes from comparative studies of student achievement and attitudes when hypermedia technologies are used rather than traditional methods (i.e., lecture and textbook). Studies using videodisc technology, in particular, report that learning occurs comparatively more rapidly and better in this type of interactive environment than in the traditional one (Henderson, 1989; Hofmeister, Lubke, & Peterson, 1988; Hughes, 1989; Johnson, 1990; Kirchner, 1988; Leonard, 1989; NSBA, 1986; Pollak & Pollak, 1990; Straker, 1988). Specifically, the integration of such technology into a course delivery system seems to:

1. Increase instructional productivity by covering more content and better meeting the needs of large and diverse classes.
2. Increase instructional alacrity by permitting more independent, individualized, and self-paced learning.

Moreover, students find the videodisc technology comparatively more interesting and appealing.

Several less-direct lines of research further support the use of hypermedia environments to promote student learning. One of these lines comes out of work in human learning; another comes out of work in human motivation.

The work of Mary Alice White at Columbia University (White, 1987) clearly suggests how hypermedia can impact learning. Recall that often central to the hypermedia environment is the use of technologies that allow students to study and to use visual information. White's work demonstrates the importance of visual imagery in today's information-based society; indeed, this work considers literacy in comprehending such imagery as being fundamental to decision making in a highly complex, technical society. Obviously, a hypermedia environment could provide an effective means for the delivery of visual images, images that are not static, as in textbooks, but dynamic. Such visuals enhance and clarify the information conveyed.

White's work can be viewed, too, as but part of a larger

research net concerned with visual organizers and their role in artificial intelligence and metacognition. This research attempts to describe how information is stored in our minds so as to identify practical teaching strategies that might increase student comprehension and memory. Apparently, methods that occasion students to attend to and process relationships among ideas can be highly beneficial in terms of comprehension and recall (Armbruster, Anderson, & Osterag, 1987), especially in text learning. Various visual categorizing schemes seem to have this occasioning power for writing and comprehension (Sinatra, 1986). However, the development of such schemes requires teaching and additional student time and effort. The potential of hypermedia environments to convey such schemes in a timely and conceptually integrated fashion is evident. Such visual categorizing schemes could be readily represented within interactive multimedia environments.

While the work of White is illustrative of research suggesting that hypermedia can impact human learning, the work of Malone and Lepper (1986) is illustrative of research that clearly suggests that hypermedia can impact human motivation, too. Elsewhere, Block and King (1987) have called attention to intrinsic dimensions of instruction that have gone largely unexplained as being factors critical to student achievement. Chief among these factors is the opportunity to learn without any external rewards but just for *fun*. Malone and Lepper provide a number of ways in which instruction can be made more fun in both personal and social ways. Both of these ways readily lend themselves to hypermedia application.

Challenge is fun and can be manipulated by varying the degree of difficulty of the material to be mastered as well as the immediacy and appropriateness of the feedback to the learner.

Hypermedia environments allow students to adjust their learning activities so that their challenges are optimal, i.e., not too easy and not too hard, but just right. The interactive nature of such environments allows students to cut their learning tasks to size, so that each task can often be achieved with different solutions of varying degrees of complexity. These environments' multimedia features then allow students to gain almost instant access to feedback about their learning progress, feedback that can be delivered in a variety of audio, visual, and written forms.

Curiosity is also fun and can be manipulated by providing students with opportunities to discover the novelties, anomalies, and complexities inherent in the material to be achieved. The interactive nature of hypermedia learning environments clearly provides students with the chance to make repeated inquiries of the databases built into the environments. Students can especially "cut" certain information of interest in one way and then recut it in another for comparative purposes. The multimedia nature of the learning environment then allows students to play with each "cut" so that its complexities might be simplified and commonalities and noncommonalities might be highlighted.

Self-control of learning is fun, too, and can be provided by varying actual or perceptual opportunities for students to choose what and how they study the material to be achieved. Obviously, the interactive nature of hypermedia learning environments provides students with multiple opportunities to make such choices about what they study. Indeed, as we have seen, if they do not feel they have enough choices of material from the databanks built into the original programs, they can generate new material from these banks or even import additional material from elsewhere. Equally obviously, the multimedia nature of hypermedia learning environments provides students with multiple opportunities to make choices about how they study. Not only can students choose from among various media for studying purposes, but they can also readily reassemble these media into a delivery package best suited to their particular learning styles.

Finally, *fantasy* in learning is fun and may be invoked by providing students with a chance to study the material to be achieved in an imaginary context or a context of more appeal. Hypermedia learning environments provide significant chances for students to couch their learning problems in contexts more relevant to them, thus freeing them to think, feel, and act in new ways. Some learners use the interactive, multimedia nature of the environments to free themselves from the practical concerns of real life. Others use them for the reverse. Either fantasy allows learners to explore ideas fully and to explore them for learning's sake.

SUMMARY

The amount of information in today's world is doubling every two and a half years and even annually in some highly technical areas. When the kindergartners of today graduate from high school, information production is likely to further accelerate, leaving new graduates twenty times more information to deal with than their predecessors who are only a few years older. This exponential increase of information can potentially improve society, but it may also bury a society that lacks the tools to collect, synthesize, and apply information. *Do students have the tools to cope?*

This chapter has suggested that the use of hypermedia learning environments can be a key factor in determining the way our future generations use information. Such environments are interactive and multimedia. In them, every student would have access to material that could be investigated interactively and in different formats at any time. In them, too, students could immediately apply their learning to either real world situations of the present or unreal world situations of the future.

This chapter has suggested that the use of hypermedia learning environments can also be a key factor in determining the way future generations *build* information. In them, all students could develop an encyclopedia of knowledge that is tailored to their own needs and interests, resulting in personalized encyclopedias of learning in their own words. Such learners would no longer passively be bound to information provided by the teacher or the textbook but actively be freed to work with information generated by themselves.

Csikzentmihalyi (1975) has identified an experiential state that reflects the satisfaction that comes from total involvement in a task, the "high" that comes from an intense involvement in an activity. He calls that state "flow." We have every reason to believe that future research will find that hypermedia learning environments generate users and builders of knowledge who not only have fun but who also experience flow with much of the material they are asked to achieve in school. These environments need only be given an informed chance (Bortnick, 1980; 1987). The school leader who understands and can apply the potential of hypermedia technology holds the key to students' greater opportunity for truly interactive learning.

- ASSESSMENT
- CURRICULUM
- EXPECTATIONS
- INSTRUCTION
- ORGANIZATION/ MANAGEMENT (CLASSROOM)

Mastery Learning

Thomas R. Guskey
University of Kentucky

Few strategies have generated as much excitement among educators in recent years as mastery learning. Few also have been implemented as broadly or evaluated as thoroughly. Programs based on the ideas of mastery learning are operating today at every level of education, from preschool to graduate and professional schools. Evaluations of these programs show that students in mastery learning classes not only learn better and reach higher levels of achievement, they also develop greater confidence in their ability to learn and in themselves as learners (Block & Burns, 1976; Block, Efthim, & Burns, 1989; Guskey & Pigott, 1988; Kulik, Kulik, & Bangert-Drowns, 1990a).

The excitement about mastery learning also has been accompanied by some confusion. Questions frequently arise about the essential elements of mastery learning, how those elements are applied, and the extent of the changes mastery learning requires of teachers who wish to implement the process successfully in their classes.

In this chapter we will try to shed light on these and other questions regarding mastery learning. We will describe how mastery learning came about, how the process is generally applied, and the kinds of improvements in student learning that typically result. We also will illustrate how mastery learning can provide practical solutions to many of the instructional problems teachers encounter in classrooms today.

THE DEVELOPMENT OF MASTERY LEARNING

Although the basic tenets of mastery learning can be traced to such early educators as Comenius, Pestalozzi, and Herbart (Bloom, 1974), most modern applications are derived from the writing and research of Benjamin S. Bloom of the University of Chicago. In the mid-1960s, Bloom was deeply involved in research on individual differences. He recognized that in school settings, individual differences among students present a tremendous challenge to teachers, even when students are grouped in grade levels by age. Bloom was convinced, however, that aspects of the teaching and learning process could be altered to accommodate better these individual differences so that more students learn excellently and, as a result, attain very high levels of achievement.

To determine how this conviction might be practically achieved, Bloom first considered how teaching and learning typically take place in group-based classroom settings. He observed that in most cases, teachers begin their teaching by dividing the material they want students to learn into smaller learning units. These units are usually sequentially ordered and often correspond to chapters in the textbook used in teaching. Following instruction on the unit, a quiz or test is administered to students covering the unit material. To the teacher, this test is an evaluation device used to determine who has learned the material well and who has not. Then, based on the results of this test, students are sorted into categories and assigned grades. To students, on the other hand, this test generally signifies the end of instruction on the unit and the end of the time they need to spend working on the material. It also represents their one and only chance to demonstrate what they have learned. After the test is administered and scored, marks are recorded in the grade book, and instruction begins on the next unit, where the process is repeated.

When teaching and learning proceed in this manner, only a small number of students usually learns well the material in the unit. In fact, Bloom found that only about 20 percent of the students in the class learn excellently what the teacher set out to teach. Under these conditions, the distribution of achievement among students at the end of the instructional sequence looks much like a normal bell-shaped curve, as is shown in Figure 5.1.

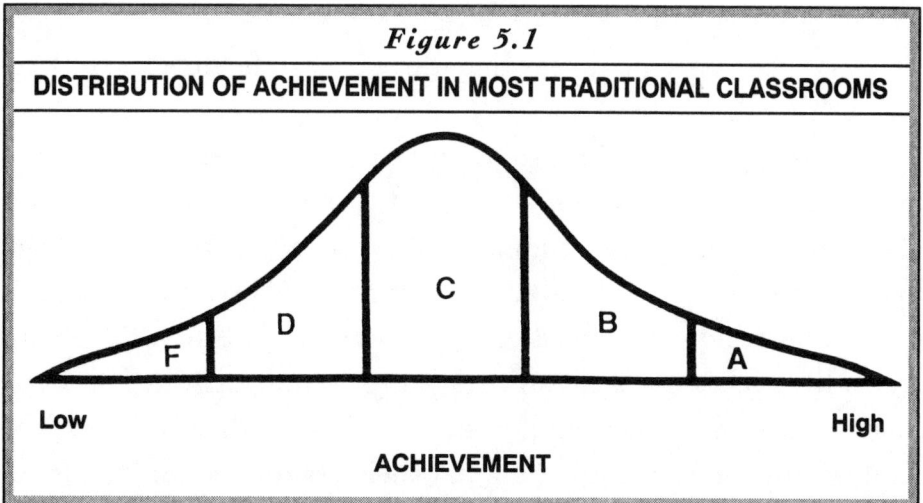

Figure 5.1
DISTRIBUTION OF ACHIEVEMENT IN MOST TRADITIONAL CLASSROOMS

Seeking a strategy that would produce better results, Bloom drew upon two sources of information. The first was knowledge of the ideal teaching and learning situation, where an excellent tutor is paired with an individual student. In other words, Bloom tried to determine what critical elements of one-to-one tutoring might be transferred to group-based instructional settings. The second source from which he drew was descriptions of the learning strategies employed by academically successful students. Here Bloom sought to identify the activities of high-achieving students in group-based learning environments that distinguish them from their less-successful counterparts.

Bloom saw dividing the material to be learned into units and checking on students' learning with a test at the end of each unit as useful instructional techniques. He believed, however, that the tests used by most teachers did little more than show for whom the initial instruction was or was not appropriate. If, on the other hand, these tests were accompanied by a *feedback and corrective* procedure, they could serve as valuable learning tools. That is, instead of using these tests solely as evaluation devices marking the end of each unit, Bloom recommended they be used to diagnose individual learning difficulties (feedback) and to prescribe specific remediation procedures (correctives).

This type of feedback and corrective procedure is precisely what takes place when an individual student works with an excellent tutor. If the student makes an error, the tutor first points out the error (feedback) and then follows up with further explanation and clarification (corrective). Similarly, academically successful students typically follow up the mistakes they make on quizzes and tests, seeking further information and greater understanding so that their errors are not repeated.

Bloom now outlined a specific instructional strategy to make use of this feedback and corrective procedure, labeling it "mastery learning" (Bloom, 1968). By this strategy, the material to be learned is first divided into smaller learning units. Usually a unit consists of the material that would be presented in about a week or two of class time. Following a teacher's initial instruction on the unit, a quiz or test is administered to students. But instead of signifying the end of the unit and being used to evaluate students, this test is used primarily to give students information or feedback on their learning. In fact, to emphasize its new purpose Bloom suggested it be called a *formative assessment*, meaning "to give information."

A formative assessment identifies for students precisely what they have and have not learned well to that point. Also included with the formative assessment are explicit suggestions to students as to what they might do to correct their learning difficulties identified on the assessment. Because these suggested corrective activities are specific to each item or group of items on the assessment, students need to work only on those concepts not yet mastered. In other words, the correctives are "individualized." They may point out additional sources of information on a particular topic, such as the page numbers in the course textbook or workbook where the topic is discussed; they may identify alternative learning resources, such as different textbooks, learning kits, alternative materials, or computerized instructional lessons; or they may simply suggest sources of additional practice, such as study guides or independent or guided practice activities. With the feedback and corrective information gained from a formative assessment, each student has a specific prescription of what more needs to be done to master the material or desired learning outcomes from that unit.

When students complete their corrective activities, usually after a class period or two, they are administered a second formative assessment. There are two major reasons for this second test. First, it is necessary to verify whether the correctives have been successful in helping students overcome their specific learning difficulties. Second, and more important, it offers students a second chance at success. Hence, it serves as a very powerful motivational device.

Through this process of formative assessment, combined with the systematic correction of individual learning difficulties, Bloom believed that all students could be provided with a more appropriate quality of instruction than is possible under more traditional approaches to teaching. He recognized that with careful planning, a teacher's initial approach to teaching is likely to be appropriate for many, and perhaps even most, of the students in the class. But because of individual differences among students, that approach is also likely to be inappropriate for some. Corrective procedures make other, possibly more appropriate, approaches available to those students so that a much larger portion of students learns well and reaches high levels of achievement.

Bloom believed that by providing students with these more favorable learning conditions, nearly *all* could learn excellently and truly master the subject material (Bloom, 1971, 1976). As a result, the distribution of achievement among students would look more like that illustrated in Figure 5.2. Note that grading standards have not been changed in any way. The same level of achievement used before to assign grades is still employed. But under mastery learning conditions, 80 percent or more of the students in a class reach the same high level of achievement that only about 20 or 30 percent do under more traditional approaches to instruction.

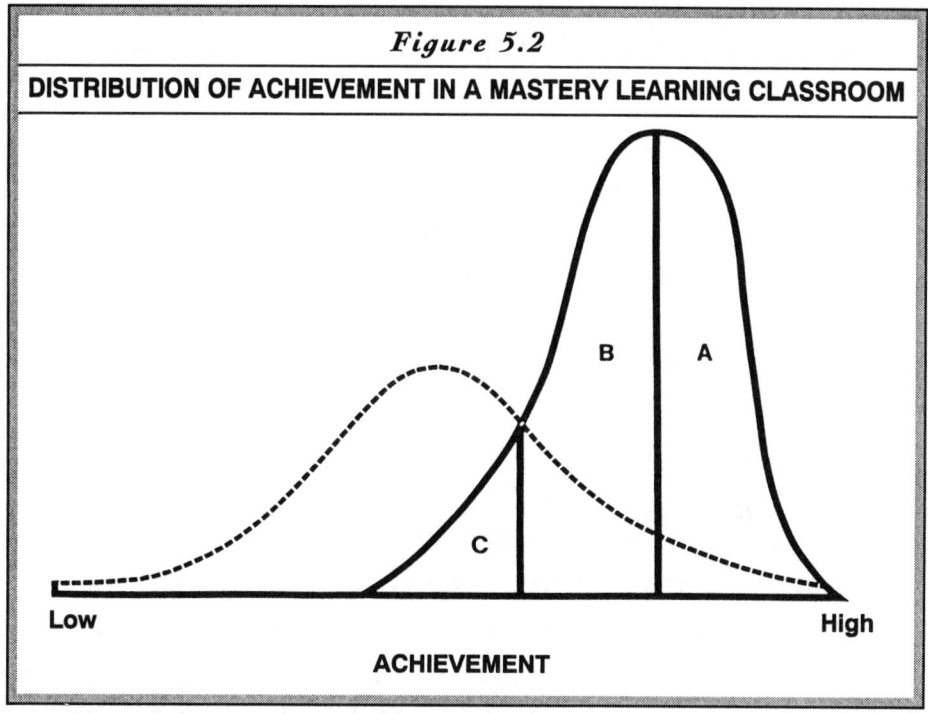

Figure 5.2
DISTRIBUTION OF ACHIEVEMENT IN A MASTERY LEARNING CLASSROOM

THE ESSENTIAL ELEMENTS OF MASTERY LEARNING

Since Benjamin Bloom first set forth his ideas, a great deal has been written about the theory of mastery learning and its accompanying instructional strategies (e.g., Block, 1971, 1974; Block & Anderson, 1975; Block, Efthim, & Burns, 1989). Still, the particular characteristics of "mastery learning" programs are known to vary greatly from setting to setting (Burns, 1987). For this reason, educators concerned with its application often have found it difficult to get a clear and concise description of the essential elements of mastery learning and the specific changes required for successful implementation.

In recent years two elements have been defined as essential to the implementation of mastery learning (Guskey, 1985, 1987a). Although the actual appearance or format of these elements may vary, they serve a very specific purpose in a mastery learning classroom and most clearly differentiate mastery learning from other instructional approaches. These essential elements are the *feedback, corrective,* and *enrichment processes* and *congruence among instructional components.*

FEEDBACK, CORRECTIVES, AND ENRICHMENT

To use mastery learning a teacher must offer students regular and specific information on their learning progress. Furthermore, that information must be both diagnostic and prescriptive. That is, the information or feedback students regularly receive should: (a) reinforce precisely what was most important for them to learn in the unit, (b) recognize what they have learned well, and (c) identify what they need to spend more time on. To be effective this feedback also should be appropriate for students' level of learning.

By itself, however, feedback will not help students greatly improve their learning. For significant improvement to occur, the feedback they receive must be paired with specific corrective activities. These correctives offer students explicit guidance and direction on how they can correct their learning errors and remedy their learning problems. And, most important, the correctives must be different from the initial instruction. Simply having students go back and repeat a process that has already proven unsuccessful is unlikely to yield any better results the second time. Therefore, corrective activities must offer students an instructional alternative. Specifically, they must *present the material differently* and *involve students differently* than did the initial teaching. This means that the correctives should incorporate different learning styles or learning modalities. In addition, corrective activities should be effective in improving performance. A new or alternative approach that does not help students overcome their learning difficulties is inappropriate as a corrective and ought to be avoided.

In most group-based applications of mastery learning, correctives are accompanied by enrichment or extension activities for students who attain mastery from the initial teaching. Enrichment activities provide these students with exciting opportunities to broaden and expand their learning. To be effective, these enrichments must be both *rewarding* and *challenging*. In general, they are related to the subject area being studied but need not be tied directly to the content of a particular unit. Hence, enrichment offers an excellent means of involving students in challenging higher-level activities such as those designed for the gifted and talented.

This feedback, corrective, and enrichment process, illustrated in Figure 5.3, can be implemented in a variety of ways. In many mastery learning classes teachers use short paper-and-pencil quizzes as formative checks to give students feedback on their learning progress. But a formative assessment can be any device teachers use to gain evidence on the learning progress of their students. Thus, essays, compositions, projects, reports, skill demonstrations, and oral presentations can all serve as formative assessments.

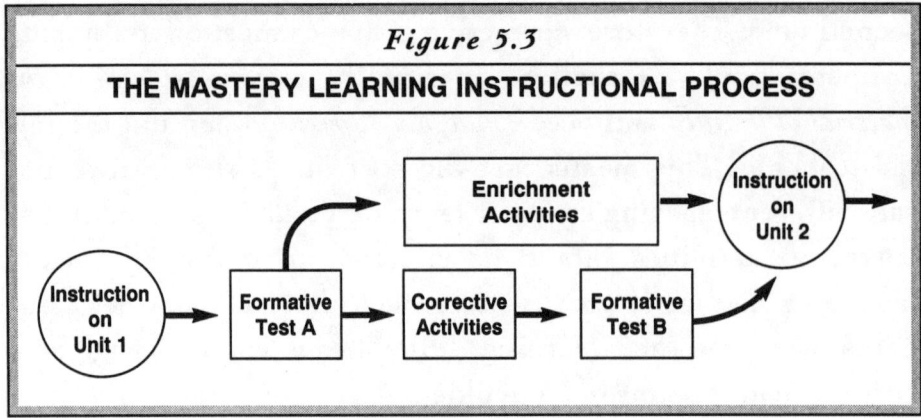

Following a formative assessment, some teachers divide the class into two groups. Then, while the teacher directs the activities of students engaged in correctives, the other students work on self-selected independent enrichment activities that are both exciting and challenging. Other teachers team with colleagues and exchange students, so that while one oversees corrective activities the other monitors enrichments. Still other teachers engage students in cooperative learning activities in which corrective and enrichment students work together in teams to ensure that all reach the mastery level. If all do attain mastery on the second formative check, the entire team receives special awards or credit (Guskey, 1990a).

Feedback, corrective, and enrichment procedures are crucial to the mastery learning process, for it is through these procedures that mastery learning "individualizes" instruction. In every unit taught, students who need extended time and opportunity to remedy learning problems are offered these through correctives. Furthermore, those students who learn quickly or for whom the initial instruction was appropriate are provided with an opportunity to extend their learning through enrichments. As a result, many more students are provided with favorable learning conditions and a more appropriate, higher quality of instruction.

CONGRUENCE AMONG INSTRUCTIONAL COMPONENTS

While feedback, correctives, and enrichment are extremely important, they alone do not constitute mastery learning. To be truly effective, they must be combined with the second essential element of the mastery learning process: congruence among instructional components.

The teaching and learning process is generally perceived as having three major components (see Figure 5.4). To begin, one must have some idea of what students are to learn—the learning objectives or goals. This is followed by instruction that, it is hoped, results in competent learners—students who have learned well and whose competence can be assessed through some form of evaluation. Mastery learning adds the additional components of feedback and correction so that teachers can determine for whom the initial instruction was appropriate and for whom an alternative must be planned.

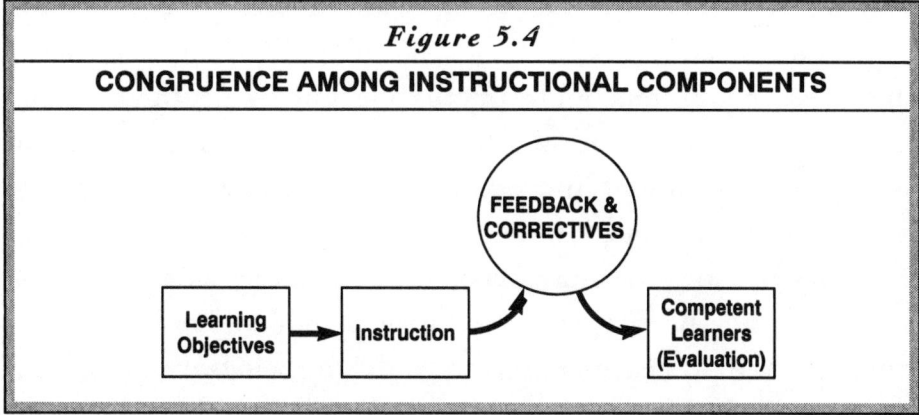

Figure 5.4
CONGRUENCE AMONG INSTRUCTIONAL COMPONENTS

Although essentially neutral with regard to what is taught, how it is taught, and how resultant learning is evaluated, mastery learning does demand consistency and alignment among these instructional components. For example, if students are expected to learn higher-level skills such as those involved in application or analysis, mastery learning stipulates that instructional activities be planned to give students opportunities to engage actively in those skills. It also requires that students be given specific feedback on their learning of those skills, coupled with directions on how to correct any learning errors. And finally, procedures for evaluating students' learning should be based on those skills as well.

Although congruence among instructional components is essential for mastery learning, it is actually an essential component of effective teaching and learning at any level. Suppose, for example, that a language arts teacher offers students feedback on their learning through short multiple-choice quizzes on grammar and punctuation but then evaluates their learning in terms of the clarity and precision with which they organize ideas in written compositions. In this case, although students receive regular feedback, that feedback is clearly not congruent with the procedures used to evaluate their learning. Students may know the rules of grammar and punctuation but be unable to apply those rules in their writing. Or they may prepare a composition with perfect grammar and punctuation but receive a low grade because of inadequate content or poor organization.

In a mastery learning class, the feedback students receive should always be congruent with the specified learning objectives and the procedures used to evaluate their learning. If students' writing skill, their organization of ideas, and the content of their writing are the criteria by which their learning is to be evaluated, they should receive diagnostic feedback based on those criteria and prescriptive guidance to correct whatever learning difficulties they may be experiencing.

This element of congruence among instructional components has led some to criticize mastery learning as simply "teaching to the test." The important issue in this regard, however, is what forms the basis for teaching. If a test is the basis of teaching and if what is taught is determined primarily by that test, then indeed one is "teaching to the test." Under these conditions, the content and format of the test dictate not only what is taught but also how it is taught. With mastery learning, it is the desired learning goals that are the basis of teaching, and these, in most cases, are determined by the teacher. In using mastery learning, teachers simply ensure that their instructional activities and the procedures they use to evaluate students' learning match what they have determined to be important for students to learn. Thus, instead of "teaching to the test," mastery learning teachers are more accurately "testing what they teach."

Admittedly, identifying the desired learning goals requires teachers to make some very crucial decisions. They must decide, for example, what concepts or skills are most important for students to learn and most central to students' understanding of the subject. But it is also important for all teachers to recognize that they are already making these decisions. Every time a test is administered, a paper is graded, or any evaluation of learning is made, teachers communicate to their students what they consider to be most important. The use of mastery learning simply compels teachers to confront these decisions more carefully and more thoughtfully than usual.

IMPLICATIONS AND RESEARCH RESULTS

There are several important implications that stem from this description of mastery learning. The first is that mastery learning is very adaptable in its application. It is possible, for example, for two teachers to implement mastery learning successfully in identical courses or grade levels using very different approaches. Both would employ the same essential elements of the mastery learning process, of course. But the way they conduct their initial teaching, the type of formative assessments they use, and the kind of corrective activities and enrichments their students engage in could all be different. In other words, there is no one best way to implement mastery learning. Successful applications depend, to a large extent, on teachers' ability to adapt the essential elements of mastery learning to fit the particular context in which they teach and the unique characteristics of their students.

A second implication is that mastery learning is broadly applicable. It is apparent to most how mastery learning might be used to teach basic skills. But the mastery learning process is equally effective when applied to instruction in higher-level skills such as problem solving, drawing inferences, deductive reasoning, and creative writing (Mevarech, 1985; Soled, 1987).

In teaching creative writing, for example, the first thing the teacher must be able to do is describe, in some detail, the difference between the composition that is creative and the one that is not. For if that difference cannot be described, what is the teacher to teach? Describing that difference is an essential prerequisite to teaching the higher-level skills associated with creative writing. As soon as that difference is described, however, a basis is also established for offering students feedback on their writing, as well as guidance in correcting their errors and making revisions, so that the composition that is not creative becomes more like one that is. In other words, a basis is established for using mastery learning, even in an advanced, highly complex subject like creative writing.

In a writing class, students' compositions serve as the formative assessments. They are submitted to the teacher and evaluated in terms of criteria the teacher has taught. In some cases, fellow students may offer evaluative feedback, with directions for doing so provided by the teacher. The compositions are then returned to students with suggestions for revision based upon those criteria. Corrective activities involve simply helping students make those revisions using different techniques than those employed in the initial teaching. Once completed, revised compositions are submitted to the teacher again as the second formative assessment.

A third implication of the essential elements of mastery learning is that most teachers do not have to alter drastically what they are doing in their classrooms to use the process. Unlike many new ideas and strategies that are designed to replace teachers' current teaching methods, mastery learning builds upon those techniques. Rather than forcing teachers to abandon the practices they have developed and refined over the years, mastery learning provides teachers with a means for improving those practices. It empowers them to make the best use of the skills they already have. Most excellent teachers are undoubtedly using some form of mastery learning already. Others are likely to find that the mastery learning process blends well with many of their present teaching strategies.

Given the demanding nature of teaching and the difficulties generally associated with approaches that require major changes or extensive revisions in teaching procedures (see Fullan & Stiegelbauer, 1991; Huberman & Miles, 1984), this is an exciting prospect.

Finally, although implementing the essential elements of mastery learning does not require drastic change, extensive research evidence shows that their use can have extremely positive effects on student learning (Block, Efthim, & Burns, 1989; Guskey & Pigott, 1988; Kulik, Kulik, & Bangert-Drowns, 1990a; Walberg, 1984). Providing feedback, correctives, and enrichments and ensuring congruence among instructional components can be accomplished by most teachers with relatively little extra time or effort, especially if tasks can be shared among teaching colleagues. Still, the careful and systematic use of these elements can lead to significant improvements.

Equally important is that the improvements that mastery learning brings about are not restricted to only student achievement indices. Mastery learning has also been shown to have very positive effects on students' attendance in school, their involvement in class lessons, and their attitudes toward learning (Block, Efthim, & Burns, 1989; Guskey & Gates, 1986; Guskey & Pigott, 1988). This has been referred to as the "multiplier effect" of mastery learning (Guskey, Barshis, & Easton, 1982), and it makes mastery learning one of the most cost-effective means of fostering educational improvement.

It should be noted that one recent review of the research on mastery learning, contrary to all previous ones, indicates that the process has essentially no effect on student achievement (Slavin, 1987). This finding surprised not only scholars familiar with the vast research literature on mastery learning showing it to yield very positive results but also large numbers of practitioners who have experienced its positive impact firsthand. A close inspection of this review shows, however, that it was conducted using techniques of questionable validity (Joyce, 1987; Hiebert, 1987), employed capricious selection criteria (Anderson & Burns, 1987; Kulik, Kulik, & Bangert-Drowns, 1990b), reported results in a biased manner (Walberg, 1988), and drew conclusions not substantiated by the evidence presented (Guskey, 1987b, 1988b). Most important, two much more extensive and methodologically sound reviews published since (Guskey & Pigott, 1988; Kulik, Kulik, & Bangert-Drowns, 1990a) verify mastery learning's consistently positive impact on a broad range of student learning outcomes.

CONCLUSION

The future of mastery learning looks particularly bright. Although the essential elements involved in the mastery learning process are different from those involved in much of traditional education, their value in enhancing the quality of instruction and improving student learning is now well established and becoming increasingly better known. Today more and more teachers are coming to recognize how necessary it is to use tests and assessments as learning tools rather than simply as devices to categorize students and assign grades. Many also are offering corrective activities to students who may need a little more time or another instructional approach to learn well. They are providing enrichment activities for fast learners who can benefit from the opportunity to extend and broaden their learning. Many, too, are working hard to ensure their instructional methods, feedback and corrective enrichment techniques, and their assessments are aligned with the learning goals they most value. For these teachers mastery learning offers the tools they need to have a more powerful influence on the learning of their students. It empowers them to be more effective and, as a result, makes teaching more rewarding and enjoyable (Guskey, 1980, 1986).

Researchers today have also come to recognize the value of the essential elements of mastery learning and the importance of these elements in effective teaching at any level. As a result, fewer studies are being conducted on the mastery learning process per se. Instead, researchers are looking for ways to enhance results further, adding to the mastery learning process additional elements that positively contribute to student learning in hopes of attaining even more impressive gains (Walberg, 1990). Recent work on the integration of mastery learning with other innovative strategies appears especially promising (Arredondo & Block, 1990; Guskey, 1988a, 1990a & b).

Mastery learning is not an educational panacea and will not solve all the complex problems facing educators today. It also does not reach the limits of the potential for teaching and learning. Exciting work is continuing on new methods aimed at attaining results far more positive than those typically derived through mastery learning (Bloom, 1984, 1988). Careful attention to the essential elements of mastery learning will, however, allow educators at all levels to make great strides toward the goal of enabling all children to learn excellently.

Teaching Innovations

6

- ASSESSMENT
- ORGANIZATION/ MANAGEMENT (SCHOOL)

Assessment as a School Improvement "Innovation"?

Richard J. Stiggins
Assessment Training Institute

In one sense, it is somewhat troubling to be called upon to prepare a chapter on the topic of the assessment of student achievement as a school improvement "innovation." Webster defines innovation as "the introduction of something new." The thesaurus lists such synonyms as *change, alteration, novelty,* and *variation.* In what sense can we consider assessment as a novelty in schools? Have assessments not always been present there? Certainly there can be no doubt that we are assessing students—at unprecedented rates. When considered together, our international, national, statewide, and local district assessments may constitute a billion-dollar per year U.S. industry.

Why, then, is it necessary in the 1990s to refer to assessment as an innovation in school improvement contexts? There are two reasons. First, we are expanding the range of methods we use to assess achievement. Second, we are redefining the meaning of assessment-competence for educators.

To understand the first reason, consider the nature of the tests commonly used in the centralized national, state, and local testing programs and compare it to the assessment needs of educators involved in local school improvement efforts. The standardized tests used in most centralized testing programs are specifically designed to provide broad-stroke portraits of student attainment of that common core of achievement that can be assessed effectively using multiple-choice test items. Very broad domains of achievement are sampled with very few test items to obtain a very general sense of student attainment levels.

Well-informed users of these tests understand that they are not high-resolution microscopes. They understand that such assessments reflect only a fraction of the full array of achievement targets we want students to hit. To illustrate, the Oregon Department of Education (1986) revealed that the commonly used norm-referenced standardized achievement test batteries cover nearly all of Oregon's essential multiple-choice testable learning skills (State Objectives). But in a follow-up study, Rhodes (1989) revealed that these skills constitute less than a quarter of all learning outcomes valued by Oregon educators.

For this reason, well-informed users understand that standardized tests, which are designed to give policymakers a general look at student achievement, typically are not sharp enough in their focus to detect the impacts of most local school improvement programs. And yet, as we move through the decade of the 1990s, we continue to find practitioners and researchers alike placing blind faith in scores on standardized tests as criterion measures of the effectiveness of school improvement efforts. The depth of this faith is reflected in the fact that an entire decade-long national program of "effective schools" research has been based on the assumption that what works in schools are those school organizations and teaching strategies that are present when standardized test scores are high and absent when such scores are low.

Quite simply, this faith in the sensitivity of these standardized test scores in local school improvement contexts is misplaced. The sense in which we must regard assessment as a school improvement "innovation" relates to our emerging awareness of the need for much higher-resolution local assessments in the future. We have begun to lay the foundation for these improved assessments with ever-clearer definitions of desired achievement targets and with a rapidly broadening sense of what it means to assess those targets effectively. These represent assessment innovations.

To understand the second reason why we must regard assessment as a school improvement "innovation" for the 1990s, we must realize that, as important as sound assessment is to student well-being, it has not been a part of the educator training curriculum in the past. Essential training in the basic principles of sound assessment is almost totally absent from teacher and administrator training programs (Schafer & Lissitz, 1987; Stiggins & Conklin, 1992). Further, in those rare instances where such training has been provided, the material covered has borne little resemblance to the assessment realities of life in schools and classrooms (Gullickson & Hopkins, 1987; Stiggins & Conklin, 1992). Still further, examination of certification requirements across the nation reveals that assessment competence is rarely required for educators to be licensed and is inadequately covered in teacher certification examinations (Wolmut, 1988).

The reason for our failure to develop and implement proper assessments in local school improvement programs is quite clear. As a community of educational practitioners, we simply did not know any better. To the extent that we act to change this state of affairs in the future, providing teachers with new tools needed to do their job, we will be innovating.

In this chapter, we will examine what it will take for us to succeed in integrating this essential assessment innovation into the ongoing functioning of schools and school improvement. To reach this goal, we will have to cover terrain that has never been successfully negotiated before. This will entail:

- Developing a very clear and highly differentiated sense of the various purposes for assessment in the school improvement context,
- Articulating a clear and specific set of achievement targets to be hit by students,
- Learning to apply the full array of assessment methods we have at our disposal, and
- Developing throughout the education community a clear understanding of how to match targets to assessment methods so as to produce high-quality information about student achievement.

Let us consider each of these points in more detail.

UNDERSTANDING ASSESSMENT PURPOSES

The first key to sound assessment is defining a clear purpose for that assessment. In the context of school improvement, we have fallen into the habit of using assessment to determine whether our improvement efforts "worked." First we change, then teach, and finally assess. This kind of thinking about assessment is acceptable in one sense but inappropriately narrow in another. Assessment can be far more than an index of success. It can be an integral part of the improvement itself. Here is how.

Think of assessment as the process of gathering information to make informed decisions (Airasian, 1991). In the school improvement situation, who are the relevant decision makers? The first, obviously, are the principal, the program developer(s), and the other upper-level manager(s). They use initial school-level achievement data to formulate improvement plans and then use subsequent data to evaluate the program's impact and to decide how to make it stronger. In order to make sound decisions and to inform the public that all is going as it should, they need periodic comprehensive achievement data that are comparable across classrooms.

However, are decision makers at the upper level the only users of assessment results? Certainly not. Yet we rarely, if ever, reflect upon who other decision makers might be or what important decisions they might make.

For instance, *teachers* use assessment results to inform decisions. They diagnose student needs, group students for instruction, assign report card grades, and evaluate their own teaching. They also use assessment as a teaching tool to clarify expectations, to help students practice hitting the target, and to help students see their own progress. Further, teachers use the power to assess as a classroom management tool—to cause students to behave in academically productive and socially acceptable ways.

If teachers had to rely solely on those periodic comprehensive assessments that the school improvement leaders used, they would be unable to function. Typical teachers can spend as much as a third to a half of their professional time on assessment-related activities (Herman & Dorr-Bremme, 1982; Stiggins & Conklin, 1992)! On average, they make decisions about how they will interact with their students at the rate of one decision every two to three minutes (Shavelson & Stern, 1981). Small wonder that yearly or twice-yearly tests are of little help.

Students also make decisions that are critical to their own well being, do they not? For instance, they set academic expectations for themselves. They decide whether to actively participate in the learning process (whether to care!). In addition, they decide what, when, how much, and with whom to study and which strategies to use. All these decisions are informed by results from teachers' day-to-day, week-to-week, and term-to-term assessments.

Let us not forget *parents*. Like students, they derive their information for decision making from teachers. Using the results of classroom assessments, parents evaluate the quality of teachers, programs, and schools; set expectations for their children; analyze home study environments; plan the allocation of family resources for their children's educations; and decide when to reward.

If teachers, students, and parents have access to sound assessment results, they can make sound decisions and students can prosper. However, consider the plight of students involved in school improvement programs where program developers rely on unsound assessments to make their key decisions, teachers rely on unsound classroom assessment to inform their decisions, and those same teachers pass their misinformation on to students and parents. I submit that this scenario represents a potential for bad decision making from which few students can recover.

If we are to avoid this kind of scenario, everyone concerned with school improvement must meet these very high standards: First, they must be crystal-clear about the decisions they make in the teaching and learning process. Then they must understand how those decisions relate to effective instruction and the well-being of students. And they must understand what specific kinds of assessments are needed to produce the accurate achievement-data they need to inform their specific decisions.

Given the current status of assessment training and the quality of classroom assessments, we have ample reason to be concerned about the nature and quality of the assessments currently informing decisions by these key "school improvement" decision makers. Remedies are available, however. They begin with the articulation of specific educational outcomes.

ARTICULATING TARGETS

Quality assessments cannot be designed in the absence of clear achievement targets. Yet we continue as teachers and administrators to be unclear about what we expect of students. For example, from among those charged with teaching students to write, how many can clearly define in writing—using words that student writers comprehend—what it means to write well? From among those charged with teaching students to read effectively, how many can precisely articulate the differences between an effective and an ineffective reader? Higher-order thinking is a national priority in schools, but those responsible for helping students hit this target often appear bewildered or confused when challenged to define what higher-order thinking really means.

Educators who cannot define their targets can neither help students hit the bull's-eye nor can they judge with any accuracy how close students are to it. The purpose of this chapter, however, is not to indict teachers for their lack of assessment literacy. Their professional preparation simply did not equip them to fulfill their critical assessment responsibilities. The point is that without a better definition of outcomes, sound assessment in the school improvement context will not be possible.

When it comes to clarifying targets we have reason to be optimistic. Nearly every national professional association of teachers—math, science, social studies, physical education, and foreign languages, among others—is carefully reexamining the valued outcomes in its field. In addition, the English/language arts community has done yeoman's work over the past decade in articulating what it means to write well (Langer & Applebee, 1987). These clearer definitions are giving birth to new and better assessments of writing proficiency all across the nation. Reading specialists have done outstanding work in articulating the differences between good and poor readers (Valencia & Pearson, 1988). And cross-discipline efforts over the past decade have helped us understand and implement stronger higher-order thinking curricula (Norris & Ennis, 1989).

The question is: How can the results of these efforts be translated into school and classroom assessment? This will take an awareness of the broad range of types of targets, a sense of how best to describe and communicate about those targets, and strategies for finding the really important targets—at the local level.

TYPES OF TARGETS

From an assessment point of view, there are many kinds of valued achievement targets. In most learning environments, we can identify at least five different kinds of targets that we want students to hit. These include:

- Specific substantive subject matter knowledge to be mastered

Examples: Number facts, science facts, history facts, spelling, vocabulary;
- Several patterns of reasoning to be demonstrated — going beyond just "knowing" to be able to use information to solve problems
  Examples: Analyzing, comparing, inferring, evaluating;
- Specific achievement-related skills to be demonstrated
  Examples: Reading aloud, speaking, foreign language dialogue, motor skills, science lab processes;
- Specific achievement-related products to be created
  Examples: Samples of writing, research reports, art or craft products; and
- Affective targets to be attained
  Examples: Attitudes, interests, values, and feelings (we do little to serve students if we teach them to do competent math, when in the end they hate math).

These different types of targets require different kinds of assessments. But until we articulate in clear and understandable terms all the different types of outcomes we value, we cannot hope to assess those outcomes well.

DESCRIBING TARGETS

Traditionally, we have been taught to articulate expectations in the form of instructional goals and objectives. While this articulation represents an excellent alternative, it is by no means the only way to describe expectations.

For example, we can communicate very effectively with students about what it means to write well by sharing with them the criteria or standards we plan to use to evaluate their writing. In this case, we might communicate both (a) the dimensions of writing to be evaluated—such as content and ideas, organization, sentence fluency—and (b) the performance continuum associated with each dimension—for example, what it means to be disorganized and to produce skillfully organized writing (Spandel & Stiggins, 1990). The rating scales and checklists we use in such assessments give us an excellent, rich vocabulary to serve as a basis for communicating about valued outcomes.

We also can communicate expectations in the form of tables of test specifications or test blueprints (Airasian, 1991). These are simple charts that cross an outline of the content to be tested along one dimension with the kinds of thinking to be tested along the other dimension. They reflect the emphasis the assessment (and, it is hoped, the instruction) will place on different categories of content and kinds of thinking. An example of such a blueprint for a tenth-grade biology unit test is presented in Figure 6.1. Test questions are then written to reflect these priorities. If students were given a copy of this test plan at the beginning of the unit of instruction, they would have a clear target to aim at as they studied.

Finally, we can articulate our expectations by providing examples of good and poor work, samples that reveal certain critical attributes or behaviors we wish to clarify for students. Or, we can give them actual samples of the test exercises that they will need to be able to handle when learning is done. Clearly, there are many ways to reveal our expectations—if we know what those expectations are.

FINDING THE IMPORTANT OUTCOMES

While national or state goals are often helpful as a beginning, they tend to be quite broad in their focus—often too broad to be effectively translated into specific school or classroom assessments.

Figure 6.1
TEST SPECIFICATION CHART

CHAPTER/SUBJECT: __BIOLOGY__
GRADE: __10__

CONTENT	RECALL	ANALYSIS	COMPARISON	TOTAL
	EDUCATIONAL OUTCOMES			
1. Cell Structure	5 Questions	2 Questions	1 Question	8
2. Cellular Reproduction	3 Questions	2 Questions	1 Question	6
3. DNA	2 Questions	2 Questions	4 Questions	8
TOTAL	10	6	6	22

Local educators must search their local curriculum for clear evidence of valued outcomes. There are many ways to do this.

For example, one can analyze textbooks to identify the content to be mastered and the kinds of reasoning to be demonstrated. Typically, the text itself is a better reflection of these priorities than any tests that might accompany it, because the tests may not cover what is taught in the book. Important outcomes can also be identified through the analysis of tasks to be performed by students, such as behaviors to be exhibited or products to be created. What are the component parts of sound performance and how does a good performance differ from a poor one—in specific terms? Yet another means of zeroing in on important instructional outcomes is to develop a few sample assessment exercises—i.e., articulate precisely what kinds of problems we want students to address, then draw inferences about the skills and knowledge they need to solve such problems.

ASSESSMENT ALTERNATIVES

Once we know what the targets look like, we can select assessment methods to match them. Let's explore what that means.

In education, we traditionally have thought of assessment as a collection of multiple-choice items. Some people believe, in fact, that the objective paper-and-pencil test is the only truly dependable, scientific, unbiased way to assess learning—no matter what the intended outcome. Nothing could be further from the truth.

While objective paper-and-pencil assessment instruments (multiple choice, true/false, matching, fill-in, and questionnaires) have valuable contributions to make in assessing important outcomes, they are but one option—an option that is not appropriate for all circumstances. Luckily, we do not have to rely on paper-and-pencil tests to do it all. We have two other general categories of options: performance assessments and personal communication with students.

PERFORMANCE ASSESSMENT

One way to assess student attainment of achievement targets is by means of observation and professional judgment (Stiggins, 1987). In fact, for certain very important targets, not only is professional judgment an acceptable way to assess, it is the only viable option. This is true of targets whose attainment manifests itself in achievement-related behaviors (i.e., communication skills, psychomotor skills, and behaviors indicative of affective states) and targets calling for the creation of complex achievement-related products (e.g., written reports, art and craft products).

If we wish to know whether students can speak a foreign language, for example, it makes absolutely no sense to give them a written test of the vocabulary. We must engage them in a realistic dialogue, observe their speech, apply internally held professional standards of proficiency, and evaluate the performance. Similarly, it makes no sense to give students a multiple-choice test of English grammar usage and then draw inferences about their ability to write. Rather, we must have them compose an original piece of writing and have a trained professional apply a clear set of standards to evaluate the quality of that writing.

Like sound paper-and-pencil tests, good performance assessments adhere to certain clearly specified rules of evidence. In particular, performance assessments require that the assessor: (1) observe the behavior as it is exhibited or examine the product and (2) apply clearly articulated performance criteria so as to make a sound professional judgment regarding the level of proficiency demonstrated. Sound performance assessment is rigorous, not casual. By that is meant that the assessor has defined a clear target, elicited a proper sample of performance, compared the student's performance to clear and public standards, and created a dependable record of performance quality.

Note that we are not referring to "intuitions" here. Forming "impressions" about achievement, having a "feeling" about what a student can or cannot do, or making "informal observations" are not synonymous with and part of, sound performance assessment. Sound performance assessments rest in a strong foundation of very careful preparation to assess. Those who violate the rules risk both doing great harm to students through the misassessment of their achievement, and perpetuating the myth that the only truly objective (fair, unbiased) way to assess is by means of objective paper-and-pencil test formats.

PERSONAL COMMUNICATION

We also can talk with students about what they have learned and how they feel about it. We do not often think of this as assessment. But in certain classroom contexts and for certain kinds of achievement targets, personal communication can provide high-quality data.

Personal communication can take many forms. During instruction, teachers commonly ask questions to assess students' understanding or extent of learning. In addition, we can develop and use highly structured group or individual interviews, conferences, and/or discussions with students. Oral exams represent yet another variation on this theme. Over and above these approaches, assessors can tap into the opinions of others, such as other teachers, parents, or students, to gain insight into the achievements of any particular student.

The major advantage in personal communication-based assessment is the added depth it can provide to our examinations of student thinking and/or attitudes. We can follow up questions with additional discussion or ask a new question to help understand how students feel about important issues. No paper-and-pencil test offers us this kind of flexibility. Of course, the trade-off is that personal communication-based assessments are much more complicated and time consuming to administer than some other options. Depending on the assessment context, though, these added costs can be controlled.

SUMMARY

Figure 6.2 provides a brief summary of the diverse and potentially useful array of assessment tools available to educators.

THE MEANING OF QUALITY

The meaning of quality is a direct function of the purpose for assessment, the nature of the target to be assessed, and the methods used to conduct the assessment. We can judge the quality of an assessment in terms of the people whom it is intended to serve and the manner in which they intend to use

Figure 6.2
ALTERNATIVE CLASSROOM ASSESSMENT METHODS

	Objective Forms	Subjective Forms
Paper and Pencil	Multiple Choice True-False Fill-In Matching	Essay
Performance Assessments	Checklist of specific attributes present or absent in behavior or products	Rating scales reflecting degrees of quality in behaviors or products
Personal Communication	Instructional questions with right/wrong answers	Interviews Conferences Discussions Opinions of others

the results. Sound assessments provide users with information they understand and can use. Accurate assessment results that are not understood by users or do not fit into the use context are of no more real value than inaccurate results. Thus, a clear sense of purpose is the first criterion for quality assessment.

Second, we can have confidence in assessments for which the target can be clearly and thoroughly described, with all of its complexity and dimensions. We can have confidence in assessments for which the method of gathering information matches both the target and the realities of the assessment context. If we wish to assess knowledge or thinking, we can use paper-and-pencil assessments, performance assessments, or personal communication. On the other hand, if our targets take the form of complex achievement-related behaviors or products, performance assessment is our only option.

Third, sound assessments provide an appropriate sample of student performance—a sample that is representative of all the questions that we could have asked if we only had enough time;

a sample that is sufficiently large to allow us to have confidence in the results. When the target is narrow, the sample may be small. But when the target is broad, the sample is large enough to lead to confident generalizations of the broad domain of interest.

And finally, sound assessments control for those sources of extraneous interference that can cause us to mismeasure student achievement. With paper-and-pencil assessments, problems could arise, for example, from poor-quality exercises, text anxiety, or distractions. With performance assessment and personal communication, add to these problems the potential for bias that is present in any subjective judgment. But none of these potential sources of invalidity or unreliability is beyond our control, if we approach the assessment task with a clear understanding of what it means to assess well.

Conclusion

A clear sense of *purpose*, a well-defined *target*, a careful *match* between context and assessment approach, appropriate *sampling* of behavior or learning to be demonstrated, and effective *control* for interference—all are critical to sound assessment. They are the practical meaning of assessment quality that needs to be the focus of assessment training for practitioners. Practitioners need to understand how to maximize the quality of assessment by knowing what can go wrong and how to prevent problems from arising. Fortunately, teacher- and administrator-training programs that meet this standard are beginning to appear.

But who will decide what the purpose ought to be in any particular school improvement context? Who will determine what it means to think or to write well? Who will set the performance criteria that guide others' judgments and decisions on critical matters? Who understands methods of sampling well enough to ensure that each assessment asks for the right information and enough information to justify its intended use later? And who will make certain that the assessments we use are free of interference so that we can have confidence in what they tell us about our students' performance and learning?

We need practitioners within school improvement programs and the educational community in general who are well prepared to respond to each of these questions and to make the relevant assessment-related decisions. We will have them if, and only if, the assessment community agrees to demystify its technology, i.e., to provide practical assessment strategies in common everyday language and to provide educators with the tools and understanding they need to assess confidently and well.

But, in addition, the educational community must face its fear of assessing educational outcomes. Many educators find the clear definition and sound assessment of achievement targets too risky. Some feel that if they were to be public about valued targets, members of their school community might find those targets to be inappropriate. Others fear that systematic assessment might produce evidence that at least some students can hit the target before we have had a chance to teach them to do so. Or even worse, assessments might reveal that some students cannot hit the target even after instruction, and everyone will know it.

Of course, balanced against these risks is the possibility that a much greater proportion of students will succeed in hitting targets if we make them clear and assess them well. Such targets and assessments would allow us to present to the community concrete and specific evidence of truly effective educational programs.

To date, the scale has consistently tipped in favor of avoiding risks. We have turned away from the issue. This is precisely why, as we move through the 1990s, we are forced to regard systematic assessment as a school improvement "innovation." High-quality assessment training is not now, nor has it ever been, demanded by or offered to teachers, administrators, or policymakers. Assessment competence—a competence essential for the well-being of students—is not required for the licensing or certification of education professionals.

As a result, those who could know about assessment do not. Those who could assess effectively do not. And those who could demonstrate the effectiveness of school improvement efforts are not in a position to conduct much-needed evaluative studies.

It need not be so. We understand what educators need to know about this "innovation," and a decade of research has taught us how to provide relevant, helpful training. We need only embrace the concept of high-quality assessment as an essential component of the school improvement process and allocate a small portion of the billions we spend in the United States on assessment R&D for assessing—on the firing line—professional development. And, of course, we need to drum up the courage to face the risks inherent in doing so.

The biggest risk in doing clear target and response assessments is that we and the public might find some programs that are not producing the kinds of outcomes we desire. But these problems can be alleviated, once discovered. Besides, as we assess, the public will find programs that are producing outcomes that are far richer and more exciting than previously realized. These productive programs can be disseminated to other schools and districts. None of this can happen in the absence of high-quality, high-resolution assessments.

- CURRICULUM
- INSTRUCTION

Direct Instruction to Accelerate Cognitive Growth

Douglas Carnine
Bonnie Grossen
Jerry Silbert
University of Oregon

Most educators associate higher cognitive functioning with the "student-dominance" end of the teacher-dominance/student-dominance continuum. The National Council of Teachers of Mathematics Teaching Standards (1991) describes the student dominance approach this way: "Learners construct their own meaning by connecting new information and concepts to what they already know, building hierarchies of understanding through the processes of assimilation and accommodation" (p. 144). The problem for teachers is that students vary tremendously in what they know (i.e., background knowledge they bring to school) and in how that knowledge develops from year to year. Low-income at-risk students enter school with less academically relevant background knowledge than other students. This gap is seldom closed during formal schooling, because the education at-risk students receive tends to lack intensity. For example, Rich and Ross (1989) found that at-risk students are engaged in academic activities for a little over 300 hours in an entire school year.

Although direct instruction's teaching techniques cause it to be classified as a teacher-dominant approach, it is very different from other such approaches. Most teacher-dominant approaches are based on textbooks that present a barrage of ideas in such a disorganized fashion that students are likely to rely on strategies that emphasize rote memorization rather than on strategies that foster understanding (Tyson & Woodward, 1989). Direct instruction is not so based.

WHAT IS DIRECT INSTRUCTION?

Direct Instruction is an intensive intervention aimed at increasing not only the amount of learning but also its quality by systematically developing important background knowledge and explicitly applying it and linking it to new knowledge. Direct instruction designs activities that carefully control the background knowledge that is required so that all students can "build hierarchies of understanding," not just those students who come to school with the appropriate background knowledge. In this process, mechanistic skills evolve into flexible strategies, concepts combine into schemata, and success in highly structured situations develops into successful performance in naturalistic, unpredictable, complex environments.

The direct instruction model grew out of Carl Bereiter's and Siegfried Engelmann (1966) research on teaching at-risk preschoolers. They recognized that closing the educational gap faced by at-risk students requires accelerating their cognitive growth in the context of restricted background knowledge. The model that evolved was designed to be effective, efficient, and manageable for elementary teachers to implement. It consisted of curricular materials, teaching techniques, staff development procedures, and a system for monitoring student progress (see Carnine, Granzin, & Becker, 1988).

THE DIRECT INSTRUCTION MODEL

The direct instruction model emphasizes frequent teacher-student interactions guided by carefully sequenced daily lessons in reading, mathematics, and language arts. Because positive self-concept can occur as a by-product of good teaching, direct instruction addresses social and affective as well as academic goals. Direct instruction assumes that all students can be taught these goals; that learning important concepts and applying them to higher-order thinking are essential to intelligent behavior and should be the main focus of an instructional program; and that at-risk students must be taught at a faster rate than typically occurs if they are to succeed in school.

COMPONENTS OF THE DIRECT INSTRUCTION MODEL

The effectiveness of the model results from the cumulative effects of components—carefully designed curricula, increased teaching time, efficient teaching techniques, thorough implementation procedures, and increased teacher expectations supported by parental involvement and, when possible, comprehensive services.

CURRICULAR MATERIALS. The curricular materials—programs in reading, mathematics, and language arts—are the heart of the model. Each program contains detailed lessons that describe how these research-based practices can be applied. The rationale for the curriculum will be illustrated in some detail later.

INCREASED TEACHING TIME. The most obvious way to increase teaching time is to lengthen the school day and the school year. But these decisions cannot be made solely by educators, nor will they be made soon. So the model focuses on teaching time more clearly under educator's control. The model places great emphasis on school schedules (i.e., the school day, the amount of time allocated to various academic subjects) and on how time is spent within each scheduled period (i.e., how much of the allocated time is spent in interactive teaching).

For example, priority subjects require ample time with schoolwide coordinated schedules for cross-classroom grouping. The teacher (and if available, the aide) become specialists in one or two of the three basic curriculum areas. And students are rotated in groups through subject areas and independent work activities. Peer tutoring and cooperative learning are also used to increase instructional time for students.

EFFICIENT TEACHING TECHNIQUES. Principles of reinforcement and a logic for resource utilization have been used to develop a number of methods for increasing teaching efficiency and student-engaged learning time. These methods include: scripted presentation of lessons, reinforcement, corrections, and procedures to teach every child by giving extra attention to the lower performers.

Learning these techniques is not easy for teachers. For example, the difficulty teachers have in learning how to correct student mistakes is reflected in the relatively long time it takes for teachers and paraprofessionals to learn to react constructively and consistently to student errors—a year (or longer) for the majority of teachers. If teachers, even those who are classroom-experienced but new to direct instruction, do not receive intensive classroom supervision, the acquisition of these skills usually takes longer.

THOROUGH IMPLEMENTATION. One important training goal of the model is to provide teachers and aides with the skills they need to teach students in both small and large groups. The structured approach to teaching makes it possible to specify the important skills that teachers and aides must have in order to perform well. During the first year of implementation, our consultants work with local supervisors and teachers on how to present the programs, where to place low performers in the classroom, how to set up classroom schedules to maximize time in academic areas, and so forth. In working with teachers, the consultants follow a strategy that models the way direct instruction teachers will eventually teach their students: Teachers are provided with explanations of why the curriculum is organized the way it is, with clear and frequent models of teaching techniques, with ongoing assessment of their progress, and with remedial assistance when necessary.

Student progress is measured in two ways—the number of lessons completed and the level of mastery of the content. In the model, instructionally referenced tests evaluate the process of instruction throughout the program, not just at the end of the year. Test results are used for evaluation in instruction as well as for remediation of problems.

TEACHER EXPECTATIONS AND ATTITUDES. Although we agree with other researchers that high expectations for all students is a key component of effective instruction, we found that expectations alone are unlikely to improve achievement scores reliably. So we have focused, also on really changing students' behavior. After teachers see at-risk children reading better than they believed possible, we find that the expectations also rise (Cronin, 1980).

DIRECT INSTRUCTION AND CURRICULUM ANALYSIS

The success of the direct instruction model with at-risk first-, second-, and third-grade students is well documented, not only in terms of student achievement in basic and cognitive skills but also in terms of student self-concept and self-esteem and of parental approval (Abt Associates, 1977; Haney, 1977). While at the heart of direct instruction is a highly sophisticated analysis of the curriculum, the educational community unfortunately has focused almost entirely on the teaching techniques, e.g., frequent questions with specific, constructive feedback offered by the teacher. So the model's full power has yet to be recognized and tapped.

Effective teaching practices cannot be understood without reference to a curriculum. Effective teaching of a rote-learning curriculum can effectively produce rote learning. In a study on water-jar problem solving by McDaniel and Schlager (1990), students in an explicit teaching condition learned a rote formula that did not transfer well in solving other water-jar problems. Quite often in research, explicit instruction is applied to content that has *not* been designed to be generalizable, such as McDaniel and Schlager's formula. These interventions should be called explicit rote teaching. The flaw, however, is in the design of the curriculum, not the explicit teaching technique.

Accordingly, the design of curriculum—the analysis and reorganization of the content of the curriculum—is *the* central aspect of the direct instruction model and has become increasingly important as the educational perspective has changed from national to international and leads policymakers to emphasize higher cognitive functioning for all students. Continuing in its tradition of concern for the welfare of at-risk students, the direct instruction development team has turned its attention to teaching complex, higher cognitive functioning. Direct instruction interventions have successfully taught at-risk students a variety of higher-level subjects: literary analysis, chemistry, earth science, legal reasoning, problem solving, critical thinking, ratio and proportions, social studies, syllogistic reasoning, and metacognition (see Carnine & Kameenui, 1992).

ANALYZING THE CURRICULUM: SOME EXAMPLES

As others have noted (Bruner, 1960; Flavell, 1971; Polya, 1973; Prawat, 1989), instruction that results in higher cognitive functioning must emphasize the organization of knowledge and important connections to other knowledge. The core of direct instruction curriculum design is to meaningfully communicate those connections—the underlying schemata of science, mathematics problem solving, history, and even art and the underlying tools of discovery. When direct instruction explicitly teaches these underlying schemata, it provides the background knowledge essential for all students to successfully engage in sophisticated problem solving and critical-thinking activities.

Why is teaching these underlying schemata so important? First, they enable students to explain and predict rather than just to memorize information. Second, the schemata are widely applicable, making them useful in a variety of problem-solving and other higher-order activities.

These advantages can best be understood through two examples, which constitute the bulk of this chapter. The first example illustrates how a schema can be widely applied in a less-structured domain—history—making the content meaningful and building a foundation for relating history to current events.

The second example is from a more-structured domain—mathematics. A schema for number relations is taught, which then serves as background knowledge for more complex schemata. By building on familiar schemata, students are not overwhelmed with too much new material at one time and are shown how new knowledge relates to background knowledge.

As you read these examples, consider the unique contribution of direct instruction: It is neither a traditional teacher-dominant approach (not a basal hodgepodge of facts, ideas, and activities) nor a student-centered approach, where students would somehow be expected to discover these schemata and learn how they apply. The direct instruction model offers a considerate alternative—a middle road.

HISTORY—A LESS-STRUCTURED DOMAIN

The long strings of dates and events in textbooks usually obfuscates the major concepts of history. For example, the traditional approach to teaching the causes of the Revolutionary War relates a series of acts imposed on the colonies by the British (e.g., the Wool Act, the Hat Act, the Iron Act, the Navigation Acts, the Sugar Act, the Stamp Act, etc.).

In contrast, a direct instruction analysis would focus on the predominant pattern in history—a problem-solution-effect pattern: people are primarily reactive, coming up with solutions that have effects that lead to further problems. For example, the way England solved some of its economic problems in the mid-1700s led to other problems, such as the American Revolution. During the mid-1700s, England needed to import raw materials for industries that often did not show a profit; moreover, the English government had debts from the French and Indian War. England's solution to these economic problems was to pass a number of revenue-producing laws that required the colonists to buy manufactured goods from England, to sell raw materials only to England, and to pay taxes on many items brought into the colonies. The effects of these laws were that the colonists smuggled goods in and out of the country and boycotted the purchase of some English goods, thus producing the conflict that eventually led to war.

The problem-solution-effect schema also is useful in teaching multiple perspectives. For example, England's solutions to its economic problems were actually problems for the colonies. With multiple perspectives, students learn that certain events represent a solution for one group, but at the same time are a problem for another group.

Most problems of history are similar in that they involve economics, though religious freedom or human rights may also be involved. The solutions can also be limited to several categories: fighting, moving, inventing, accommodating, or tolerating. The limited number of causes and solutions makes it possible to teach all students the problem-solution pattern in history background knowledge and guide them in applying it, as Kinder and Bursuck (1991) point out:

> Consider the invention of the cotton gin. Generally, the isolated fact that Eli Whitney invented the cotton gin is taught; however, the need for the cotton gin at that time and the historical effects of that invention usually are not made clear. The problem-solution-effect analysis showed these causal connections. Unlike the cotton grown in Egypt, most of the cotton grown in the southern United States was short-staple cotton. The short fibers made it difficult and expensive to remove the seeds—another economically based problem. The solution was Eli Whitney's machine that removed the seeds.

The effect was that much more cotton could be cleaned in a day, farmers could sell more cotton, and they were in turn motivated to grow more cotton, which ultimately increased the need for slaves (p. 273).

Looking at the bigger picture of history also reveals significant shifts in the patterns of human response to problems. For example, most history books present a list of new discoveries made during the Enlightenment without indicating clearly that this type of problem solving was a rather sudden shift from when humans relied more on worship and religious faith as solutions. In this case, people's faith was severely shaken by the discovery that the Earth orbited around the sun rather than being positioned in the center of the universe and, therefore, possibly was not the center of God's attention and personal engagement. Rather than relying entirely on God, humans began to rely more on themselves to solve their problems.

MATH PROBLEM SOLVING—
A MORE STRUCTURED DOMAIN

In the history analysis, students are taught the essential background knowledge—the problem-solution-effect pattern—and the most common causes of problems and types of solutions. Students then apply this background knowledge to a wide range of historical events. In mathematics, by contrast, students do not apply the same schema in a broad fashion. Instead, they learn to extend their background knowledge of a familiar strategy so that it can accommodate new types of problems. The following example illustrates how the simple concept of a number line has been extended to produce related strategies for solving probability, ratio, and function problems in a direct instruction mathematics program (Engelmann & Carnine, 1991a).

Building on the number-line concept, the concept of number families is taught. In a number family, the sum of the numbers on top of the arrow equals the "big" number to the right of the arrow:

$$\underset{\longrightarrow}{1 \quad 5} \; 6$$

This family links statements of addition to each other and to subtraction:

$$1 + 5 = 6 \qquad 6 - 5 = 1$$
$$5 + 1 = 6 \qquad 6 - 1 = 5$$

Fifty-five of these families lead to all 200 addition and subtraction facts.

Number families also link more difficult addition and subtraction problems. Missing numbers are found using either addition or subtraction, depending on the location of the missing number:

$$31 \; \square$$

If a "small" number is $\longrightarrow$ 46, the small number is missing:

$$46 - 31 = 15.$$

If the "big" number is missing, one must add

$$31 \longrightarrow 15$$

in, $\longrightarrow \square$ the "big" number is missing: $31 + 15 = 46.$
These problem-solving properties then serve as background knowledge for solving simple verbal problems (see Figure 7.1).

Students extract information from the problem and place the values on a number-family arrow, a form of mapping. The following self-talk would be used to solve problem 1 in Figure 7.1: "The first sentence, 'Juan had sixteen more stamps than Frank had,' indicates that the problem tells about a difference. The difference is always a small number. Sixteen is the difference. I write 16 first on the arrow. The person or thing with more is the big number;

that name goes at the end of the arrow. Juan has more, so I write Juan at the end of the arrow. Frank has to be the other small number." This is the result of the analysis to this point:

  16   Frank

————————————————▶ Juan

The self-talk continues: "The problem tells me that Juan had 28 stamps, so I cross out Juan and write 28:

  16   Frank 28

————————————————▶ ~~Juan~~

Now I have one missing number, Frank. Frank is a small number, so I subtract to find the value for Frank . . . 28 – 16; Frank had 12 stamps."

Students learn to use the same strategy to solve the other comparison problems in Figure 7.1. Regardless of which values are missing or whether the problem states who had more or who had fewer, the same strategy works.

With this strategy as background knowledge, students are then taught slight variations for temporal sequence and classification problems. Once students set up the number family, they insert the numbers they know and then solve the problem (see Figure 7.1). For example, to solve classification problems (problem 9 in Figure 7.1), students identify the subsets (trucks and other vehicles) of the larger set (total vehicles) and then write 12 for trucks and 86 for total vehicles. Because the "big number" is given, the students subtract: 86 – 12. There are 74 other vehicles on the ferry.

The strategy for solving classification problems then serves as background knowledge for solving data-analysis problems such as this one:

> The ferry company wants to know how many trucks and other vehicles use the morning and afternoon

Figure 7.1
SIMPLER VERBAL PROBLEMS

Comparison Problems:

1. Juan had 16 more stamps than Frank had. Juan had 28 stamps. How many did Frank have?

        16   Frank   28
    ———————————→ ~~Juan~~

2. Frank had 16 fewer stamps than Juan had. Juan had 28 stamps. How many did Frank have?

        16   Frank   28
    ———————————→ ~~Juan~~

3. Juan had 16 more stamps than Frank had. Frank had 12 stamps. How many did Juan have?

        16   ~~Frank~~   12
    ———————————→ Juan

4. Frank had 16 fewer stamps than Juan had. Frank had 12 stamps. How many did Juan have?

        16   ~~Frank~~   12
    ———————————→ Juan

Temporal Sequence Problems:

5. Tina had some berries. She gave away 40 berries. She ended up with 312 berries. How many did she start out with?

        312
       ~~End with~~   ~~Lose~~   40
    ———————————→ Start with

6. Tina had some berries. Then she picked 40 berries more. She ended up with 352 berries. How many did she start out with?

                  40
    Start with   ~~Get~~   352
    ———————————→ ~~End with~~

7. Tina had 352 berries. She gave away some. She ended up with 312 berries. How many did she give away?

        312
      ~~End with~~   Lose   352
    ———————————→ ~~Start with~~

8. Tina had 352 berries. She picked 40 berries more. How many did she end up with?

        352   40
    ~~Start with~~   Lose   ~~Get~~
    ———————————→ End with

Classification Problems:

9. There were 86 vehicles on a ferry. 12 of the vehicles were trucks. How many other vehicles were on the ferry?

        12
      ~~Trucks~~   Other   86
    ———————————→ ~~Vehicles~~

ferry. The ticket-taker has receipts for 226 vehicles on the morning ferry and 160 on the afternoon ferry. Because of a special tax on trucks, the ticket-taker knows that 38 trucks were on the morning ferry and 81 were on the afternoon ferry.

Having learned how to map a single classification problem, students learn that they can think of data analysis problems as classification maps stacked one on top of the other (the rows) and as classification problems lined up side by side (the columns):

	Trucks	Other Vehicles	Total
Morning ferry	38	a.	226
Afternoon ferry	81	b.	160
Total for the day	c.	d.	e.

The units for the classification problem across the top are trucks, other vehicles, and total vehicles. The units for the classification problem along the side are morning ferry, afternoon ferry, and total for the day. To complete the table, students must recognize that the columns and the rows are number families.

For example, in the first row, the number family for the morning ferry, 38   [a] ⟶ 226, yields a subtraction problem, 226 − 38. The answer, 188, is the number of other vehicles on the morning ferry (cell a). Using the number family strategy for the classification problems embedded in the table, students can solve for any missing value in the table.

The data analysis strategy serves as background knowledge for a variety of naturalistic survey activities that involve first collecting and then analyzing data. For example, students can survey the preferences of boys versus girls regarding different types of movies, such as action versus comedy movies, or collect data on the number of cars versus bicycles on streets with bike lanes and streets without bike lanes. The range of applicability is immense. Even more important, because of the way the program builds on prior knowledge, the likelihood of success is great.

Number family analysis is a powerful example of how extending background knowledge in a clear, systematic way to form new schemata contributes to both understanding and efficient learning. With a teacher as their guide, students can experience number families as one of Gelman's (1986) "root meanings":

> A focus on different algorithmic instantiations of a set of principles helps teach children that procedures that seem very different on the surface can share the same mathematical underpinning and, hence, root meanings (p. 350).

How Well Does Direct Instruction Work?

Researchers from within and outside the United States have investigated direct instruction with students at different ages and with different needs. Their findings attest to direct instruction's potential to contribute to students' competence and confidence. While over twenty studies have investigated the application of our curriculum analysis to higher-order thinking (Carnine & Kameenui, 1992), the most extensive research has been carried out with the ordinary elementary-grade curriculum.

FINDINGS FROM INDEPENDENT RESEARCHERS

STUDENTS. The National Follow Through Project included a large-scale longitudinal study of over twenty different approaches to teaching economically disadvantaged K–3 students. At the project's peak, 7,500 participated each year. Follow Through evaluation data were then gathered and analyzed by two impartial, independent agencies—Stanford Research Institute and Abt Associates respectively (Stebbins, 1976; Stebbins, St. Pierre, Proper, Anderson, & Cerva, 1977). Abt, in particular, compared experimental students with control students on three types of measures: basic, cognitive, and affective. A crude metric of overall effectiveness can be found by combining positive and negative effects and dividing by the total number of comparisons; for example, in the cognitive skills area, 10 significant negative effects combined with 20 significant positive effects divided by 100 total comparisons would yield an overall effect of +10 percent. The actual percents are summarized in Figure 7.2 for the nine largest models.

Note that the traditional basal and the inductive, constructivist approaches (the bottom five models in Figure 7.2) not only have fewer positive outcomes than the direct instruction model, but also have even more negative than positive outcomes period. This pattern of negative outcomes occurs with affective measures as well as with academic measures.

The various Abt reports also provided median grade-equivalent scores by site and by sponsor for four Metropolitan Achievement Test measures: Total Reading, Math, Spelling, and Language. The means for these data, by model (converted to percentiles) for students entering kindergarten, are presented in Figure 7.3 on a one-fourth standard deviation scale—scores for entering first-grade students, who had one year less instruction, are lower.

With this display, differences among sponsors are easily detected, and a normative reference is provided. The average achievement expectation for disadvantaged children without special help was thought to be twentieth percentile. So we have

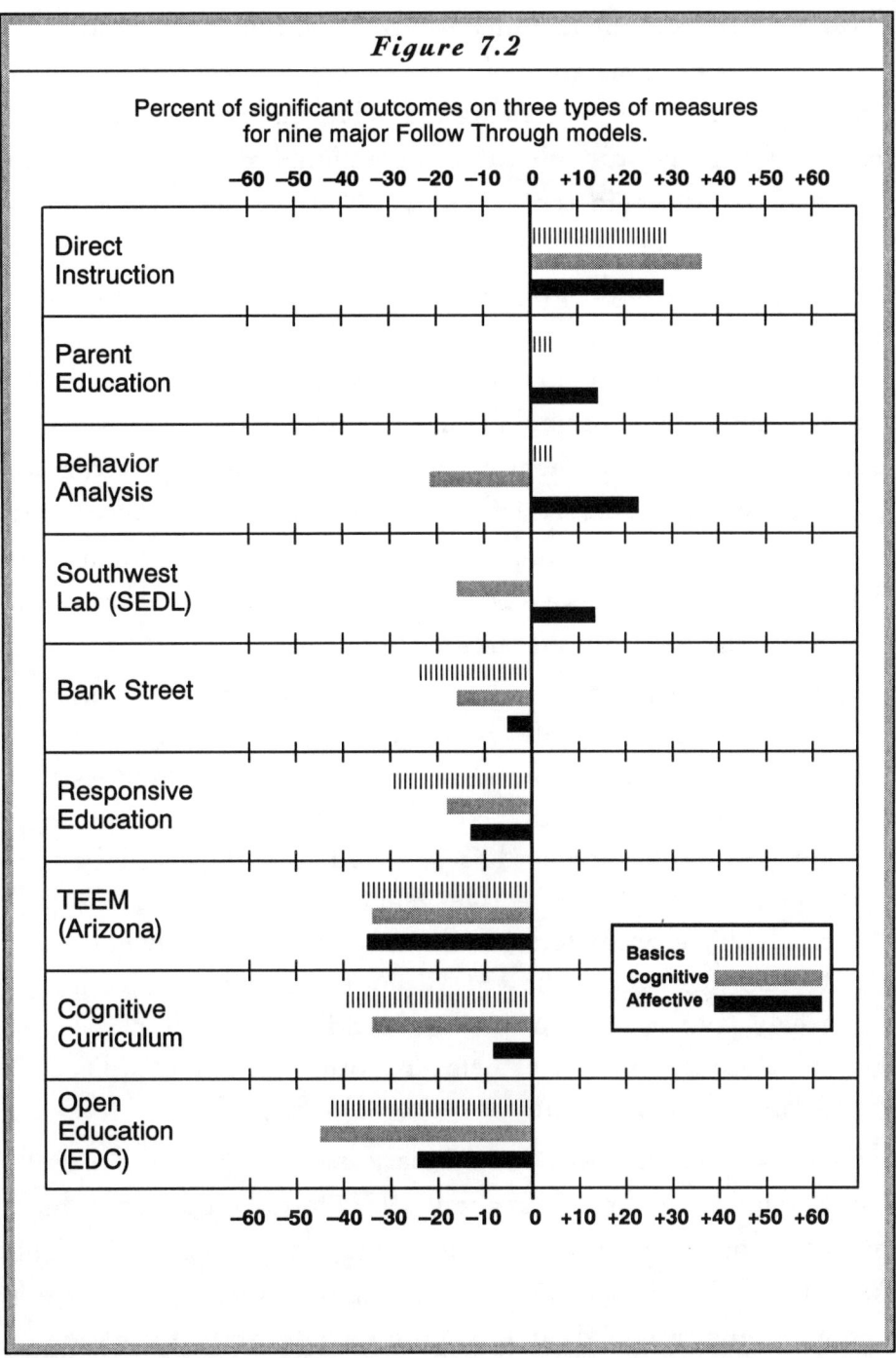

Figure 7.2

Percent of significant outcomes on three types of measures for nine major Follow Through models.

chosen this percentile as our baseline in drawing the graphs.

The major objective of the Direct Instruction Follow-Through Program was to bring the achievement levels of disadvantaged primary students up to the national median. Figure 7.3 indicates that direct instruction students are close to or at national norms on all measures. On the other hand, students in many other follow-through programs performed worse than they would have been expected to perform without any intervention.

Abt researchers noted that direct instruction students achieved well not only in these basic skills areas but also in the cognitive skills areas of reading comprehension, math problem solving, and math concepts. Further, direct instruction students' scores were quite high in the affective domain, suggesting that competence enhances self-esteem and not vice versa (Stebbins et al., 1977). This last result especially surprised Abt researchers, who wrote:

> The performance of Follow Through children in Direct Instruction sites on the affective measures is an unexpected result. The Direct Instruction Model does not explicitly emphasize affective outcomes of instruction, but the sponsor has asserted that they will be consequences of effective teaching. Critics of the model have predicted that the emphasis on tightly controlled instruction might discourage children from freely expressing themselves, and thus inhibit the development of self-esteem and other affective skills. In fact, this is not the case (Abt, IV–B, p. 73).

PARENTAL INVOLVEMENT. In an analysis of the Follow Through parent data for all models, Haney (1977) found moderate to high parent involvement in all the direct instruction school districts. Parents significantly disagreed with the view that there is not much parents can do about changing the educational situation in

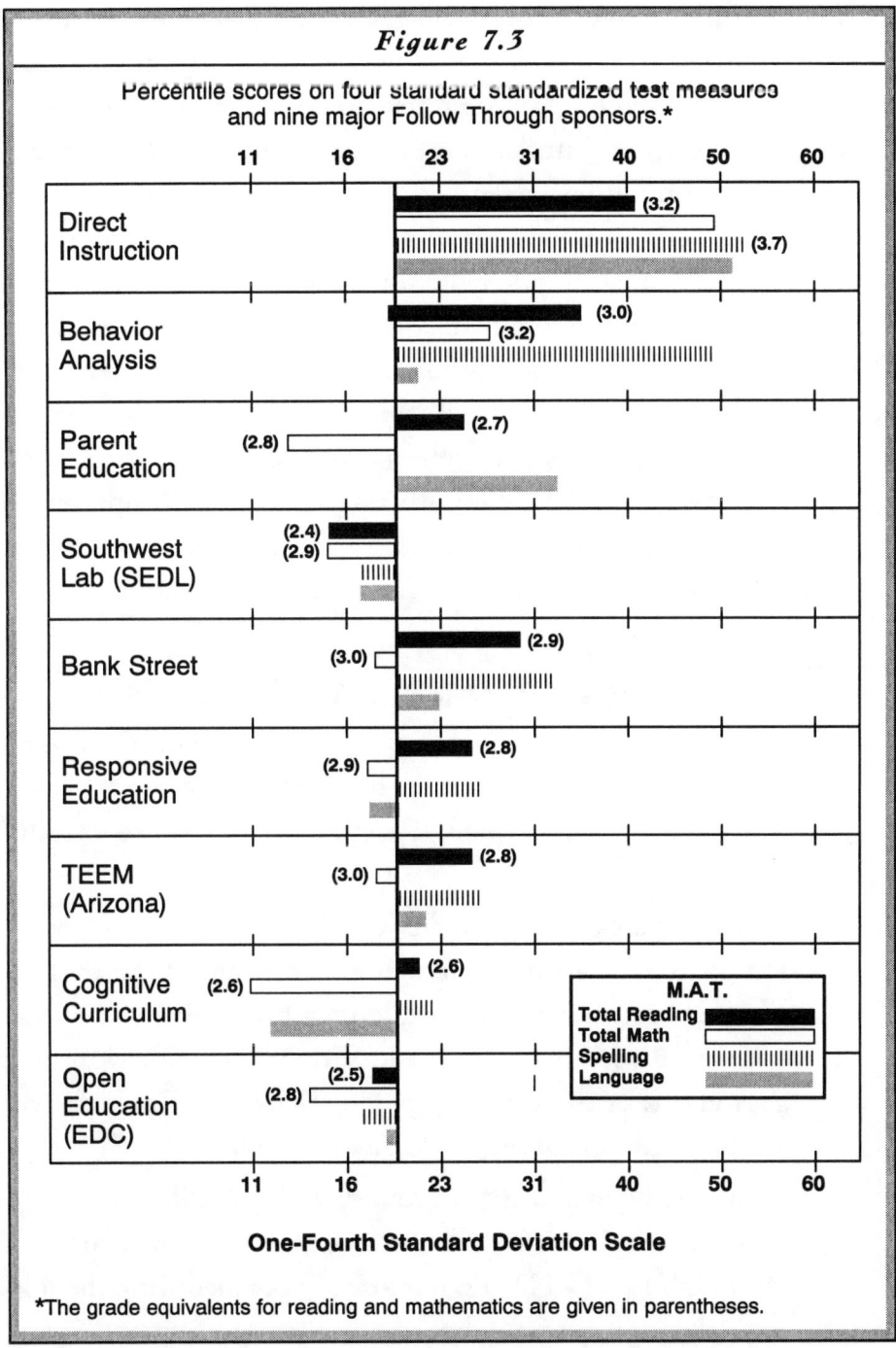

Figure 7.3

Percentile scores on four standard standardized test measures and nine major Follow Through sponsors.*

*The grade equivalents for reading and mathematics are given in parentheses.

their community. These parents viewed school as helpful not only to their children but also to themselves, particularly in terms of learning about teaching, learning how to help at home with their children's schoolwork, understanding better how their children learn, and meeting other parents.

Another very interesting finding had to do with a comparison of parents of students from different schools who were receiving instruction from different follow-through models. Parents of direct instruction students most frequently felt that school had appreciably helped their children academically. Because children in direct instruction classrooms had significantly higher scores than other follow-through children, this parental perception corresponded not only with the goals but also with the actual accomplishment of the direct instruction model.

FINDINGS FROM DIRECT INSTRUCTION RESEARCHERS

The preceding data were collected and analyzed by impartial agencies. The direct instruction follow through model conducted a number of supplementary studies, which are briefly summarized below.

1. A greater measurable and educationally significant benefit of .6 to .8 grade equivalents is present at the end of the third grade for those students who received an extra year of direct instruction; i.e., they began in kindergarten rather than in first grade (Becker & Engelmann, 1978; Gersten, Darch, & Gleason, 1988).

2. Significant gains in IQ are found, which are largely maintained through third grade. Students entering the program with high IQs (> 111) do not lose IQ points during the follow through years, though one might expect some

regression over time. And students entering with low IQs actually gain IQ points—entering K students with IQs below 71 gain 17 points and entering first-grade students gain 9.4 points. Gains for the children with entering IQs in the 71–90 range are (first grade) 15.6 and (kindergarten) 9.2 points (Gersten, Becker, Heiry, & White, 1984).

3. Studies of low-IQ students (< 80) show that the program is clearly effective. In fact, these students gain nearly as much each year, in reading (decoding) and math, as the direct instruction students with higher IQs. These gains are more than a year per year on the Wide-Range Achievement Test (WRAT) in reading and a year per year on the MAT Total Math (Gersten, Becker, Heiry, & White, 1984).

4. Longitudinal studies of direct instruction and comparable non-direct instruction students have followed these students after leaving third grade. All the significant differences favored the direct instruction students: five on academic measures, three on attendance, two on college acceptance, and three on reduced retention rates (Gersten & Keating, 1987).

5. Additional evaluation research is now showing that the model generalizes across both time and communities. The Department of Education's Joint Dissemination Review Panel validated educational programs as exemplary and qualified them for national dissemination. All twelve Direct Instruction Follow Through projects were submitted for validation, eleven of which had eight to ten years of data on successive groups of children. Collectively, these projects' schools sampled a full range of students: large cities (New York, San Diego, Washington, DC), middle-sized cities (Flint, MI; Dayton, OH; E. St. Louis, IL);

rural white communities (Flippin, AR; Smithville, TN); a rural black community (Williamsburg, SC); Latino communities (Uvalde, TX; E. Las Vegas, NM); and a Native-American community (Cherokee, NC). One hundred percent of the projects were certified as exemplary in reading and mathematics for the primary grades.

FUTURE DIRECTIONS

The technical goal of direct instruction is to reveal and communicate the underlying order of knowledge—the logic of science, the poetic unity of art, the underlying sense of the universe—in a way that this order can be understood, applied, built upon, or transformed into new knowledge. The search for underlying schemata is unending; it is hoped that the history and math analyses illustrated in this chapter will be replaced by better ones over time. New analyses need to be developed in a broad range of higher-order applications, particularly problem solving and reasoning. Finally, students must do more than problem solve and reason; they must be able to communicate to others the hows and whys of these applications through oral and written expression.

A quite different, but equally important, communication goal is to explain (1) that direct instruction is not a traditional "teacher-dominance" approach, as represented by typical textbooks, and (2) that direct instruction does believe students should be able to engage *successfully* in "student-dominated" activities. The designers of direct instruction never thought that systematic, intensive, directed instruction should fill up every minute of the school day year after year. Rather, direct instruction was designed to use as little time as possible in preparing children to succeed in those activities that are common in school and life, including student-dominated ones. The direct instruction teacher structures learning to the minimum extent necessary to ensure success in its initial phases, but gradually steps back as students are able to cope successfully with the unstructured situations of life, including higher-level thinking.

Unfortunately, most educators believe that systematic, intensive teacher-directed instruction, even in initial learning, is incompatible with higher-order thinking. This is probably true in the absence of a curriculum analysis that identifies and develops underlying schemata. However, neither intensive teaching from most basals nor switching to student-dominated process approaches will develop higher-order thinking in most at-risk students. In discussing a study of a carefully implemented student-dominated approach to literacy with Hispanic students, Reyes (1991) found that instead of feeling like

> "members of the literacy club" as Frank Smith (1986) refers to readers, the students wrote comments in their journals and literature logs like: "I hate reading," "The book is too boring and too long," or "Please tell me a bit about the book so I'll know what it is about." These revealed that the students were *outside* the club. The students provided many hints that they needed help in mastering the literacy tasks, but their pleas went unheeded by the teachers who felt that it was only a matter of time before the kids would get the hang of it. The process needed time. The teachers hesitated "imposing" their expertise in the selection of books. They advised students to keep trying, that they would eventually find a book of their liking (p. 4).

These students ran out of time. They made no discernable improvement in literacy over the course of the school year. What educators need to realize is that intensive, explicit instruction of underlying schema is crucial for at-risk students. In writing about the education of African-American students, Delpit (1988) noted: "If such explicitness is not provided to students, what it feels like to people who are old enough to judge is that there are secrets being kept, that time is being wasted, that the teacher is abdicating his or her duty to teach" (p. 287).

In a recent review of intervention techniques and programs for improving academic performance, Elliott and Shapiro (1990) point out the need for direct instruction to better explain what it can accomplish and why:

> Future research issues related to direct instruction do not need to center upon demonstrations of its effectiveness. These data exist and are convincing. More important, however, efforts need to be devoted to examining how these strategies can be adopted more widely into the educational system. . . . It is unfortunate that the technology and resources exist for accelerating the academic performance of low-achieving youngsters, but continue to go relatively untapped (p. 654).

It may be that the only way teachers will come to better understand direct instruction is by using it. In a description of the evolution of teachers' attitudes toward direct instruction during the course of an implementation mandated by court order, Cronin (1980) reported that most of the teachers initially disliked several of its features—the scripted questions for teachers, in-class supervision, and prescribed teaching techniques. After six months, however, the teachers reported that their students were reading at a level they thought unimaginable for inner city minority students; the teachers' attitudes toward direct instruction changed dramatically.

- ASSESSMENT
- CURRICULUM
- EXPECTATIONS
- INSTRUCTION

Instructional Alignment

S. Alan Cohen
University of San Francisco

Lots of things explain student achievement. For example, we can explain a child's academic performance as a function of home background, parent involvement, language development, emotional stability, racism, poverty, and so on. Or we can explain it by the quality of the school's instruction. How we explain it determines what we do about it.

Here are two reasons why we should explain it as a function of instruction. First, as educators, we control instruction. We have little control over home background, parent involvement, language development, emotional stability, racism, and poverty. Second, these latter factors take years to affect academic achievement. Language development takes place over many years; the effects of racism take generations to erase. But effective instruction takes seconds to work and is more powerful than all these linguistic and psychosocial factors.

This chapter describes instructional alignment, one variable that explains why instruction is so powerful when it is done well. At this stage of research, instructional alignment is a fundamental component of effective instructional design. Alone it can explain 50 percent of the variability in academic performance scores (Cohen, 1987). Combined with accommodating cognitive entry skills prerequisite to a lesson (Bloom, 1976), P Ratio (Cohen, 1971) [also known as *time on task*], use of correctives (Block & Anderson, 1975), and use of appropriate reinforcers (Lysakowski & Walberg, 1982), alignment makes instruction powerful enough to reverse the twenty-year decline in academic achievement currently plaguing U.S. schools.

WHAT IS INSTRUCTIONAL ALIGNMENT?

Instructional alignment describes the degree of congruence among stimulus conditions of instruction, assessment, and intended outcome (Cohen, 1984a & b; 1987). We say instruction is aligned when three components of a learning activity match: (1) what the instructor intends as the outcome, (2) what the learner does during instruction, and (3) what the assessment demands.

Alignment is simple to understand if we accept three assumptions:

ASSUMPTION 1: All important instructional outcomes are behaviorally definable.

Many educators do not believe this. For example, Bloom (1987) accepts this assumption for basic but not for higher-level skills. Goodman (1987) goes further than Bloom. He insists that we cannot measure whole language reading instruction outcomes.

Obviously, if we define instructional outcomes as invisible

cognitive effects occurring somewhere in the head or as invisible affects occurring somewhere in the heart, then we cannot analyze their stimulus conditions and, therefore, cannot align instruction. Defining instructional outcomes as human performances does not deny cognition or affect. This assumption merely requires us to constrain our fields of accountability to what students do, rather than what we wish, guess, infer, or hope they do.

ASSUMPTION 2: A behavior involves both an action and contingent stimulus conditions.

Contingent means not only that they occur contiguous to the action but also that they control the action's quality and rate. Reading behavior, for example, is not merely a first grader saying a word. It involves that action contingently linked to various events preceding, concurrent to, and following the word. We do not learn to say a word; we learn to say a word on the occasion of specific contingent events. To understand a behavior, we must spot the critical features of those events—the ones to which the actions are contingent. Researchers call those events *contingent stimuli.*

ASSUMPTION 3: A precise observation can be a valid and reliable test.

Many instructional outcomes must be observed in the learner's spontaneous behavior, not on a piece of paper. We call such observations *performance indicators* (PIs for short). When we include PIs in our definition of test, alignment is feasible. For example, if we define enjoying literature as an instructional outcome, we can align instruction when the test is a child laughing at a funny story, crying at a sad story, or sitting riveted to a suspenseful story. Laughing, crying, and sitting riveted on the occasions of specified literary and social events are PIs. They cannot be observed with pencil-and-paper tests.

How Does Alignment Work?

First, the instructor designs an assessment that represents a demonstration of desired performance. We call this the instructional designer's "moment of truth." Translating into action an idea of what we want our students to learn strips us of self-delusions. We may start out thinking we know what we mean by "reading for main ideas." But when we design test items that demonstrate that noble outcome, self-doubt rears its discomforting head. Which outcome do we choose:

1. Reads a random paragraph and selects one of five statements "that best expresses the main idea"?
2. Writes statements of the main idea?
3. Informally says what the main idea is without a teacher prod?
4. Discusses what the writer "really meant"?

That moment of truth arrives when we ask ourselves: "What actions do we want to observe that make us say that students have it, can do it, or know it?"

Second, we analyze the critical features of the stimulus conditions associated with this criterion performance to ensure that those same conditions occur in instruction. Now the first question is modified to: "What actions do we want to observe under what stimulus conditions that make us say that students have it, can do it, or know it?" The four different main idea behaviors above represent differences in stimulus conditions. These critical features of stimulus conditions are the substance of instructional alignment.

Third, we design instruction to ensure that students perform the criterion actions in the presence of the contingent stimulus conditions represented in the assessment performance. In other words, we teach for the test.

Let us consider these steps more closely.

STEP ONE: DEFUZZIATING, OR, WHAT'S WORTH TEACHING?

The toughest part of aligning instruction is trying to define the instructional outcome. Pretend we are preparing a fifth-grade arithmetic lesson, the outcome of which is to understand the multiplication concept. We discriminate this outcome from knowing how to multiply, a prerequisite entry skill to our lesson but different from the outcome we seek.

Both the prerequisite entry skill and the lesson outcome are cognitive events. We cannot align instruction to cognitive events because they are invisible. So we ask ourselves: "What actions or performances that occur on the occasion of contingent events or stimuli do we observe that make us say a student has mastered the multiplication concept?" When we see a fifth grader write or say "25" to the stimulus condition: "How much is 5 times 5?" we say that she can multiply. When she responds to similar events for a number of paired values, we infer that she knows her multiplication tables. That inference about the invisible phenomenon of knowing is based on observing events immediately contingent to her responding actions. But knowing her multiplication tables is a prerequisite, not the actual performances we associate with understanding the multiplication concept. What critical features of those contingent events differentiate the two behaviors?

We answer that question by designing criterion performance items and by deciding which ones deal with the *understanding* the multiplication concept as discriminated from the *knowing how to multiply* outcome. We call this *defuzziating the fuzzies*. That is because in alignment terms, understanding the multiplication concept is a fuzzy. It must be changed from an invisible cognitive event to an overt action and its critical contingent events.

For example, we might choose to observe as understanding the multiplication concept what a fifth grader does or says in relation to such arithmetic problems as:

Sum these values: 18, 10, 10, 5, 6, 10, 11, 22, 5, 5, 10, 19, 3, 5, 10, 17, 5, 10, 10, 5.

Tommy arrays these twenty values in a column and sums them one at a time. Terri first counts the number of 10s, multiplies them by that sum (10 × 7), and records 70. She does the same thing with the 5s (5 × 6), recording 30 in the column, and then jots down the remaining seven values before summing the column. Tommy knows how to multiply. Terri knows how to multiply, too, but she also understands the multiplication concept.

So the first step in aligning instruction is to answer the tough question: "What action and its contingent events demonstrate the cognitive or affective outcome we seek?" And the method we use to answer this question is to design criterion performance items that represent that outcome.

STEP TWO: ANALYZING CRITICAL FEATURES OF CRITERION PERFORMANCE INDICATORS

To demonstrate Step 2, consider this social studies fuzzy: A student understands the U.S. government's separation of powers principle. We always start with a fuzzy. Then we proceed directly to the criterion PI or test item. We prefer to ignore behavioral objectives because they usually describe one set of words (". . . understanding the relationship among . . ., etc.") with another set of words (Given an excerpt from the daily newspaper in which . . ., etc."). Language is too ambiguous for the precision demanded in instructional alignment. Instead, we design criterion performance items. They allow us to see actual performances rather than verbal descriptions.

Notice that we design the post-instructional assessment *before* we design the lesson. We analyze the stimulus conditions of the PIs and pencil-and-paper test items that differentiate one outcome from others. The lesson will then be designed to teach to the test.

For example, we ask of each item we design: "To what stimulus conditions do we want to link the learner's signal that he or she understands the separation of powers principle?" Here are some possibilities:

1. Students signal when a TV news sound bite on the National Security Agency's secret war connects with the separation of powers principle taught in their civics classes.
2. Students signal by writing short answers to such questions as . . .
3. Students signal in incidental conversation.
4. Students recite the role of each branch of government and explain how each is forbidden by law to assume the other's functions.

INSTRUCTIONAL ALIGNMENT

5. Students perform within time limitations.
6. Students debate the War Powers Act as a separation of powers issue.
7. Students write a paper on the extent to which the Korean, Vietnam, Panama, and Iraq "police actions" were a violation of the separation of powers principle.
8. Students present a ten-minute public speech on the War Powers Act as a separation of powers issue.

Each of these outcomes has a number of possible variations in stimulus conditions. For example, number 7 could be done at home, in class, with or without available references, and so on. Which combination of stimulus conditions we choose to define this social studies outcome is more than an assessment decision. It determines how we teach the competency, for the lesson development will hinge on the posttest's stimulus conditions. For example, if we teach students number 4 above, then we cannot expect them to perform numbers 1, 2, 3, 6, 7, and 8.

Now consider three examples of analyzing stimulus conditions for another area, the teaching of reading.

Example 1: Joseph says /dog/ each time the teacher presents a flashcard with the letters d-o-g. He demonstrates that he learned an action (saying *dog*) in the presence of certain stimulus conditions (when flashed the printed word on a card). Call this TASK 1. Five minutes later, the word *dog* appears in Joseph's basal reader story. He is expected to read the word with the same efficiency demonstrated in TASK 1. Call this TASK 2.

In both tasks, Joseph is expected to perform the act of saying *dog*. But the stimulus conditions of Task 1 and Task 2 are misaligned.

> Example 2: Consider the daily reading lesson in which Joseph sits with seven bluebirds (the "middle" achievement group) and orally reads selections from his reader, guided by the teacher's rhetorical questions. Call that TASK 1. Late in the spring, the school district "evaluates" the reading program's effect by presenting pages different from those in his basal reader, under time limits, in an individual rather than group setting, and on the occasion of stimuli radically different from those of instruction. This is TASK 2.

The stimulus conditions of each task obviously vary from each other. They misalign.

> Example 3: Consider the whole language movement in reading instruction. This movement occurred because of its concern with the misalignment between intended and actual outcomes of language arts instruction.

This example is tinged with irony, since whole language advocates consider alignment a Skinnerian-tainted scourge on the instructional scene. Nevertheless, concern for critical features of instructional stimuli spawned the movement.

Consider its origins. Appalled at the decline of reading in U.S. society and at the "blanding" of U.S. reading instruction, whole language advocates promoted the notion that reading instruction must mimic "natural" language behavior (Goodman, 1989). However, the actions involved in "natural" reading behavior do not differ from those in "artificial school reading" behavior. In both cases, readers visually scan text, say things, do not say things, etc. They act the same.

But their actions occur on the occasion of different contingent stimulus events. For example, whole language reading actions are not supposed to be contingent upon artificial phonic exercises. Instead, whole language reading actions are supposed to be contingent to children's literature, reading, speaking, and writing stimuli normally found in the natural language environment (Stahl & Miller, 1989).

The whole language movement is obsessed with defining those "natural" events, an obsession with stimulus conditions shared with instructional alignment advocates. What separates them from the instructional alignment camp is at least one surface issue—avoidance of being tainted as "behaviorists"—and one substantive issue—willingness to define these stimulus conditions at the instructional stage but not at the assessment stage.

STEP 3: THE MATCH

In its most technical sense, alignment refers to the match between any two or more behaviors. We also use the term *misalignment* to describe the extent to which two behaviors or tasks vary in their stimulus match. We need both terms, because in the research, we cannot measure an alignment effect except in contrast to degrees of misalignment.

We can align one test with another test, a test with instructional activities, a test or instructional activities with intended outcomes, one instructional activity with another, and so on. Any two or more tasks can be analyzed for the degree of stimulus condition match. For example, Wishnick (1989) analyzed alignments between items on commercially published norm-referenced tests (NRTs) of reading achievement and a school district's local criterion tests of instructional outcomes. She checked the length, level, and print density of the two pairs of test items. She checked such stimulus conditions as the mode of question answering (multiple choice, short answer, etc.). When both tests had multiple-choice items, she checked the number of options, the features of each option that determined whether it was a correct or an incorrect answer, and so on. Wishnick found that the degree to which stimulus conditions of the local test aligned with the NRT's stimulus conditions explained over two-thirds of the NRT score variability.

Alignment's greatest appeal and the feature most relevant to school reform is the three-way match among intended outcomes, assessment, and instructional strategies. By defining outcomes as demonstrated criterion performances, we ensure that end of the match. To ensure the match between assessment and instruction, we use various strategies.

For example, all lessons present extended practice with performances whose actions and contingent stimuli are similar to those that appear on the criterion test. If the lesson outcome is a mere regurgitation of facts, students at least have a model of performance items in front of them as they learn the target outcome. When the outcome is not simple regurgitation, students have copies of the posttest during instruction. The teacher delivers instruction with the same posttest in his or her hand. For example, if the posttest says: "Write a 250-word essay discussing the symbolism of Melville's *Pequod*," students know this before instruction begins. Assuming students have in their repertoires the skills needed to write a 250-word essay, the instruction would provide practice in writing one about the *Pequod*. Instruction might begin with practice in writing 100-word statements about symbolism in various pieces of literature but would eventually lead to symbolism associated with the *Pequod*. The final practice before the test would be a 250-word essay discussing the symbolism of Melville's *Pequod*. In other words, we teach to the test.

Teaching to the test raises, of course, two fundamental issues. One deals with alignment's hidden agenda. The other deals with its ethics.

ALIGNMENT'S HIDDEN AGENDA. Alignment's apparent purpose is to make every student academically excellent. Alignment, however, has an equally important hidden purpose. It monitors educators' responses to the most critical educational question of all: "What's worth teaching?" Alignment consistently reminds us how easily we hide questionable teaching acts behind such fuzzies as "love of literature," "appreciating music," "getting along with others," "understanding Ahab's obsession with the white whale," "writing good essays," "knowing the causes of Hitler's rise to power."

But when we defuzziate these invisible outcomes as criterion performances that specify events and contingent actions, we confront that previously described "moment of truth" with all its discomfort. For any fuzzy we choose as an outcome, many stimulus variations apply. But only a few can be chosen. This makes the choice of those few a value judgment. Aligning instruction makes those values transparent and apparent by the forms they take as criterion performances. Therein lies discomfort for those not used to making value-based decisions. The popular term for this decision process is *accountability*.

THE ETHICS OF TEACHING TO TESTS. From the alignment perspective, hiding instructional outcomes behind fuzzies is inefficient and therefore unethical. Instructional inefficiency is unethical for the same reason that medical inefficiency is unethical. Inefficiency's effects damage people.

Producing mathematically illiterate citizens, when we do not have to, is unethical. Producing children who can substitute consonants but hate to read books is unethical. Producing normally distributed academic achievement scores based on tests that misalign with instruction, when we do not have to, is unethical. Blaming teachers or parents for test scores that show little schooling effects because they are misaligned with what was taught is unethical. Requiring children to daily attend a school in which an unaligned curriculum causes so many of them to experience academic failure year after year is unethical.

In contrast, using exemplary criterion test items or PIs to define instructional outcomes and teaching to those criteria increase the probability that all students will achieve excellence. That seems ethical to us. When aligning instruction, the ethical question is never: "Should we teach to the test?" The question is "What should we test?" which returns us to that fundamental value question: "What's worth teaching?"

WHERE DOES ALIGNMENT COME FROM?

Twenty years ago, instructional designers in industry and the military used the term *alignment* routinely. When the war on poverty infused funds into schools, some of their products showed up in inner city classrooms. These products were considered "innovative" because they looked different from conventional textbooks. Some of them came as kits rather than as textbooks. Others took the form of programmed instruction. The strategies imbedded in these products were substantively different, too. They applied research findings from the experimental analysis of behavior, which is to instructional design what physics is to bridge building. The most important findings dealt with the operant principle of stimulus control; instructional designers renamed it *instructional alignment.*

OPERANT THEORY

Most instructional designers were students of B. F. Skinner (1951, 1953, 1957), who had earlier revolutionized learning research. Two of Skinner's ideas generated the alignment construct. One idea destroyed simplistic Watsonian behaviorism. Skinner relegated S-R psychology to a few basic physiological actions. He replaced the reflex with operants, because animals are proactive, not reactive. According to Skinner, all animals, especially humans, act to elicit events (stimuli) from their environments. We act, and the environment responds.

Those acts not only elicit reinforcing events, but they occur on the occasion of other events as well. Therefore, we cannot design instruction as a set of stimuli to which learners respond robotically. We can, however, arrange events so that these self-initiated, proactive actions link to those occasions. We can, for example, leave a book about dogs on a child's desk, and we can bet a normal child will look at it, say *dog*, smile, etc. If we manipulate those stimulus conditions cleverly, we can soon have him saying *dog* and smiling when the word appears in print.

Skinner's second idea derived from this view of proactive in contrast to reactive behavior. According to Skinner, a behavior cannot be described without those contingent stimulus conditions. Without the book, good feelings, interest, and the smile, the word *dog*, as any whole language expert will attest, is merely an action, not the reading behavior we seek. The behavior is the entire contingency system. To call two actions the same behavior when the contingent stimulus conditions vary is self-deluding.

This new definition of behavior has produced sixty years of experimental research in stimulus control, with enormous implications for instruction. Consider, for example, the common practice of stating a lesson goal such as: "Knows the causes of the Civil War." What does *knowing* mean? Cognitivists would argue that something analogous to a knowing faculty exists in the brain. However, when evidence of knowing is demanded, all cognitivists become behaviorists. They expect to see a behavior.

What might this knowing behavior look like? It could take the form of circling (the action) "True" or "False" for ten statements about causes of the Civil War (stimulus events, also called *conditions*). Or it could take the form of writing answers (the action) to five short-answer questions (stimulus conditions), which, in turn, is a far cry from writing (the action) a 500-word essay on the Civil War's causes (stimulus conditions). Those are three different behaviors, and the ability to do one does not guarantee the ability to do the others. Furthermore, writing (the action) the essay at home without time constraints (stimulus conditions) is not the same behavior as writing (the action) in school against time (stimulus conditions). And all these behaviors are different from the PI of discussing (the action) these causes informally with a peer (stimulus conditions).

An infinite variety of stimulus conditions represents "knowing." To assume that some central knowing faculty exists that generates generalized knowing behaviors, independent of varying contingent events, contradicts mountains of empirical data that experimental researchers have produced for six generations. Yet Skinner's second contribution causes us considerable distress because it requires us to decide which behaviors we want our students to demonstrate. The cognitive model is, therefore, considerably more comforting. Unfortunately, it does not generate large effects as consistently as Skinner's operant model. When Skinnerian researchers defined such behaviors as an action with its contingent stimuli, they produced the steepest learning curves in psychological research history (Ferster & Skinner, 1957).

CURRICULUM ALIGNMENT

Southwest Regional Educational Labs introduced the stimulus control construct to public schools. They called it *curriculum alignment*. They trained Los Angeles inner city teachers to align their instruction with the district's performance objectives (Niedermeyer, 1979; Niedermeyer & Yelon, 1981; Levine, 1982). The results were spotty, and it is easy to see why in hindsight.

First, the Lab's principal investigators assumed that increased student mastery would reinforce teachers' alignment efforts. Unfortunately, the aversive events associated with efforts to align instruction were more potent than the reinforcing events associated with student mastery.

In addition, most performance objectives used in Los Angeles did not specify the stimulus conditions' critical features. By analyzing the objective, teachers could not predict exactly what might appear on an instructional assessment. For example, schools would list as a performance objective: "Students will recall main ideas of paragraphs read." Such objectives omit the critical features of the stimulus condition. Does recall mean select a statement among five that vary slightly or five that are widely different? Does recall mean to write one "from memory"? Does recall mean to say it to a teacher in private or in front of the class? Most teachers are not trained in learning theory; they do not know that small variations in stimulus conditions cause large performance variations. So Los Angeles teachers simply taught whatever they wanted as a main idea lesson, as if there were a trainable main idea brain faculty or as if a main idea "habit" could be shaped.

Southwest Regional Lab's experiences alerted me to the importance of precision when defining stimulus conditions. That is why I use the term *instructional* rather than *curriculum* alignment. It implies more precision.

ALIGNMENT RESEARCH

Instructional alignment has always been an assumption of good instructional design, but why suddenly elevate it to a school reform variable? In 1981 we published a research report (Cohen & Stover, 1981) based on Stover's award-winning doctoral dissertation (Stover, 1980). One journal referee recommended not publishing the report because it ". . . simply demonstrated that if we teach something to kids, and measure what we do, we get results." He was right about that but wrong about the study's significance. While the rest of the educational community sought higher cognitive skills and manipulated self-esteem to generate tiny learning effects, we had used rather mundane instruction to generate six to ten times those effects. Stover's study reminded us how large aligned instruction's effects could be with so little instructional effort.

ALIGNMENT STUDIES

Stover (1980) taught math word problem solving to sixth

graders. One group learned to create diagrams to solve word problems. Another group learned to eliminate extraneous information. A third group learned to manipulate the arithmetic paradigm needed to solve the problem. In this experiment, each group was the other's control, but each group received test items aligned to all three treatments. Thus, for each group, one item set was aligned, and the rest were misaligned.

Alignment learning effect sizes were enormous, ranging from 1.4 to 3.5 sigma after only three forty-five-minute lessons. The journal referee was right—instruction works. But its potency depends upon the degree of alignment between stimulus conditions of instruction and assessment. And that potency easily reaches two and three sigma effects. Could alignment generate these effects routinely? The Stover study launched a decade of instructional alignment research.

THE KOCZOR STUDY. When we want our fourth graders to "know Roman numerals," precisely what do we mean? Slight variations in answering this question cause enormous variation in instructional outcome.

Koczor (1984) taught fourth graders to write Roman for Arabic numerals. After her students demonstrated competency, she gave two versions of the same test, each to half the group. One version presented Roman numerals. Students wrote Arabic equivalents, the exact behavior taught. The other version presented Arabic numerals, a "slight" variation in stimulus conditions. Students wrote Roman numerals. That slight variation caused a 40 percent difference in the number correct. It must be noted that these fourth graders were the highest achievers in an upper-middle-class community. Their general scholastic achievement scores were at or above seventh-grade level.

Most teachers would simply say they "taught Roman numerals" and pay little attention to critical differences in stimulus conditions, especially among such high achievers. Reinforcing the response to: IV=? shapes a different behavior from reinforcing the response to: 4=?. In human learning, tiny variations make a big difference.

Koczor's study consisted of similar short experiments in various typical fourth-grade skill and content areas. Alignment routinely generated 1 to 2 sigma effects.

THE TALLARICO STUDY. Another award-winning alignment experiment taught second graders a peculiar "test-wiseness" skill. When Cohen (1977) analyzed commercially published Norm-referenced Test (NRT) stimulus conditions, he found ten to fifteen critical stimulus features across varying grade levels that explain significant reading score variability. One feature was the use of more than one correct answer option at the primary level. In about 60 percent of the items either of two answers was reasonably correct. The "best" correct answer, however, was more denotative, less metaphorical.

Tallarico (1984) taught disadvantaged second graders how to select the more denotative alternative. He provided practice with feedback on items whose stimulus conditions matched NRT items on this feature. On the NRT norms, a difference of about .7 sigma represented a full year's growth in "reading ability." Tallarico's experimental group outperformed the placebo group with a 1.2 sigma effect. In only two thirty-minute sessions, by providing instruction aligned with this critical stimulus feature, his experimental second graders gained more than "a year's growth" in "reading ability."

This approach to NRTs has elicited the charge that too

much aligned instruction "invalidates" the NRT (Mehrens & Kaminski, 1989). Mehrens and Kaminski call it "cheating." We, of course, call it effective instruction (Cohen & Hyman, 1991) and charge Mehrens, Kaminski, and some of their psychometric colleagues with using tests unethically. If these test scores are used to make educational policy decisions, to determine a child's instructional placement, or to determine access to educational opportunity, then aligning instruction with NRTs is an ethical imperative.

THE ELIA STUDY. Elia (1986) manipulated alignment between instruction and testing by teaching twenty-four target words under varying stimulus conditions (in a sentence, phrase, or paragraph). She also manipulated the instruction-to-test match on the dimension of word vs. word variant. Each subject learned eight words plus four word variants (*exist, existing*) under each contrasting condition, one condition per day for three days. The day after each instructional segment, one-third of these low socio-economic status fourth graders was tested with words and variants systematically varied over the three stimulus conditions. One-third of the items generated an aligned condition score, and each remaining third generated scores for successively less aligned conditions.

In this study, misalignment represented traditional classroom instruction-to-test mismatch; most teachers often teach a word in a paragraph but test it in a sentence. Or the student learns the word *exist*, but the test measures *existing*. Alignment explained 23 percent of the posttest score with differences between aligned and less-aligned instruction reaching about 1.8 sigma.

THE FAHEY STUDY. Treatment-aptitude interaction analysis is a classic way to judge an educational treatment's potency. The logic is that using treatment and aptitude in an ANOVA design allows us to observe treatment's effect compared with aptitude's expected large effect. Aptitude usually explains from 15 percent to 40 percent of academic achievement test score variability. When a treatment approaches a quarter of that magnitude, educators might take note.

Considering the large alignment effects in our early studies, we proposed that alignment might be a better yardstick than aptitude to assess instructional treatments (Cohen, 1987). We demonstrated that proposal in Fahey's (1986) study.

The purpose of the study was to compare the main effect—variations in directed practice—with both aptitude and alignment effects. Subjects were community college students trying to improve their "ability to read for main ideas."

Two important findings emerged. Under mild misalignment representing "traditional" teach-to-test incongruities, aptitude generated its usual strong effect. But as the task demand increased in difficulty, alignment effects increased. In fact, lowest-aptitude students under aligned conditions in the most difficult level of the treatment performed better than the high-aptitude students under traditional conditions of mild misalignments. The difference was 1.2 sigma after 1.5 hours of instruction. Here, alignment eradicated aptitude's effect; for lower achievers, a little alignment apparently went a long way.

THE GRABY STUDY. Graby (1987) proposed that alignment's effect could be observed as a cognitive phenomenon. He predicted that varying stimulus conditions caused varying cognitive connections. He said that two groups learning the "same skill," as usually defined by teachers, will develop different cognitive structures when contingent stimulus conditions of instruction vary.

He taught two groups of high-achieving high schoolers how to figure the area of a trapezoid. Instruction was identical except for variations in the contexts. One group learned to estimate areas of shapes. The other group learned the same things, but the shapes were called lawns, backyards, football fields, and so on.

Half the test items were aligned to each context. The alignment effect reached 2 sigma, and a measure of cognitive connectedness clearly discriminated the two groups. Graby was not only right, but he set the stage for our subsequent research in using the alignment/misalignment construct to teach transfer of learning.

TRANSFER STUDIES. If Sally successfully estimates a trapezoid's area in math class, why can't she estimate her lawn's area when she purchases grass seed at the local garden shop? Some teachers blame Sally's inability to transfer (Perkins & Salomon, 1988) or to apply her school learning. I explain her performance in terms of alignment.

Sally's problem is analogous to the difference between d-o-g on the flashcard and d-o-g on the text page. They are misalignments. Selecting the main idea of a paragraph in reading class but not understanding the historian's point of view in a tenth-grade social studies text is an instructional alignment problem. Understanding the separation of powers principle in civics class and missing its relevance to debates over the War Powers Act is not a lack of the student's ability to apply what he learns. It is a mismatch between the civics teacher's intended and achieved outcomes.

Graby (1987) approached transfer through cognitive theory,

but he ended up manipulating an alignment/misalignment variable. Our most recent studies approach transfer more directly as a fuzzy outcome, and we assume its discriminating stimulus features can be defined as a criterion performance. This allows us to design instructional practice with the same stimulus conditions.

Our first study defined transfer as (1) the score on a chemistry math conversion test presenting problems that become progressively less aligned with those practiced during instruction; and (2) the score representing the number of these same problems for which the student correctly identifies the aligned and misaligned contingent stimuli.

Nolen (1991) taught community college chemistry students to spot aligned and misaligned features among chemistry "conversion" problems. In these classes, a conversion problem was not considered solved unless the student provided both the correct answer and a description of how the critical stimulus features aligned and misaligned with previous problems. By shaping an expectancy that any new chemistry problem will vary from the previous one, he taught them the "habit" of analyzing stimulus features. We call this habit *cognitive stretching.*

Two comparison groups received identical instructional modules that taught the conversion skill using a modeling method. One comparison group's modules contained fewer practice items replaced by training in cognitive stretching. A third control group was baseline. Instructional time was constant across treatment levels. Alignment effects explained 20 percent to 40 percent of the posttest variance. Differences between means ranged from over 1.4 to about 2 sigma in favor of the cognitive stretching group.

In another study, high schoolers are learning to interpret regression lines in math under two different conditions, one of which teaches cognitive stretching. The other is an identical treatment, less the cognitive stretching. Transfer is defined as the score on solving problems in social science and in economics, two content areas not being taught.

In a study of fifth graders, degrees of alignment are carefully controlled, and transfer is being analyzed across skill and content areas. One comparison involves scores representing transfer from math to social studies compared to the reverse transfer.

CONCLUSION

A most stunning implication of our alignment research is the probability that almost all children can learn to levels of excellence almost everything we teach in school. Bloom (1968, 1973, 1976) has been saying this for over twenty years, while Block (1971) outlined a method for achieving this in 1971. Yet today we know more about what constitutes appropriate instruction than Bloom or Block was able to describe twenty years ago.

For example, we know that when learners have the academic entry skills prerequisite to a specific learning task, they tend to learn efficiently (Bloom, 1976). We know that when low-aptitude learners enter an aligned instructional system that guarantees mastery of prerequisite competencies, their learning rates eventually reach speeds of the highest learners (Stone, 1984). We know that if we hold clock time constant but increase percentage of time learners attend to the instruction, their learning rates increase significantly (Ben Peretz &

Bramme, 1990, Carroll, 1963; Cohen, 1971;). We know which stimulus conditions provide appropriate reinforcers (Lysakowski & Walberg, 1982).

And now we know that instructional alignment can make low aptitude children perform as well as high-aptitude students (Stone, 1984; Fahey, 1986; Elia, 1986). In our early alignment experiments we recognized its power to force us to think carefully, critically, and precisely about our outcomes. This alone helped us focus on creating outcomes closer to real-world applications. Now alignment has enabled us to operationize transfer as an observable outcome rather than as a process, and the first cognitive stretching studies are showing promising results.

But twenty years have passed, and academic achievement in the U.S. has continued to decline. The educational community still has not accepted Bloom's claims, even with the emergence of empirical data to support them. Nor has the community accepted Block's methods, though his outline has grown to a complete essay (see Block & Anderson, 1975; Block, Efthim, & Burns, 1989).

Therefore, we expect that the educational community will also ignore instructional alignment. Here are six reasons why.

1. Alignment effects are deceiving. They are too powerful for such a simple idea. If we teach what we test, or test what we teach, then almost all children will achieve excellence. If what we test is what we want children to do or be like, then we can produce superior academic performers.

How simple, but how deceiving! Initially alignment deceived us, too. We thought it was a simple technicality of instructional design. By 1987, however, we were convinced that alignment was a magic bullet (Cohen, 1987), a sort of educational penicillin, an instructional infusion that could reform U.S. schools. It generates greater effects directly on student achievement than any other school reform. In spite of its complexity, it is more do-able than eradicating poverty and racism and more cost effective than trying to implement a children-at-risk model. Unfortunately, it is not as sexy.

2. Teachers are trained to teach, but they are not trained to design instruction.

Discriminating a stimulus condition's critical features is as unfamiliar to most teachers as piloting a space capsule. No teacher training program I know provides alignment training. No state teacher credentialling guidelines require this competency.

3. Aligning requires educators to define their most cherished myths.

Apparently, that frightens many of them. They prefer to believe in literary appreciation rather than to define it. Are they terrified of operationalizing love of reading, critical thinking, creativity, and understanding a poem? Or are they terrified because these definitions are value judgments for which they might be held accountable? They also recognize instructional alignment's power to force us to declare precisely what we want to test and teach. Some things are just too uncomfortable to do even when we know we should.

4. We can avoid these uncomfortable decisions by believing that some outcomes' stimulus conditions remain illusive and undefinable.

Love of reading, understanding the concept of multiplication, critical thinking, higher-level problem solving, and music appreciation *are* popular "outcomes" that many educators believe escape the instructional designer's proclivity for operationalizing. But because some outcomes are certainly fuzzy right now, it does not follow that they cannot be operationized into specified contingency systems in the future, if we have the courage to do it.

    5. Many educators think that teaching to tests lies along a narrow continuum stretching from demeaning to dishonest.

Even in the current antitesting milieu, social values demand a normal distribution of academic performance. Our society apparently views education as another game that produces winners and losers. The proof, we are told, is that any test administered to a large enough group will "naturally" generate a random distribution of scores.

Indeed, it is natural to have differences, unless we introduce an intervention designed to eliminate them. Instruction is intended to be that intervention. With alignment as its fundamental component, instruction can guarantee academic excellence for almost all children. Should we withhold that intervention because the norm-referenced testing tradition has institutionalized the belief that test items must misalign with instruction in order to generate a normal distribution of school effect?

The major reason our children do not achieve excellence is because we think our tests are supposed to be misaligned with our instruction. What irony! We manufacture a misalignment, and then we declare it inevitable. And when someone aligns tests and instruction, we call them cheaters (Mehrens & Kaminski, 1989)!

6. Perhaps it is not irony at all. Perhaps it is intentional.

Perhaps some people suspect that aligned instruction endangers the social order. Have we deluded ourselves into thinking that the Jacksonian revolution marked the end of social oligarchies in North America? Has the great American experiment merely changed some social ascendency rules and the nomenclatures for class identity? Is it possible that money and birth still define aristocracy and power, that the king is called president, that noblemen are CEOs, and that the school is charged with maintaining that hierarchy through such constructs as random score distributions?

- Curriculum
- Instruction
- Organization/ Management (Classroom)

Mastery Teaching

Madeline Hunter
University of California, Los Angeles

Mastery teaching is a way of thinking about and organizing the decisions that all teachers must make before, during, and after teaching. Those decisions are based on research but should be implemented with artistry.

The theory undergirding mastery teaching applies to all students regardless of age, ability, or ethnicity, to all content, to all levels of thinking, and to all models of teaching or learning. Mastery teaching is not specific to direct teaching, to any particular level of learning or thinking, or to a "way to teach"!

Mastery teaching began a quarter of a century ago, when we at the Graduate School of Education, University of California, Los Angeles, addressed the question "How do you create a teacher whose decisions and actions are based on research and who is both artistic and effective?" Back in those days (which were not good at all in teacher education!), many people believed that teachers were born, not made.

We would not accept such a fatalistic stance. We had seen too many bumbling beginners grow into absolute virtuosos in the classroom. Conversely, we had seen charismatic individuals, the Pied Pipers of education, continue year after year to turn out happy, excited illiterates. Charisma was great, but it was neither essential nor sufficient to the performance of a truly effective and artistic teacher.

We turned first to the research on teaching. What little there was could have been summarized by the statement "If you took all the truly effective teachers in the world and laid them end to end, they'd be a lot more comfortable!" We found little that would help us design a more effective teacher preparation program.

The problem was that researchers had been looking for what a teacher was, hoping to identify a predictor to be used in selecting successful candidates for teacher education. It soon became clear (and still is!) that there is no one trait or personality type that guarantees success in teaching.

So we left the ivory towers of research and went to the classrooms of the United States and Canada. There we found an (not *the*) answer. It was not what teachers were, it was what they *did* as they planned for instruction, interacted with students during instruction, and evaluated and replanned after instruction.

Our contribution to teacher education is that, because of our knowledge of the psychological cause-effect relationships between what students did and how much they learned, we were able to label psychologically and teach professional behaviors that had higher probability of accelerating students' learning. We now define teaching as a "constant stream of professional decisions that when implemented increase the probability of learning."

We estimate that a "thinking" teacher (not a direction follower) makes approximately 5,000 professional decisions each day. The questions teachers pose, whether these questions are directed to the group or to an individual, how long teachers wait for answers, their responses to answers, where their eyes go—every action of the teacher—has a potential effect on student learning. No wonder teachers go home exhausted! Their professional decisions, when implemented, have the potential for either increasing learning, producing nothing, or, albeit unintentionally, interfering with learning. It is important that teachers learn to make decisions that predictably achieve the first effect.

We wondered how we could reduce the complexity of these 5,000 decisions, and the research that would support them, so they could be made effectively by beginning teachers. As we looked for commonalties, we discovered that all teaching decisions could be placed in just three categories.

These categories include every decision a teacher makes, regardless of the age, ethnicity, or ability of the student; regardless of the content or skill being learned; and regardless of the teaching model or the level of thinking or learning strategies of the student. Our categorization is not limited to direct teaching of/or less complex thinking. It applies to all models of teaching, such as discovery, cooperative learning, computer-assisted instruction, concept attainment, "hands-on," or observational learning. Our categorization is based on the temporal order of the decisions being made. No one category is most important. All are essential to artistic, effective teaching that leads to successful learning. Also, as new research emerges, we have found that the results from both curricular research and cognitive psychology fit with and add depth to the decisions. Ours is a dynamic teacher decision-making model that is continually being augmented and refined by new research findings in both cognition and curriculum.

CATEGORIES OF DECISIONS

CONTENT

The first decision a teacher must make is in content: what is to be learned? The curriculum guide, course of study, and state mandates define the general focus of learning. This first teaching decision concerns which aspect of that general content will be the specific focus for this student or group of students at this point in time.

In the distant past, content decisions were based on astrology. Students' birthdays were the best predictors of what would be taught. Instead of astrology, we now use psychology, which validates that everyone can learn the next thing beyond that which is already known. Learners differ in rate of learning and size of the learning step, not in random sequences of learning.

Some learnings are sequential; that is, each new learning is based on an essential prior learning having been accomplished. Many operations in mathematics are typical of a "dependent sequence." Division cannot be learned before addition and subtraction. Other learnings are independent in their order of acquisition. Common fractions can be learned before or after decimal fractions. In such an "independent sequence" the order of learning makes no difference.

Consequently, a teacher must determine whether the content to be learned is part of a dependent or an independent sequence. If the learning is in an independent sequence, the teacher need not diagnose because specific prior learnings are not essential to the achievement of the new learning. If the sequence is dependent, the teacher needs to task-analyze that learning objective and then diagnose where students' learning leaves off and new learning needs to begin. Students then focus their learning efforts on what next needs to be learned, not on what already has been accomplished or on what is not possible to accomplish at this point. While such diagnosing used to be an arduous task of paper-and-pencil testing and correcting, now it often can be accomplished by brief questions with signaled answers or even by informal observation.

As we task-analyzed writing to discover why some students "couldn't write," for example, we found several independent sequences, including conventions of punctuation, spelling, capitalization, descriptive words, variety and complexity of sentence patterns, form, type, and so on. More importantly, we found several dependent sequences and learned that some missing skills had never been taught.

An example of a dependent sequence for writing would be (1) making recognizable symbols for words (correct spelling is independent; it can be learned before writing or in subsequent editing), (2) forming phrases and sentences, (3) creating related sentences, (4) creating a paragraph, (5) creating related paragraphs, (6) creating a report or essay, (7) creating a cogent, artistic piece with thesis, introduction, and conclusion.

Now, with the teaching focus on the skills of writing as "content," we find that all students can learn to write better. They will never write equally well because some students are more endowed with this ability than others, but all can increase their skills if they are well taught. We teach the skills of reading, solving math problems, and ball playing, too. Writing, thinking, imaging, and functioning in cooperative learning also respond to instruction. This does not always mean "direct instruction."

A current content focus is on "thinking skills," which, like writing, *all* students—not just the gifted—can learn, albeit to different degrees. Again, a dependent sequence mandates that one cannot think without information. Our objective of "higher-level thinking" is dependent on a student's having knowledge that he or she comprehends and can apply to a new situation.

Our prediction is that a new content area will be "imaging" (not imagining, which is a creative task). Imaging is the process of activating something in long-term sensory memory. This too used to be thought of as a skill of only "right-hemispheric processors." Now we know that while facility in imaging varies, it too responds to instruction and practice. Because it is such an enabling tool in accelerating learning and remembering, it needs to become the deliberate content of teaching.

In summary, a teacher's first decision is the content focus of the learning opportunity being planned, whether that content is specific information, concepts and generalizations, or cognitive, affective, and psychomotor skills. To make that decision, the teacher must create or have available a task analysis to determine whether there are essential prior learnings and, when necessary, diagnose to determine their presence or absence.

Decisions may always be delegated. The teacher's decision may be to have the student decide what needs to be learned, whether it has been learned, when to go on, when to do additional practice, or when to go back and relearn. But these are delegated decisions; the teacher is the professional in charge and is responsible for increasing the probability of successful accomplishment.

LEARNING BEHAVIORS

The second decision that every teacher must make is directed to the behavior or strategy the student will use to learn. This is the only area where models of teaching differ.

It is important that teachers become sophisticated in the varying learning styles of students. It is equally important that teachers create opportunities for students to develop their less-preferred styles, to "bring up their valleys while enhancing their peaks." Consequently, unless a teacher is giving practice in a particular modality, a multimodality learning behavior is indicated. While "thinking skills" start as content to be learned, once acquired they become the learning behavior used to solve problems or acquire new content or skills.

In discovery learning, information and feedback come from the student behavior of observing, hypothesizing, and validating or impeaching the hypothesis. In cooperative learning, information and feedback come from interaction with peers. In computer-assisted instruction, information and feedback come from the computer. In concept attainment, information comes from student-generated examples with feedback from the teacher. In "hands-on," information and feedback come from manipulation. In observational learning, information and feedback come from observation and subsequent practice.

The more instruction and practice students receive in many strategies, the more they are able to select and adapt them to the demands of the learning task and situation. In the same way that there is not one best food, medicine, mode of transportation, or occupation, there is not one best way to learn or to teach. While students may have learning preferences, instruction and practice in various ways of learning enable them to become more flexible, proficient, resilient, and successful in learning situations throughout life.

In the late fifties we learned that there must be perceivable student behavior to validate that learning had or had not occurred in order to guide the teacher's subsequent decisions. Throughout the interaction of teaching and learning, the teacher has four alternatives: (1) Move ahead—the students have attained the content or skill; (2) The students are getting it—they need more practice; (3) The students do not know it—go back and reteach; (4) "Abandon ship—today's not the day." This last decision sometimes needs to be made. On a windy, rainy Friday afternoon or when there is much confusion, it is better to let the "dust settle" and plan a more successful lesson for tomorrow.

These four alternatives can be selected only on the basis of perceivable student output that supplies the necessary information. Those famous (or infamous) "behavioral objectives" of the sixties became our "instructional outcomes" and criterion-referenced tests of the nineties. Instead of "hoping they have learned," we now must know that students have or have not achieved the intended learning. Thus, our instructional decisions are based on evidence rather than on wishful thinking.

THE INSTRUCTIONAL OBJECTIVE. The point of intersection of students' outcome behavior and the content to be learned become our instructional objective or learning outcome. It is the instructional objective that has built accountability and precision as the scientific launching pad to support the artistry of teaching. The objective can be short term, the result of one instructional episode. It can be medium range, the result of several days or weeks. It can be long range, the result of a unit, a year, or several years of instruction: outcome-based education. The latter forms the basis for criterion-referenced tests, which validate that students have achieved intended outcomes, unlike norm-referenced tests, which rank students in comparison to each other.

It is assumed that before a teacher begins to plan for a particular day's teaching, the following determinations will have been made:

A. Within each general content area, the teacher will have determined the particular strand for immediate diagnosing and teaching. For example, in the general content area of reading, the teacher might diagnose and plan for enjoyment of reading, identifying main idea, separating fact from opinion, increasing decoding skills, or predicting outcomes.

B. The teacher will have identified a major target objective in that content and diagnosed students' achievement in relation to that objective. For example, the teacher will identify which students do or do not enjoy reading or can or cannot identify main idea, separate fact from opinion, use beginning consonants to decode words, or predict outcomes. Diagnosis identifies the instruction students need in content and learning behaviors in order to accomplish a particular outcome.

C. On the basis of diagnosis, the teacher will have selected the objective for each group's subsequent instruction. For example, "The learners will select books they enjoy"; "The learners will identify the main idea and underline it"; "The learners will place 'F' by statements that are facts and 'O' by those that are opinions"; or "The learners will predict subsequent events." This objective, which can be at any cognitive, affective, or psychomotor level, will become the basis for instruction and subsequent guided and independent practice.

Only after these decisions have been made is the teacher ready to plan for instruction regardless of whether the plan is implemented by input from the teacher, by materials, or by the students themselves in discovery or cooperative learning. This planning model includes elements necessary for every mode of learning, not just direct instruction.

TEACHING BEHAVIORS: THE THIRD CATEGORY OF DECISIONS

It is in the third category of teaching decisions that we find the art of teaching, which is based on the science of pedagogy. The way the teacher incorporates research-based principles of learning separates the pedestrian teacher from the artist. Many of these principles have been around for a century but not deliberately used. Many also are recent findings from brain research and cognitive psychology.

Once the teacher has determined (or delegated to students to determine) the content to be attained, the input learning behavior that has the highest probability for successful attainment, and the perceivable student output behavior that will validate that outcome, the teacher must anticipate which psychological factors have the highest probability of eliciting successful student learning effort. We only list in this chapter the factors that influence motivations to learn, rate and degree of learning, retention, and transfer. Several publications and videotapes available through the author describe and demonstrate the translation of knowledge about these factors into teaching behaviors (see also Barker & Hunter, 1989d; Hunter, 1984, 1987c, 1988a, 1989c, 1990, 1994; Hunter & Gee, 1988).

FACTORS THAT AFFECT MOTIVATION TO LEARN. From research we gleaned those factors that were demonstrated to have potential for increasing the probability of students' motivation to learn: control, attributions, interest, success, knowledge of results, feeling tone, and level of concern. We also separated intrinsic motivation (where the task is the goal) and extrinsic motivation (where the task leads to the goal) from the confusion of internal motivation (where the student initiates the effort) and external motivation (where the pressure to perform comes from outside the student). We dispelled the myth that one is saintly and the other sinful. The skilled teacher selects from all variables in motivation to move students toward more and more intrinsic motivation and a "zest for learning" outcome.

In the last decade we have incorporated the research from attribution theory to affect students' motivation to learn. According to this theory, the causal agent to which a student attributes past success or failure (ability, effort, task, or luck) is a major determiner of a student's decision to put forth effort to achieve the present learning. As a result, skilled teachers now emphasize effort as the major cause of successful learning because effort is the only thing the student completely controls. If success results from effort, the student obviously has the necessary ability, so self-esteem is enhanced. This is why the first teaching decision regarding content is so critical. If despite effort a student fails, she or he must not have the ability to be successful. Therefore, there is no point in putting forth further effort, and self-esteem is diminished.

FACTORS THAT AFFECT RATE AND DEGREE OF LEARNING. Beginning with Wundt, Pavlov, Watson, and Thorndike, scientific inquiry sought to reveal factors that affected the rate and degree of learning. As Binet built his predictions about school success around IQ and Terman created the Stanford Binet, educators developed a fatalistic stance dependent on the recorded IQ in the student's folder. Students with low IQs were believed to learn slowly and not well.

Recent research, though, has given us more optimistic

insights into one of the most complex thing in the universe: the human brain. While we still are a long way from completely understanding it, we have derived teaching and learning techniques from neuropsychological research that have potential for increasing the rate and degree of each student's learning. Teachers can, for example, apply techniques such as eliciting the brain's "alerting response" by using students' names and also by relating learning to students' prior knowledge and experience, by accelerating learning by massing practice to facilitate new learning, and by distributing practice for long retention.

It is estimated that we use only a very small percentage of our brain power. In the same way that we have learned to run faster, jump higher, and live longer than ever before, we are learning how to learn better, remember longer, and transfer that learning to new situations that require creative problem solving and responsible decisions. It is the deliberate and artistic use of this knowledge that makes teaching a profession.

FACTORS THAT AFFECT RETENTION. It is to no avail if what a student has "learned" is not remembered for subsequent use. Consequently, teachers need to be aware of and incorporate these factors that contribute to retention: meaning, degree of original learning, feeling tone, distributed practice, and transfer. Teachers, for example, should make sure something is well understood and can be applied before moving to another learning with which the first learning could be confused, as well as being careful to build networks of connections among learnings. Designing learning experiences that deliberately and artistically incorporate these factors increases the probability that students will remember what has been learned while reducing the time spent in practice.

FACTORS THAT PROMOTE TRANSFER. Transfer is the process of old learnings affecting, either positively or negatively, the acquisition of new learning or products of that learning. As a result, teachers' awareness of behaviors that promote transfer can reduce the time needed for new learning. Also, transfer is the heart and core of all thinking, creativity, problem solving, and productive, responsible decisions. Specific facts do not transfer, only concepts, generalizations, and discriminations transfer. This observation takes us back to the content decision: that which is worthwhile to teach. Content must be examined for its generalizability to new situations.

New research in curriculum is revealing those concepts and generalizations that are essential to productive existence. Teachers, for example, teach that all wars result from an infraction of beliefs or economic resources. This generalization can then be applied to the Revolutionary War, the Civil War, or Star Wars.

DESIGNING EFFECTIVE LEARNING OPPORTUNITIES

The theory behind the three categories of decisions in mastery teaching is similar to the theory of nutrition. Everyone needs protein, vitamins, minerals, and fiber, regardless of age, ethnicity, customs, value system, or current state of health. However, people need these nutrients in varying amounts and in different forms.

It is the same for the "nutrients" of learning. They are "served" in different forms, but they all result from decisions (regardless of who makes them) in content, learning behaviors, and teaching behaviors. You do not see the cook's decisions, you see only the resultant meal. In the same way, you do not see the teacher's decisions, you see the learning opportunity: the "lesson."

Unfortunately, the most famous aspect of mastery teaching is not our categorization of teaching decisions with the research on which they're based, but the resultant sequence of decisions made while *planning* a lesson: that famous (or infamous!) "Lesson Design."

Doug Russell, while a supervising teacher at the UCLA Lab School, was dismayed by the chaotic way student teachers went about designing lessons, so he created a sequence of decisions to be made when planning a lesson. Seeing its rich potential for more effective planning, I worked with him and we subsequently published *Planning for Effective Instruction* (Hunter & Russell, 1977).

This planning sequence was so new, practical, and useful that educators seized on it, and "Lesson Design" became the "Sermon on the Mount"; any deviation became sinful. "Check lists" of "steps" emerged from educators who didn't realize that there is nothing that must be in every lesson.

A skilled observer of teaching is never looking for the presence or absence of anything but is looking for the appropriateness of what is happening and for the artistry of the teacher in causing it to happen. We believe, however, that a systematic consideration of seven elements, which research has shown to be influential in learning, should be deliberately examined for inclusion or exclusion in designing any learning opportunity regardless of content, learner, or model of teaching.

For each instructional session, the teacher must consider the following seven elements separately to determine whether, for the *particular* content or skill objective for *these* students in *this* situation, that element should be included, excluded, or combined with another element. If the element is included, how to effectively design, sequence, and integrate it into an artistic "flow" of instruction is the essence of the planning task. "Decide, then design" is the foundation on which successful instruction is built. Teacher decision making is the basis of this approach to teaching. To reiterate, there is nothing that must be in every lesson.

All lesson design (not all teaching) begins with articulation of an instructional objective that specifies perceivable student behavior that validates achievement of the precise content, appreciation, process, or skill that is to be the learning outcome. When *designing* lessons, seven questions need to be considered in a certain order as each element of a teaching sequence is derived from and has a relationship to previous elements. When the design is implemented in teaching, the sequence of elements that are included is determined by the professional skill and artistry of the teacher.

Questions that must be answered in planning are:

1. What Independent Practice Will Cement the Learning of This Objective and Develop Automaticity?

Teachers, like all professionals, are successful only when the client no longer needs them. All teaching has as its purpose to make the student as independent as possible. When lessons are carefully planned, student independence becomes much more probable.

Once students, during instruction, can perform with minimal errors, discomfort, or confusion, they are ready to develop fluency and increase accuracy by practicing without the supervision and guidance of the teacher. Only at that point can students be given an independent assignment.

It is important that in independent work the student does

what already has been practiced under teacher guidance rather than some new or "inverted" endeavor. An "inverted" assignment is one where a skill is taught and its reciprocal is practiced. It is as if you taught a child how to untie shoes and take them off and then assigned the independent practice of putting them on and tying them or you taught addition and then assigned a practice sheet of subtraction. The same situation is created by teaching students to solve word problems and then asking them to generate word problems; by teaching punctuation of written sentences and assigning creation of sentences requiring that punctuation; by teaching how to recognize a topic sentence and then requiring generation of topic sentences.

2. What Guided/Monitored Practice Will Enable Students to Achieve This Objective?

The beginning stages of learning are critical to future successful performance. Initial errors can "set" and be difficult to eradicate. Consequently, students' initial attempts in new learning should be carefully monitored and/or guided so that they are reasonably accurate and successful. Teachers need to work with the group or circulate among students to make sure instruction has "taken" before "turning students loose" to practice independently. Under teacher guidance, the student needs to perform all (or enough) of the task so that clarification or remediation can occur immediately, should it be needed. In that way, the teacher is assured that students will perform the task correctly rather than practicing errors when working by themselves.

If a teacher does not begin the planning by translating the objective into activities that could be used in guided/monitored and independent practice, it is much more likely that unnecessary information and activities will be included or that necessary information or skills will be omitted. This procedure is similar to the behavior of experts who frequently "work backwards."

3. What Instructional Input Is Needed?

To plan instructional input needed to achieve the target objective, the teacher must anticipate what information or skill is essential for the student to accomplish the intended objective. Sometimes no input is needed because it was previously done, and today's objective is to develop speed and fluency. Often, though, students are expected to achieve an objective without having been taught that which is essential in order to do so. Task analysis is the process by which component learnings or skills essential to the accomplishment of an objective are identified.

Once the necessary information, process, or skill has been determined, the teacher needs to select the means for "getting it in students' heads." Will it be done by discovery, inquiry, teacher, book, film, record, filmstrip, field trip, diagram, picture, real objects, demonstration, individually, collaboratively, or in a larger group? The possibilities are legion. This is where models of teaching differ.

4. Should There Be Modeling, and What Type Will Be Most Effective?

It is facilitating for students not only to know about but also to see, feel, or hear examples of an acceptable finished product (story, poem, object diagram, graph) or to observe a process modeled (how to identify the main idea, weave, kick a ball, or determine effective ways of thinking or making decisions while fulfilling the assignment). It is important that visual input of modeling be accompanied by the verbal input of labeling the critical elements of what is happening (or has happened) so that students are focused on essentials rather than distracted by transitory or nonrelevant factors in the process or product. For example,

> "I am going to use my thumb to work the clay in here like this so the tail has a firm foundation where it is joined to the body of the animal. In that way, it's less likely to break off in the kiln."

> "Watch while I do this problem (experiment) and I'll tell you what I'm thinking as I work."

> "Notice that this story has a provocative introductory paragraph that catches your interest by the first question the author asks."

There are times when there should be *no* modeling. If divergent thinking is desired, models should have been observed in previous lessons (poetry, texture, descriptive words, movement, and so on). But on the day the students are to create, a model may tempt them to imitate rather than use their own creativity.

5. How Will I Check for Understanding?

During learning, the teacher needs to know whether students are acquiring the information and/or skill necessary to achieve the instructional objective. This ongoing diagnosis may be secured by:

    a. Sampling: Posing questions to the whole group in order to focus everyone on coming up with an answer and to develop readiness to hear the affirmation or impeachment of his or her own answer, then calling on members representative of strata of the group (most able, average, or least able) so that the teacher can estimate progress of the class. Note that at the beginning of learning, correct answers are most enabling. Therefore, incorrect answers are to be avoided.

b. Signaled responses from each member of the group: Selection of first, second, third, fourth alternative by showing that number of fingers, putting pencil straight up for "don't call on me for this question," making a "c" with a hand when examples are correct and an "i" when they are incorrect. First letters, math operations, and punctuation can all be hand signaled. Use of counting sticks and pointing to a place in the book or to parts in a diagram or object are examples of the many signals that can validate learning. Signaled responses have changed from the original "Thumbs up-down" to visual, right-hemispheric manifestations of the answer.

c. Choral response: The strength of a choral response from the group can indicate the general degree of accuracy and comfort with the learning but not what *each* student knows.

d. Individual private response: A brief written or whispered-to-teacher response makes students accountable for demonstrating possession of or progress toward achievement of the needed information or skills.

Examples:

Signals—

"Signal whether you add, subtract, multiply, or divide by making that sign with your fingers."

"Show a 'c' with your fingers if what I say is correct; an 'i' if incorrect. Don't do anything if you're not sure."

"Raise your hand when you are ready to answer this question."

"On your microscope, point to _____."

Private Responses—

> "Write the names of the three important categories we have discussed."

> "Do the first part of this problem on your paper."

The teacher "audits" cooperative learning and individual discovery by moving around, listening, and posing questions. On the basis of "ongoing diagnosis" the learners will move on or the teacher will give additional practice, reteach, or "abandon ship" and replan for tomorrow.

6. Should the Student Know the Objective and Its Purpose?

This element of planning involves communicating to students what they will learn and why that accomplishment is important, useful, and relevant to present and/or future life situations. For example,

> "As you work with these magnets, see if you can develop some generalizations that apply to all magnets."

> "You were slowed down yesterday because you had trouble with _____. Today we are going to practice so you develop more speed and accuracy."

> "We are going to work on the correct form of letter writing so that you can write for the materials you need in your social studies project."

> "Today you are going to practice ways of participating in a discussion so each of you gets turns and you also learn from other people's ideas."

> "Knowing the objective and why it is important is not the pedantic 'At the end of today's lesson you will be able to _____.'

Note that in designing a lesson, the teacher generates the objective as presented to the student, not as presented in the teacher's plan book, which might state, "The learner will use correct form in writing a letter"; "The learner will derive generalizations about magnets."

Usually students will learn more efficiently if they know what the learning will be and why it is important in their lives. There are times when the students should not know the objective because it will distract them or "turn them off." ("Today you are going to learn the difference between colons and semicolons" could elicit, "Who cares?")

7. What Anticipatory Set Will Focus the Students on the Objective of Today's Lesson?

Anticipatory set results from a *brief* activity that occurs at the beginning of the lesson or when students are mentally "shifting gears" from one activity to the next. The purpose of anticipatory set is to elicit attending behavior as well as a focus on and a mental readiness or "set" for the content of the ensuing learning. That set may (but does not need to) include review of previous learning that will help the student achieve today's objective, not routine review of old material. That set also may give the teacher some diagnostic data needed for achievement of the current objective. An anticipatory activity should continue only long enough to get students "ready to go" so that the major portion of instructional time is available for the accomplishment of the current objective.

Examples of activities that produce anticipatory set are:

- Give synonyms for overused words when the objective is improvement in descriptive writing.
- Create word problems to go with a numeral problem on the chalkboard when the objective is meaningful computational practice.

- Review the main ideas of yesterday's lesson that will be extended today.
- State ways a skill might be useful in daily life when the objective is to develop fluency with that skill.
- Practice speedy answers to multiplication facts for a quick review before today's math lesson on two-place multiplication.

An anticipatory set is not needed if students are already alert and "ready to go" because of previous events that built the bridge or transition into today's learning.

SUMMARY

To reiterate, not all seven elements will be included in every lesson. It may take several lessons before students are ready for guided and/or independent practice. Also, mere presence of an element in a lesson does not guarantee quality teaching. A teacher may use an anticipatory set that spreads rather than focuses students' attention. ("Think of your favorite food. Today we are going to talk about cereals.") Input may be done ineffectively. The modeling may be distracting. ("I will cut this chocolate cupcake in fourths.")

Questions about these seven elements are guides in planning for artistic and effective learning opportunities, not mandates! Simply "knowing" the seven elements in planning for effective instruction will not ensure that those elements are implemented with artistry. Also, simply having a "knack with kids" will not ensure that those elements that promote successful learning will be included in instructional planning. Both the science and the art of teaching are essential.

It is the belief of the writer that knowledge of the three categories of teaching decisions and the research on which they are based plus deliberate consideration of seven elements that can promote effective learning constitute the launching pad for planning and implementing artistic learning opportunities that achieve greater student progress toward any objective or goal. Teachers' progress in mastery teaching can be dramatically accelerated by coaching and supervision if observers consider those same three decision categories in designing an effective professional learning opportunity and then implement their decisions in artistic and productive instructional conferences.

MASTERY TEACHING RESEARCH

Where is the research that would support this teacher decision making? The basic cause-effect relationships upon which the mastery teaching model rests can be found in any beginning psychology text that describes research-based factors that affect human motivation, increase the rate and degree of learning, and facilitate the retention and transfer of that learning to creative problem solving.

The model's effectiveness itself was first validated in "Project Linkage," where it was implemented in a failing (sixth percentile in national achievement scores) inner city school in Los Angeles. An independent evaluator report on file with the California State Department of Education verified that with no other new intervention, the year's median gain by students doubled as measured by the same standardized tests used the previous years, which had shown a steady decrease in achievement during the previous ten years.

Since then, the model has often been used in concert with other interventions. A good example is the Napa Project (Hunter, 1986a), which demonstrated achievement gains while the teachers were using the model and achievement drops when they stopped. While there were some flaws in research methodology in this project (Mandeville & Rivers, 1989), as well as omissions in the complete model application (Hunter, 1988c; Mandeville & Rivers, 1989), teachers and project directors were enthusiastic about the obviously productive results in student learning and professional satisfaction. Sousa and Donovan (1990) found statistically significant achievement gains in four out of six academic areas. I have responded to many who, not understanding that it was a teacher decision-making model, simple in conceptualization but incredibly complex in artistic application, thought it was a rigid way of conducting only teacher-directed lessons (see Hunter, 1986a & b, 1987a & b, 1988b & c).

The greatest validation comes from the daily experiences of teachers who are using mastery teaching principles to make professionally informed decisions that result in accelerated student learning regardless of the model of teaching being employed. As a result, this teacher decision-making model is being used in every state, every province in Canada, and literally all over the world. In November 1990, the European Council of International Schools featured it at their conference for 3,000 educators from Russia to Africa.

FUTURE OF MASTERY TEACHING

After a quarter of a century of use (and, unfortunately, some abuse), mastery teaching has benefited those students whose teachers understood the decision-making model as a process for describing and planning learning opportunities that were implemented with artistry rather than as a "way of teaching." As a result, teaching has finally attained full status as a profession for it now is based on a core of research-validated knowledge, which is used by decision-making professionals who are constantly adding additional research-based knowledge and skills to enhance their effectiveness.

- CLIMATE
- ORGANIZATION/ MANAGEMENT (CLASSROOM)
- ORGANIZATION/ MANAGEMENT (SCHOOL)

Peer Coaching: Quality Through Collaborative Work

Pam Robbins
Private Educational Consultant

One of the major movements of the 1990s and toward the twenty-first century has been teacher empowerment. Its goal is to promote the involvement of teachers as key decision makers in bringing about quality in all aspects of the educational process. But teachers cannot achieve this quality alone; they must be organized through collaborative structures. To accomplish this, teachers must be involved in a *shared decision-making* process.

As with many movements in education, teacher empowerment has been interpreted in a variety of ways. Several collaborative structures have been developed—shared leadership, shared decision making, principal's advisory councils, mentor or lead teacher programs, and peer coaching. This chapter will examine only one of these structures: peer coaching.

WHAT IS PEER COACHING?

Peer coaching is a confidential process through which two or more professional colleagues work together to reflect upon current practices; expand, refine, and build new skills; share ideas; conduct action research; teach one another; or problem solve within the workplace. Though "peer coaching" seems to be the most prominent label for this type of activity, there are a variety of other names: peer support, consulting colleagues, peer partners, and peer sharing and caring. Regardless of how these relationships are labeled, what they all have in common is a focus on the collaborative development, refinement, and sharing of craft knowledge—a practice that is sorely lacking within the walls of many schools.

The ultimate form peer coaching takes is as individual and unique as the people who engage in it (see Figure 10.1). As this figure indicates, peer coaching activities can be formal or informal. Most formal arrangements take place within the classroom and are based on an observation while class is in session. Informal coaching activities, with the exception of co-teaching, generally take place outside of the classroom. Many teachers have commented that working informally together initially has created a trust among colleagues that later served as a powerful foundation for more formal, in-classroom peer coaching arrangements.

FORMAL, IN-CLASSROOM COACHING: TEACHER GENERATED

Some peer coaching involves colleagues formally working together to share classroom observations of teaching in general. In these instances, there is generally a preconference, an observation, and a postconference.

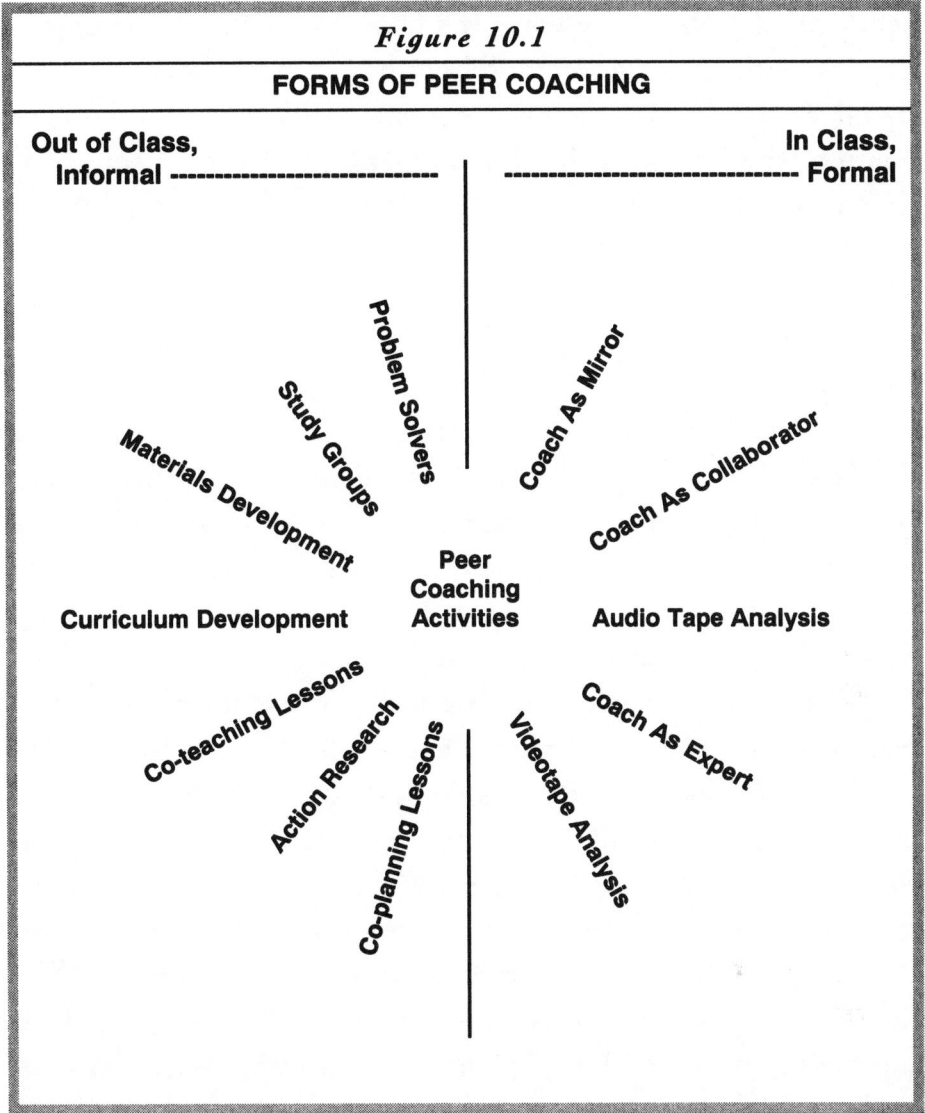

Figure 10.1
FORMS OF PEER COACHING

THE PRECONFERENCE. In the preconference, the teacher who functions as the coach asks the inviting teacher (the teacher who has requested to be coached) to explain the lesson purpose, what led up to the lesson, and what will follow. The coach might also want to discuss student characteristics and class norms for behavior as well as any concerns about the lesson or observation. Sometimes the coach and inviting teacher might arrange a signal, so that if the lesson is not going as was expected and the inviting teacher wants the coach to leave, this can be conveyed with ease.

The inviting teacher then specifies the focus of the observation. Generally, the focus is something about which the teacher is genuinely curious. It might have an instructional, curricular, or student emphasis.

The inviting teacher and coach next decide together how the data might best be collected. Essentially, it is as if the teacher is a researcher in his or her own classroom and the coach is the data collector. The discussion between colleagues usually includes talk about where the coach should sit or stand to collect data and whether or not the coach should interact with students.

The inviting teacher clearly controls the focus of the observation to take place and determines the parameters for the discussion of the lesson in the postconference that will follow. The coach's role is to facilitate the inviting teacher's thinking about the lesson to afford a "dress rehearsal" prior to the actual teaching performance. This facilitation usually includes probing and clarifying questions that serve two purposes. Generally, they help the teacher fine-tune thinking about the lesson and, at times, develop a "fall-back" plan just in case the lesson does not go as desired. These questions also assist the coach in clarifying the desired focus for the observation and in specifying how the data is to be collected.

The preconference generally concludes with the coach asking for feedback about what she or he did during the conference to facilitate the teacher's thinking prior to the lesson. This feedback allows the coach to reflect and determine which coaching strategies are helpful so that these can be repeated in future sessions. Asking for feedback in this way also models a spirit of reciprocity. It is as if the coach is committed to working just as seriously in the coaching role as the teacher is in the teaching roles. This spirit of reciprocity ultimately contributes to the establishment of a trusting relationship.

THE OBSERVATION. The topics upon which coaches focus data-collection efforts are varied. Some examples include higher-order questioning skills, teacher-student interaction, student time on task, physical proximity, wait time, use of motivation variables, verbal flow, use of a particular instructional strategy and its effects, active participation, or the effects of a particular curricular approach. The inviting teacher determines the particular focus so that he or she feels "in control" of the discussion about the observed teaching.

In no way is evaluation a part of the coaching interaction. For example, if the inviting teacher asks the coach to determine if there is "appropriate pacing" in the lesson, the coach needs to ask, "If pacing is appropriate, what will I see?" Such a stance allows the coach to avoid being put in a judgmental role. She or he then needs to simply record the presence or absence of those behaviors specified by the inviting teacher.

In the early stages of a peer coaching relationship, the inviting teacher often picks a "safe" focus—one that typically will yield positive data. As trust builds between coach and teacher and the two have the opportunity to experience switching roles, the inviting teacher might be more willing to experiment, take risks, and "let his or her rough edges show" (Little, 1982). The teacher and coach soon realize that it is precisely these rough edges that give one something to hang on to in order to examine the practice of teaching. As one teacher commented as she grew more comfortable with the peer coaching process, "Anything worth doing is worth doing poorly at first!"

Coaching should be a dynamic process. The focus of coaching visits will change as the inviting teacher wishes. On one occasion, an inviting teacher asked her coach to record the questions she asked, how many seconds she waited before eliciting student responses, which students responded, and what they said. When the inviting teacher examined her data, she discovered that she consistently called on some students first, while asking others to "elaborate on the answer." This meant that those students routinely called upon to elaborate always had more wait time. For this reason the inviting teacher decided to be more conscious of which students she called upon and in what order. During the next observation she asked the coach to focus on collecting data about the response patterns so that she could determine if she met her personal objective of distributing the opportunity for wait time.

Prior to the observation, the inviting teacher usually tells his or her class about the coach's visit: "Mr. Klein will be coming in to watch me teach today. At another time, I will be visiting his classroom. At this school, teachers believe in learning from one another." Many teachers have commented that statements such as these model, at an adult level, the type of cooperative learning they are promoting in their own classrooms among students. It also models a stance of life-long learning.

THE POSTCONFERENCE. After the observation, a postconference is held. These postconferences can differ dramatically and are of three types: mirroring, collaborative, and expert. Which type is used depends on the preference of the inviting teacher, preferences often influenced by the time available to meet, the trust between coach and teacher, and the history of the coaching relationship.

The *mirroring postconference* takes the least time and does not provide a lot of dialogue about the observation. In this type of postconference, the coach's role is that of a confidential, objective observer and data collector, and the teacher is left to do the analysis alone. In the postconference, the coach simply says, "Here's the information you asked me to collect. If you have any questions, please let me know." The data from the observation and any notes from the preconference are then handed over to the inviting teacher.

The *collaborative postconference* takes more time and allows for dialogue usually characterized by a mutual discussion of the teaching that was observed. The coach asks the inviting teacher to reflect upon what was expected or planned to happen and what actually happened. The inviting teacher also analyzes what teaching and student behaviors contributed to the lesson outcomes and determines what changes might be made if the lesson were to be taught again. At the end of the conference, the coach solicits feedback about the coaching strategies she or he employed.

Throughout the postconference, the discussion is guided by the parameters set forth by the inviting teacher in the preconference. It is the inviting teacher who ultimately decides what to do with the data. Sometimes in the collaborative conference, the coach helps plan the initial lesson in the preconference and in the postconference, collaboratively analyzes the lesson, and helps replan it if it is to be taught again. This type of postconference might take as long as thirty to fifty minutes and involves a much deeper and more mutual analysis of the data.

The *expert postconference* involves a coach who has more

experience or expertise than the inviting teacher at either a particular grade level or with a particular instructional or curricular technique. So in the postconference, the expert facilitates the teacher's analysis of the lesson, much as the coach does in the collaborative conference, but the expert often also teaches as a part of the pre-and postconference.

One novice teacher, for example, asked her coach to analyze the variety of ways she asked students to actively participate in her lesson. The coach wrote down specific examples of active participation used during the lesson observation. In the postconference, the novice reflected "I used 'think, pair, share,' choral responses, and signaling . . . but I wish I could have used additional strategies. Could you share some others with me?" The coach responded to the novice's question with another: "What other techniques have you tried in previous lessons?" The novice recalled her use of response cards and of individual chalkboards. If the novice had not been able to recall any techniques that she used in the past, the expert might have shared some of those he had seen others use and then asked the novice to consider the following question: "Which techniques might best suit this lesson and your style of teaching?" In another form of expert coaching, the expert invites the novice to observe him or her teach. This observation is followed by a discussion.

In this example, the expert facilitated the novice's reflection and rehearsal of strategies used in the past. This reflection/rehearsal served to increase the likelihood that these strategies could be recalled quickly and used in the future, even when the expert coach was not there. Such facilitation strengthened the novice's ability to help herself—a vital survival skill in many isolated classrooms.

Even in the expert conference, the inviting teacher has control over what happens and how the data are to be collected. The expert postconference usually takes thirty minutes to an hour. Trust is a critical factor, because some teachers fear that to acknowledge an instructional difficulty or to ask for assistance might be seen as an open admission of incompetence (Rosenholtz, 1989).

The mirror, collaborative, and expert forms of postconferences are not a developmental continuum. They represent a range of options for interaction between inviting teacher and coach. For example, the inviting teacher might work with an expert coach for one observation in order to learn more about teaching social skills in cooperative learning. In the next coaching session, the inviting teacher might ask the same coach to collaboratively plan, observe, and discuss a lesson on social skills. The third time they work together, the inviting teacher might ask the coach to function as a mirror and to observe student time on task in a cooperative learning lesson. The collective goal of these coaching sessions is to facilitate the teacher's ability to reflect upon and analyze teaching and its consequences. Teachers play the role of action researchers in their own classrooms. They are assisted by the coach, who serves as a data collector and in some cases as a co-investigator.

FORMAL, IN-CLASS COACHING: IN-SERVICE GENERATED

So far we have seen that some peer coaching involves pre- and postconferencing tied to in-classroom observations focused on a particular aspect of teaching selected by the inviting teacher. Other forms of formal, in-class coaching involve observations and conferencing tied to the application of a specific in-service strategy or curricular approach.

Here, the purpose of coaching is to facilitate skill transfer of the strategy/approach from a workshop to the workplace. In this instance, the focus of the observation is not steered by the inviting teacher but determined by the workshop content. If the workshop has addressed the elements of a specific lesson strategy, such as concept attainment, for example, the coaching process revolves around the implementation of this strategy in the classroom.

This in-service-generated approach to peer coaching has been shown by research to facilitate skill transfer (Joyce & Showers, 1980). But if it is the only form of coaching that teachers experience, the process may become routine—coaching as "unreflective practice" (Hargreaves, 1989)—and the aspects of the lesson about which the teacher is genuinely curious may go unaddressed (Robbins, 1984).

INFORMAL, OUT-OF-CLASSROOM COACHING

In addition to the formal in-classroom coaching structures already discussed, teachers have experimented with a variety of out-of-classroom forms of coaching. For example, they have co-planned lessons, cooperatively developed interdisciplinary units, created grade-level appropriate cooperative learning materials, analyzed and discussed videotape teaching episodes, problem solved, met in study groups to discuss topics of interest, and taught one another new instructional and curricular approaches. Many teachers have commented on the value of keeping reflective journals about their learnings. What these efforts have in common is the element of peer support in the quest to refine, expand, and enhance knowledge about the teaching profession. These approaches make learning about the business of teaching accessible within the workplace to all teachers.

PEER COACHING CONSIDERATIONS

Whether a formal in-class or an informal out-of-class activity, peer coaching should possess certain characteristics. Most important, it should be *voluntary*. When coaching is mandated because it is written into a plan or endorsed by administration, it runs the risk of becoming what Hargreaves (1989) has appropriately labeled "contrived collegiality"—an activity that forces unwanted contacts among unconsenting adults, consuming already scarce time.

How often peer-coaching partners meet is a function of professional need or desire as well as of programmatic opportunity (which is often tied to school budget). Many peer-coaching partners meet professionally at least twice a month so that each individual can play the role of both inviting teacher and coach.

Released time to participate in peer coaching is provided through a variety of means. Some teachers use "prep periods." Others work in trios so that "teacher one" can take two classes to release "teacher two" to observe "teacher three." Many peer coaches meet, too, through a variety of programmatic means. Some peer-coaching programs use a librarian so that the coaching teacher's class learns study skills while their teacher is out peer coaching. Still others involve guest lecturers who teach students about a subject related to their course of study. At times, the principal or vice principal will take a class. A few peer-coaching programs use substitute teachers—often referred to as "guest teachers" to enhance their status with students! When substitutes are used, it is useful to provide them with training to assist them in managing the classroom. Many schools request the same substitute on the same day each week to provide a measure of continuity for students. Teachers report worrying about loss of student contact time even though the gains they report from participating in peer coaching are great. They also indicate that it is important to inform parents about peer coaching and its goal to enhance learning.

Coaching pairs should be formed by allowing teachers to select their own partners on the basis of similar/dissimilar interests, areas of expertise, friendship patterns, geographic proximity, teaching styles, or grade levels. Some teachers, for example, purposefully form duos and choose partners who have a similar style to theirs; others find it more challenging to stretch and form a partner with a teacher who has a different style; still others change partners each semester. Some have formed trios so that A observes B, B observes C, and C observes A. In one district an entire grade-level team worked together where one teacher preconferenced with the rest of the team, then taught the same lesson in each team member's classroom, and later postconferenced with the entire team.

Who works with whom in peer coaching or for how long ultimately reflects and rewards teacher choice. It should always be acceptable for a peer coaching pair to "get divorced." A more detailed description of the peer coaching process can be found in *How to Plan and Implement a Peer Coaching Program* (Robbins, 1991).

How Well Does Peer Coaching Work?

Teachers at schools where peer coaching is implemented have reported profound benefits (see Robbins, 1991): a better understanding of teaching, increased skill in reflection and self-analysis, an improved sense of professional skill, renewal, recognition by peers, increased collaboration within the school, collegiality, enhanced teaching performance, greater articulation across grade levels, a larger resource bank of successful practices, and increased student growth. These benefits are so significant that they motivate teachers to persist with coaching activities in spite of budget cutbacks that in some schools have eliminated the possibility of using substitute time for coaching activities. Teachers feel comfortable experimenting with new practices, laughing at mistakes, and working together. School is an exciting place to be—for staff and students. At Wells Junior High School in Wells, Maine, for example, peer-coaching activities preceded the development of a collaboratively run school, a school ultimately characterized by shared decision-making structures for leadership functions related to instruction and curriculum.

WHERE IS PEER COACHING HEADED?

In spite of their potential virtues, however, collaborative practices such as peer coaching are not easily put into place. There are, in fact, several barriers to the development of any form of collaborative work within a school, especially contextual ones. Because peer coaching is an activity that goes on within a school, its ultimate form must take into account and be responsive to these contextual factors. Variables include not only those associated with the unique context of the specific school (e.g., other activities competing for teacher time, budget, and schedule) but also the broader political, social, and historical factors that impact the implementation of coaching.

One major factor influencing the implementation of peer coaching is the isolation that has traditionally characterized the teaching profession. So nationwide, reform agendas and political action such as Mentor or Lead Teacher legislation are calling for collaborative work among teachers as a prescription for revitalizing the teaching profession, improving workplace conditions, and enhancing the teaching and learning process. The rationale for this thrust has several dimensions.

- Collaborative work among teachers demonstrably promotes greater reflection about teaching. As a result of this reflection, teachers have the capacity to implement those practices responsive to the changing societal demand for the education of our students (Glickman, 1990).

- Collaborative institutions also enhance performance and reinforce continuous improvement (Fullan, 1990b). Collegial workplaces are more likely to implement and sustain an innovation because people are constantly talking about, focusing on, and reflecting upon it within the workplace. The innovation becomes a part of the daily life of the school and serves to connect teachers across classrooms.

- Collaboration in the form of coaching sustains the effects of specific skills and strategies taught in workshops so that they are transferred to the workplace (Joyce & Showers, 1980).

- The quality of teacher interactions outside of the classroom affects the quality of their future actions within the classroom (Little, 1982).

Because the rationale for collaborative arrangements appears to make perfect sense, many districts have jumped on the peer-coaching bandwagon. But frequently these efforts fail. There are a myriad of reasons for this failure. Following is a list of frequently encountered problems and suggested guidelines for averting them.

PROBLEM 1

Many districts swiftly respond to reform agendas by mandating the implementation of programs of collaborative work. These "top-down, well-intended" mandates rarely consider the implications of such action.

For many schools, such action is familiar and fuels the existing lore that prevails about school changes—"if you wait long enough, this too will pass." Individuals within such schools frequently are deprived of critical readiness-building activities. "Information" is often rumor or hearsay; emotions frequently run high and people feel invaded—coerced, resentful, and powerless. "Implementation" is often similar to the installation of a new household fixture—collaboration is simply attached with bolts to the existing structure, with little regard for whether the internal systems can handle its weight. Such attachments do not take into account the individual culture of a school, the conventional pattern of teacher isolation, the lack of precedence for collaborative work or roles, the characteristics and beliefs of individuals in the school, the history of past innovative reform efforts at the school, or the workplace norms that would impact such an enterprise. Consequently, the innovation may take hold only briefly and usually will disappear or "self-destruct" as soon as the pressure for implementation subsides.

> **GUIDELINE I.** There is a need for a readiness phase prior to program implementation. During this time, information about peer coaching, including examples and visitations, should be provided, and key people should be involved in a commitment-building process. The organizational barriers to the program should be identified and plans made to overcome them. For example, existing workplace norms,

those unwritten rules that govern behavior, should be examined to see if they are consistent with peer-coaching activities. If they are not, plans need to be made to modify these norms or create new ones. The rationale or relevance of peer coaching needs to be demonstrated. Individuals need to feel that it is feasible to participate. And those who will be affected by the program need to feel involved in decisions about its structure. Trust must exist or be created between program planners and implementers.

PROBLEM 2

In many instances, funds are allocated for collaborative work activities such as peer coaching, but the training necessary to equip individuals to take on these new collaborative roles is not provided or is provided only in a minimal way with little or no follow-up. Because many teachers have not spent time in others' classrooms, they often feel uncomfortable even entering. Once in, they frequently fumble to converse because many times their only prior experience with working with another adult in the classroom has been conferring with an administrator during evaluation. The peer-coaching experience is a foreign one. Because colleagues do not know how to begin talking about teaching, their feelings of discomfort rise.

GUIDELINE 2. Providing funds to support peer coaching is not enough. Training and follow-up activities must be provided to support teachers in new roles. Training should involve theory, demonstration, practice, feedback, shadowing experiences of peer-coaching preconferences, observations and postconferences, application opportunities with discussion, and problem solving. Individuals involved in the training should meet periodically to review, refine, and expand coaching skills, teach and learn from one another, problem solve issues of implementation within the collaborative group, and celebrate success. Figure 10.2 is an example of how peer-coaching training might be structured (Robbins, 1991).

PROBLEM 3

In most schools, teachers have never experienced a peer-coaching or mentor role; hence, when asked to function in one of these roles, individuals tend to invent it as they go along (Little, 1990). In the California Mentor Teacher program, for example, mentors functioned more as resource providers, sharing materials and equipment, rather than working within the classroom, giving novice teachers feedback about their performance, and teaching about craft knowledge (Little, 1990 quoted in Fullan, 1990). The mentors expressed discomfort with giving advice or offering feedback that might be perceived as hurtful. Many commented that even "drumming up business" was difficult. They explained that often individuals within the school did not know what a mentor was, what she or he did, or how affiliating with the mentor might be perceived by colleagues. In these situations, colleagues often went through the motions of collaboration, but their work lacked vitality and curiosity about practice.

> **GUIDELINE 3.** Peer-coaching roles and functions should be discussed and clarified. Models should be provided for roles that have no historical precedence. Support groups should be organized for mentors so that they can share successful practices and problem solve.

PROBLEM 4

Even in schools where true collaborative cultures have

Figure 10.2
OVERVIEW OF PEER-COACHING TRAINING SESSIONS

Session 1: **Overview of the Research on Peer Coaching**
- **A context for peer coaching**
  - the history of the teaching profession
  - collaborative goal structures in schools
  - peer coaching, school norms, and culture
  - social and technical principles of coaching
  - organizing for peer coaching
- **Exemplary peer coaching models**
  - ways to coach within classrooms
  - other structures for peer coaching

Sessions 2, 3:
- **Overview of observation instruments for coaching: from mirroring to coaching**
  - interaction analysis
  - time off task
  - drop-in observation
  - script taping
  - checklists
  - verbal flow
  - making your own instrument

Session 4:
- **Factors influencing peer-coaching relationships: How we look, what we value**
- **A model of factors influencing teacher thinking and behavior**
  - modality preferences
  - educational beliefs
  - cognitive style
  - learning styles

Session 5:
- **Advanced conferencing skills**
  - the memory research: foundation for coaching
  - preconferencing
  - observing
  - postconferencing

Session 6:
- **Fine tuning communication skills**
  - mediational questions
  - probing for specificity
  - identifying and staying aware of presuppositions

Session 7:
- **Change theory and effective staff development practices**
  - what the research says
  - implications for peer coaching
  - planning for maintenance

been created, opportunities for collegial contacts among teachers are frequently limited by the finances available to support released time for collaborative work and shared observation of teaching. Bureaucratic conditions, such as schedules and routine duties, provide barriers to collaborative work time as well. In addition, parents as well as teachers often fear that time taken to build collegial relationships among staff members will result in the loss of quality instructional time for students. "Guest teachers" or substitutes, who might release teachers to partake in collaborative work, often cannot provide for continuous progress in the classroom because they are not aware of the lessons that have preceded or will follow.

GUIDELINE 4. Time is a major factor in peer-coaching success. Planning efforts should address where time can be made available within the duty day for peer coaching partners or work groups to carry out their activities. What else is going on within the school, how many groups of individuals will be affected by schedule changes, the time taken away from other activities, and the time needed to implement training and follow-up activities should be considered in the planning process. How each school resolves the issue of time is a function of its individual characteristics and of the needs and desires of the school community. Some schools have addressed this issue by offering financial compensation for hours worked beyond those contracted for. Other schools have focused study groups on different scheduling options in order to plan how time for collaborative work might be arranged.

PROBLEM 5

Another variable affecting potential collaborative work is the existence of strong norms of isolation within the culture of most schools. This is not surprising when one considers the physical structure of schools:

> The most important single property of classrooms, viewed from a schoolwide perspective, is their spatial scattering and isolation throughout school buildings. Because teachers work in different places at the same time, they do not observe each other working (Dreeben, 1973, pp. 450–473).

Or as Glickman (1990) suggests, it seems as if "the one-room schoolhouse is repeated every few yards down the corridor."

These physical conditions, along with the multitude of activities that consume the teacher's time within the four walls of the classroom, limit the prospects for success for any form of collaboration among teachers and perpetuate the norms of isolation. As a consequence of this reality, many teachers have expressed curiosity as to "how they measure up" to other teachers. Yet they hesitate to seek opportunities that would enable them to visit other teachers' classrooms.

GUIDELINE 5. In the planning process, consider the impact of the history of the teaching profession as a potential barrier to getting started. Many school cultures have never included collaborative work among teachers. In these settings, trust-building activities to promote a readiness to share, problem solve, and teach one another must take place in order to build a desire for in-classroom coaching activities. People should first have positive, safe experiences in order to change values and beliefs about the potential benefits to be derived from the coaching experience. These "safe experiences" can include discussing instructional or curriculum ideas during a faculty meeting, sharing successful practices, or carrying out structured problem-solving activities in small groups.

PROBLEM 6

Many teachers report waning enthusiasm for coaching about six to eight months into the program. Sometimes this is a function of the effort it takes to participate in coaching activities—for example, preparing for a substitute and the aftermath of a substitute.

>**GUIDELINE 6.** Recognize that even after a peer coaching program is implemented, a state of entropy frequently sets in. Coaching takes much energy and competes for time with other vital aspects of the teacher's work life. There is a need to build in on a regular basis celebration for and renewal of coaching efforts. Make sure that coaching practices focus on issues teachers care about. Provide opportunities for teachers to share insights and learnings. Continually monitor program effects and discuss the data. Revise the program based on feedback.

PROBLEM 7

Often teachers feel overwhelmed by having so many things to do. One staff brainstormed seventy-eight things they were collectively doing in the month! Coaching can be seen as just one more thing to do rather than an opportunity "to work smarter, not harder," as one teacher put it.

>**GUIDELINE 7.** Monitor and adjust peer-coaching activities. Involve staff in talking about program successes and program needs. Make modifications accordingly. Staff members should consider how peer coaching can be integrated with other site-level activities so that rather than being an "add-on," it can provide valuable support for a variety of aspects of daily classroom life. If a school is focusing on whole language, for example, suggest that peer coaching

might be used to facilitate the implementation of new approaches related to whole language.

PROBLEM 8

In some schools the theme is "Let's do in-service X this year; then next year we can do in-service Y." When this becomes the theme in schools, teachers are hesitant to devote the time and energy to become involved, knowing that the focus of in-service efforts will change the next year. At other schools where small groups of faculty members become highly involved in coaching and others are not, there evolves a notion among staff members of an "elite, in-group" and an "out-group." Resentment triggered toward the implementers becomes a strong negative force within the school culture.

GUIDELINE 8. Build peer coaching into a long-range plan for staff development. Work to make coaching "a way of life" at the school. Peer-coaching activities should be discussed regularly at faculty meetings and should have priority placement on the agenda. They should be supported by the school budget. Some teachers have found it useful to reflect upon and write about their activities in peer-coaching journals. New members of the school community should be offered the chance to shadow peer-coaching activities to increase their awareness of potential benefits and invite their involvement. Peer coaching should be accessible to all members of the school.

PROBLEM 9

Teachers at some sites report that one factor in the failure of peer-coaching efforts is a lack of administrative support. There is frequent talk about its value, but few opportunities are provided within the bureaucracy to make peer coaching work.

GUIDELINE 9. Principals have busy work lives characterized by competing priorities. However, if they truly value peer coaching and want it to work, they need to provide administrative support in both symbolic and expressive ways (Peterson, 1981). Principals who value peer coaching should "walk like they talk." This involves not only talking and writing about peer coaching in a supportive way, but also allocating funds for peer-coaching activities, providing time for discussion and celebration of peer-coaching activities, and facilitating release time opportunities for peer coaching. Some principals have taught classes to release teachers to observe others. Some have offered to be coached or to serve as a coach. Principals at successful peer-coaching sites communicate about it regularly—at board meetings and parent-teacher meetings, in newsletters, with teachers, and with students. They are available to listen to, address, and respond to teachers' concerns.

PROBLEM 10

Peer coaching requires a cooperative goal structure. Many schools operate with competitive or individualistic goal structures. The ease with which peer coaching is implemented will be strongly affected by the way individuals at the site are used to working together.

GUIDELINE 10. Model collaborative work throughout the school. One of the major impediments to coaching is that it breaks the familiar paradigm of working in isolation. To promote success in peer coaching, provide structures for collaborative work at all levels of the school. This can include grade-level team meetings, cross-grade-level team meetings, shared decision making in faculty meetings, team teaching, cross-school visitations, principals shadowing one another, advisor-advisee programs, and cooperative learning in classrooms. Collaborative work needs to become a norm in the school!

Many schools have been overwhelmed by a variety of problems affecting the implementation of peer coaching, yet others have succeeded by setting to work in spite of them. For those working to ensure the success of school improvement and staff development, peer coaching offers one avenue for building the essential collaborative norms of practice. Peer coaching and its modified forms of peer support provide flexible structures, responsive to a variety of school variables that enable staffs to address the changing needs of students and society. Teachers talking about teaching—reflecting on how they do what they do—helps develop trust and genuine appreciation and acceptance of others. Feelings of isolation and passivity give way to an environment of collaboration and professional growth. Collaboration becomes central to teachers' daily work. As one teacher put it, "The norm has changed from 'what others do is not my business' to 'what we do here at school is everybody's business, and business is booming' " (Raney & Robbins, 1989).

- CURRICULUM
- FACILITIES
- INSTRUCTION
- MOTIVATION

Teaching for Literacy

Peter Winograd
Connie Bridge
University of Kentucky

School people interested in improving teaching for literacy must deal with a wealth of innovations and insights that are simultaneously exciting and frustrating. Much has changed in our understanding of reading and writing instruction, yet much of what we read seems difficult to implement in real classrooms. Consequently, we find ourselves caught in the "problem of professional uncertainty: Despite decades of research and reflection, no one is exactly sure how children learn to read or how best to teach them" (Fraatz, 1987, p. 26).

This chapter will not solve this problem. However, we would like to offer some suggestions to educators as they go about choosing research-based school improvement innovations to help their students become better readers and writers. We start by sharing our perspectives on the teaching of literacy. Then we present three promising innovations in the teaching of reading and writing based upon recent research and successful practice.

A Perspective on Teaching for Literacy

We view literacy as one of the ways people make sense of their experiences and involve themselves in relationships and communities. Like Smith (1985) and Vygotsky (1978), we believe that individuals use reading and writing to learn about themselves, others, and the world.

This broad perspective on literacy challenges the traditional dominant perspective in literacy instruction that views reading and writing as a series of discrete and isolated skills. Indeed, we think the single most important innovation in the teaching of literacy in the last fifteen years has been the shift in the "common wisdom" regarding the nature of literacy and literacy learning (e.g., Anderson, Hiebert, Scott, & Wilkinson, 1985). We have moved from the view of reading and writing as a series of hierarchical skills, each to be mastered in turn, toward the view of literacy as a social activity involving a contextualized set of interrelated skills, strategies, beliefs, and attitudes.

Our experiences as teachers and as researchers in implementing our broad perspective on literacy have centered on inexperienced readers and writers who are just beginning to learn to read or write or who have been unsuccessful in their initial efforts to become literate. Thus, when we think about innovations in the teaching of literacy, we focus on those that enhance children's introduction to and involvement in reading and writing. We also think about innovations that are not necessarily conceptually new but that entail using old ideas in new ways.

In the following sections, we will examine three important innovations that derive from this perspective on literacy and literacy instruction. These include the importance of creating literate environments in classrooms, of helping students become strategic readers and writers, and of using constructive assessments.

Three Literacy Innovations

INNOVATION # 1: CREATING LITERATE ENVIRONMENTS IN WHICH CHILDREN READ AND WRITE AUTHENTIC TEXTS FOR AUTHENTIC PURPOSES

As educators consider ways to improve literacy instruction, one guideline should be that any innovation must result in students spending more time reading and writing authentic texts and engaging in authentic tasks. Authentic *texts* are those written by genuine authors (of all ages) for the purposes of entertaining, informing, enlightening, or engaging the reader. Since authentic texts can vary in quality—real authors sometimes write very poorly—authentic texts are also those books, articles, student-produced writings, and so forth, that children and teachers find intrinsically interesting, worth reading, and worth sharing. Such texts stand in stark contrast to those constructed merely to give students "practice" in using the skills of decoding or comprehension.

Authentic *tasks* are the kinds of activities that students perceive as worthwhile and that require them to use reading and writing to accomplish purposes that are meaningful both in and out of school. Authentic tasks, like authentic texts, can vary in quality, so authentic tasks are also those activities that involve students in reading or writing for entertainment, information, enlightenment, or engagement. Such tasks can be contrasted with activities like worksheets and skill pads that require students to apply reading and writing skills in a "decontextualized" manner.

Why are authentic texts and authentic tasks so important from the perspective of literacy instruction? Researchers in emergent literacy have gathered strong evidence that children who learn to read without formal instruction are ones who grow up in highly literate home environments in which loving adults read aloud to them from favorite storybooks using the "lap technique" (McCracken & McCracken, 1986) and answer their questions about print (e.g., Teale & Sulzby, 1986). The parents of these children report that they did not set out to teach the child to read but that they merely wanted to share with the child some favorite stories, especially ones they used to enjoy.

Some of the most promising innovative literacy programs are, indeed, those systematically designed to provide preschoolers with the "lap" experience of hearing good books read aloud. Many of these programs target new mothers and parents receiving public assistance and teach them the importance of sharing books with their preschoolers and ways of engaging their children with print. Some programs even help parents of limited reading ability improve their own skills through the sharing of easy books with their children (e.g., Edwards, 1990).

Teachers, too, can capitalize on the social nature of literacy by creating environments in their classrooms that resemble highly literate home environments. Teachers can set the stage for literacy instruction by developing reading and writing centers in their classrooms. They and their students fill the reading center with printed materials of various types, such as fiction and nonfiction books, magazines, newspapers, TV guides, cookbooks, encyclopedias, atlases, almanacs, and so on. They fill the writing center with the "write stuff," including paper of various sizes and colors, pencils, crayons, chalkboard and chalk, magnetic boards and letters, typewriters, and word processors. Such classroom reading and writing centers along with daily storybook read-aloud sessions and opportunities to write have proved to be essential in getting children to interact with print (Teale & Sulzby, 1986). Also essential are chances for children to share their writing with classmates and to give and receive feedback about their writing processes and products (e.g., Graves, 1983).

The rationale behind classroom reading centers or classroom libraries is that immediate access to books increases the amount of independent reading by children (e.g., Morrow, 1989), perhaps by 50 percent over classrooms without such centers or libraries (Bissett, 1969). Given the strong evidence that time spent in free reading is positively associated with gains in comprehension and vocabulary (Anderson, Wilson, & Fielding, 1988), the addition of classroom libraries may be especially powerful in those classrooms where the only reading is done from individual pupil's books in a basal reading series.

Simply setting up classroom centers or libraries may not be enough, though. The physical layout and organization of the library corner are also crucial to its success. Researchers (e.g., Morrow & Weinstein, 1986) stress the importance of specific teacher activities in piquing children's interest in books and in teaching them how to choose books and how to care for them. In short, teachers teach students how to become lifelong readers.

One essential activity in an environment that fosters lifelong readers is reading aloud daily from good children's literature and other texts (Trelease, 1985). Reading aloud is beneficial in several ways, especially for young children and low achievers (Bridge, 1989). For example, by reading aloud, the teacher models how sophisticated readers interact with text, thereby increasing students' comprehension and vocabulary test scores (Cochran-Smith, 1988).

So far we have argued that exposing children to literate environments full of quality literature and engaging activities is crucial for helping them take their first steps toward becoming readers and writers. As we shall see, the issue of quality texts and tasks is equally crucial as teachers set about the important goal of helping children extend and refine their abilities as readers and writers.

Researchers and practitioners have expressed concern over the detrimental effects that accrue when the materials used during instruction have been adapted to fit "readability formulas" or written simply to provide exercises in specific skills (e.g., Anderson, Osborn, & Tierney, 1984). Strict vocabulary and sentence-length controls resulted in beginning reading selections characterized by strings of short, stilted sentences and by plots that unfolded in unnatural and uninteresting ways (e.g., Brennan, Bridge, & Winograd, 1986). In the upper grades, the "dumbing down" of textbooks and the lack of "considerate" writing resulted in too many texts that violated critical characteristics known to affect reading comprehension—organization of ideas, author style, page layout, and content difficulty and familiarity (e.g., Armbruster, Osborn, & Davison, 1985).

One innovation that has emerged from the concern over contrived instructional texts is the increased use of "predictable" or "patterned language" materials in early reading instruction (Bridge, 1986). These are materials with an underlying structure that enables the reader to anticipate the next word, phrase, line, or event. Many classic tales, such as "The Little Red Hen" and "The Three Billy Goats Gruff," have predictable plots and repetitive lines that enable the novice reader to join in and read along. Other predictable books have lots of rhyme, rhythm, and repetition that support children's early efforts to decode and comprehend what they read.

Another innovation that emerged from the concern over contrived instructional materials has been the increased interest in thematic units or webs (e.g., Pappas, Kiefer, & Levstik, 1990). Such units are a feasible way of integrating a rich variety of well-written books, magazines, and other primary sources into and across a wide range of content areas studied by children. Themes can deal with a variety of topics, including the concepts of change, explorations, giants, and journeys; they cut across the disciplines of science, social studies, mathematics, and literature; and they are appropriate for a variety of grade levels. Pappas, Kiefer, & Levstik (1990), for example, show how the theme of "explorations" can be used to involve children in reading and writing personally relevant texts and engaging in authentic activities related to exploring the natural world, exploring the future, exploring with language, exploring the imagination, and exploring the arts.

Theme-centered units also create a richer, more natural context in which reading and writing become meaningful, purposeful activities rather than contrived experiences in which students are involved in low-level tasks focusing on isolated skills. Theme-centered units provide multiple opportunities to surround reading with writing (Lytle & Botel, 1988). As students delve into a topic, they write before, during, and after the reading. The consequent integration of reading and writing with the content areas is a major improvement over the traditional focus on discrete skills (e.g., Allington, 1983; Anderson, 1984).

INNOVATION #2:
HELPING STUDENTS BECOME
STRATEGIC READERS AND WRITERS

Creating literate environments in which children read and write authentic texts for authentic purposes is the most basic and critical innovation for improving the teaching of literacy. Let us now turn our attention to another critical innovation: helping students become strategic readers and writers.

Even in the most literate environment some students need more support, guidance, and instruction than others. Most often these are students who have not figured out the processes of reading and writing for themselves or students whose experiences with print have been especially painful or frustrating. In addition, there will be times when most students need some guidance because they will be encountering unfamiliar or specialized texts or particularly difficult tasks. Thus, a number of researchers have emphasized the importance of helping children develop learning strategies.

The emphasis on teaching children learning strategies rather than just skills grew out of the realization that traditional skills instruction provided children with little guidance in how to comprehend what they were reading (e.g., Durkin, 1978–79). In contrast, teachers who helped their students develop learning strategies provided explanations of how to construct meaning, how to check to see if the ideas made sense, and what to do if problems in comprehension occurred.

What are learning strategies and how can they be taught? Educators interested in these questions can find a great deal of information in the research literature dealing with instruction in thinking and cognition (e.g., Jones & Idol, 1990), learning strategies (Pressley, et al., 1990), and with metacognition (e.g., Paris & Winograd, 1990). When we refer to learning strategies in reading, for example, we mean purposeful actions that individuals can take to promote their enjoyment and understanding of texts. Some of these strategies include previewing the text, setting purposes for reading, activating prior knowledge about the topic, visualizing while reading, paraphrasing, making predictions, raising questions, reading ahead or rereading, taking notes, and making graphic organizers.

In our own work, we have found it useful to organize the strategies we teach into ones that students can use *Before Reading* (e.g., previewing, setting purposes, activating prior knowledge); *While Reading* (e.g., checking and clarifying comprehension, understanding different levels of meaning); and *After Reading* (e.g., reviewing comprehension, responding to and applying different kinds of reading). Our intent, and that of other researchers dealing with learning strategies, is to provide students with a repertoire of flexible ways to plan their reading, regulate their comprehension, and evaluate their progress.

Similar processes are involved in writing. Students need help in learning how writers plan their compositions before they write, record their ideas, and then revise their compositions as they clarify meaning (e.g., Calkins, 1986). Teacher modeling, direct instruction, and teacher and peer conferences are ways to help young writers plan and revise their compositions and become more adept at communicating clearly and concisely.

We want to emphasize, however, that strategies are not to be learned by rote by all students. What makes a strategy effective is that it is selected or invented by a learner to fit his or her purposes and to fit the demands of a particular task (Paris,

Lipson, & Wixson, 1983). A strategy is a purposeful action used appropriately and flexibly by the learner.

A number of programs and instructional techniques have been developed for teaching students strategies that can be applied to reading and writing. We favor approaches that include three key features. First, teachers model the strategies so that students have a process to emulate. For example, Palincsar and her colleagues (e.g., Palincsar, Ransom, & Derber, 1989) favor an instructional technique in which teachers use dialogue to model four strategies—predicting, generating questions, clarifying points in the text that were unclear, and summarizing. Initially, teachers lead the dialogue and model the strategies. Students gradually accept these leadership responsibilities. Other researchers (e.g., Afflerbach & Johnston, 1984; Duffy, Roehler, & Hermann, 1988) suggest that teachers "think aloud" or provide a running commentary on their reasoning as they construct meaning, confront and solve problems, and respond to what they have read. Whether teachers use conversations or think aloud, they provide students with models of how an expert performs a particular task. Through such approaches, teachers can help students understand why certain strategies are appropriate, how to apply the strategies that have been selected, how to monitor the effectiveness of the strategy, and how to use fix-up strategies when necessary.

The second key feature of sound instruction in strategy is that teachers provide clear and complete explanations of the strategies they use and model. The lack of clear explanations has been documented in many traditional approaches to teaching reading comprehension (e.g., Durkin, 1978–79; Pearson, 1984). Thus, many current approaches take great pains to ensure that students understand what the strategy is, why it is important, how to employ it, when and where it is appropriate, and how to evaluate its use (Winograd & Hare, 1988). Paris and his colleagues (e.g., Paris, Cross, & Lipson, 1984), for example, used metaphors and group discussions to help children learn a variety of strategies, including planning for reading and monitoring comprehension. Their studies indicate that children respond positively to metaphors like "Be a reading detective" (evaluating the reading task) and "Road to reading disaster" (detecting comprehension failures). Such explanations take time, but they are important for children who need guidance in learning how to comprehend.

The third important feature of effective strategy instruction is that students work cooperatively. Johnson and Johnson (this volume) address the advantages of cooperative learning in more detail, but we feel that it is essential to emphasize that cooperative learning allows students to work together to discuss ideas and share strategies as they read. Such oral discussions stimulate metacognitive insights that are so central to the effective use of learning strategies. When students can analyze and talk about their own reading behaviors, they make thinking public and create better opportunities for understanding how and why they should use particular strategies (Paris, Lipson, & Wixson, 1983). Cooperative learning is also important because it enables students to both give and receive help from their peers, behaviors that seem to lead to higher achievement and lowered anxieties (e.g., Webb, 1982).

Educators can help students become thoughtful learners by explicitly teaching them to use learning strategies. We want to stress, however, that it is critical that such strategy instruction take place within the context of the literate environment that we described earlier. The best way to ensure that students actually implement the strategies they are learning is to ensure that they are engaged in composing and comprehending meaningful texts (Winograd & Paris, 1988).

INNOVATION #3: IMPROVING THE ASSESSMENT OF LITERACY

Our third suggestion for improving the teaching of literacy focuses on the critical need to improve the assessment of literacy. We share the widespread view that traditional forms of reading and writing assessment have driven instruction in inappropriate ways. We also share the increasingly accepted view that authentic assessments are a crucial and supportive part of authentic instruction.

The measurement of literacy is perhaps the most popular topic when educators get together to talk about ways to help children become better readers and writers. Much of this interest comes out of the realization that there is a tremendous gap between current views of reading and writing instruction and traditional methods of assessment (e.g., Shepard, 1989). Recall our earlier discussion regarding how the skills view of literacy has changed to the view that reading and writing are social activities involving a contextualized set of interrelated skills, strategies, beliefs, and attitudes. Unfortunately, most traditional assessments of literacy are still based upon the outdated skills view and are thus limited to group-administered multiple-choice tests of low-level skills such as grammar, punctuation, word decoding, sight vocabulary, and comprehension of isolated sentences or short paragraphs. Moreover, many of these tests are administered to large groups of students who fill in bubbles on multiple-choice answer sheets, an intimidating context to say the least.

The gap between current views of reading and writing and traditional methods of assessment creates a number of problems for educators and students. Let us consider four of these problems in more detail.

First, traditional assessments remove literacy from real purposes and uses, test low-level skills in isolation, ignore the prior knowledge and motivation of the student, and violate the principles of literacy as we understand them today (e.g., Johnston, 1984; Wixson & Peters, 1987). If new literacy curricula (e.g., integrated language arts, whole language) are based upon different and incompatible models of literacy, then traditional tests cannot adequately measure the outcomes of such innovations and improvements. Misaligned tests and curricula force teachers to abandon innovative curriculum goals to prepare students for skill-based tests.

Second, many traditional assessments prohibit the use of learning strategies that we identified as an important innovation in instruction (e.g., Winograd, Paris, & Bridge, 1991). In reading, for example, teachers help students preview, make predictions, take notes, read ahead, or reread. But reading tests are usually timed exercises that penalize students who attempt to use these kinds of strategies. Writing tests also may prohibit the student from applying the composing strategies they have been taught. They are required to write on a designated topic about which they may or may not have any prior knowledge. They are given a limited amount of time to compose and to reflect on what they have written and no opportunity to confer with others before they revise (if they are allowed to revise at all).

Third, traditional approaches to assessment redefine the goals of education in ways that are counterproductive to students' motivation (e.g., Johnston & Winograd, 1985; Nicholls, 1989). When success in school is reduced to the knowledge demonstrated on traditional tests, the goals of reading and writing instruction are reduced to comparative success on tests rather than involvement in the literate community. Students who are losers in such a competitive environment experience increasing anxiety, low self-esteem, cynicism about teachers and school, and a devaluation of education (Paris, Lawton, Turner, & Roth, 1991).

Finally, traditional assessments provide information that is of limited use and is easily subject to misuse and misinterpretation (e.g., Neill & Medina, 1989). Traditional assessments provide data that are presented as if they are accurate measures of a district's success or of student learning. But these tests are not valid measures of teaching or of learning; rather, they are measures of students' accumulated knowledge, test-taking skills, and socioeconomic status (e.g., Guskey & Kiefer, 1989). These measures are rarely understood by students or their parents and fail to provide useful information to teachers.

Educators interested in implementing innovative forms of literacy instruction must pay equal attention to implementing innovative forms of literacy assessment. In other words, innovations in literacy instruction must be matched by congruent innovations in literacy assessment.

One such important innovation in literacy assessment that has received widespread attention and acceptance has been the use of reading and writing portfolios (e.g., Graves, 1983; Tierney, Carter, & Desai, 1991; Valencia, 1990). Portfolios are "purposeful collections of student work that exhibit the student's efforts, progress, and achievements in one or more areas" (Paulson, Paulson, & Meyer, 1991, p. 60).

The use of portfolios in reading and writing is based upon the recognition of several critical assumptions. First, literate behavior is complex and cannot be captured by a single test or conveyed by a single score. Portfolios contain multiple measures of performance that can provide a more complete and accurate understanding of student growth. Second, the assessment of literacy should be based upon performance with authentic texts and authentic tasks that are representative of those found in literate environments. Instruction and assessment should be congruent and aligned. Third, student participation in constructing portfolios and evaluating their contents is crucial. Portfolios are intended to increase students' ownership of their learning; portfolios are done *by* students rather than *to* them.

What kinds of information should be included in a reading and writing portfolio? Specific contents will depend upon the age and needs of the students and the sophistication and theoretical viewpoints of the teachers, but here are three suggestions that appear fairly often in the literature on portfolios:

1. Samples of students' work in progress. Students can keep lists of topics they are interested in exploring, drafts of current manuscripts, and other records of work in progress. Portfolios that include work in progress are useful to students because they enable them to work on important projects over time. Such portfolios are also useful to teachers because they afford teachers insight into students' growth over time.
2. Samples of the students' best pieces of work. A number

of educators have students select the best examples of their written work. These might include samples of different kinds of writing (e.g., persuasive, informative, creative) done during the year; writing produced in response to something the student has read; or writing that took place in content-area classes (such as a report in science or social studies). In each of these cases, students write a brief evaluation of why they selected this piece as one of their best.

3. Lists of books read throughout the year. Students can easily keep such lists with a minimum amount of paperwork. Hansen (1987), for example, suggests that students simply record the title of the book, the author, and whether they only read it, shared it, or wrote about it. At key points during the year, students can write up a brief self-evaluation of what books or authors they found most worthwhile.

We want to emphasize that portfolios are opportunities for self-evaluation. Teachers can have input as well, but the key to a successful portfolio is that the students themselves gather, display, and reflect on their own work and their own progress. Such portfolios provide students with a concrete and systematic means of self-appraisal and self-management. As Paulson, Paulson, & Meyer (1991, p. 61) state: "If carefully assembled, portfolios become an intersection of instruction and assessment: they are not just instruction or just assessment, but, rather, both."

Portfolios can, of course, serve a number of purposes, as long as those purposes do not conflict. For example, the portfolios we just described in which students select their best pieces of work and identify their favorite authors or books are extremely useful for parent-teacher conferences or to pass on to the teacher in the next grade. But many teachers also find portfolios useful for diagnostic purposes, especially when such portfolios contain daily classroom observations, interviews and checklists aimed at assessing the child's motivations and attitudes toward reading, interviews that focus on the child's ability to engage in self-evaluation, and results of other formal or informal assessments.

We should stress here that collecting, organizing, and interpreting the results of multiple measures contained in portfolios can be time-consuming work for students and teachers. Some teachers are rightly skeptical about the new emphasis on portfolio assessment because it requires large investments of time and effort. Any kind of assessment that simply adds to already full workloads is unlikely to be well received by either teachers or students. Thus, a crucial aspect of improving assessment is ensuring that teachers and students have the time and support they need to make sense of these more complex measures of growth.

We have focused primarily on portfolio assessment as one of the most crucial innovations in the assessment of literacy, but we should note that portfolios fit in well with current trends in performance-based assessment (see Airasian, 1991; Stiggins, this volume; Wiggins, 1989) and other current movements in large-scale assessment techniques. The important thing to keep in mind about assessment at any level is that it should reflect and support the kinds of instruction that we have described in the sections dealing with creating a literate environment and helping students become strategic readers and writers. If we have learned any lesson from the last few years, it is that when assessment and instruction are in conflict, instruction suffers.

SUMMARY

Educators need to perceive reading and writing as ways that people make sense of themselves, their experiences, and their relationships rather than as a series of discrete and isolated skills. Such a perspective will ease the task of deciding which research-based innovations should be implemented and which ignored. From our perspective, three general innovations are crucial.

First, educators should focus on those changes that enable students to spend more time reading and writing authentic texts for authentic purposes. Teachers need to surround students with materials worth reading and worth sharing and to provide students with systematic opportunities to use reading and writing for pleasure and for information.

Second, educators should consider ways to implement the kinds of instruction that will enable all children, especially those whose experiences with literacy are limited, to become strategic readers and writers. Helping students become adept at using reading and writing strategies can be accomplished in a number of ways, including teacher modeling, clear explanation, and cooperative learning.

Third, it is absolutely critical that educators improve the assessment of literacy so that teachers and students find evaluation to be a source of insight rather than of anxiety. Increasing the use of alternative methods of assessment, particularly the use of portfolios that enable students to reflect on their own work, will go a long way toward helping students gain a better sense of themselves as lifelong readers and writers.

These three innovations will not solve the problem of professional uncertainty in the area of literacy. However, if we can make these kinds of changes, we should find that teaching for literacy becomes more rewarding both for our students and for ourselves.

- CURRICULUM
- INSTRUCTION

Writing Across the Curriculum

Carol Dixon
Harold Horn
University of California, Santa Barbara

"How can I have my students spend time writing? I don't have time to cover everything in the curriculum as it is!" This cry is often the response when teachers are asked to include writing as a regular part of all subject area classes.

The response reflects two underlying issues. One is the tremendous pressure teachers feel to deal with the explosion of information that has occurred during this century. Teachers and students are literally drowning in facts, and the result is often a rush to "cover" a certain set of information so that the next class can begin where this one stops. In this context, writing may be seen as a dispensable extra, something that would take time away from learning the required information. Yet even when the facts are learned, mere possession of information is not enough. The learning environment is damaged when the learner is asked simply to amass a sequence of information provided by some outside source. Such information can be easily tested by the teacher, but it is quickly forgotten by the learner, unless that learner has assimilated the facts into schemata of his or her own design.

The second issue comes from a mistaken belief that all teachers are being asked to "be writing teachers" and to include writing for the sake of improving writing skills. Teachers often feel insecure in their ability to teach writing (e.g., "I'm not an English teacher."). They also see writing as something that would take time away from the important concerns of the content curriculum, their area of expertise. As Nistler (1990, p. 366) reflects, "We are a minimum competency district. We don't have time in the day for the frill of free writing."

The effect of these concerns is that writing is seldom used as a tool for learning. When students are asked to write in their subject area classes, it is most often as a vehicle for testing their acquisition of facts or providing evidence that they have completed a required assignment. These uses of writing only reinforce an almost universal student apathy toward learning. Students subjected to "read your text and answer the questions at the end of the chapter" pedagogy learn only that reading and writing are unexciting, mind-numbing activities. When worksheets and workbooks are added to the teaching mix, students often respond in ways that make it clear that they regard the whole enterprise as a useless waste of time. Teachers who are teaching a subject because they love the subject matter in turn often assume that "these kids just don't want to learn. There's something wrong with them."

Well, just what is wrong with kids, and how can writing help cure it? Most human beings do not like to be bored. They would rather spend their time trying to solve a tough problem than doing endless repetitions of an easy task—as long as they have a chance of succeeding at that difficult task. Writing can be a tool for creating knowledge. When it is used in that way, writing increases the overall effectiveness of instruction, even though it may take time away from some other activities.

The goal of this chapter is to suggest a way to increase the overall effectiveness of instruction through an approach frequently referred to as "writing across the curriculum." We will discuss what we mean by that label, describe some of the activities that might be used in a writing across the curriculum approach, provide examples of student writing that could result from such activities, and review briefly some of the evidence that such an instructional approach does make a positive difference in the learning that takes place.

WHAT DOES WRITING ACROSS THE CURRICULUM MEAN?

Writing across the curriculum does not mean simply having students perform the physical act of writing in each of their classes, nor is it a "canned" program that can be accomplished by following a few simple steps. Rather, writing across the curriculum means a teaching perspective that uses writing as a vehicle for constructing understanding and for developing reflective and analytical judgment. Further, this teaching perspective assumes that writing will accomplish the goals of developing reflective and analytical judgment only when it is about something for some significant purpose and when it is "engaged" writing where the writer uses it to explore his or her own attitudes and experiences (Barnes & Barnes, 1990).

Hand in hand with the belief that writing must be engaged and must be done for some significant purpose is the realization that writing, reading, listening, and speaking are all facets of the same construction process and are inextricably intertwined. Unfortunately, discussions of writing across the curriculum often tend to treat writing as if the writing activities can be considered independently. However, we do not believe that students can be expected to write with passion on any subject until they have had a chance to grapple with that subject by reading about it and by working through its implications in a setting that also encourages speaking and listening to others before attempting a private written analysis. Although research has not yet directly examined the relationship between writing and the development of reflective judgement (Davidson, King, & Kitchener, 1990), it does provide support for the conclusions that both reading and writing can play a significant and related role in the development of reflective and analytical judgment (Applebee, 1984; Emig, 1977; Langer, 1986; Langer & Applebee, 1987; Shanahan & Tierney, 1990) and that "different writing tasks . . . may lead to different kinds of learning, . . . not simply to different amounts of learning" (Marshall, 1990, p. 162).

How Should Writing Across the Curriculum Work?

Developing reflective judgement does not happen quickly or easily. It cannot be accomplished by a few hours a week in one classroom or on one subject area, nor can it be accomplished in isolation without regard to the rest of the curriculum. Rather, it must be the conscious aim of a student's total school experience. Unfortunately, in classrooms today the major vehicle for providing the reading, listening, and speaking context for developing reflective judgment through writing is often an impoverished textbook. Assuming that the very nature of the marketplace in an open, democratic society will always place constraints on what publishers include in texts, a given textbook may never be completely adequate.

One answer is to supplement textbooks with exciting literature, not just in the English classroom but across the curriculum. In an effort to "cover" all subject area information at a given grade level, textbook authors often end up saying nothing of any interest to anyone. A supreme moment in American history, Pickett's Charge, has been reduced thusly in a secondary history text (we will use history as the subject matter of choice for our argument, but unfortunately our conclusions hold true in every discipline):

> On July 1, 1863, the two armies met near the small town of Gettysburg, Pennsylvania. For three days, the Confederate troops tried without success to break through the Union lines. On the afternoon of July 3 came the climax of the battle. General George Pickett led 15,000 soldiers against the heart of the Union's defense. "Pickett's Charge," as it was called, ended in failure. (Drewry, O'Connor, & Freidel, 1984, p. 348)

Using such a passionless text as a basis for classroom discussion, with the goal of generating meaningful student learning, is a challenge for even the most gifted of teachers. How can this simple recitation of facts capture students' imagination? How can they be expected even to remember the facts beyond the forthcoming multiple-choice test, let alone synthesize those facts into a thoughtful piece of writing?

Contrast the textbook with a piece of historical literature:

> . . . The Federal soldiers on the eastern ridge looked west; they were veterans and they had been in many battles, but what they saw now took their breath away. Some of them had seventy-five years yet to live and some of them had no more than ten minutes, but until they died they remembered the scene that now presented

itself. There it was, for the last time in this war, perhaps for the last time anywhere, the fearful pageantry and color of war in the old style, beautiful and majestic and hideous; fighting men lined up in double and triple ranks, a solid mile from flank to flank, slashed red flags overhead, sunlight glinting off polished musket barrels—the flower of Lee's army coming forward, unhurried, for the great test that would determine whether there would hereafter be one nation or two between Canada and the Rio Grande... and whether Americans on American soil could continue to own other men and women, or be owned by them, as cattle and horses are owned. (Catton, 1952, p. 314)

Supplementing the texts with more powerful pieces of writing will help. However, in addition to supplementing the texts we must also use approaches to instruction that can bring a meaningful context to student writing. English teachers have in recent years concluded that something was very wrong in the traditional approach to teaching their subject matter. Their conclusions have significance for teaching across the curriculum. Traditionally, the English teacher had acted as a kind of high priest or priestess in the classroom, interpreting the meanings of the sacred texts for students. Difficult literature would be placed in front of the learners, and the teacher's task would be to explain the meaning of that text and the motives of its author. The result has been a passive classroom where students are asked to assimilate the teacher's knowledge and parrot it back on objective tests or, at best, to write an essay so preconceived as to force student thinking down to the lowest possible levels.

English teachers have begun to replace this traditional pedagogy with reader-response techniques in which students are empowered to reach their own conclusions about the meaning of a text. The teacher's interpretation becomes only one of many competing interpretations in a classroom of ideas. Students are invited to reach their own conclusions, judging competing notions before setting these conclusions down on paper. Not only do students gain control of their own thought processes but also factual information almost magically is internalized far more efficiently because it has a real function—that of supporting one's ideas.

Anyone who has been a teacher for more than ten minutes knows that most students do not enter a classroom with a fervent desire to interpret texts, let along write about them. One hard lesson for new teachers is that students are in their classroom because they have to be there. Many students see the classroom as a boring, uncomfortable, often embarrassing place where they must "serve time." Given any alternative, most adolescents would rather be at the beach. With the absence of any real sense of urgency, how then can students be encouraged to interpret a piece of text, share that interpretation with others, and build enough enthusiasm to write a thoughtful and reflective composition or research report on the subject?

Providing stimulating text to supplement the textbook information and addressing the reading in ways that give students a voice in the process of constructing meaning provide a starting point. But by themselves they are not enough to ensure the kind of reflective and analytical thinking we desire. For us, the most crucial aspect of what we would describe as effective use of writing across the curriculum lies in an approach to instruction that changes the nature of the writing tasks students are asked to perform before they are expected to develop a final, formal written project. Carefully chosen informal writing activities can so involve students with a text that the actual writing of a final "polished" text becomes a natural part of a process that generates higher-level thinking and interpretation while reinforcing the construction and retention of knowledge.

Effective informal writing tasks are ones that validate student decision making. Writing tasks that can accomplish this result range from group activities, like cooperative learning jigsaw activities; readers' theater presentations; and text rendering, where "new texts" are composed orally; to informal written compositions such as quick writes and entries in learning logs. While these and other strategies have up to now been the province almost exclusively of the English department or the Reading/Language Arts curriculum, we are convinced that they can be of use in making writing an important tool for learning in every subject area. The following brief descriptions are presented as examples of the kinds of student interactions and writing that each activity might engender.

QUICK WRITES

Every once in a while during a lesson or classroom exchange, it is useful for teacher and students to reflect on the learning that, it is hoped, has been taking place. Asking students to put their thoughts on paper during a two- or three-minute quiet time gives them a chance not only to reflect for a moment but also to assimilate and formulate their own thinking for future activities, such as class or small-group discussions.

Quick writes are just what the name implies. They are not intended to be finished pieces of writing but, rather, brief works that capture current thinking and ideas or questions about a topic. However, keeping quick writes in some sort of organized format, rather than on miscellaneous slips of scrap paper, often ensures that ideas from them find their way later into more polished final products. Following are two examples of quick writes.

The Great Compromise was an argument for how many representatives are to go to Congress from each state. The bigger the state the more representatives.

Science is very important because if we didn't have it we wouldn't have our easy ways of communications (TV, radio, telephone). Life would be much harder because we wouldn't have appliances (washer, dryer, toasters, stove/oven, etc.) to make life easier. We also wouldn't have any cures or vaccines for the sick. We wouldn't know where things come from or how they/it came about, and we wouldn't be living a life that we live now.

LEARNING LOGS

Learning logs are sometimes thought of as a form of journal. They are usually longer and more reflective pieces than quick writes and are kept in some kind of organized format such as a special notebook. Learning logs often serve to bring partial closure to a topic or to raise new issues. A learning log notebook can also be a convenient place to collect quick writes, allowing some of the ideas from them to be incorporated into later learning log-writing. Teachers often ask students to use a learning log during the last few minutes of class time to summarize the day's lesson:

> Today I learned more meanings of mass. I learned that there are ten physical properties even though we're only learning four and they are density, hardness, odor, and color. I learned that when we do chemistry we'll be using math.

This kind of summation helps students organize the lesson in their own minds while the information is still clear. If confusion remains, the learning log provides an opportunity for that confusion to surface while there is time for further clarification.

> I kind of understand what the covalent bonding is but if I had to draw it I wouldn't know how to draw an example. There are some connections that are being made but it takes me awhile. Does the ionic bonding differ from the covalent bonding? I don't understand anything about the ionic bonding. I understand the valence stuff, the electron.

Writing in learning logs may take a variety of forms. Often they are used to help the students imagine themselves personally involved in the event, as in the following log written after a lesson about the Fugitive Slave Law:

> We Northerners think that it is the stupidest law ever. Because the slaves are free when they come here, and they are happy living here. But then they make up some stupid law that they can take their slaves back to the South.

or this learning log in the form of a letter written in a science class:

> Hypatia,
>
> Hey girl, what's up? Well now it's the year 1990 (A.D.) and I'm in science class right now. So you were the one who discovered or actually invented the astrolabe, eh. Well times have changed and so has the technology. You should see some of the stuff we have. For instance we've got telephones, radios, televisions, fax machines, computers, cellular phones, video games (the most popular one, Nintendo), microwaves, VCR's, compact discs (portable ones too), and stereos. Water comes in a turn of a knob. The same goes for heat, gas, energy, etc. I bet you wished you lived during this time. Everything that we have now makes our life a luxury compared to when you lived. Well, because of the smart people like you that lived during your time or

around then, we have an easier life. Thanks. Oh, by the way, did I tell you that people can go to space nowadays?

Like quick writes, learning logs are not intended to be polished pieces of writing and need not be read in detail by the teacher. Instead, learning logs are done for the benefit of the student, even to the extent that students may be allowed to refer to their learning logs as a way of reviewing their thinking during specified examinations.

TEXT RENDERING

A traditional way to force students to interpret a piece of text has been to have them read a selection and then answer teacher-posed questions. Reading through such answers is frequently a disheartening experience, because students are seldom interested in their own responses and are in a hurry just to get the task finished. Text rendering, on the other hand, results in a community of students interpreting a piece of text together in a mutually supportive atmosphere. In text rendering, a group of students are asked to read a piece of text together, either silently or aloud. As the text is being read, each student is asked to highlight or underline portions of the text that seem significant in any way. These significant parts may range from single words to entire sentences. When all are finished, students read aloud, in no particular order (Quaker meeting style), parts of the text that they have interpreted as being somehow significant. If another student has chosen the same words, students may repeat a portion of the text already illuminated, which usually gives a sense of validation to both students.

Instead of producing a confusing mishmash of quotations, the restructuring of the text informs and enlightens. Participants listen carefully to others' choices, and pieces of text read aloud seem to flow almost effortlessly from one idea to another, usually developing a recurrent theme or message. Text rendering almost invariably emphasizes the same key portions of the text the teacher would have targeted, but now the students have ownership, and this leads effortlessly to a class discussion of the material. The discussion, in turn, often culminates in a natural move to writing, in a quick write or a learning log, because the student now has something real to say. Quick writes after a text rendering exercise usually reflect careful student thought:

> Observing is something very important and I didn't realize that. It's one of the main ways of discovering patterns.

Simultaneous text rendering of two contrasting pieces of text can also be extremely effective. For instance, half of a class might read a selection of quotations of Thomas Jefferson while the other reads quotations of Alexander Hamilton. In text rendering, the participants tend to read their piece of text when a preceding piece of text provides a natural bridge or contrast. If the text rendering were structured in such a way that a quotation of Jefferson was always followed by one of Hamilton, or vice-versa, the result would tend to dramatize the differences in two political philosophies, again with the students rather than the teacher taking ownership. Even when text rendering is not followed by the production of an actual piece of writing, the effect of the text rendering is itself the verbal "writing" of a new text, one that reflects the students' construction of knowledge.

READER'S THEATER

Reader's theater also offers a uniquely effective way for students to explore the meaning of a piece of text in a communal activity before they are asked to interpret the text in either a formal or an informal written activity. In reader's theater the written text becomes a script, which is then presented informally orally, usually without the use of props or other stage action. Teachers may ask students to compose formal scripts from a given piece of text by rewriting it, with the intention of presenting the resulting playlet to the entire class. Careful interpretation of the text is, of course, a necessary part of this activity as the script is organized and written.

However, an informal approach to reader's theater is probably more appropriate in most classroom situations. When the classroom teacher wants the class to focus on a particular selection, he or she can ask students working in small groups to create a brief unwritten script based on the page in question by simply dividing up the text as it stands. After assigning parts and practicing for a few minutes, several of the groups then present their production to the class. A reading of Thomas Paine's *Common Sense* might result in the following (Fast, 1945, pp. 24–25):

(Student One)—In no instance hath nature made the satellite larger than its primary planet;

(Student Two)—and as England and America, with respect to each other, [reverse] the common order of nature,

(Student Three)—it is evident that they belong to different systems: England to Europe—America to itself...

(All together)—In short, independence is the only bond that can tie and keep us together...

Like text rendering, reader's theater brings the written word to life in a way that serves to highlight and illuminate the construction of meaning. It again accomplishes the composition of a text without the physical act of producing a written product. At the same time, this close attention to text written by authors more skilled than the students helps them internalize models of what text can be that may assist them when they come to their own writing.

COOPERATIVE LEARNING AND WRITING

Lively debates often accompany group activities. Certainly the emotional level of a class working in groups is at a far higher pitch than when the teacher is lecturing and students are listening. Adrenaline begins to flow as students anticipate making their point. This is especially true when each student has different information to share, such as in a cooperative learning "jigsaw" activity. Here students are making a presentation to classmates who are relying on them to be coherent, because each student must produce a written argument that reflects knowledge from all of the assigned readings, not just the section read by the individual student. Johnson and Johnson (1984) have pointed to other reasons for this enthusiasm, with some interesting by-products:

> Involved participation in cooperative learning groups inevitably produces conflicts among the ideas, opinions, conclusions, theories, and information of members . . . such controversies promote increased motivation to achieve, higher achievement and retention of the learned material, and greater depth of understanding (p. 15).

We believe that learning is further enhanced when cooperative activities cause students to reflect on the meaning they are constructing. One of the greatest hindrances to students remains the practice of presenting the subject matter in isolated factual tidbits to be learned in preparation for periodic objective tests, the hope being that students will at some future time be able to use these facts for higher-level thinking activities—activities that seldom occur. We ask students to work at the knowledge level, knowing that they need to be analyzing, synthesizing, and evaluating. Synthesizing the information learned during a cooperative learning group activity into a composition, based on a specific hypothesis, places students in a situation where they must also analyze and evaluate. By supporting their arguments with information learned during the activity, they are developing critical thinking skills, and, almost incidentally, learning the facts. The compositions that result reflect a depth of understanding seldom achieved from lectures followed immediately by reading:

> I do not believe the War of 1812 should have been fought. There were arguments against (Federalist) and for (Republican) involvement, as well as ulterior motives, such as acquisition of territory. But, the U.S. was not prepared for war, and the nation was divided in public opinion. In the end, there were no real tangible gains directly from the fighting, The war really should have been avoided. The Federalists were against the war because . . .

Cooperative groups provide opportunities for powerful writing and reading activities that promote higher-level thinking as well as the retention of factual detail because that detail is placed in a meaningful context by students. Students who approach course work with a little passion, carefully cultivated in the classroom, are far more apt to carry learning away with them. One student's concluding paragraph based on the hypothesis that "the Black Revolution was good for America" reflects some of that passion:

> if a whistle kettle is not removed from the fire, the whistle (will) go off . . . . America is only great through her people, and when people are educated and prosperous then so is America. We black Americans have gone from the times of accepting "for colored only" signs and

sitting at the back of the bus. We have contributed much to this country that we helped build. We only wanted to feel a part of it not apart from it. Although the statistics . . . show that we are well behind white Americans we have at least been given the opportunity to be a part. We have not overcome all things that have happened to us as a race but we will. Our revolution was and is good for America, because America could not grow with such an injustice hanging over her head.

AN APPROACH TO INSTRUCTION, NOT A BAG OF TRICKS

The techniques we have described are only a few of the approaches possible when writing across the curriculum is the goal. We have chosen them to provide a picture of how writing across the curriculum, for us, represents a way of approaching instruction rather than a static program of given activities wearing a particular label. "From such a perspective, writing becomes not a measure of students' understanding, but a means of achieving it. It becomes an instructional tool that can shape at the same time it deepens our students' conception of the subjects they address in their writing" (Marshall, 1990, p. 175).

All of these techniques do take time, and the writing involved in them is "first draft" rather than polished perfection, but over time they pay off. The evidence that they are worth the time and effort they require comes from a number of sources. First and foremost are the reports of teachers and students, such as those whose work we have cited in this chapter. Examples of student work such as these clearly demonstrate the kind of reflective and analytical thinking we would like all students to be engaged in during their school years.

Fortunately, these examples are not the result of the experiences of a few isolated, idiosyncratic teachers and students. The spectacular spread of a concept born in a small regional activity, the Bay Area Writing Project, into a chain of 159 National Writing Project sites, provides ample evidence that teachers across the entire range of curriculum areas have found value in using writing approaches such as these. But no matter how enthusiastic their original reception, curriculum innovations have a hard time surviving over the long term. In order to flourish they must usually find acceptance over more than one curriculum area. Certainly English and language arts teachers have been the most active participants in most writing projects. However, the continued growth of the projects makes it clear that teachers of other subject areas are also coming to see the value of engaging students in writing to learn rather than simply writing to regurgitate.

Considerable research evidence also has been compiled during the last ten years that further substantiates the value of a writing across the curriculum approach. Writing in the *Handbook of Reading Research, Vol. II,* Tierney and Shanahan (1991) cite studies at the sixth-grade (Copeland, 1987), eighth-grade (Colvin-Murphy, 1986), high school (Hayes, 1987), and college (McGinley, 1988; Penrose, 1988) levels that support the value of writing for long-term learning when students are asked to use writing for reflection and analysis. "What has emerged from this research is a consistent finding: Writing prompts readers to engage in thoughtful exploration of issues, whether it be in the context of studying science, social studies, or literature" (Tierney & Shanahan, 1991, p. 268). They conclude that "writing and reading together engage learners in a greater variety of reasoning operations than when writing and reading are apart or when students are given a variety of other tasks to go along with their reading" (Tierney & Shanahan, 1991, p. 272).

The evidence suggests that as the level of understanding increases, students may actually arrive at the desired end-point sooner because understanding provides a solid foundation for each new idea or piece of information. Classes become less dependent on the teacher and much more a community of scholars, where "reading and writing [are] presented as means of taking part in the dialogues—written and spoken—that constitute the conversation of mankind" (Barnes & Barnes, 1990, p. 43).

A Final Comment

"Today, we as teachers face the awesome responsibility of educating our students to become more adept at thinking analytically, critically, and reactively; at being better able to solve problems and make wise decisions that can lead toward a better society" (Tonjes, 1991, p. 7). If this is to be accomplished, "the acquisition of knowledge and thinking skills need to be embedded within each other, rather than competing for educational primacy, as is too often the case now" (Russell, 1990, p. 9).

Writing must be used as a tool for learning to think. It can lead students beyond the acquisition of isolated facts to those synthesis and evaluation levels of thinking that make learning intriguing enough to pursue for its own sake. Each learner needs to have the opportunity to develop those higher-level thinking processes that writing, when used as a tool for learning, almost uniquely can provide.

SCHOOLING INNOVATIONS

- CLIMATE
- COMMUNITY/PARENT INVOLVEMENT
- EXPECTATIONS
- LEADERSHIP
- MOTIVATION
- ORGANIZATION/ MANAGEMENT (SCHOOL)

Learning from Accelerated Schools

Henry M. Levin
Stanford University

The Hollibrook Elementary School in Houston enrolls over 1,000 students, many of them recently arrived immigrants from Central and South America. About 90 percent of the students are from families with incomes below the poverty line. In 1988, the school's fifth graders were about two years behind grade level in reading and language arts and behind grade level in mathematics as well. By the spring of 1991, Hollibrook fifth graders were performing slightly above grade level in their composite score and fully one year above grade level in mathematics (McCarthy & Still, 1993). More than this, the Hollibrook Elementary School had become a place of joy for its students, staff, and parents. Through hands-on activities, research, discourse, imagination, and creativity, the school had been transformed to a place of excitement and a beehive of activity.

The 99th Street School in the Watts section of Los Angeles has about 700 students, of which two-thirds are African-American and one-third are Hispanic. Prior to the 1990–91 school year, 99th Street was one of the bottom twenty schools in achievement among the 650 schools in Los Angeles. Gangs, vandalism, fighting, poor attendance, high teacher turnover, and low achievement were chronic conditions at 99th Street. By 1992, even after having weathered the worst urban riot in U.S. history, 99th Street's reading scores had jumped from the eighteenth percentile to the thirtieth percentile, over six times the average gain for the district. Students were involved in artistic projects and research, student behavior problems had waned, and for the first time parents were actively involved in the school. And this was just the beginning as the school began to make deeply rooted changes to achieve its school dream.

At the Eugene Field School in Hannibal, Missouri, some three quarters of the kindergarteners enter school at least six months behind in language development. Despite starting behind the norm for their age, almost 90 percent are above grade level in reading by the end of the second grade. Field had a 77 percent drop in major discipline referrals between 1987 and 1988 and 1991 and 1992, and retention of students in grade fell almost 80 percent over the same period. The school has become a center for creative and exciting activities among students and staff with a doubling of parent participation.

Before 1990 Burnett Academy was considered to be the bottom middle school in San Jose, California, with problems of violence, gangs, low test scores, and enrollments considerably below capacity in a system of school choice. About 80 percent of Burnett's students were taking remedial subjects. By

1992–93, all eighth graders were enrolled in algebra and all seventh graders in pre-algebra. The school had constructed a highly enriched humanities curriculum that combined a social studies, an English, and a foreign languages experience in which all students participated. Achievement scores in reading and writing rose dramatically, with writing scores going from the bottom in the district to the district average in two years. Student research projects abounded, especially in the sciences and technology, and fighting had become largely passe on campus.

Although these four schools are in different parts of the country and have strikingly different student populations, they have three things in common. First, their enrollments consist predominantly of students from poverty backgrounds who are at risk of educational failure. Second, although they were formerly among the bottom schools in their districts in terms of student progress, all have had dramatic success in increasing student achievement and involvement in challenging educational activities and raising parent participation within existing resources. Third, all have committed themselves to an unusual program that replaces remediation with academic enrichment and acceleration.

Hollibrook, 99th Street, Eugene Field, and Burnett are just four of the more than 300 schools located in twenty-five states in 1992–93 that adopted the approach of the Accelerated Schools Project. This project was established at Stanford University in 1986 after an exhaustive five-year study on the status of at-risk students in the United States. Our study defined at-risk students as those youngsters who are unlikely to succeed in schools as schools are currently constituted. Such students are heavily concentrated among minority groups, immigrants, non-English-speaking families, single-parent families, and poverty populations.

Recent estimates suggest that on a national basis, about 30 percent of students in primary and secondary schools are educationally at risk and that this proportion will continue to rise sharply in the future with immigration and the increased incidence of children in poverty (Levin, 1986; Pallas, Natriello, & McDill, 1989). In many of the major cities of the United States the majority of students are educationally at risk.

At-risk students enter school behind other children academically, and they get farther and farther behind the longer they are in school. Over half fail to complete high school, and those who do are performing academically at the eighth-grade level. These educational deficiencies translate into poor life chances with respect to employment and income as well as to political and social participation in U.S. society.

The Stanford study found that the inability of existing schools to advance the education of at-risk students is hardly an accident. Most schools that enroll such children embrace organizational, curricular, and instructional strategies that contribute to reduced expectations and stigmatization of at-risk students, uninspiring school experiences, and a devaluation of the rich talents of teachers and parents. In the absence of change, students will be subjected systematically to an experience that will assure only glacial progress and high failure rates.

Accelerated schools were designed by the Stanford project to have exactly the opposite results by bringing at-risk students into the educational mainstream by the end of elementary school. Our premise was very basic: At-risk students must learn at a *faster* rate than more privileged students—not at a slower rate that drags them farther and farther behind. An enrichment strategy is called for rather than a remedial one.

It may seem strange to talk of acceleration for at-risk students. Educators usually reserve accelerated programs for their "gifted and talented" students, those who perform at the very top of their grade levels. Yet one cannot help wondering why we channel so much enrichment to help our best students get even better while we deliberately slow the pace of learning of children who lack educational advantages.

Acceleration works just as well for at-risk students. One recent study randomly assigned at-risk students to remedial, average, and honors classes in seventh-grade mathematics. At the end of the year, the at-risk students in the honors class—which provided pre-algebra instruction—outshone those in the other two groups (Peterson, 1989). Knapp, Shield, & Turnbull (1992) evaluated instruction in 140 classrooms in fifteen schools serving at-risk students. Over a school year it was found that high-content instruction designed to create meaning and understanding was more effective in increasing knowledge of advanced skills and at least as effective in providing basic skills as the more traditional remediation and basic skills-and-drill approach. Indeed, this approach is consistent with trends among educators who have specialized in the study of "gifted" children. For example, John Feldhusen, a noted authority on gifted and talented education, has concluded:

> Schools should abandon efforts to identify "gifted students" as though they were a biologically distinct category of human beings and concentrate instead on: (1) searching for talent or strengths in all children, (2) searching for those who might have very high levels of talent or precocity in a "worthwhile area" of human endeavor, and (3) seeking to provide the best instruction possible to help youth develop their talents to the fullest (Feldhusen, 1992).

It is these three goals set out by Feldhusen that are embedded in accelerated schools.

INSTITUTIONALIZING CHANGE

However, moving from an idea to institutional change is never easy. In order to develop a strategy for creating accelerated institutions, we found that we would have to make three major changes in U.S. schools, changes that were in deep conflict with current practices (Levin, 1988).

BASIC PRINCIPLES

1. Unity of Purpose

Most schools that educate at-risk students seem to lack any central purpose. Rather, they are a composite of individuals and programs that seem largely disparate and piecemeal with no unifying vision. Planning, implementation, and evaluation are typically done independently and by different groups. Teachers tend to see their responsibilities extending no farther than carrying out good teaching practices in self-contained classrooms, while remedial specialists work in isolation from each other and from the regular school program.

Acceleration requires the establishment and pursuit of a common view of what is desirable that serves as a focal point for the efforts of parents, teachers, staff, and students. The vision of an accelerated school should focus on bringing children into the mainstream, where they can more fully benefit from school experiences and opportunities. Developing this vision requires the combined efforts and commitment of all parties involved: staff, parents, and children. Unity of purpose refers to both a vision or dream of what the school can be and a plan for action that will get the school there. It is more than just a statement of intentions. That is, there must be agreement on how the school will function to get there with a common set of values, beliefs, and practices about the purpose and role of the school and the participation of all of its members.

2. School-Site Empowerment

Existing schools for at-risk students are largely run according to decisions made by entities that are far removed from the school site and classroom. Federal and state governments and central offices of school districts have established a compendium of rules, regulations, directives, policies, laws, guidelines, reporting requirements, and "approved" instructional materials that serve to stifle educational decisions and initiative at local school sites. It is little wonder that administrators, teachers, parents, and students tend to blame factors "beyond their control" for the poor educational outcomes of at-risk students. And compliance with these policies ensures failure, not success, as the historical record has shown.

An accelerated school requires that schools take responsibility for the major decisions that will determine educational outcomes. If the school is to achieve its vision of educational success, administrators, teachers, and other staff, parents, and students must participate in making informed decisions regarding school activities. Important areas of school-site decisions include some or all of the following: curriculum, instructional strategies, instructional materials, personnel, and allocation of resources inside of the school. Such decision making requires active support from the district's central office in the form of information, technical assistance, staff development, and evaluation as well as an overall system of accountability.

3. Building on Strengths

Schools with large numbers of at-risk students tend to highlight the weaknesses of their students, staff, funding, administrative support, and so on, as an explanation for poor performance. A particularly heavy emphasis is placed on the recitation of the flaws of at-risk students and their parents. But good pedagogy builds on participants' strengths to overcome areas of weakness rather than dwelling on them.

Accelerated schools seek out the strengths of their students and other participants and use those strengths as the foundation of their programs. In this respect, students are treated as gifted and talented students, whose strengths are identified and then used as a basis for enrichment and acceleration. The strengths of at-risk students are often overlooked because they are not as obvious as those of middle-class students. But our research has shown that at-risk children bring assets that can be used to accelerate the learning process. These include an interest and curiosity in oral and artistic expression, the ability to learn through manipulation of appropriate learning materials and interesting applications, the capability of delving eagerly into intrinsically interesting tasks, and the capacity for learning to write prior to mastering reading skills.

But the process of building on strengths is not limited just to students. Accelerated schools also build on the strengths of parents, teachers, and other school staff. Parents and teachers are underutilized resources in most schools. Parents, because they want their children to succeed, can be powerful allies if they are placed in productive roles and provided with the skills to work with their children. Teachers bring the gifts of insight, intuition, and organizational acumen to the instructional process, gifts that are often untapped by the mechanical curricula that are so typical of remedial programs. Accelerated schools acknowledge the gifts of teachers and parents and build on those strengths in fulfilling their visions.

COMBINING THE PRINCIPLES

An accelerated school is not merely a conventional school with new principles or special programs grafted onto it. It is a dynamic environment that transforms the entire school and its operations. The emphasis is on the school as a whole rather than on a particular grade, curriculum, staff development approach, or some other limited strategy. The goal is high academic achievement for *all* students.

The three principles of unity of purpose, site-based empowerment, and building on strengths are woven together in virtually all of the activities of the accelerated school. The school is governed by its staff, students, and parents, and priorities are pursued by task groups that follow a systematic inquiry process for problem solving, implementation, and evaluation.

In practice, the accelerated school process generally leads to the use of rich language (writing, speaking, listening, reading) across all subjects, even mathematics, with an early introduction to writing and reading for meaning. The curricula reflect a sense of high expectations and a tie to the students' cultures. Active learning experiences are provided through independent projects, problem solving, and applying learning to concrete situations. By applying academic concepts and skills to real-life problems and events, students see the usefulness of what they are learning.

The organization of accelerated schools allows for a broad range of participants and a collaborative approach in which students' families play a central role. Indeed, success depends on parents working with staff and students to help make school decisions by participating in the decision-making bodies of the school.

LESSONS LEARNED

It takes about six years to fully transform a conventional school to an accelerated one. This transformation is done largely within existing budgetary resources, so no major change in resource requirements is needed to initiate the process. Over the long run, however, we do believe that some of the specific needs of at-risk students can only be met through greater investments in both their schools and home situations (Levin, 1989). In 1992–93, only a few of our 300 accelerated schools were even old four years old. However, even schools with only two or three years of experience have shown extraordinary gains in student achievement, student and teacher attendance, parental involvement, reductions in student mobility, and the establishment of inviting and stimulating school programs. These evaluations are based both on year-to-year changes and on comparisons with matched control schools (e.g., Knight & Stallings 1992; McCarthy & Still, 1993).

These gains have included bringing student achievement above grade level from well below grade level (McCarthy & Still, 1993); dramatically increasing parent participation in school events and student assistance (English, 1992; McCarthy & Still, 1993); reducing pupil mobility (McCarthy & Still, 1993); dramatically increasing student and teacher attendance (English, 1992); and improving teacher and student expectations and attitudes relative to a matched control school (Knight & Stallings, 1992).

In our assessment of the growing movement toward accelerated schools, we have learned a number of lessons that we are using to improve the implementation of the accelerated school model. These include the need to devote considerable attention to capacity building, the need for more staff time, the need to resolve particular leadership issues, and the challenges of underutilized talent in the schools, the need to tap the potential of parents, and the need for a new way for the district to support individual schools.

CAPACITY BUILDING

Merely stating that a school is accelerated does not make it so. The school needs to acquire the capacity to establish a unity of purpose, make responsible decisions, and build on the strengths of students, staff, parents, and community (Levin, 1991). This has been an important focus for our comprehensive source book on accelerated schools (Hopfenberg, et al., 1993). Certainly, school staff have not been trained to function in this way, nor have their schools reinforced these patterns of behavior. Much of the transformation to an accelerated school comes directly from learning by doing. As school staff and community work at it, they become experts at the process. But in order to get the process started, they must take a number of steps that are carried out over much of the initial year in which an accelerated school is launched.

It is usually necessary to provide some training in making decisions within groups. Rarely do principals, teachers, and school staff have this experience. Meetings in traditional schools tend to be highly structured and to run in a routine and often authoritarian fashion. Teachers, in particular, usually consider meetings a waste of time. School staff rarely view meetings as having the potential to be productive and to accomplish major goals on behalf of the school. Accordingly, school staff need experience in working together and in giving special attention to group process and participation, acquisition and sharing of information, and working toward decisions. In addition, they need exposure to inquiry-oriented processes that help them identify and define challenges, look for alternative solutions, and implement those solutions (Accelerated Schools Project, 1991b).

These needs can be met through special training in the appropriate areas. But in addition, involvement in the accelerated school process itself is an important part of building capacity. In order to initiate such changes, we have designed a process for launching accelerated schools (Accelerated Schools Project, 1991a). Virtually all training is based upon constructivist principles by engaging trainees in activities in which the principles and practices of accelerated schools are embedded. Schools begin by working together to learn in great detail about themselves. Staff, parents, and students gather for discussion extensive baseline information about the school, including its history, community, students, strengths, and the challenges that face it. After extensive research and analysis, they construct a detailed report on the school, which is the subject of a deep discourse that results in consensus on "who they are."

Next, in a series of meetings of both the entire school and smaller components of staff, the participants focus on building a vision of a school that will work for students, staff, and community and that will be reached over a six-year transition period. This vision will be the focus of accelerated school implementation. Staff members prepare for the vision process by informally discussing dreams and possibilities. Parents and students are also involved in the vision-setting through activities that focus on their dreams. The discussions and consensus are used to construct a vision of the school that will be the focus of all future school activities.

The third phase involves comparing the vision with the baseline report. Clearly, almost always there will be a large gap between the vision and the existing situation. School staff are asked to work on setting out all of the things that must be done in order to move from the present situation to the vision of the future. Of course, they amass a very large number of changes that must be made, often between forty and fifty major alterations.

The fourth step takes this long list of changes and reduces it to a few initial priorities that will become the immediate focus of the school, because no organization can work effectively on more than three or four major priorities at a time.

The task facing the staff is to select those three or four priorities. This exercise can generate very animated discussions that get to the heart of staff concerns. The dynamics of the discourse are themselves useful because they make the staff realize that they are responsible for change and for choosing those areas where they must begin. After the priorities are agreed on, the first task committees are established. These are the small groups that will work on the priorities that have been established. Staff are usually assigned to each group, usually through self-selection as well as through the establishment of a coordinating or steering committee for the school.

Once the governance system is established, the school participants are trained in inquiry methods and additional tools for working effectively together. The inquiry process combines discourse, information gathering, research and analysis, hypothesis testing, brainstorming, design and pilot testing of action plans, implementation, and assessment. Since most of these activities are rare in schools, establishing the process requires considerable training, practice, and application under the watchful eye of a coach or mentor. Over several months the cadres and steering committee of the school learn how to use the inquiry process by addressing the priorities that have been set out. When all of the previous parts of the process are brought together into a school that is actively moving toward its vision using the inquiry system and the three principles, the school is viewed as accelerated.

Our experience suggests that how the process is carried out is at least as important as what is done. Schools tend to treat reform as a list of steps that can be carried out mechanically, after which there will be magical results. When such results are not forthcoming, the reform is call inadequate, and the search begins for a new magic formula. At the heart of the accelerated school is a focus on the participants as the reform package and on the process by which they formulate their needs, goals, and priorities as well as how they define and solve problems and implement and assess solutions. Accelerated schooling involves the transformation of the school from a community that is dominated by mechanical practices imported from outside "expertise" to one in which responsibility, expertise, and efficacy are internal. We have found that the process of getting there requires leadership, inspiration, hard work, and sufficient time to model and practice what is learned, rather than the mechanical completion of staff development activities.

TIME NEEDS

It takes time, over and above usual teaching demands, for a school staff to work together to define challenges and to search for and implement solutions. In contrast to secondary schools where two out of seven periods of "prep" time are often given for meetings, planning, preparation, and so on, elementary school schedules do not provide such "luxuries." Other than about an hour a week for faculty meetings and occasional periods for staff development, there is no time provided for working together on the accelerated school process. The lack of time is as great a bottleneck as the underfunding of schools attended by at-risk students (Levin, 1989).

We have taken the following steps to maximize the amount of time available for focusing on the school agenda. Since the accelerated school process is a whole-school effort, all faculty meetings and staff development days are devoted to the accelerated process. Previously established committees, if needed, are folded into accelerated school activities. Attempts are made to secure additional time through the scheduling of particular activities that can be partially or fully staffed by the visiting school district teams in the arts, sciences, and physical education. By freeing up available time formerly devoted to other activities, most of our schools have obtained at least the minimum time necessary to create an accelerated school. Small grants have been obtained from foundations to pay for substitutes and for meetings outside of regular school hours. While these solutions are helpful, they are piecemeal. We believe that school systems need to recognize that if site-based decision-making and responsibility are to be effective, elementary school staff require "prep" time just as secondary school staff do.

LEADERSHIP NEEDS

In the traditional school, the role of the principal is primarily one of policy enforcement of rules, regulations, mandates, procedures, and deadlines. The demands on the principal to fulfill the myriad requirements of policy compliance leave little time or energy for instructional leadership. In contrast, the principal in an accelerated school has a different role. The principal is responsible for coordinating and facilitating the activities of decision-making bodies as well as for obtaining the logistical support that is necessary in such areas as information, staff development, assessment, implementation, and instructional resources.

A good principal in the context of the accelerated school is one who is an active listener and participant, who can identify and cultivate talents among staff, who can keep the school focused on its mission, who can work effectively with parents and community, who is dedicated to the students and their success, who can motivate the various actors, and who can marshal the necessary resources. The principal must also have keen analytic and planning skills in order to coordinate the school's many ongoing activities and initiatives without creating burnout among staff. Finally, the principal is the "keeper of the dream," helping staff overcome temporary disappointments or setbacks. Principals must make the transition from control and policy enforcement to inspiration, facilitation, coordination, and acceleration. Not all will be able to make the transition, and selection and training of future leaders of accelerated schools must be promoted through both intensive staff development and the transformation of traditional administrator training to programs based upon principles of acceleration.

SCHOOL TALENT

One of our most rewarding discoveries in the pilot schools has been the amount of talent embodied in school staff. As teachers and other staff members begin to embrace a problem-solving mode in which their ideas count, they generate many creative ideas for accelerating student progress. We believe that teachers in existing schools are being underutilized and that there is far more talent in the schools than most people recognize. The accelerated school process seems to unleash that talent so that ideas count in ways that more traditional staff roles do not permit. Further, through the practice of mutual support and sharing insights, the entire school benefits from the enormous potential that is normally hidden in classrooms or repressed by drill and practice and teacher-proof curricula. We continue to find new ways of helping schools build on the talents of teachers and other staff.

PARENT POTENTIAL

A second pleasant surprise has been the enormous potential to harness parental support and involvement in accelerated schools. Our pilot schools have built their programs of parental involvement on a simple assumption: parents love their children and want them to succeed. We have found that if the schools can connect this assumption to manageable parental activities and responsibilities, parents will become involved in their children's education and in the school. Particular approaches include helping parents help their children succeed by providing classes, parent meetings, and individual counseling. Equally important is creating an atmosphere in which the parents always feel welcome. This can be achieved by providing a reception center, encouraging cordial attitudes on the part of the staff, and helping parents develop and implement programs.

These approaches result in parents' widespread participation in school and home activities that support their children. Some of our pilot schools have obtained representation of over 90 percent of the parents at major school functions and close to 100 percent at parent-teacher conferences. Parent volunteers provide regular assistance in classrooms and at school events. Parents are attending sessions on assisting their children educationally and applying what they learn at home.

SCHOOL DISTRICT SUPPORT

Finally, we have learned the need to obtain school district support for accelerated schools in the form of technical assistance, staff development, and evaluation as well as bottom-line performance expectations rather than compliance requirements (Levin, 1991). Accelerated schools will function best if school districts work with individual schools to set targets for improvement as well as develop accountability systems to monitor that improvement. Once there is agreement on goals, school districts should waive all superfluous procedural requirements. In their place, central office personnel should help schools reach their goals.

For example, if there is a particular concern with student performance in a particular subject, the curriculum and evaluation divisions of the central office should assign personnel to work with the school-level task force in evaluating student performance, defining the problems, providing information on alternative solutions, and assisting in implementation. Such assistance is also needed in placing staff development within such a problem-solving context. In principle, all central office personnel should devote at least half of their time to helping individual schools reach their goals. Schools should be evaluated only in terms of their progress toward meeting their goals, and central office staff should be evaluated by schools on a periodic basis for their effectiveness in helping schools. This would turn around the evaluation process. Even school board members should see their main roles as creating the conditions under which accelerated schools can succeed in reaching their performance goals.

Two Myths

We have learned that there are two powerful myths about school reform. First is the widespread view that the only way to dramatically improve the schooling of at-risk students is with vast increases in funding. The case for increased school funding is a powerful one on the basis of cost-benefit and cost-effectiveness studies (Levin, 1989). However, lack of funding cannot be used as an excuse to waste present resources. To be sure, there are enormous unmet needs among at-risk students and their families, but only a portion of the students' educational needs can be met with additional resources. What is imperative is that we use existing resources to create dramatic educational breakthroughs for at-risk students. To argue that additional funding is needed before we can begin is just another excuse not to get started. We need to fight for more school support while simultaneously creating the conditions under which that support will be highly effective. Indeed, this is likely to be a far more effective political strategy for attracting additional funding than simply demanding more resources to apply to conventional schooling strategies.

We have found that the transformation to an accelerated school can be made primarily by reallocating existing resources to free up time and make other provisions for staff development and accelerated school activities. To our knowledge, none of our schools has obtained additional funding that exceeds even 1 percent of its budget to pursue the accelerated school process. We believe that the basic transformation to and operation of an accelerated school can be done largely within existing resources.

A second myth is that there are curriculum packages, educational technologies, or stylized teaching practices that, if adopted, make the difference between school failure and school success. In our experience, the ability to energize a school and get it to focus productively on a common set of objectives, using the talents of staff, parents, and students, is far more important than any particular curriculum package or teaching method. A school that functions in this way discovers and develops the methods and content that contribute to bottom-line success in a way that integrates curriculum, instructional strategies, and school organization. In contrast, the endless quest for piecemeal reforms such as new curriculum packages, educational technologies, and teaching methods in the absence of more far-reaching reforms is likely to be fruitless and expensive (Cuban, 1984).

FUTURE OF ACCELERATED SCHOOLS

The establishment of accelerated schools for at-risk students has gotten off to a promising start with considerable encouragement from the broader educational community. We have tried to use the lessons that we have learned over these early years to improve the process of initiating and supporting accelerated schools, to develop an effective training program, to work more closely with school districts, to help schools find ways of obtaining more time to plan, and to build on the enormous talents of both school staffs and parents. These lessons have also sparked three new initiatives.

First, we have found that expanding the possibility of the accelerated school movement will require a national network of centers with the capacity to collaborate with schools in their own geographical areas. The movement will necessarily be limited if it is connected to only a single center at Stanford. We have established the first four of a larger number of university-based satellite centers in San Francisco, Los Angeles, Houston, and New Orleans and a district-based satellite in the Denver area as well as a state-based center in Massachusetts.

The satellite centers are expected to play leading roles in their geographical areas in both research and training for accelerated schools as well as to provide technical assistance to such schools. These centers have established pilot accelerated schools that provide hands-on experiences for their staffs as well as training for student teachers and administrative interns. It is hoped that such schools will provide a laboratory for transforming both teacher and administrative training and will create local models of success that can be replicated.

Second, we have recognized that we need to set national training standards that must be met by the staffs of satellite centers and accelerated schools. Accordingly, we have established an eight-day training workshop for accelerated schools coaches that can be used to provide the knowledge and some of the initial skills required for establishing accelerated schools. This workshop emphasizes an understanding of accelerated practices that will be implemented at school sites following the training. These practices should be immediately adopted by the school following the workshop to reinforce what has been learned. Further, all coaches are mentored over the first year by staff from our national center with regular communications and mentorship visits to school sites. We are attempting to assure that all schools have access to trained facilitators who can provide follow-up and guidance at the school site.

Third, we have learned that sending children who have experienced accelerated elementary education to traditional middle schools or junior high schools can undo the earlier successes. Traditional middle schools have low expectations for at-risk students and do not build on the gains of accelerated students. Accordingly, we have begun to establish middle schools that are premised on the same principles as our elementary schools. By 1992, we had launched about a dozen middle schools and will be expanding the number through the establishment of middle-school satellite centers. It is our belief that accelerated practices can be as effective in middle schools as in elementary schools and that ultimately high schools will adopt the same practices so that at-risk students and all students can experience an articulate education that is fully accelerated.

- COMMUNITY/ PARENT INVOLVEMENT
- CURRICULUM
- INSTRUCTION
- ORGANIZATION/ MANAGEMENT (CLASSROOM)
- ORGANIZATION/ MANAGEMENT (SCHOOL)

Early Childhood Education

David P. Weikart
High/Scope Educational Research Foundation

Early childhood education as we know it today both here and abroad is of fairly recent origin. Various histories of early childhood education (e.g., Cleverley & Phillips, 1986, Osborn, 1991) illustrate the extent to which children, especially females, were often regarded as liabilities and subject to indifference instead of nurturing. Indeed, only in the 1900s were such practices as infanticide by exposure or a more gentile form of discarding infants called "potting" (which the infant Moses experienced) generally called into question. Such disposing of children was finally accepted as illegal, and governments attempted to reduce the practice.

During earlier periods, child labor was valued in industrial areas and on the farms. While often horrendous, the conditions of child labor were frequently better than the squalor and poverty in which the vast majority of families lived. But in the 1800s a number of French and German reformers began to understand the process of child growth and development. They began to sense that childhood is different from adulthood and that children are not just miniature adults. Pioneers such as Froebel, starting in 1826, and Montessori, starting in 1907, began to make an impact on actual programs for large numbers of children.

In their recent book *How Nations Serve Young Children*, Olmsted and Weikart (1989) bring together the histories of early childhood in fourteen countries ranging from Nigeria to China to Germany. It is clear from each of these histories that the modern thrust of early childhood care and education has come only since the post–World War II period. However, the current state of early childhood education has evolved in a step-by-step process over many years in most of these countries.

In the United States, the real thrust of change came in the 1950s with the growing awareness that something needed to be done for children with special needs. The focus was initially on the handicapped, but it was quickly extended to impoverished children as the awareness of civil rights issues spread into education. Terms such as "culturally deprived" were used in the early 1960s before the advent of Head Start. As people realized that the problems of these children were the result of social indifference to their culture and needs, the term "culturally deprived" changed to "economically disadvantaged."

In the early 1960s, a series of small projects began that preceded National Head Start. These studies looked seriously, from a research basis, at the question of how such young people can be helped through early education. Most of their findings have now been brought together in the Consortium for Longitudinal Studies' (1983) book, *As a Twig Is Bent*. While the results of these projects differ because of varying experimental designs, populations sampled, duration of study, and so forth, the overall conclusion is that high-quality early childhood education programs can make a long-term difference in the lives of children.

THE CASE FOR EARLY EDUCATION

For many reasons a preschool education is a particularly appealing intervention. Education has been the traditional means by which people have improved their prospects for productive and satisfying lives.

Many poor children are handicapped when they enter school because they have not had the chance to develop the skills, habits, and attitudes expected of children in kindergarten and first grade. This lack of development is manifested in low scores on tests of intellectual or scholastic ability. And while poor children may be developmentally advanced in other respects, their lack of preparedness for school can also lead to their unnecessary (preventable) placement in special education classes, to being held back a grade, to repeated scholastic failure, and to dropping out of high school.

So, given the chance to attend high-quality preschool programs, poor children can learn the skills, habits, and attitudes expected of them in kindergarten and first grade. Thus, they get a better start toward success in school and in life.

This idea of giving poor children a "head start" took hold with educators and social scientists in the 1960s. As many experimental preschool child development programs were mounted, a limited number of scientific evaluations of these programs were made. As might be expected, most studies assessed the short-term effects of such programs; only a handful have been able to examine their effectiveness ten years or more after the programs' end.

The most carefully drawn studies of preschool child development programs suggest a pattern of cause and effect that stretches from early childhood into the adult years. The weight of the evidence from all the studies suggests that:

- Poor children who attend a high-quality early childhood development program are better prepared for school, intellectually and socially.
- This better start probably helps them achieve greater success in school. Far fewer poor children who have attended good preschool programs need special education classes or have to repeat a grade.
- Their greater success in school tends to lead to greater success in adolescence and adulthood. Their rates of delinquency, teenage pregnancy, and welfare usage are lower; and their rates of high school completion and subsequent employment are higher.

HIGH/SCOPE PERRY PRESCHOOL STUDY

Compelling evidence on the value of early childhood education comes from a long-term study of the Perry Preschool Project in Ypsilanti, Michigan, conducted by the nonprofit High/Scope Educational Research Foundation (Berrueta-Clement, Schweinhart, Barnett, Epstein, & Weikart, 1984). The purpose of the study was to explore whether participation in a high-quality early childhood education program would have long-term effects.

The Perry Preschool Project is a longitudinal study begun in 1962 of 123 disadvantaged African-American youths from a single school district. At ages three and four, these youths were randomly divided into two groups—an experimental group that received a high-quality preschool education and a control group that received no preschool training. The two groups were then studied on an annual basis from ages 3 to 11; again at ages 14, 15, and 19; and currently at age 28. Among the hundreds of variables considered were the children's abilities, attitudes, and scholastic accomplishments; their involvement in delinquent and criminal behavior; their use of welfare assistance; and their employment patterns.

The study's results indicate that good preschool programs can lead to consistent improvement in poor children's achievement throughout their school years, a reduced delinquency and arrest rate, a reduced teenage pregnancy rate at age nineteen, and a decreased rate of dependency on welfare at age nineteen. Among statistically significant results through age nineteen were the following:

- In education, fewer children were classified as mentally retarded, more completed high school, and more attended college or job-training programs.
- In the world of work, more hold jobs, more support themselves by their own or their spouses' earnings, and there is more satisfaction with work.
- In the community, fewer have been arrested for criminal acts, there has been a lower birth rate, and fewer have needed public assistance.

The Perry Project has become a standard reference for those who argue in favor of early education. Its acceptance is widespread. The American Psychological Association (Price, Cowen, Lorion, & Ramos-McKay, 1988) has selected it as one of twelve validated methods for reducing social problems of adolescence. This endorsement occurred after a committee of scientists carefully reviewed research from 900 intervention programs. The Committee on Economic Development (1985), after reviewing the Perry Preschool Project economic study, labeled early education a major investment opportunity for the business community.

THE CURRICULUM. The Perry Preschool Project used the High/Scope Curriculum (Hohmann & Weikart, in press, Hohmann, Banet, & Weikart, 1979; Weikart, Rogers, Adcock, & McClelland, 1971). In its first year, the curriculum was centered loosely around traditional nursery school activities. After the first year, the theories of psychologist Jean Piaget became influential and the curriculum was reorganized accordingly. The fundamental premise of the High/Scope Curriculum is that children are active learners and construct their own knowledge from activities they plan and carry out with the support of adults. This concept of active, self-generated learning affects all aspects of the curriculum from teacher training to parent involvement.

Such an approach implies a consistent daily routine, because the children have to be able to follow up on their plans and ideas. The adherence to routine gives children control of their time, which helps them develop a sense of responsibility and independence. The daily routine includes a "plan-do-review" sequence and incorporates cleanup as well as small-and large-group activities. This cycle permits children to make choices about their activities and keeps the teacher involved in the whole process.

Planning gives children consistent opportunities to express their ideas and intentions to adults and to see themselves as individuals who can make decisions and act on them. The children experience the power of independence and the joy of working with attentive adults and peers. Since the children are responsible for executing their plans, the adults do not lead work-time activities. The adult's role during work time is first to observe how children gather information, interact with peers, and solve problems. Adults then join the children in play activities to encourage them and to help them set up problem-solving situations.

The final phase of the plan-do-review cycle gives children an opportunity to represent their experiences in a variety of developmentally appropriate ways. They can draw pictures or make models of what they did, review their plan, or describe the activities they undertook. This opportunity for reflection gives the child a sense of personal control and success.

The curriculum is organized around "key experiences" that underlie the development of thought—based in part on Piaget's theory of cognitive development. The experiences are divided into eight main categories that are further subdivided: active learning, using language, representing experiences and ideas, classification, seriation, number concepts, spatial relations, and time. Experiences in computer literacy and movement/dance are being added. The key experiences create a frame of reference that helps the teachers assess the children's progress so that they can work with the children at each stage of their development and structure their own (adult) interactions with the children. They are not a framework of instructions delivered by a teacher to the child.

Although the High/Scope Curriculum is based on a particular theoretical perspective, it is an open framework approach. This means that people can use it in many disparate situations with many different kinds of children. It is now widely used throughout the United States and in many other countries, including the Australia, Chile, Peru, Bolivia, Ecuador, Colombia, the Netherlands, Norway, Portugal, Mexico, and the United Kingdom.

THE VALIDITY OF THE STUDY. The High/Scope Perry Preschool study was designed as a true experiment, with subjects randomly assigned to experimental or control groups. Another strength of the study is that it repeated the experimental-control group design annually for five successive waves of children. The experimental children attended two years of preschool and received 2 1/2 hours per day of the center-based program, plus a weekly family visitation for 1 1/2 hours. The children then entered a regular kindergarten. Although the study sample is small compared to cross-sectional surveys, nearly all of the subjects are still available to the project. The study located and interviewed all but five of the now twenty-eight-year-old subjects. Such availability eliminates most of the problems of attrition that plague so many longitudinal studies, even those that last only a few years.

Data from the study have been internally consistent over the years: there is no indication that the control group did better than the experimental group at any point. The data collected from subjects' own reports have been corroborated by data collected by outside agencies. For instance, arrest records, documented on police blotters, corroborate the participants' reports of arrests; official school records confirm the findings of testing and interviews of subjects by project staff; and computer files of the Michigan Department of Social Services match the participants' reports on their use of welfare.

The study chose to collect variables meaningful to society

rather than those important mainly to psychologists. The effort thus focused on "real-world" success as well as on test scores, using such indicators of outcomes in school as special education placement, school attendance, retention in grade, remedial education placement, and school completion. Outside of school, the study focused on participation in the labor force, crime and delinquency rates, and birth and welfare rates.

COST-BENEFIT ANALYSIS. The High/Scope Perry Preschool study includes the most complete cost-benefit analysis of early childhood education yet undertaken. A first, rudimentary effort made in 1971 looked at scholastic placement from a cost-savings viewpoint. A second, major effort was carried out under the direction of an economist using data collected from the schools through 1973. The most recent report presents a new economic analysis based on data collected through 1982 from schools, police and courts, and social services.

The cost-benefit analysis, covering fifteen years of follow-up data, indicates that this type of program can be a good investment for taxpayers. The major cost (in constant 1988 dollars, discounted at 3 percent annually) is the initial investment of about $6,500 per participant per program year. This cost includes items of school operation that are usually overlooked, such as building depreciation, clothing, volunteers, and so on. The costs of postsecondary education added $964 to the total cost. The major benefits for the taxpayers were savings per participant of $7,005 for special education programs, $4,252 for crime, and $22,490 for welfare assistance. Participants were expected to pay $6,495 more in taxes because of increased lifetime earnings (predicted from their improved educational attainment).

The total benefits to taxpayers amount to about $39,278 per

participant, which is nearly six times the initial cost of the one-year program or three times the cost of the two-year program. The return is large enough that even a two-year program that was only half as effective as the program studied would still yield a positive return on investment. The savings from special education alone are equivalent to the cost of a one-year program.

The Perry data indicate the great importance of high-quality educational experiences during the transition from infancy to the elementary school years, at ages three, four, five, and six. This finding can be generalized to any youngster, poor or middle class. Although the educational, social, and economic results for middle-class children might not be as dramatic as those for disadvantaged children, because middle-class children tend to have more advantages to begin with, the preschool years are clearly crucial for all children.

OTHER FOLLOW-UP STUDIES. The High/Scope Foundation is also engaged in a study of young adults in Ft. Walton Beach (FL) and in Greeley (CO) who had been involved in the National Planned Variation Head Start Project of 1970–71. In these projects, the High/Scope Curriculum was implemented by local staff, who periodically consulted with the High/Scope staff. Third-party evaluators (Marshall Smith, then Dean of the School of Education at Stanford University) reported positive results during the operation of the project.

High/Scope is currently studying the differences between the now young adults who participated in the early childhood projects and those who did not. The majority of the original sample have been identified, located, and interviewed, resulting in 625 individuals. If the data obtained on these young people show the same results as the data from those who participated in the original Perry Project, there will be strong evidence that a high-quality early childhood education program—at least as exemplified by those that used the High/Scope Curriculum—can have a significant impact in different geographic situations with different Head Start populations and typical Head Start staff. Until the study is complete, however, generalization to groups other than those similar to High/Scope's original sample should be limited.

FACTORS THAT CONTRIBUTE TO SUCCESSFUL LIFE PATTERNS

It would seem worthwhile to attempt to identify the dynamic social factors that lead to a life pattern of success—broadly defined as one that is self-supporting and law abiding. A preliminary attempt was made in the Perry Preschool Project's eight in-depth case studies of preschool participants at age nineteen. The purpose of the case studies was to develop issues for discussion.

The case studies indicated that four factors most consistently differentiated those whose lives are successful from those whose lives are not: parental and family support for education; positive role models, particularly those who demonstrate the value of schooling; a sense of responsibility that extends beyond oneself; and an active, goal-oriented approach to life. Basic attitudes about education are probably already ingrained when a child enters school, be it preschool or kindergarten. Although preschool may not be able to change a negative family attitude, it does appear that it can reinforce or give concrete direction to a positive one.

Role models are present or absent in the children's families regardless of whether the children attend preschool. Nonfamily role models first appear most influential around junior high school, but if students are not part of the school success flow, they are likely to miss the opportunity to be exposed to teachers and other positive role models in junior high. In helping put children on the success track, preschool can indirectly affect life outcomes.

A sense of responsibility seems to stem from one's family values, but goal orientation appears to be a personality characteristic formed by a multitude of inner and outer forces. Yet preschool may reinforce what the child already brings with him or her. The preschool experience may be an important early step on the road to independence. Successful young adults have a sense of responsibility for others and believe they can take care of themselves and those for whom they feel responsible. Preschool can give youngsters a year or two to develop these social values before they face the more formal demands of public school.

Preschool may also instill a certain confidence in a youngster that ultimately contributes to a more active goal orientation. All of the successful participants viewed themselves, more or less, as self-made people. While acknowledging the importance of their families or other role models in their achievements, the young men and women always came back to their internal motivation. They believed in themselves, often more than others believed in them.

In an earlier study of parents and infants, High/Scope found that children who are active participants in problem-solving processes and who perform well academically had mothers who interacted with them from infancy on in ways that were verbally supportive and responsive. Conversely, children who are not involved in problem-solving processes and who perform more poorly academically tended to have mothers who did not so interact.

FACTORS THAT CONTRIBUTE TO SUCCESSFUL PRESCHOOL PROGRAMS

Successful preschool programs are the result of numerous variables. Some are known; others are still being discovered. High/Scope has studied the effects of three different preschool curriculum models on the subsequent lives of children through the age of fifteen in the High/Scope Curriculum Comparison study (Schweinhart, Weikart, & Larner, 1986). At the ages of three and four, sixty-eight preschoolers in Ypsilanti, Michigan, were randomly assigned to one of three curriculum groups. Fifty-four of the children (79 percent of the original sample) were then interviewed at age fifteen.

The three curricular approaches differ mainly in the degree of initiative required of teacher and child—whether the primary role of each is to initiate or respond. The first approach, inspired by the psychological theory of B. F. Skinner and other behaviorists, may be called the programmed learning or direct instruction approach. Briefly, in this approach the teacher initiates clearly defined, structured activities and the child responds and receives positive reinforcement. The second, an open framework approach, is based largely on the cognitive development theories of Jean Piaget and is represented by the High/Scope Curriculum as described above. Its activities involve specific "key experiences" that promote intellectual and social development. The third, a child-centered approach, consists of elements of traditional nursery school programs. Based on Freudian psychoanalytic theory, this type of curriculum allows the child to express needs and interests, while the teacher responds and encourages free play.

Although earlier reports from the study found no significant differences in results from any of the three different approaches, the most recent findings have raised some questions about direct instruction or behaviorist programs, at least for disadvantaged children at the preschool age. These results also refocus attention on the importance of the surrounding environmental events that permit general social and behavioral learning rather than simply on the knowledge content itself.

High/Scope's latest report shows that the three preschool curriculum groups differed little in their patterns of IQ and school achievement over time. However, according to participants' reports at age fifteen, the group that attended the direct instruction preschool program engaged in twice as many delinquent acts as did the other two groups, including five times as many acts of violence against property. The direct instruction group also reported relatively poor relations with their families, less participation in sports, fewer school job appointments, and less reaching out to others for help with personal problems. These findings, based on one study with a small sample, are by no means definitive; but two other studies have raised some of the same questions (Karnes, Schwedel, & Williams, 1983; Miller & Bizzell, 1983).

WHY THE HIGH/SCOPE CURRICULUM WORKS FOR CHILDREN

What makes high-quality early childhood education experience at three to five years of age so powerful that it changes children's lives and experiences as they reach young adulthood? In the early 1960s, the theory was that early intervention through education would improve children's intelligence. Yet most studies have failed to provide evidence that such experiences raise children's IQ significantly for any length of time. Even the High/Scope Perry Preschool study findings (Berrueta-Clement, et al., 1984) report similar IQ levels for both control-group and experimental-group participants a decade after intervention. The data from the Consortium of Longitudinal Studies (1983) and Head Start (Cicerelli, 1969; McKey, et al., 1985) all report essentially the same outcome. Only a few studies such as the High/Scope Curriculum Comparison study (Schweinhart, et al., 1986) report long-term IQ gains.

Since IQ does not seem to be responsible for the long-term changes in children's lives, what is? Perhaps it is the academic content that early education provides. Most adults agree that children need to learn certain skills early on to be successful in later schooling. Yet the High/Scope Curriculum Comparison study, among others, found that children who participated in direct-teaching curriculum, with its structured approach to teaching reading, math, and language, did not do any better academically in a decade of follow-up than children who participated in child-initiated learning programs. In fact, the young adults who as children had participated in the direct-teaching model evidenced some serious alienation from school, family, and society. Clearly, academic content, at least as a structured objective, is not the link between the experiences of early childhood and successful adult performance.

The best estimate of what permits a high-quality early childhood experience to significantly influence adult performance seems to be the development of specific personal traits. Erik

Erikson (1950) points out that the natural psychological thrust of three- to five-year-olds is toward developing a sense of initiative, responsibility, and independence. Lilian Katz (1985) discusses the importance of dispositions such as curiosity, friendliness, and cooperation that young children develop at this age range and how effective preschool programs support the development of such traits. However, these personal traits and dispositions are elusive. They cannot be "taught" or inserted as a "theme" into a program of instruction. They can only develop under appropriate circumstances.

HIGH/SCOPE'S CURRICULUM PROCESSES AND OUTCOMES

So what specific circumstances and program strategies support the development of such traits? Attempts to answer this question are important undertakings of early childhood policy and training organizations. The National Association for the Education of Young Children (Bredekamp, 1987) has outlined a set of standards for developmentally appropriate education that forms a basis for educational quality. The High/Scope Curriculum Comparison study helped validate developmentally appropriate curricula that provide ample opportunity for child-initiated learning processes that result in positive, lifelong outcomes.

High/Scope's high-quality early childhood curriculum relies heavily on *active learning* and *child-initiated experiences* during which children express their intentions, plan and carry out their play experiences, and reflect on their accomplishments. The processes described in Figure 14.1 are the key events in child-initiated, adult-supported events that High/Scope's curriculum planners believe lead to the outcomes listed—positive habits, traits, and dispositions.

Figure 14.1
HIGH/SCOPE CURRICULUM PROCESSES AND OUTCOMES

PROCESSES	OUTCOMES
Children express intentions.	Initiative
Children generate experiences.	Responsibility Curiosity Independence
Children reflect on experiences.	Divergent Thinking Trust
Children gain control.	Sense of Personal Control

CHILDREN EXPRESS THEIR INTENTIONS. High-quality programs provide numerous ongoing opportunities for children to express their own intentions. Initially, children express their intentions through both gestures and actions. For example, an infant picks one toy rather than another, or a preschooler points to a toy or takes the adult's hand and walks to the material she or he wants to play with. As children mature, they can inform others of their intentions: "I want the wagon." "I'm gonna play with the blocks." As they become writers and readers, children begin to express their intentions in more detail, through written plans, models, blueprints, and detailed discussions with peers and adults. The High/Scope Curriculum calls children's expression of intent "planning"—children not only plan during the designated "planning time" but also throughout the day.

CHILDREN GENERATE EXPERIENCES. As well as encouraging children to express their intentions, a high-quality program must offer opportunities for the children to act on them. Effective action comes about when a child makes choices; is actively involved with people, materials, events, and ideas; and has enough time for trial-and-error, generating new ideas, practicing, and succeeding. Personal independence is the key to active learning by self-motivated children. In the High/Scope Curriculum, children act on their intentions during "work time." Throughout other parts of the day children's choices are somewhat limited by specific materials or decisions made by others, but they are still free to use materials and respond to situations in ways that make sense to them.

CHILDREN REFLECT ON THEIR EXPERIENCES. Along with providing opportunities for children to express their intentions and generate their own experiences, a high-quality curriculum must provide opportunities for children to reflect on their activities and accomplishments. Children reflect on their experiences with increasing verbal ability and logic as they mature. Through this process, they begin to match words to their actions and construct memories and insights they can modify as their understanding increases. In the High/Scope Curriculum the time set aside for this process is called "recalling" or "review."

These three essential aspects of high-quality curriculum— *children's expression of intent,* their *independently-generated experiences,* and their *reflections*—are central to our definition of child-initiated learning. Their outcomes, important to lifelong learning, include the development of important traits, such as initiative, curiosity, trust, confidence, independence, responsibility, and divergent thinking—traits valued by society.

CHILDREN GAIN CONTROL. When children experience the High/Scope program, they develop control—power not over people or things but over themselves—and self-discipline. Understanding what is happening in our environment, realizing that those around us are genuinely interested in what we say and do, and knowing that our work and effort will often lead to success is the type of control that promotes personal satisfaction and motivates us to be productive. While no single factor assures success in life, the *sense of personal control* is certainly a major factor. And high-quality early childhood programs can support and strengthen this feeling.

NEW DIRECTIONS

The major focus of early educators in the 1980s was on expanding programs to accommodate children. The Perry Preschool Project data were used extensively by advocates during this time to convince both federal and state governments to provide the necessary funds for such spaces. The issue of the 1990s is changing from quantity to quality of programs. With the advent of large-scale increases in funding of Head Start by the federal government and the parallel expansion of funding by states and day care monies through block grants to states, the number and types of programs available to young children will be extended rapidly.

The long-term problem remains—the delivery on the promise of early education. Operating programs of questionable quality offers, at best, a safe haven while parents are at work or otherwise absent. At worst, such programs can actually be detrimental to a child's growth, particularly in creating health and psychological problems. If low-quality or mediocre programs are publicly financed, they drain resources from the tax system that could be better spent elsewhere to support children and families or to correct our failure to act by building better police forces or employment training programs to provide services later in life.

A number of observers in the field have suggested, through extensive contact with programs, that the typical U.S. early childhood care and education program is "outcome neutral"— causing neither harm nor benefit to its participants. Thus, the major issue is how to deliver a high-quality program that can significantly help children.

Some would argue that program accreditation, increased rates of pay, improved teacher education, and more professional credentials are the best means of dealing with quality issues. The problem is, of course, that if the answer to providing high-quality programs lay solely in these issues, we would be satisfied with the public schools. Schools are accredited; teachers have a credential based on at least four years of college education; and the pay, while not outstanding, is acceptable.

While it is a good assumption that pre-service education leads to better-prepared staff, alternative solutions to the problems of quality in the early childhood field need to be recognized. Presently, a major discussion within the field is whether the focus should be on the expansion of generic pre-service teacher education programs or on support of curriculum models that can be applied and supervised through in-service training programs. The High/Scope Curriculum as a well-researched and effective program model is an illustration of the latter approach.

Some basic assumptions are useful. First, high-quality programs with positive outcomes for children, families, and communities broadly defined are possible. Second, ready access by community members for employment in childhood care and education programs is important, recognizing the intimate connection of such programs to the community. Third, the rapid expansion of the field and the need for many new staff in the very near future require an immediate response.

Guided by these assumptions, the choice is either to emphasize a generic education approach working with all teacher education institutions, especially community colleges, to provide improved pre-service education or to emphasize a model-program approach that focuses on training supervisors in the direct delivery of validated curriculum. Wade Horn, former commissioner of the Administration of Children, Youth, and Families, calls this the "smorgasbord versus the gourmet" approach, and Lilian Katz, professor at University of Illinois, calls it the "coverage versus mastery" approach.

The model program approach is a viable strategy to meet the current needs and to improve standards in the short run. In order to be considered, however, a model program must at least have the following:

1. It must represent a coherent system based on a developmentally valid theory or belief system.
2. It must be a documented approach so that it can be understood and utilized by a wide range of individuals from different educational and social backgrounds.
3. It needs a staff training system so that it can be transferred successfully from the model developers or initial demonstration program implementers to a wide range of normally operating classrooms or care settings.
4. The model must actually be utilized in a wide range of settings to be certain that it really works and is not just a grandiose system without any real application.
5. It must be validated by significant research to show it

5. It must be validated by significant research to show it works when it is well implemented so that it is worth wide-scale implementation.

6. It needs a developed monitoring system to ensure that it is actually in operation when it is said to be employed. Too often, model programs are given "lip service" but are never actually instituted in programs attempting to use them.

7. The model needs an assessment system of child outcomes that supports the service or curriculum practice, indicating the extent of growth being achieved by the child; and an open system that will improve parental understanding and investment in the program and communication with parents.

The High/Scope Training of Trainers approach to large-scale application illustrates the use of a model program. The High/Scope Curriculum has been under development since 1962 and has achieved the standards as a basic model curriculum outlined above. The Foundation has now trained over 1,000 leaders in early childhood care and education to implement the High/Scope Curriculum throughout early childhood care and education programs in the United States with funding from the Ford Foundation, Head Start, and hundreds of local groups.

The central focus of the High/Scope model training program is on the development of agency supervisors or coordinators as trainers so that local curriculum supervision expertise in the model exists. This approach is used because it reduces the costs of training within the agency. It permits distributed learning by the staff—full implementation of High/Scope Curriculum takes about three years. It provides for adaptation to local needs and cultural sensitivity. And it allows for parental input directly to the training staff during the process of the training.

The High/Scope Training of Trainers program is also focused on bringing all child care and education groups together within a community, as supervisors from each agency train together in a common group. There is little to recommend separating staff for categorical group training from day care, Head Start, home day care, school-based programs, and so on. This whole-group approach develops a network of local supervisors who can then share training and provide support to each other over time. Training cross-agency by supervisors greatly improves their skills and abilities.

High/Scope operates a national registry in which people who achieve endorsement are awarded membership. The registry provides for the monitoring of ongoing work and retraining opportunities as new information is developed for the curriculum. It further extends contact among trainers for shared training beyond local agency training groups. And, of course, it is designed to give professional identity.

The High/Scope Training of Trainers program is operated in cooperation with graduate training institutes throughout the country. Wherever a program is located, linkages are established with local training institutions. In 1989, 399 people participated in the program. Many of these received fourteen to sixteen hours of graduate credit if they did not already have their Master's or Ph.D. degrees.

SUMMARY

Since the early 1960s, well-designed research projects have explored the issues in early childhood growth and development that lead to high-quality care and educational programs for all children. The essential ingredients of high-quality educational programs are known. The challenge is to apply these principles in programs throughout the country to improve the lives of children and families.

15

- CLIMATE
- COMMUNITY/PARENT INVOLVEMENT
- EXPECTATIONS
- LEADERSHIP
- ORGANIZATION/ MANAGEMENT (SCHOOL)

Effective Schools: The Evolving Research and Practices

Lawrence W. Lezotte
Effective Schools Products

In his book *The Conflict in Education in a Democratic Society*, Robert Hutchins (1953) suggests that education for all may be the greatest idea that the United States has given the world. However, the world is entitled to know whether this means that everybody can be educated or simply that everybody must go to school. As we approach the end of the twentieth century the United States has made significant progress toward Hutchins's vision. Each state has established a system of free public education for all of its children. Each has established compulsory-schooling laws that require that every child attend those free public schools or their equivalent. While the struggle to assure *universal access to quality schools* is far from over, it is nevertheless true that all students are required to attend school for at least a minimum number of years, regardless of their race, gender, or social class.

The 1954 U.S. Supreme Court decision *Brown vs. the Board of Education of Topeka, Kansas* represented a milestone in the struggle to assure equal educational opportunity for all. That general principle is now established, even though court cases continue that involve more subtle legal questions regarding access to public education.

After the 1950s, the battle line for democratic education shifted. Researchers began to ask whether minority students, especially African Americans, were participating in the schools' programs and services in proportion to their numbers in the population. Here again, some progress has been realized but much more is required.

Now minority children are still overly represented in special-education, low-track, and other remedial programs. They lag behind their nonminority counterparts in rates of graduation, proportion going on to postsecondary education, and participation in more academically rigorous programs, especially mathematics and science. Researchers documenting the problem have begun to identify programs and other strategies that seem to be helpful in assuring more success for more students, especially those groups who have profited little from schooling in the past.

THE EFFECTIVE SCHOOLS MOVEMENT: AN HISTORICAL PERSPECTIVE

One of the programs that has resulted from this research and has become widely used by educators throughout the United States is school improvement based on effective schools research. This program has been described by some as the "effective schools movement." It represents a program of school reform that is based on research and descriptions of effective school practices that now span about twenty-five years.

This brief description of the effective schools movement is organized around five relatively distinguishable periods. The first period discussed the problems of definition and the subsequent search for the "effective school." In the following period, a series of case studies designed to capture the organizational culture of the identified "effective schools" was completed. The third period represented a critical transition from describing the effective school to creating more effective schools, one school at a time. In the fourth period, the larger organizational context and the local school district came to play an important role in school improvement; how the school district could enhance or impede improvement of schools, one school at a time. Finally, there is some discussion of the current federal and state policies and programs that are being implemented to ensure the availability of more effective schools for more children.

PHASE I: SEARCH FOR EFFECTIVE SCHOOLS

The story of the effective schools movement began in July 1966 with the publication *Equality of Educational Opportunity* by James Coleman and his colleagues (1966). The controversial findings that Coleman et al. reported became widely disseminated and debated. This excerpt from the Coleman study summarizes the issue of effective schools:

> Schools bring little influence to bear on a child's achievement that is independent of his background and general social context . . . this very lack of an independent effect means that the inequality imposed on children by their home, neighborhood and peer environment [is] carried

along to become the inequalities with which they confront adult life at the end of school. For equality of educational opportunity must imply a strong effect of schools that is independent of the child's immediate social environment, and that strong independence is not present in American schools (Coleman, Campbell, Hobson, McPartland, Mood, Weinfeld, & York, 1966, p. 325).

Coleman et al. clarified the effective schools public policy issue by bringing into sharp contrast the question of whether student achievement derives more from the homes from which children have come or the schools to which they are sent. They said that the issue has been, and is likely to continue to be, fundamental to the discourse on student achievement for a long time to come. The issue is basic in that it serves to question the usefulness of increasing public investment in public schools if, in fact, schools do not (and seemingly cannot) make a difference.

Unfortunately, public acceptance of the Coleman hypothesis still constitutes a formidable obstacle to the advancement of educational equity and to the general improvement of student achievement through schooling. Fortunately, though, several researchers did not accept it. Initially working independently of one another, they began to formulate a research strategy that, if successful, would begin to challenge the hypothesis. Their strategy was to go into the real world of public schools and see if they could identify individual schools that represented clear exceptions to Coleman's theory. The first-generation studies conducted by these researchers became the foundation for the research base of the effective schools movement.

Though further syntheses of the effective schools research

have been published, readers who are interested in an in-depth syntheses of the early research and public policy debate should read Ronald Edmonds's (1978) paper in a compilation of articles from *Educational Leadership* (Brandt, 1989) "A Discussion of the Literature and Issues Related to Effective Schooling." The papers, which can be found in the first section of this compilation, do a good job of "tracking" the effective schools research, associated policy issues, and the research criticisms.

Collectively, these syntheses indicate that the validity of Coleman's theory remains largely intact if one judges student achievement by means of "broad-gauged," standardized, norm-referenced measures designed to find differences among the test population—differences in measured student performance on such measures do tend to be more directly associated with home and family background factors. If, however, one measures student achievement by assessing student mastery of the taught curriculum, then the differences in school-to-school effects become more marked, and a stronger case is made for the school effect. The conclusion is that the issues of measurement have been, and probably always will be, at or near the center of the debate on effective schools.

Because of the centrality of the measurement questions, any discussion of school improvement must begin with the question: "What should we be willing to accept as observable, measurable evidence of school effectiveness or school improvement?" To help schools with the issue of acceptable evidence of school improvement, the following conceptual definition of an effective school is offered:

> An effective school is one that can demonstrate the joint presence of quality (acceptably high levels of

achievement) and equity (no differences in the distribution of that achievement among the major subsets of the student population).

These criteria must be operationalized in the state and local setting and demonstrated in outcome terms reflective of the school's learning mission.

Besides demonstrating that Coleman et al. are right or wrong, depending on how student achievement is measured, effective schools case study research has also proven them just plain wrong in one sense. This literature clearly demonstrates, in numerous settings, that there are schools that are able to attain remarkably high levels of pupil mastery of essential school skills, even though these schools are serving large proportions of economically poor and disadvantaged students, minority and nonminority. The criticisms of the effective schools research have been many and pointed, but the one fact remains: Some schools are able to achieve these extraordinary results. As long as such places exist, the effective schools debate is not a discussion of theory but a discussion of commitment and political will.

PHASE II:
DESCRIPTIONS OF EFFECTIVE SCHOOLS

During the second major period of the effective schools movement, the attention of researchers turned toward the internal descriptions of these effective schools. Ironically, the search for effective schools captured the interest of social scientists and policymakers but not necessarily of educational practitioners. School leaders, teachers, and local boards of education began to take a more active interest in the effective schools research as the descriptions of the effective schools made their way into the literature and language of the educational community.

During this period, researchers sought to answer the following general question: "In what ways do effective schools differ from their less effective counterparts?" Their research methodology generally consisted of three steps. First, effective schools, based on measured outcomes, were identified and paired with schools that were similar in all respects except for the more favorable student outcome profile. Next, field researchers were sent into these "pairs of schools," where they conducted interviews, observations, and surveys designed to develop as rich a description as possible of the life of these schools. Finally, the data were analyzed with the following question in mind: "What are the distinctive characteristics of the effective schools that seem to set them apart from their less effective counterparts?"

From the field research emerged descriptions of certain characteristics that seemed to describe how these schools were able to maintain their exceptional status. These five factors were described by Edmonds (1979) in his early research:

- The principal's leadership and attention to the quality of instruction
- A pervasive and broadly understood instructional focus
- An orderly, safe climate conducive to teaching and learning
- Teacher behaviors that convey the expectation that all students will obtain at least minimum mastery
- The use of measures of pupil achievement as the basis for program evaluation

Since that original listing, numerous other studies have cross-validated the original findings. Some of the more recent studies have described additional factors, and others have sought to make the original Edmonds factors more explicit and more operational. New studies have also looked closely at elementary schools, as did Edmonds in his original research. Other more recent studies have also taken the characteristics or factor theory of the effective school to the secondary levels. In addition, the researchers have now documented the existence of the correlates in settings other than those that were characterized as serving primarily economically poor and minority student populations. Finally, the research has been expanded to include studies in other countries, particularly in Great Britain.

What are the major conclusions that seem to emerge from this expanding array of descriptive studies of the organization and operation of effective schools? First, schools where students master the intended curriculum do share a describable list of institutional and organizational variables that seem to coexist with school effectiveness. Second, these core factors seem to be robust in that they have endured across the various studies. Third, the effective school can and generally does stand alone, even among its counterparts in the same local school district. The major implication is that the institutional and organizational mechanisms that coexist with effectiveness can be attained by individual schools, one school at a time. This suggests that effective schooling is within the grasp of the teachers and administrators who make up the teaching community of the single school.

With the publication of these descriptions of the effective school, practitioners and community members began to take a more active interest. It became clear that more schools could organize themselves to achieve these extraordinary results. The important question began to refocus itself: How could the knowledge about these effective schools become the basis for the purposeful transformation through planned change programs for even more schools?

PHASE III: CREATING MORE EFFECTIVE SCHOOLS—ONE SCHOOL AT A TIME

When school practitioners began to discover that the effective school could be characterized by a relatively short list of alterable school variables, some educators began to see new possibilities for their schools. Their reasoning seemed to proceed along the following lines: If these individual schools had the wherewithal to make their schools effective, as suggested by the original effective schools descriptions, then individual schools ought to accept the responsibility for doing so. The original research provided little guidance as to how the effective schools became effective (that is, the processes involved). In the more common language of the 1980s, the effective schools research provided a vision of a more desirable place for schools to be but gave little insight as to how best to make the journey to that place.

As a result, three problems emerged. First, in many cases, central offices and local boards of education, not knowing a better way, tried to mandate that their local schools become effective, the sooner the better. This led to the conclusion by many teachers and building-level administrators that the effective schools process was just another "top-down" model of school improvement. Second, many principals were told that they were responsible for making their schools effective and that it was a matter of administrative responsibility. As a result, principals often erroneously concluded that they were expected to make their schools effective by themselves. This created anxiety and a great deal of resistance, for the principals had not been trained to be agents of change. Their evaluations generally had been based on the efficient management of school processes rather than results. Additionally, principals could not understand how their low-achieving students could learn when many, if not most, of these students came from low-income families. Third, teachers began to see the effective schools process as an administrative mechanism that implied that teachers were not already doing their best, given the existing working conditions. To many teachers, creating a "more effective school" meant simply "working harder."

Given these apparently insurmountable problems and the resistance they engendered in the major "stakeholders" to more effective schools, why was the movement not stopped in its tracks? The survival of the effective schools movement against these significant obstacles seemed to depend heavily on the implementation strategies used by schools. This overview will focus on the processes used by Edmonds and Lezotte as they responded to the numerous invitations to work with schools. Their experience was repeated by many other facilitators of effective schools research, with some variations in the processes.

A review of the available research literature produced several guiding principles for successful school change. They are:

- The single school must be preserved as the strategic unit for the planned change.
- Teachers and other members of the school community must be an integral part of the school improvement process; principals, though essential as leaders of change, cannot do it alone.

- School improvement, like any change, is best approached as a process, not an event. Such a process approach is more likely to create a permanent change in the operating culture of the school that will accommodate this new function called continuous school improvement.
- The research would be useful in facilitating the change process but it would have to include suggestions of practices, policies, and procedures that could be implemented as a part of the process.
- Finally, like the original effective schools, these improving schools must feel that they have a choice in the matter, and, equally important, they must feel that they have control over the processes of change.

With these guiding principles, the task of creating school plans to take the school from its current level of functioning toward the vision of effectiveness as represented in the research was undertaken. Literally hundreds of schools launched their effective schools processes. Some did it with help from the outside; some chose to proceed on their own. Some followed the guidelines of the lessons we had learned, even without knowing the research per se; others chose to try to implement change and ignore what the research on successful change has reported.

As a result of this diversity in approaches, we can say that effective schools research worked for some and not for others. Fortunately, it has worked for enough schools so that a growing number can proudly claim that they have the results to prove that more of their students are learning, and learning at a higher level. These schools feel empowered to commit their professional energies to the proposition that even more students can and will learn in their schools in the future.

Two major conclusions can be drawn from the lessons from this period of the effective schools movement. First, while researchers do not have all the answers, the literature on successful change clearly establishes that some strategies of planned change do indeed work better than others. Second, the process of school improvement based on the effective schools research takes time, involvement, and commitment. Whenever one tries to gloss over any one of these essential prerequisites, the results are soon diminished. Clearly, when effective schools processes are followed appropriately, school improvement is reaffected. However, when effective schools processes are not implemented properly, they fail to produce more effective schools.

PHASE IV: DISTRICTWIDE PROGRAMS BASED ON EFFECTIVE SCHOOLS RESEARCH

The early efforts to implement programs of school improvement based on the effective schools research clearly supported the individual school as the strategic unit for change. Effective schools research emphasizes that if school improvement is going to occur, it will take place one school at a time. Experience with the school-by-school model has taught a number of valuable lessons that taken together serve to reinforce the districtwide concept associated with this phase of the effective schools movement.

Two forces seem to have combined to reinforce the current emphasis on the overall district planning model. First, the effective schools model represented a viable, manageable, and therefore attractive district response to the local call for a program of school improvement. The second force evolved when individuals working with the effective schools process at the school level realized that individual schools exist as a part of the larger legal, political, and organizational setting of a local school district. It became clear that one could successfully effect school improvement at the individual school level and still ignore this layered context. It also became clear how difficult it would be to sustain it on a long-term basis. Furthermore, when an individual school's faculty set out on their own to plan and implement their program, they often found themselves being challenged by their colleagues or, at least, being impeded by district-level policies, patterns, and practices.

These two forces were joined, and a new, stronger formulation of the effective schools process resulted. This formulation still places great emphasis on school-level change but now also emphasizes the larger organizational context and its role in supporting and enhancing the individual school's efforts. The formulation builds upon the notion of a district plan that supports school change. In this plan, the policies, programs, and procedures generally thought to be beyond the control of a single school are aligned to support the effort.

There are two challenges that are faced in the district planning process. First, the plan must address the necessary changes in district-level policies and programs to ensure that school-level change can occur. Second, the plan must not go so far as to mandate what each school must do in its improvement plan. The first set of challenges, when handled successfully by the district planning group, gives guidance, direction, and the human and financial resources to the school-level improvement process. However, if this plan goes too far, the sense of ownership and empowerment leading to the essential commitment at the school level gets lost.

The current emphasis on the district model for sustained

school improvement serves several valuable functions. It acknowledges:

1. There are no unimportant adults in the school system.
2. The roles of the superintendent and the members of the board of education are critical in providing leadership and vision for school improvement.
3. There is a need to couple more tightly and ensure alignment between the school site and the district office.
4. School-level personnel are central to school effectiveness, and all other personnel should stand ready to do whatever they can to be of assistance.

Early efforts at implementing effective schools produced an expanded list of individual schools that benefit from these efforts. But as each preceding phase builds upon and adds to what has gone before, the fundamental belief that all students can and will learn is reinforced.

ASSUMPTIONS FOR DISTRICT AND SCHOOL-BASED SCHOOL IMPROVEMENT

An important set of basic beliefs undergirds our internal renewal model.

1. Only two kinds of schools exist in the United States: improving schools and declining schools.
2. Every school can improve regardless of current levels of success.
3. The potential for improvement already resides in every school.
4. In school improvement, no adults in the school are unimportant.

5. School improvement is a process, not an event.
6. The people working in the school now—teachers, administrators, support staff, and others—are in the best position to manage the change process. We are not convinced that there is a significant and enduring role for the outside person or agency. That is contrary to many of the innovations that we have tried in the past. In the past we have thought that improvement would come by bringing in a new curriculum, a new approach by classroom organization, or whatever. We have finally come to realize, by looking at both effective schools and other successful organizations in the private sector, that the people inside the organization are in the best position to improve the outcomes of that organization.
7. Teachers and administrators are already doing the best they know how to do, given the conditions under which they find themselves.
8. Internal renewal requires that an ongoing discourse on school improvement be established and sustained in each school and in the district as a whole.

ESSENTIAL PREREQUISITES FOR DISCOURSE ON SCHOOL IMPROVEMENT

Most schools have a "design defect"—a lack of structure, organization, or functioning to assure an ongoing discourse on school improvement. It is almost as if the architect of the public school left off the "back porch" on which this conversation was to occur. The absence of rituals and structures calling for an ongoing discourse on improvement means that when you begin to talk about school improvement in most schools, people perceive that you are asking them to participate in an unnatural act. People will say something like this: "Why do we have to be involved in school improvement? We are already doing a good job. If it's not broken, don't fix it." What they are saying with that language is that to talk about school improvement in most schools is not a natural occurrence.

Correcting this design defect requires three essential prerequisites:

1. School-based discourse on school improvement among the adults who work in a school requires a common language, a language of improvement. In order to launch a systematic program of school improvement in your school or district, you have to plan a strategy for introducing all staff members to the common language of school improvement.

2. A team structure must be created through which this discourse can—and will—flow. Such a collaborative, school-based, school-improvement team needs to consist of a cross section of teaching faculty, the principal of the school, and others—both in and outside the school. This discourse on school improvement should not be limited simply to that group, but that group is in a position to take leadership and provide the language for discussion that will lead to making plans for improvement.

3. Finding time in each school for this group to meet is essential. One major shortcoming in our schools today is the limited time staff members have to meet and talk about school improvement. Local boards of education and the superintendent must convince the community that this time to meet and to talk about school improvement is

absolutely critical. Creating more time for planning, curriculum review, and staff development is going to be a major challenge to local boards of education for two reasons. First, time is a code word for money; more time will cost more money—and that is always a problem. Second, and as important, most people in the community believe that the only time a teacher is at work is when he or she is in the presence of students. This belief will create some tension in most communities when teachers are given released time to meet and talk about school improvement. But these three prerequisites—a common language, a school improvement team, and time—are essential for creating viable discourse on improvement in our schools.

SCHOOL IMPROVEMENT—THE DECADE AHEAD

Much of what is likely to happen to the effective schools movement in the early 1990s is predictable, given the momentum it has gathered recently. However, the model of school improvement based on the effective schools framework will likely undergo significant modifications and refinements in the decade ahead.

The metaphor of the journey has been used to describe the process of school improvement based on the effective schools research. In using this metaphor it is useful to note that, as in any journey, the effective schools process of school improvement has: a destination, a mode of transportation, and a map to be followed throughout. The journey metaphor with its three parts is a useful framework for discussing the anticipated changes in school improvement that are likely to occur in the decade of the 1990s.

THE EFFECTIVE SCHOOLS DESTINATION

By the end of the 1980s, the battle lines regarding school improvement became clearly drawn. The effective schools framework and its advocates can share the credit or blame for this clarification and the attendant lines that subsequently were drawn. From the beginning, the effective schools research suggested that the primary mission of the schools ought to be "learning for all." As the advocacy of this mission became more widely known, if not accepted, it became clear where the political opposition would, and did, gather. Those who favored either the custodial mission or the mission of sorting and selecting students organized and began their counterattack. The excellence advocates called for "teaching for learning for only a few (given limited resources)." Those who advocated that schools serve as the family that "many poor children never had" began to advance with the notion of nurturing first and learning second—if time permitted.

How these struggles will be resolved is not yet clear. What is clear is that this nation is going to have to come to terms with the child care issue, or it will have neither good schools nor reliable custodial care—except for the economically advantaged. A nation with as many "at-risk" children as ours is an "at-risk" nation.

In the decade of the 1990s, the debate regarding the evidence to be used in judging school effectiveness or school improvement will probably intensify. The position of the effective schools advocates is clear. At the moment there is no consensus as to what this country will accept as evidence of school improvement. If and when consensus is reached, and assuming it does focus on *the mission of learning for all,* the effective schools framework will surely help the nation's schools get from where they are to their chosen destination.

A related issue surrounding the destination (or mission) debate has to do with curriculum content itself. The effective schools process has helped clarify two other "truths" that are most unsettling because of their inherent conflict. On the one hand, it is true that virtually all students tend to learn well those things on which they spend the most time. On the other hand, it is true that the curriculum of the public schools must be "trimmed back" because the schools are trying to teach too much content in too little time and with too few resources.

Currently, the mission of many teachers is to cover content. The effective schools model asks teachers to commit themselves to assuring that their students learn the content they cover. To be successful in this mission, they will have to abandon aspects of the curriculum content. This abandonment is going to be an extremely delicate issue and is likely to become volatile before it is settled. The 1990s are likely to be recorded as the decade of the great curriculum debates. These debates probably cannot be avoided, since it is unlikely that the political processes will provide enough resources to teach all that we must know in our rapidly changing society. Such debates should be welcomed and should include a broad cross section of educators and community representatives.

Ron Edmonds said, "We can, whenever and wherever we choose, successfully teach all students . . ." I would like to add to that statement the phrase "whatever we choose" but doing so assumes that we can agree on what it is that we want *all* students to know.

MODE OF TRANSPORTATION

On the journey to school improvement the means to get a school from where it is to where it wants to go seem both clear and compelling. The democratization of the U.S. public school is the means for successfully making the journey. The top-down, outside-in mandates approach to change has been tried and found wanting because so few educators at the local level are willing to own the change. Without ownership and commitment and the enthusiasm they engender, few ideas have the potency required for long-term success. A new organizational form—one that invites teachers and administrators to work collaboratively as partners in the process of school reform—represents our best hope for sustained school reform.

Several changes are needed, however, if this democratic form of school organization is to deliver on its promise. In the 1990s these changes must take hold, or else the "old order" will probably reaffirm its "grip" on our public schools. First, administrators must be trained to work in the network organization. Second, teachers must come to believe that the democratic school is worth the time and energy required to make it work. Third, the necessary time for discourse and training becomes a priority for the local boards of education. Finally, from research and proven practices, powerful visions of what can be done must be delivered, through democratic organizations, to improve the schools. Ron Edmonds said, "We already know more than we need in order to do that." I would like to amend that statement by adding for emphasis, "we already know *more about what to do and how to do it* than we need in order to do that."

THE MAP

During the last decade the effective schools journey has followed a map of the correlates or characteristics of effective schools as they were identified in the original studies. These correlates have displayed a resiliency that amazed many. It is unlikely that any of the correlates will be found to be unimportant. However, two changes in the map for effective schools are likely to occur in the future. First, the research on effective schools is going to be joined even more closely with the effective teaching research, and the resulting syntheses are going to make it even clearer how mutually reinforcing and powerful these paradigms are as instruments for successful school transformations.

Second, the characteristics of effective schools are likely to evidence a significant growth in the 1990s. A number of the schools have been relying on the effective schools research as the framework for their school improvement program. After three or four years, many claim that they have successfully met the criteria described in the research on the correlates of effective schools. These educators ask if there is anything that comes after, or goes beyond, these standards. The concept of second-generation correlates attempts to incorporate the recent research and school improvement findings and offers an even more challenging developmental stage to which the schools committed to the "learning for all" mission ought to aspire.

There are two underlying assumptions to keep in mind. First, school improvement is an "endless journey." Second, the second-generation correlates cannot be successfully implemented unless the first-generation correlate standards are present in the school. In one sense, the second-generation correlates represent a developmental step beyond the first and, when successfully accomplished, will move the school even closer to the mission of *learning for all.*

Safe and Orderly Environment

THE FIRST GENERATION. In the effective school there is an orderly, purposeful, businesslike atmosphere that is free from the threat of physical harm. The school climate is not oppressive and is conducive to teaching and learning.

THE SECOND GENERATION. During the first generation, the safe and orderly environment correlate was defined in terms of the absence of undesirable student behavior (e.g., students fighting). In the second generation, increased emphasis will be placed on the presence of certain desirable behaviors (cooperative team learning). These second-generation schools will be places where students actually help one another.

Since schools as workplaces are characterized by their isolation, creating more collaborative/cooperative environments for both the adults and students will require substantial commitment and change in most schools. Several changes will be required. First, teachers will have to be taught the "technologies" of teamwork. Second, the school will have to create the "opportunity structures" for collaboration. Finally, the staff will have to nurture the belief that collaboration, which often requires more time initially, will help the schools be more effective and satisfying in the long run.

But schools will not be able to get students to work together cooperatively unless they have been taught to respect human diversity and appreciate democratic values. These student learnings will require a major and sustained commitment to multicultural education.

Climate of High Expectations for Success

THE FIRST GENERATION. In the effective school there is a climate of expectation in which the staff believes and demonstrates that all students can attain mastery of the essential school skills, and they believe that they have the capability to help all students achieve that mastery.

THE SECOND GENERATION. During the second generation, the emphasis placed on high expectations for success will be significantly broadened. In the first generation, expectations were described in terms of attitudes and beliefs that suggested how the teacher should behave in the teaching-learning situation. Those descriptions sought to tell teachers how they should initially deliver the lesson. High expectations meant, for example, that the teacher should evenly distribute question-asking to all students and provide each student with a more equal opportunity to participate in the learning process. Unfortunately, this "equalization of opportunity," though beneficial, proved to be insufficient to assure mastery for many of the learners. Teachers found themselves in the difficult position of having had high expectations and having acted upon them and still finding that some students did not learn.

In the second generation, the teachers will anticipate this and they will develop a broader array of responses. For example, teachers will implement additional strategies such as reteaching and regrouping to assure that all students do learn to achieve mastery. Implementing this expanded concept of high expectations will require the school, as a cultural organizational system, to reflect high expectations, since most of the useful strategies will require the cooperation of the school as a whole. Teachers cannot implement most of these strategies working alone in isolated classrooms. High expectations for success will be judged not only by the initial staff beliefs and behaviors but also by the organization's response when some students do not learn.

Instructional Leadership

THE FIRST GENERATION. In the effective school, the principal acts as an instructional leader and effectively and persistently communicates that mission to the staff, parents, and students. The principal understands and applies the characteristics of instructional effectiveness in the management of the instructional program.

THE SECOND GENERATION. In the first generation, the standards for instructional leadership focused primarily on the principal and the administrative staff of the school. In the second generation, instructional leadership will remain important; however, the concept will be broadened and leadership will be viewed as a dispersed concept that includes all adults, especially the teachers. This is in keeping with the teacher-empowerment concept and recognizes that principals cannot be the only leader in a complex organization like a school. With the democratization of the organizations, especially the schools, the leadership function becomes one of creating a "community of shared values." The role of the principal will be changed from that of a "leader of followers" to that of "a leader of leaders." Specifically, the broader concept of leadership recognizes that leadership is always delegated from the followership in any organization. It also recognizes what teachers have known for a long time and good schools have capitalized on since the beginning of time; namely, expertise is generally dispersed across many, not concentrated in a single person.

Clear and Focused Mission

THE FIRST GENERATION. In the effective school there is a clearly articulated school mission through which the staff shares accountability and an understanding of and commitment to the instructional goals, priorities, and assessment procedures. Staff accept responsibility for students' learning of the school's essential curricular goals.

THE SECOND GENERATION. In the first generation, the effective school mission emphasized teaching for learning for all, with two issues coming to the fore. First, did this really mean all students or just those with whom the schools had a history of reasonable success? When it became clear that this mission was inclusive of all students, especially the children of the poor (minority and nonminority), the second issue surfaced. It centered itself around the question: Learn what? Partially because of the accountability movement and partially because of the belief that disadvantaged students could not learn higher-level curricula, the focus was on mastery of mostly low-level skills. In the next generation, the focus will shift toward a more appropriate balance between higher-level learnings and those more basic skills that are truly prerequisite to their mastery.

Finally, a subtle but significant change in the concept of school mission deserves notice. Throughout the first generation, effective schools proponents advocated the mission of "teaching for learning for all." In the second generation, the advocated mission will be "learning for all." The rationale for this change is that the "teaching for" portion of the old statement created ambiguity (although this was unintended) and kept too much of the focus on "teaching" rather than "learning." This allowed people to discount school learnings that were not the result of direct teaching. Finally, the new formulation of "learning for all" opens the door to the continued learning of the educators as well as the students.

Opportunity to Learn and Student Time on Task

THE FIRST GENERATION. In the effective school, teachers allocate a significant amount of classroom time to instruction in the essential skills. For a high percentage of this time, students are engaged in whole-class or large-group, teacher-directed, planned learning activities.

THE SECOND GENERATION. In the second generation, time will continue to be a difficult problem for the teacher. As a matter of fact, in all likelihood, the problems that occur with too much to teach and not enough time to teach it will intensify. In the past, when the teachers were oriented toward "covering curricular content" and more content was added, they knew what to do in response—"speed up." Now teachers are being asked to stress the mission that assures student mastery of the content covered. How are they to respond?

In the next generation, teachers will have to become more skilled at interdisciplinary curriculum, and they will need to learn how to practice "organized abandonment" comfortably. They must be able to ask the question "What goes and what stays?" One reason that many of the mandated approaches to school reform have failed is that in every case, the local school was asked to do more! One of the characteristics of the most effective schools is their willingness to declare that some things are more important than others and to abandon some less important content so as to dedicate enough time to those areas that are valued the most.

The only alternative to abandonment would be to adjust the available time that students spend in school so that those who need more time to reach mastery would be given it. The necessary time must be provided in a quality program that is not perceived as punitive by those in it or excessive by those who will have to fund it. These conditions will be a real challenge indeed!

If the American dream and the democratic ideal of educating everyone is going to move forward, we must explore several important policies and past practices. For example, on the issue of time to learn, if the children of the disadvantaged present a "larger educational task" to teachers and if it can be demonstrated that this "larger task" will require more time, then our notion of limited compulsory schooling may need to be changed. The current system of compulsory schooling makes little allowance for the fact that some students need more time. If we could get the system to be more mastery-based and more humane at the same time, our nation and its students would benefit immensely.

Frequent Monitoring of Student Progress

THE FIRST GENERATION. In the effective school, students' academic progress is measured frequently. A variety of assessment procedures are used. The results of the assessments are used to improve individual student performance and also to improve the instructional program.

THE SECOND GENERATION. In the first generation. the correlate was interpreted to mean that the teachers should frequently monitor their students' learning and, where necessary, the teacher should adjust his or her behavior. Several major changes can be anticipated in the second generation. First, the use of technology will permit the teachers to do a better job of monitoring their students' progress. Second, this same technology will allow students to monitor their own learning and, where necessary, adjust their own behavior. The use of computerized practice tests, the ability to get immediate results on their homework, and the ability to see correct solutions developed on the screen are a few of the available "tools for assuring student learning."

Another major change that will become more apparent in the second generation is already underway. In the area of assessment the emphasis will continue to shift away from standardized norm-referenced paper-and-pencil measures and toward curricular-based, criterion-referenced assessments of student mastery. In the second generation, the monitoring of student learning will emphasize "more authentic assessments" of curriculum mastery. This generally means that there will be a decreased emphasis on the paper-and-pencil, multiple-choice tests and an increased emphasis on assessments that take the form of products of student work, including performances and portfolios. Teachers will pay much more attention to the alignment that must exist between the intended, taught, and tested curriculum.

Two new questions are being stimulated by the reform movement and will dominate much of professional educators' discourse in the second generation. The two important questions are: "What's worth knowing?" and "How will we know when they know it?" In all likelihood the answer to the first question will become clear relatively quickly because we can reach agreement that we want our students to be self-disciplined, socially responsible, and just. The problem comes with the second question "How will we know when they know it?" Educators and citizens are going to have to come to terms with that question. The bad news is that the question demands our best thinking and will require patience if we are going to reach consensus. The good news is that once we reach something of a consensus, the schools will be able to deliver significant progress toward these agreed-upon outcomes.

Home–School Relations

THE FIRST GENERATION. In the effective school, parents understand and support the school's basic mission and are given the opportunity to play an important role in helping the school achieve this mission.

THE SECOND GENERATION. During the first generation, the role of parents in the education of their children was always somewhat unclear. Schools often gave "lip service" to the desire to have parents more actively involved in the schooling of their children. Unfortunately, when pressed, many educators were willing to admit that they really did not know how to deal effectively with increased levels of parent involvement in the schools.

In the second generation, the relationship between parents and the school must reflect an authentic partnership. In the past when teachers said they wanted more parent involvement, more often than not they were looking for unqualified support from the parents. Many teachers believed that the parents knew how to get their children to behave in the ways that the school desired if they truly valued education. It is now clear to both teachers and parents that the parent involvement issue is not that simple. What is clear is that parents are often as perplexed as the teachers regarding the best way to inspire students to learn what the school teaches. The best hope for effectively confronting the problem—and not each other—is to *build* enough trust and enough communication to realize that both have the same goal—the effective school and home for all children!

SUMMARY

School improvement is like a journey. As with any journey, one needs to choose the destination, select the means of transportation, and select a map to follow as a guide. The concept and supporting effective schools research are especially well suited for the school improvement journey. In using the effective schools framework, the destination is both clear and compelling—learning for all. That destination speaks about "equity in quality" for all students. The means of transportation to this destination is equally clear and just as compelling. The process calls for a collaborative school-based team empowered with the right and responsibility to take the school from wherever it is and bring it closer to the mission of learning for all. Finally, we have the large and evolving body of effective schools research, the process of disaggregating student outcome data, and the assessment of school environments for the presence or absence and the strength or weakness of the effective schools characteristics. This is indeed a detailed and compelling map to guide the school teams' efforts on their journey to school improvement.

Successful school improvement based on the effective schools framework, like the effective school itself, is the outcome of a change strategy implemented through the efforts of many individuals. It requires commitment and time. It also represents the collective interests and commitment of a "community of shared values."

Creating more effective schools through the effective schools framework will only occur in those schools and districts in which the necessary patience, persistence, pride, and partnership are evident. The future belongs to those educators who have the vision of educating all children and the courage to act on that vision. The exhilaration that will be felt by those who dare to act will more than compensate for the risk taking such actions require.

- CLIMATE
- EXPECTATIONS
- MOTIVATION
- ORGANIZATION/ MANAGEMENT (SCHOOL)

Invitational Education

William W. Purkey
University of North Carolina, Greensboro

Invitational education has a much wider focus of application than is typically discussed in other self-theories. It is deliberately aimed at broader goals than students and their achievement alone. It is geared to the total development of all who interact within the school. It is concerned with more than grades, attendance, and even perceptions of self. It is concerned with the skills of becoming (Stafford, 1990, p. 5).

Invitational education (Purkey & Novak, 1984, 1988; Purkey & Stanley, 1991) is a theory of practice designed to create a total school environment that intentionally summons school people to realize their relatively boundless potential. Invitational education addresses the global nature of schools, the entire gestalt. Its purpose is to make schooling a more exciting, satisfying, and enriching experience for everyone involved in the educative process. Its method is to offer a guiding theory, a common language of improvement, and a practical means to accomplish its stated purpose.

The term "invitational education" was chosen because the two words have special meaning. The English word *invite* is probably a derivative of the Latin word *invitare*, which means to offer something beneficial for consideration. Translated literally, *invitare* means to summon cordially, not to shun. The word *education* comes from the Latin word *educare*, which means to call forth something potential or latent. Literally, invitational education is the process by which people are cordially summoned to realize their relatively boundless potential in all areas of worthwhile human endeavor. Implicit in this definition is that invitational education is an ethical process involving continuous democratic interactions among and between human beings.

Figure 16.1 highlights the major qualities of invitational education. It will be helpful to keep this diagram in mind as invitational education's foundations, assumptions, areas, levels, and dimensions are introduced.

THE FOUNDATIONS OF INVITATIONAL EDUCATION

Invitational education is based on two interlocking foundations: the perceptual tradition and self-concept theory. These two perspectives, supported by decades of scholarly research and writing, give invitational education its substance and structure.

THE PERCEPTUAL TRADITION

In invitational education, a most important question is "What is the fit between educators' perceptions and students' perceptions?" The perceptual tradition (Combs, 1962) maintains

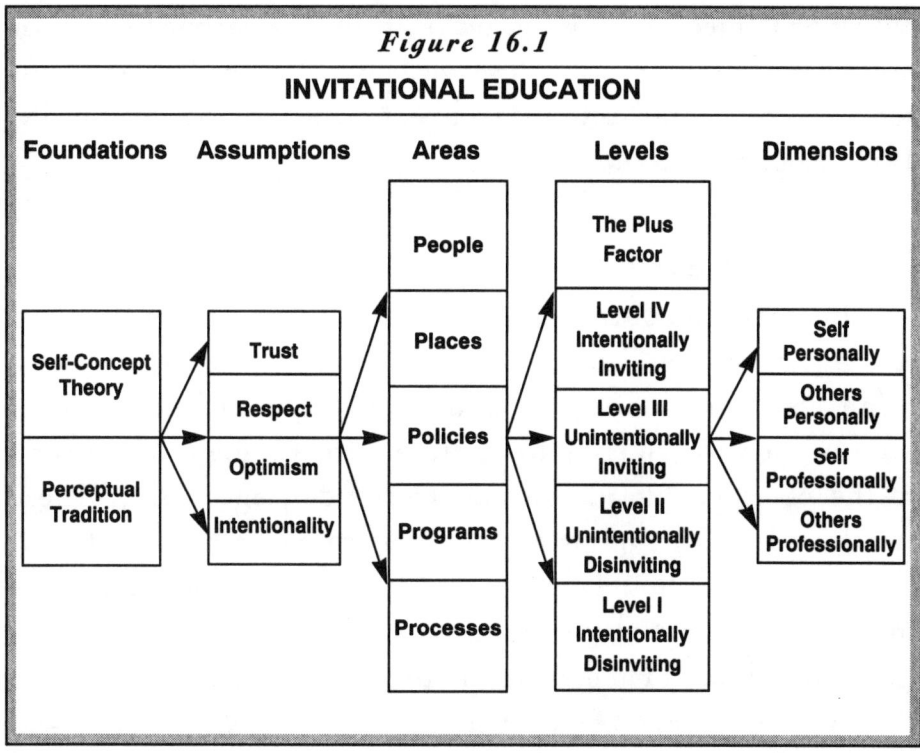

Figure 16.1
INVITATIONAL EDUCATION

that human behavior is the product of the unique ways that individuals view the world. The perceptual viewpoint places consciousness at the center of personality. It proposes that people are not influenced by events so much as by their *perceptions* of events.

SELF-CONCEPT THEORY

A second important question in invitational education is "Who am I and how do I fit in the world?" This question derives from the second foundation of invitational education: self-concept theory. Self-concept is a complex and dynamic system of learned beliefs that each person holds to be true about his or her personal existence. The theory maintains that behavior is mediated by the ways an individual views her- or himself and that these views serve as both antecedent and consequence of human activity (see, e.g., Jourard, 1968; Purkey, 1970, Rogers, 1969).

BASIC ASSUMPTIONS

Invitational education is unlike any other system reported in the professional literature in that it provides an overarching framework for a variety of educational approaches to school improvement. Invitational education offers a logical extension to the perceptual tradition and to self-concept theory. These two foundations, supported by a vast research literature, provide, in turn, a humanistic, person-centered rationale for the four basic assumptions of invitational education. These assumptions give invitational education purpose and direction and take the form of propositions reflecting *trust, respect, optimism,* and *intentionality.*

TRUST

Education is a cooperative activity where process is as important as product. A basic ingredient of invitational education is a recognition of the interdependence of human beings. Attempting to get others to do what is wanted without involving them in the process is a lost cause. Each individual is the highest authority on his or her personal existence. Given an optimally inviting environment, each person will find his or her own best ways of being and becoming.

RESPECT

People are able, valuable, and responsible and should be treated accordingly. An indispensable element in any successful school is shared responsibility based on mutual respect. This respect is manifested in the caring and appropriate behaviors exhibited by everyone in the school as well as in the places, policies, programs, and processes they create and maintain.

OPTIMISM

People possess untapped potential in all areas of human endeavor. The uniqueness of human beings is that no clear limits to potential have been discovered. Invitational education could not be seriously considered if optimism regarding human potential did not exist. It is not enough to be inviting; it is critical to be optimistic about the process. No one in a school—not a student, teacher, principal, counselor, parent, librarian, supervisor, or whoever—can choose a beneficial direction in life without hope that change for the better is possible. From an invitational education viewpoint, seeing people as possessing untapped potential determines the curricula devised, the policies established, the programs supported, the processes encouraged, the physical environments created, and the relationships established and maintained.

INTENTIONALITY

Human potential can best be realized by places, policies, processes, and programs specifically designed to invite development and by people who are personally and professionally inviting with themselves and others. An invitation is defined as an intentional act designed to offer something beneficial for consideration. Intentionality enables educators to create and maintain consistently caring and appropriate schools characterized by purpose and direction. It takes intentionality to consistently and dependably invite the realization of human potential. Intentionality is so important in invitational education that it receives special attention later in this chapter under "levels" of functioning.

These four essential propositions of invitational education—*trust, respect, optimism, and intentionality*—offer a consistent "stance" through which educators and others can create and maintain an optimally inviting environment. While there are other elements that contribute to invitational education, these propositions are key ingredients.

THE FIVE AREAS

Invitational education focuses on five areas that exist in every school and that contribute to the success or failure of each student (Figure 16.2). In the same way that everyone and everything in hospitals should invite health, so everyone and everything in every school setting should democratically and ethically invite the realization of human potential. This involves the people, places, policies, programs, and processes. These five P's make up the educational ecosystem in which individuals continuously interact.

PEOPLE

While everything in life adds to or detracts from success or failure, nothing is more important in life than people. It is the people who create a respectful, optimistic, trusting, and intentional society.

PLACES

The physical environment of the school offers a starting point in invitational education, because places are so visible. Almost anyone can recognize smelly restrooms, cluttered offices, peeling paint, or unkempt buildings. Fortunately, places

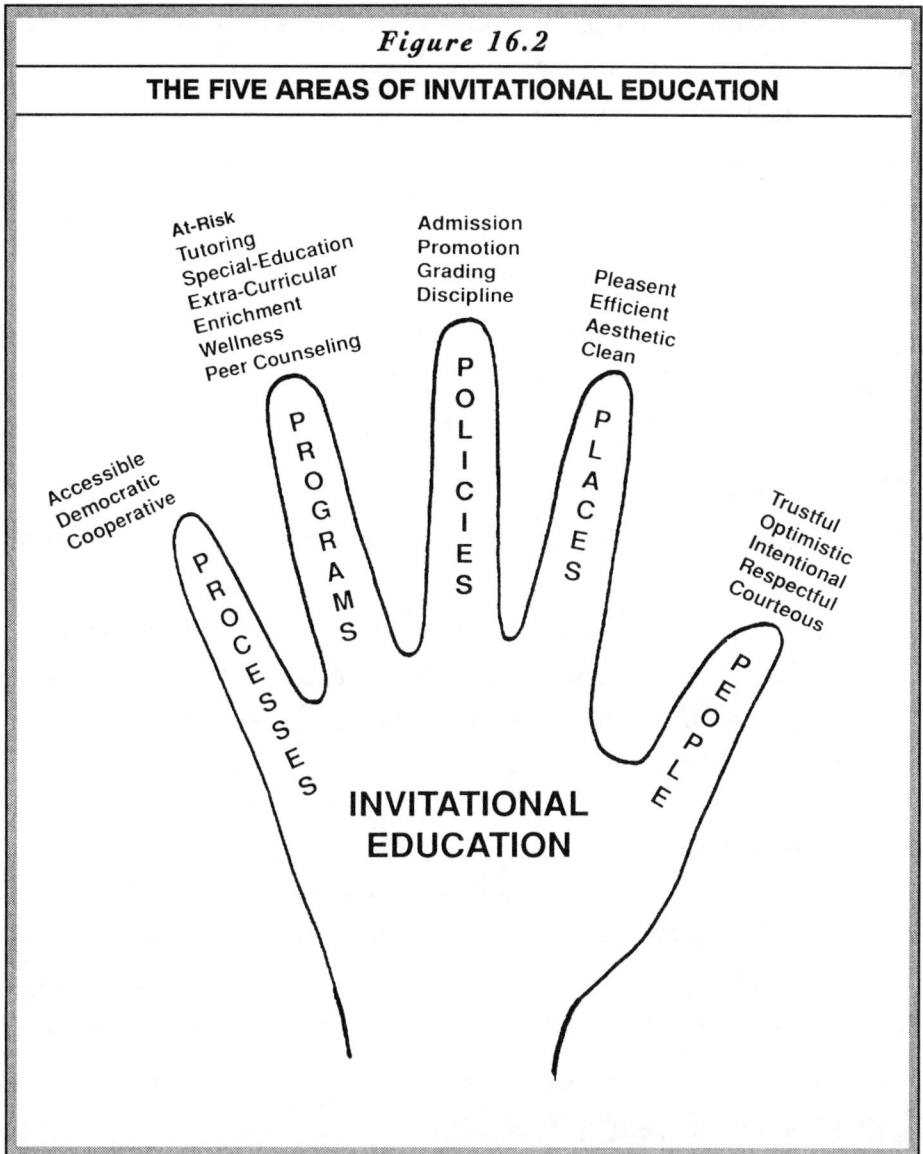

Figure 16.2

THE FIVE AREAS OF INVITATIONAL EDUCATION

are the easiest to change because they are the most visible element in any school environment. They also offer the opportunity for immediate improvement.

POLICIES

Policies refer to the procedures, codes, and rules, written or unwritten, used to regulate the ongoing functions of individuals and organizations. Ultimately, the policies created and maintained communicate a strong message regarding the value, ability, and responsibility of people.

PROGRAMS

Programs have an important part to play in invitational education because in many schools they focus on narrow goals that neglect the wider scope of human needs. For example, programs that label people can influence self-perceptions that negate the positive purposes for which these programs were originally created.

PROCESSES

The final P, processes, addresses the ways the other four P's function. Processes address such issues as cooperative spirit, democratic activities, collaborative efforts, ethical guidelines, and humane activities. They focus on how the other P's are conducted.

LEVELS OF FUNCTIONING

In addition to building on the perceptual tradition and self-concept theory and centering itself on trust, respect, optimism, and intentionality, invitational education identifies levels of functioning. Being human, everyone functions at each level from time to time, but it is the level at which one typically functions that determines one's approach to life and one's success in personal and professional living. To reach the highest levels of functioning requires intentionality and self-discipline.

It is useful here to contemplate the complexity of invitational education. Many educators think they already understand the concept of "inviting." They see it as simply doing nice things — sharing a smile, giving a hug, saying something nice, or buying a gift. But invitational education is far more than giving "warm fuzzies," sharing "strokes," forming "hug stations," or walking around with IALAC ("*I Am Lovable And Capable*") newsprint. While these may be worthwhile activities when used caringly and appropriately, they are only manifestations of a theoretical "stance" one takes. This stance determines the level of personal and professional functioning. The following levels provide a check system to monitor each of the five P's (people, places, policies, programs, and processes) found in and around any school.

INTENTIONALLY DISINVITING

The most negative and toxic level of human functioning involves those actions, policies, programs, places, and processes that are deliberately designed to demean, dissuade, discourage, defeat, and destroy. A classical example of intentionally disinviting behavior in action may be seen in the play *Amadeus*. It is Salieri who is intentionally disinviting — with great destructive skill — to Mozart.

In the educational setting, intentionally disinviting functioning might be seen in a teacher who is purposely insulting, a school policy that is intentionally discriminatory, a program that purposely demeans students, or an environment intentionally left unpleasant and unattractive. An illustration of intentionally disinviting functioning was provided by a high school teacher.

> After attending a workshop in invitational education, this teacher sent a note to the principal pointing out that the girls' bathroom needed soap, paper towels, and tissue. Her note was returned to her mailbox at the end of the day with this remark written across the bottom: "What do you think this place is—the Hilton?"

With such an intentionally disinviting stance, is it any wonder that teachers in this particular school are so apathetic and students so unruly?

UNINTENTIONALLY DISINVITING

People, places, policies, programs, and processes that are intentionally disinviting are few compared with those that are unintentionally disinviting. The great majority of disinviting forces that exist in and around schools are the result of a lack of stance. Because there is no philosophy of trust, respect, optimism, and intentionality, school policies are established, programs designed, places arranged, processes evolve, and people behave in ways that are clearly disinviting although such was not the intent.

Schools that typically function at the unintentionally disinviting level spend a lot of time wondering: "Why do we have such a high dropout rate?"; "Why are the teachers so unhappy in this school?"; "Why are our SAT scores so low?"; "Why do we have so many discipline problems?" Educators who function at the unintentionally disinviting level are often viewed as uncaring, chauvinistic, condescending, patronizing, sexist, racist, dictatorial, or just plain thoughtless. They do not intend to be hurtful or harmful, but because they lack consistency in direction and purpose, they act in unintentionally disinviting ways.

Examples of unintentionally disinviting forces at work can be seen in almost any school. The sign that reads "No One Allowed in School Before 8:15 A.M." (although the temperature is below zero); the policy of reserving the best parking space for the principal; the tendency to answer the office phone with a curt "Jackson Junior," or teachers who consistently kick students "in the but" ("This is a good paper, Mary, *but* . . ."). Educators who function at the unintentionally disinviting level do not intend to be disinviting, but the damage is done. Like being run over by a truck, intended or not, the victim is still dead.

UNINTENTIONALLY INVITING

Educators who usually function at the unintentionally inviting level have stumbled serendipitously onto ways of functioning that are often effective. However, they encounter difficulty when asked to explain *why* they are successful. They can describe in loving detail *what* they do but not *why* they do it.

An illustration of unintentionally inviting functioning might be seen in "natural-born" teachers. They may be successful in teaching because they exhibit many of the trusting, respecting, and optimistic qualities associated with invitational education. However, because they lack the fourth critical element, intentionality, they lack consistency and dependability in the actions they exhibit, the policies and programs they establish, and the places and processes they create and maintain.

Young educators often function at the unintentionally inviting level. While they are likeable, entertaining, enthusiastic, and graduate just in time to save education, they lack intentionality regarding why they are doing what they do. These teachers are somewhat akin to the early barnstorming airplane pilots. Pioneer pilots did not know exactly why their planes flew, what caused weather patterns, or much about navigational systems. As long as they stayed close to the ground, followed a railway track, and the weather was clear, they were able to function. But when the weather turned bad or night fell, they became disoriented. In difficult situations, those who function at the unintentionally inviting level lack dependability in behavior and consistency in direction.

The basic weakness in functioning at the unintentionally inviting level is the inability to identify the reasons for success or failure. Most people know whether something is working or not, but when it stops working, they are puzzled about how to start it up again. Those who function at the unintentionally inviting level lack a consistent stance—a dependable position from which to operate.

INTENTIONALLY INVITING

When educators function at the intentionally inviting level they seek to consistently exhibit the assumptions of invitational education. Intentionality can be a tremendous asset for educators, for it is a constant reminder of what is truly important in education.

A beautiful example of intentionality in action is presented by Mizer (1964), who described how schools can function to turn a child "into a zero." Mizer illustrated the tragedy of one such child, then concluded her article with these words (p. 10):

> I look up and down the rows carefully each September at the unfamiliar faces. I look for veiled eyes or bodies scrounged into an alien world. "Look, Kids," I say silently, "I may not do anything else for you this year, but not one of you is going to come out of here a

nobody. I'll work or fight to the bitter end doing battle with society and the school board, but I won't have one of you coming out of here thinking of himself as a zero."

In invitational education, *everybody* and *everything* adds to, or subtracts from, connecting with students. Ideally, the factors of people, places, policies, programs, and processes should be so intentionally inviting as to create a world where each individual is cordially summoned to develop physically, intellectually, and emotionally. Those who accept the assumptions of invitational education not only strive to be intentionally inviting but also, once there, continue to grow and develop, to reach for the "Plus Factor."

THE PLUS FACTOR

When people watch the accomplished musician, the headline comedian, the world-class athlete, or the master teacher, what he or she does seems simple. It is only when people try to do it themselves that they realize that true art requires painstaking care, discipline, and deliberate planning.

At its best, invitational education becomes "invisible" because it becomes a means of addressing humanity. To borrow the words of Chuang-tse, an ancient Chinese philosopher, "It flows like water, reflects like a mirror, and responds like an echo." When the educator reaches this special plateau of invitational education, what he or she does appears effortless. Football teams call it "momentum," comedians call it "feeling the center," world-class athletes call it "finding the zone," fighter pilots call it "rhythm." In invitational education it is called the Plus Factor.

A good example of this factor in action was provided by Ginger Rogers, the famous actress and dancer. When describing dancing with Fred Astair, she said, "It's a lot of hard work, that I do know." Someone responded: "But it doesn't look it, Ginger." Ginger replied, "That's why it's magic."

Educators who function at the highest levels of inviting become so fluent that the carefully honed skills and techniques they employ are invisible to the untrained eye. They function with such talented assurance that the tremendous effort involved does not call attention to itself. At its best, invitational education requires implicit, rather than explicit, expression.

DIMENSIONS

The goal of invitational education is to encourage educators to enrich their lives in each of four basic dimensions: (1) being personally inviting with oneself, (2) being personally inviting with others, (3) being professionally inviting with oneself, and (4) being professionally inviting with others. Like pistons in a finely tuned engine, the four dimensions work together to give power to the whole movement. While there are times when one of the four dimensions may demand special attention, the overall goal is to seek balance and harmony between personal and professional functioning.

BEING PERSONALLY INVITING WITH ONESELF

To be a beneficial presence in the lives of students, it is essential that educators first invite themselves. This means that they view themselves as able, valuable, and responsible and are open to experience. Educators who adopt the invitational education model seek to reinvent and respirit themselves personally.

Being personally inviting with oneself takes an endless variety of forms. It means caring for one's mental health and making appropriate choices in life. By taking up a new hobby, relaxing with a good book, exercising regularly, learning to laugh more, visiting friends, getting sufficient sleep, growing a garden, or managing time wisely, educators can rejuvenate their own well-being.

BEING PERSONALLY INVITING WITH OTHERS

Being inviting requires that the feelings, wishes, and aspirations of others be taken into account. Without this, invitational education could not exist. In practical terms, this means that the social committee might be the most vital committee in any school.

Specific ways to be personally inviting with others are simple but often overlooked. Getting to know colleagues on a social basis, sending friendly notes, forming a car pool, remembering birthdays, enjoying a faculty party, practicing politeness, and celebrating successes are all examples of invitational education in action.

BEING PROFESSIONALLY INVITING WITH ONESELF

Being professionally inviting with oneself can take a variety of forms, but it begins with ethical awareness, a clear and efficient perception of situations and oneself. In practical terms, being professionally inviting with oneself means trying a new teaching method, seeking certification, learning new skills, returning to graduate school, enrolling in a workshop, attending conferences, reading journals, writing for publication, and making presentations at conferences.

Invitational education requires that educators not "rust" on their laurels. Keeping alive professionally is particularly important for educators because of the rapidly expanding knowledge base regarding teaching and learning. Perhaps never before in North American education have knowledge, techniques, and methods been so bountiful. Canoes must be paddled harder than ever just to keep up with the knowledge explosion. Invitational education involves not only encounters with students in caring and appropriate ways. It also involves the educator's relationship with the content of what is being taught.

BEING PROFESSIONALLY INVITING WITH OTHERS

The final dimension of invitational education is being professionally inviting with others. This involves such qualities as treating people not as labels or groups but as individuals. It also requires honesty and the ability to accept less-than-perfect behavior.

In everyday practice, being professionally inviting with others requires careful attention to the policies introduced, the programs established, the places created, the processes manifested, and the behaviors exhibited. Among the countless ways that educators can be professionally inviting with others are to have high aspirations, fight sexism and racism in any form, work cooperatively, behave ethically, provide professional feedback, and maintain an optimistic stance.

Professionals who combine the four dimensions of invitational education into a seamless whole are well on their way to mastering invitational education. The successful educator is one who balances the four dimensions to sustain energy and enthusiasm for teaching, learning, and living.

How Invitational Education Works

The first part of this chapter has presented invitational education as a guiding theory of practice based on the perceptual tradition and self-concept theory. Invitational education offers a common language for school transformation involving trust, respect, optimism, and intentionality. It highlights areas, levels, and dimensions of functioning. The second part of this chapter demonstrates invitational education in action.

Invitational education has been applied in many diverse educational settings, including elementary and secondary schools, entire school systems, and higher education (Purkey & Schmidt, 1990). In addition, over 150 schools throughout the United States and Canada have received the "Inviting School Award" presented by the International Alliance for Invitational Education, centered at the University of North Carolina at Greensboro. A list of these schools may be obtained by contacting the Alliance.

It will be useful to take an in-depth look at one public junior high school in North Carolina where invitational education has been adopted: Douglas Byrd Junior High School, Cumberland County (NC). Because of its many challenges, Byrd was an excellent testing ground for invitational education.

DOUGLAS BYRD JUNIOR HIGH SCHOOL

In the Spring of 1990, Douglas Byrd Junior High School was the largest junior high school in Cumberland County and the seventh-largest junior high school in North Carolina. It was 59 percent Caucasian students, 34 percent African American, 4 percent Native American, 2 percent Hispanic, and 1 percent

Asian. Over 50 percent were on free or reduced lunch, 38 percent were listed under *Chapter 1*, and over 50 percent were classified as "at risk." Of the twelve Cumberland County Junior High Schools, Douglas Byrd had, as of June 1990, the highest dropout rate and the highest absentee rate and ranked among the bottom of the twelve schools in California Achievement Test scores.

Teachers and administrators at Byrd were dedicated professionals who had worked hard over the years but had indicated frustration at reaching at-risk youth by means of conventional classrooms. Administrators and support staff expressed great concern over the proportion of time spent on crisis intervention while striving to maintain standards of excellence. Parents voiced the desire to help but felt overwhelmed by the lack of other parents willing or able to engage themselves in the school. The professionals of Douglas Byrd in the spring of 1990 were dedicated but fatigued by the continued challenges and disappointments.

THE STAR PROJECT

The introduction of invitational education at Byrd Junior High School became possible, in part, by a grant from RJR Nabisco. In 1990 the company initiated the *Next Century Schools* program. The goal of RJR Nabisco was to stimulate bold, visionary, and sustainable change in public education.

The grant money enabled Byrd to organize two pilot classes called STAR—Students Together Achieving Recognition. This involved a "school-within-a-school" demonstration site for at-risk youth. The thirty-eight students in the STAR classes were recommended by their sixth-grade teachers. The students had a wide range of academic achievement levels, but their elementary teachers thought they might have difficulty in adapting to a large junior high school with over 1,300 students.

STAR was designed to help increase standardized test scores and reduce dropout rates not only for the two pilot classes but also for the whole school. The goal of STAR was to create a total school environment that enhances the abilities, strengths, and worth of everyone who lives and works at Douglas Byrd Junior High School.

Invitational education was chosen by the school personnel as the best model to facilitate a climate of shared decision making, and shared responsibility and a shared vision of school transformation. The hope was that the project would expand and impact on the entire school population not only of Byrd Junior High School but also of all of Cumberland County and beyond.

INTRODUCTION OF INVITATIONAL EDUCATION. When Douglas Byrd Junior High School received notification of their RJR Nabisco grant, the principal, STAR project director, and central office administrators contacted the author. They had concluded, after reviewing materials on numerous workable models and strategies ("The Comer Process," "Higher-Order Thinking Skills," "Learning Styles," and others), that invitational education offered their best hope of *systemically* transforming Douglas Byrd Junior High School.

In a series of meetings held during the summer of 1990, a team of educators from Byrd Junior High School met with the author to establish plans whereby invitational education could be adopted by Byrd Junior High. The plans included a one-day opening-of-school celebration involving Byrd educators, students, and parents; a leadership training program on invitational education at the University of North Carolina at Greensboro; and a continuing series of small-group workshops to be held at Byrd.

THE OPENING-OF-SCHOOL CELEBRATION. In August of 1990 all Byrd teachers and staff, six invitational education consultants, and representative groups of Byrd parents and students gathered at a Fayetteville hotel for a full-day in-service. It was considered important to get everyone away from Byrd in order to "break the mold" of traditional thinking. At this meeting all participants were introduced to the concept of invitational education, given a *Phi Delta Kappa Fastback* describing *Invitational Education* (Purkey & Novak, 1988), and divided equally into five "P strands" (People, Places, Policies, Programs, and Processes).

Each strand was facilitated by a consultant on invitational education who specialized in a particular strand. Each of the five strands considered three questions that related to its particular P: (1) What are we doing well already? (2) What could we do better? and (3) How do we do it? The day also featured entertainment by Byrd faculty and lunch at the hotel.

Strands listed their ideas on newsprint and presented their thoughts to the entire group. These were typed up, duplicated, and served as an initial action plan. Each strand and its invitational education consultant formed a team that worked together at intervals throughout the school year.

LEADERSHIP TRAINING AT UNCG. In addition to ongoing small group workshops at Byrd Junior High School conducted by invitational education consultants with their strands, five leaders of each strand traveled to Greensboro for a full-day training session. This session employed the "Five P Relay." The relay involved (1) placing participants in their P groups, (2) having each group set five clearly defined "do-able" goals, (3) circulating their goals through the other four groups, who identified possible obstacles and ways to overcome them, and (4) returning the list of goals, obstacles, and ways to overcome obstacles to the original P group. Each of the five groups then developed an action plan. The Five P Relay allowed everyone to have input and accept ownership for all five P's.

CONTINUING IN-SERVICE WORKSHOPS AT BYRD. At intervals throughout the 1990–91 school year, the five P strands came together with their invitational education consultants to work on their school improvement projects. These projects focused on such areas as classroom discipline, cooperative learning, teaming, and student evaluation. Regardless of focus, the guiding theory and common language were always that of invitational education. Invitational education was the glue that held everything together.

END-OF-YEAR SUCCESS PICNIC. A faculty picnic concluded the 1990–91 school year with singing, games, and hoopla. The picnic was preceded by a closing two-hour seminar at which the five invitational education consultants shared their impressions of what had happened during the school year.

ABSTRACT OF EXTERNAL EVALUATION

The major findings of the invitational education component of the STAR Project for 1990–91 were gathered by an external consultant working under contract with the STAR Project at Douglas Byrd Junior High School. The complete evaluation reports for 1990–91 and 1991–92 may be obtained by contacting the STAR Project, Douglas Byrd Junior High School, Cumberland County Schools, Fayetteville, NC 28304.

Findings were summarized under the 5-P Format of invitational education: People, Places, Programs, Policies, and Processes. Here are some of the results:

People
: Teacher average daily attendance showed significant improvement.

    Student average daily attendance showed significant improvement.

    Parent attendance at PTA meetings increased 100 percent.

    Teacher/student recognition programs were initiated.

Places
: Significant improvements were made in physical environment.

    Significant increase in student use of the library was achieved.

    Two new faculty workrooms were opened and a chain-link fence was removed from breezeways.

    Special tables for faculty were added in Byrd cafeteria.

Programs
: Number of dropouts at Byrd decreased by 44 percent.

    California Achievement Test (CAT) scores improved significantly.

    PSAT scores of ninth graders showed a significant improvement in most areas.

    Fifteen partnerships with civic groups were arranged.

	Fourteen student assemblies were held, compared to two in 1989–90.
Policies	Nine students received long-term suspensions, compared to fifteen in 1989–90.
	Short-term suspensions decreased from ninety-seven to eighty.
	144 students were retained at grade level, compared to 157 in 1989–90.
Processes	3,099 hours were committed to staff development, compared to 220 in 1989–90.
	Evaluations on Adjective Checklists, *Wayson School Climate and Context Inventory*, and STAR Project Year-End Assessment all indicated significant improvement in faculty and staff morale.

From all indications, the invitational education STAR Project was an overwhelming success. This success echoes the successes experienced at numerous other locations throughout the United States and is described by contributors to the ERIC/CAPS monograph *Invitational Learning for Counseling and Development* (Purkey & Schmidt, 1990). For example, in 1989 the governor of North Carolina recognized East Davison High School, Thomasville (NC), by arriving on the high school lawn by helicopter and praising the Invitational School for cutting its dropout rate in half.

THE FUTURE

This chapter has introduced invitational education and explained the process of inviting school success. It described the total school environment, consisting of people, places, policies, programs, and processes and demonstrated how invitational education can influence each of these. While creating inviting schools is no easy task, they can be created and maintained by educators who are committed to making their schools "the most inviting place in town."

Increasingly, invitational education is finding its way into health care facilities, management workplaces, and parenting. Wherever it goes, it carries the basic message that human potential, while not always evident, is always there, waiting to be discovered and invited forth. Equally important, invitational education offers a concrete, practical, and successful way to accomplish its stated purposes.

- ASSESSMENT
- CURRICULUM
- EXPECTATIONS
- ORGANIZATION/ MANAGEMENT (SCHOOL)

Outcome-based Education: From Instructional Reform to Paradigm Restructuring

William G. Spady
The High Success Network, Inc.

Interest in what people are calling Outcome-based Education (OBE) is sweeping U.S. school districts and state capitals. Everyone is talking about student outcomes and the need for improving them. As always, this kind of school improvement imperative gets translated into a variety of state policy actions, and, in this case, state policy initiatives that mention or even imply the words "Outcome-based" are getting enormous attention.

To those of us who have been heavily involved with various aspects of this concept for the past twenty years or so, this flood of attention represents a mixed blessing. One's optimistic self says: "It's about time! People are finally paying attention to the power and potential in this concept. Let's get on with helping them do it well!" But then one's pessimistic self replies: "Help? Help! Most of what they're calling OBE isn't *real OBE* at all, and the bandwagon is out of control. Is there no end to people's ability to confuse, distort, and misrepresent a perfectly sound concept?"

Well, both selves are accurate. There is enormous interest these days in the truly sound aspects of OBE among both state policy shapers and local educators. And in a great many cases, people do hold incredibly simplistic or distorted views of what OBE means and what to do about it.

In what follows, I hope to provide some clarification of these issues by focusing on three things: (1) OBE's fundamental meaning and defining features; (2) its evolution as a reform concept in K-12 education over the past twenty-five years; and (3) the state of the advances that are being made within the OBE movement in the United States.

THE FUNDAMENTALS OF THE OBE CONCEPT

The term "Outcome-based" is very straightforward. Outcome-based means OUTCOME-based—not time-based, curriculum-based, or procedure-based with outcomes added on. It also means Outcome-BASED—not outcome-oriented, outcome-related, or outcome-like while everything else is going on as usual.

KEY OPERATIONAL FEATURES

When you put the terms outcomes and based together, you get a concept that has the following distinguishing features and implications:

1. OUTCOMES are the starting point and bottom line of everything that happens in an educational system. Defining what you want all students to know, be able to

do, and be like as the consequence of their learning experiences precedes any other program design, delivery, or evaluation process. Unless and until you have clearly defined and described what you want successful student learning to look like, there is no rationale for putting any other program component or strategy in place.

2. BASED means that focus, priorities, planning, design, organization, decision making, delivery, and evaluation all emanate from one fundamental source. That source is the successful learning results you are seeking. When a system does in fact become outcome-BASED, the calendar, the schedule, the clock, the age of the students, the name of the program, the pages in the textbook, the name of the course or program, the curriculum, the testing program, the bell-curve, past practices, the Carnegie Unit, and a host of other organizational features of schools as we know them cease to be the reason why or when things are done.

3. Schools define and clearly communicate to students and parents the performance criteria and standards that represent the intended learning and outcomes expected of all students in all areas of study. Assessment and grading are carefully matched to (i.e., aligned with) these criteria, and every student is eligible for high marks provided that he or she meets or exceeds the criteria.

4. Program design is carried out backwards; that is, staff begin at the point where they want students' learning to ultimately peak or culminate, and they consistently, systematically, and creatively design the essential learning

experiences for that to happen successfully back (or "down") from there. When culminating demonstrations (i.e., outcomes) are complex, design almost inevitably takes on an interdisciplinary character.

5. Time is thought of and treated as a flexible resource rather than as a predefined and inflexible absolute. This approach to time and learning opportunities supports the fundamental tenet of OBE that differences in students' learning rates rather than inherent limitations in their ability to learn account for major differences in learning success. Therefore, OBE teachers use a variety of flexible-time/multiple-opportunity strategies that are based on the notion that one single/fixed/prescheduled/routine opportunity to learn impedes optimum performance in virtually all students and puts instruction on an assembly-line schedule that cannot possibly be responsive to differences in student prerequisite learning and aptitudes. Thus, features like extending opportunities to learn and giving credit for it after fixed marking periods are over and grading in pencil are common features of OBE schools and classrooms.

6. Specialized programs and curriculum tracks for students deemed to be exceptional in one way or another are few and far between. This reflects a strong assumption on the part of OBE practitioners that is borne out in their expectations for students and the results they get: namely, that almost all students are capable of learning well what the "most-able" students learn sooner than others. Consequently, different courses, tracks, and programs serve no purpose if all the students are

essentially capable of learning the best things in the curriculum, and *you want them to.* Consequently, all kinds of strategies abound for expanding student opportunities to succeed at high levels of challenge and to receive grades commensurate with their eventual achievements.

7. Related to these issues of grouping, tracking, and opportunities for success are marked alterations in typical patterns of grading, offering credit, reporting progress, and advancing students through a program of study. These arrangements fall into a category called performance validation (rather than evaluation), whose prime, all-American example is Boy Scout and Girl Scout merit badges. The notion, which parallels various forms of professional licensure, is that students receive formal acknowledgement for meeting clearly defined standards and criteria successfully whenever those standards are met. Time and relative lack of success while learning to reach the high standard are usually discounted. The principle that this set of issues embodies is that clear, high standards (i.e., culminating outcomes) can be met by all students, so formal recognition should be tied directly to them, not to the calendar.

Although previously published work on OBE (Levine, 1985; Spady, 1981, 1989), as well as our current unpublished work in the High Success Program, clearly suggests that other aspects of a full-blown OBE implementation could be enumerated, these seven characteristics by themselves signal a radical departure from the time-based/calendar-driven model of practice that typifies today's (and yesterday's) educational system.

Using outcomes as *the* basis of program design, curriculum content and organization, instructional decision making, instructional processes and delivery patterns, student assessment, standard setting and grading, student grouping and advancement, and school operations and structures is a new and puzzling concept to both educators and policymakers. If you add to this list the implications of using time as a flexible resource and of eliminating the bell curve as a definer of competitive standards for success, the whole conceptual picture of traditional education goes up for grabs.

It is no wonder, then, that some educators and policymakers cannot make the necessary conceptual leap to view OBE in this proper light, simply because their entire pattern of thinking about education is thoroughly grounded in time-based, curriculum-based, and procedure-based examples and experiences. Consequently, what they attempt to do—and this typifies a great many state "reform" initiatives that use the term *outcomes* somewhere in their language—is to tack outcome requirements onto the system as it now exists rather than address the needed changes in the system itself. That is what I meant earlier in using the terms *outcome-related* and *outcome-oriented*. People want to address and achieve outcomes, but they do not know how to conceive or operationalize a system that is truly *outcome-based* in character.

What is missing from their attempts, many of us have found, is a framework for viewing schooling and learning in a different light; one that is grounded on different assumptions than those underlying the policies and practices that most of us have grown accustomed to, and one that operates according to a different set of principles and priorities than do our current schools. This framework, we have discovered, is relatively simple. It consists of three major premises (i.e., starting points and assumptions) and four key principles for decision making and action. Together, they account for the seven operational features just described and for many rapidly evolving ideas about profound school reform and restructuring that are surfacing within the circle of OBE implementers nationally.

OBE'S MAJOR PREMISES

Although there are minor variations in use within the OBE community, most district OBE implementation efforts clearly articulate the following three premises as literal statements of philosophy and commitment:

ALL STUDENTS CAN LEARN AND SUCCEED

SUCCESS BREEDS SUCCESS

SCHOOLS CONTROL THE CONDITIONS OF SUCCESS

Let us consider them one at a time.

ALL STUDENTS CAN LEARN AND SUCCEED. This first premise is about learners. Its language conveys a message that traditional educators and public citizens often find difficult to accept: namely, that all students have the ability to learn the best of what we have to teach, *but not on the same day in the same way.* This latter condition is directly implied in the premise, but I find that it catches most people by surprise whenever it is stated. What this condition points out is how routinely we assume that "on the same day in the same way" is the natural order of things. In virtually no classroom of students will one find all of them capable of achieving a given thing on the same day at a high level of performance, simply because their backgrounds for learning it, their inclination to learn it, and their rate of learning it will certainly not be identical. With that we have no argument, except to say that through systematic interventions built around OBE's four "power principles," students commonly labeled "at risk" and originally placed in low-level courses are now learning successfully in demanding academic high school courses. Notable examples will be presented in the next major section of the chapter.

The issue, then, comes down to whether one believes that *when* a student learns something is more important than *whether* he or she learns it successfully, or the reverse. OBE advocates endorse the latter option: "whether" is the given, and "when" becomes the variable. Conventional schooling places the premium on "when" and readily compromises on "whether."

SUCCESS BREEDS SUCCESS. OBE's second premise is about learning and the influence that previous learning success has on subsequent learning success. In essence, this premise is about what a lot of educators call "self-fulfilling prophecies." In this case, the prophecy has two mutually reinforcing sources, one cognitive and the other affective. The cognitive version implies that the stronger the learning background of the student, the easier it will be to learn related things successfully—hence, OBE's major emphasis on explicitly addressing prerequisite learning and assuring that it is sound. The affective version relates to a tight connection among performance, judgments received, self-concept, self-confidence, expectations of success, motivation and persistence, and subsequent performance—a self-reinforcing spiral of success, mediocrity, or failure.

SCHOOLS CONTROL THE CONDITIONS OF SUCCESS. The third premise is clearly about schools and the people who work in them. The premise directly implies that schools establish the ground rules and conditions under which learning, evaluation, and the labeling of that learning occur. Schools can set up conditions that make it extremely difficult, if not impossible, for all students to learn successfully; or they can define and organize the conditions so that it happens. Simply put: the conditions that define and influence student learning success in school are not immutable; they are simply the way that some group of consenting adults agreed (probably several generations ago) that they should be.

Tradition and inertia die hard, but die they can. So OBE advocates argue that educators do not have to accept unworkable and counterproductive conditions as inevitable. Instead, they have direct control *in their own classrooms* of at least four things that, singly and in combination with each other, can profoundly alter both the conditions and the patterns of success in their rooms. They are:

1. Where they place their instructional focus;
2. How long, how often, and when they provide students with opportunities for learning;
3. What learning they expect from which students, and how they reward it; and
4. How they design and organize curriculum.

OBE'S FOUR "POWER" PRINCIPLES

What OBE implementors have discovered is just how much control they do in fact have over these four conditions and how changing them in certain directions can affect student success. The keys to changing those conditions lie in the four principles that actually drive and determine the action side of OBE. They are often seen as "power" principles because in combination and in alignment with each other they can have exceptional power in generating more and higher student learning success. The guiding message to teachers is to apply the four principles *consistently, systematically, creatively,* and *simultaneously* and watch the patterns of student success amaze and delight you.

As it turns out, each principle relates directly to one of the four conditions of success. Hence, the condition changes when a different and more powerful operating principle is brought to bear on it. The four power principles in their common abbreviated form are:

1. **CLARITY OF FOCUS** on Outcomes of Significance;
2. **EXPANDED OPPORTUNITY** and Support for Learning Success;
3. **HIGH EXPECTATIONS** for All to Succeed; and
4. **DESIGN DOWN** from Your Ultimate Outcomes.

PRINCIPLE 1. The "Clarity of Focus" principle is the driving force of OBE for it puts into place the essence of the Outcome-based approach: outcomes of significance. Appropriately, some people feel that it should be renamed the "Focus on Outcomes" principle because that is the real function it serves within a total OBE system. In either event, Principle 1 sets in motion program direction, design, delivery documentation, and decision making—all grounded on the learning results that really matter for students in the long run. Without it, nothing can be outcome-based.

To illustrate its centrality to the entire OBE concept, this Clarity of Focus principle lies at the heart of the first three operational features of OBE discussed earlier and is significant in numbers four, six, and seven as well. It governs the determination of what outcomes will be pursued, provides a base for all curriculum, instructional, and assessment design, gives a clear criterion meaning to performance standards and grades, serves as the focus and priority of instruction, and provides the rationale for all instructional decision making and for the alignment of curriculum and instruction.

Moreover, principle 1 also raises the issue of what outcomes are worth pursuing and compels educators to deal with the issue of what learning will be most significant for students in the long run. Two common sayings among OBE implementors that relate directly to this issue of significance are:

"Not all outcomes are created equal";

and

"If everything is a priority, then nothing is a priority."

What these two sayings point out is that by defining and focusing on outcomes, educators are inherently making choices about what is most important for students to learn and demonstrate and these choices reflect and embody their priorities of some content and competencies over others. Making such choices is a matter of judging what, among all of the available content, is going to affect most the quality and success of the student's life beyond the immediacy of the classroom. In what my colleagues in the High Success Program call our strategic design work, educators examine at least eight critical factors that affect the nature and significance of outcomes. Our goal is to enable educators to use these eight factors wisely in shaping the direction and priorities of their instructional experiences for students.

PRINCIPLE 2. This principle, commonly called "Expanded Opportunity," is the vehicle most responsible for calling into question the inflexible, time-defined nature of the educational system's curriculum organization, instructional delivery system, student assessment and credentialing practices, placement and advancement practices, organizational structure, employment contracts and conditions, and funding mechanisms. It also lies at the core of OBE's second and fifth operational characteristics described earlier and directly supports its sixth and seventh as well.

In practice this Expanded Opportunity principle has compelled educators to come to grips with the three key dimensions of time and opportunity and to ask themselves why schools routinely place such arbitrary and counterproductive constraints on each:

1. Duration—how long opportunity lasts;
2. Frequency—how often opportunity occurs; and
3. Timing—when exactly opportunity occurs.

In addition, this principle has provided practitioners with a related window on their curriculum-structuring and delivery practices. Specifically, they have addressed three distinctive aspects of instructional time and opportunity:

1. Teaching Time—The time taken to provide students with instructional assistance on given segments of the curriculum;
2. Learning Time—The time given students before they are made ultimately accountable for demonstrating success on given segments of the curriculum; and
3. Eligibility—When students are allowed and/or required to learn given segments of the curriculum.

Without going into detail about these aspects of time and

opportunity, the two key questions OBE practitioners are continually compelled to address are:

> Why are we so arbitrarily and unnecessarily constraining the duration, frequency, and timing of teaching time, learning time, and eligibility for our students?

and

> What could we do to expand opportunities for and experiences of success of all our students every day?

At least one answer, some believe, is that our current system of schooling is modeled after the late-nineteenth-century organizational wonder, the assembly-line factory, where the schedule rules everything and the line grinds on unrelentingly. Students are simply expected to do particular things at particular times within particular time constraints because, for generations, that is how things have been set up to operate in school. OBE simply calls that entire mode of operating into question.

PRINCIPLE 3. OBE's "High Expectations" principle has three distinctive dimensions, is explicitly manifested in operational characteristics three, six, and seven, and indirectly influences number one as well. The first of these dimensions concerns what proportion of students the system wants, expects, and allows to succeed (i.e., receive high marks and commensurate recognition). The second relates to how high standards for acceptable performance are set. And the third reflects the quality of outcomes and curriculum that are available to all students to pursue and attain. OBE's straightforward position on these three dimensions is: All, High, and High.

OBE schools do not have quotas on how many students

can do well and be recognized for it, they set acceptable performance standards very high for all work, and they eliminate low-track, low-expectation curricula for their students. The results sometimes amaze staff, who never thought that "their" students had "that" kind of potential. That, of course, is the point behind the High Expectations principle, and it brings home a saying that has become popular in OBE schools: "Students will rise to our *lowest* expectations of them!"

The subtle meaning that teachers have discovered about this saying is that if low performance by students is accepted by a teacher, the teacher's expectations for those students are not very high, because, if they were higher, the performance would have to be higher before it would be accepted. This means, in effect, that students will rise to whatever level of "minimum" that teachers establish, even if the minimum is high.

For example, in many OBE schools, not only are teachers' minimums remarkably higher today than they were before OBE, but also the percentages of students meeting those higher standards are far greater than before. The same holds for the elimination of low-track and remedial courses. As soon as the curriculum gets more demanding, levels of learning success increase simultaneously, clearly suggesting that many students are far more capable than their traditional curriculum placement assumes. Stories about schools such as Alhambra and South Mountain High Schools in Phoenix eliminating General Math courses because of high failure rates by large percentages of ninth-grade students and replacing them with OBE Algebra programs in which virtually all students succeed have, in fact, become wonderful examples of "High Expectations" at work.

Readers interested in developing a richer background in

examples of this kind should investigate the quarterly journal of the Network for Outcome-based Schools, *Outcomes*, the quarterly journal of the National Center for Outcome-based Education, *Quality Outcomes-Driven Education, COBE News*, the newsletter of the Center for Outcome-based Education, and *Connections*, the newsletter of the High Success Network. These journals and newsletters regularly contain articles by practitioners who share the results of their OBE implementation experiences, and they provide vehicles for the exchange of both data and perspectives about the rapid spread and evolution of Outcome-based practice.

PRINCIPLE 4. OBE's "Design Down" principle raises a number of issues and ironies that go to the heart of the concept. First, "Design Down" is about designing back from the place teachers want student learning to culminate. The common message in OBE schools is: "Design down from where you want students to end up!"

But does "down" mean from the end of a lesson or a unit of instruction? or a course? or a whole program of study? Or is it even about the specific curriculum content at all? While the field has not found consistent answers to these questions, two trends are clear.

First, the concept of "significance" addressed earlier has elevated the focus well beyond lessons and units in many OBE schools. The small increments of information contained in those two small segments of curriculum do not qualify as significant in their own right. This means that courses are likely to be the smallest segments of learning in which the notions of "Design Down" and "significance" are being simultaneously addressed by more advanced OBE implementors.

Second, almost universally, advanced OBE curriculum design is focusing on higher-order competencies and processes as the culminating targets of instruction, not subject content and details. Therefore, curriculum design and instructional planning focus on putting in place the knowledge, competence, and orientation "enablers" that make successful demonstrations of these complex processes eventually possible, sometimes in complex, interrelated ways.

What these two trends mean from a practical point of view is:

1. "Design Down" cannot be separated in practice from "Clarity of Focus" and "High Expectations," because both of the latter have a major bearing on what the target outcomes from which one designs down are actually going to be;

2. "Design Down" cannot be done in isolation if the nature of the culminating outcome requires instructional input from many sources; and

3. The higher the starting point in a design process (i.e., Exit or Program Outcomes rather than Course or Unit Outcomes), the greater is the common "Clarity of Focus" among staff, the less focus there is on content detail, and the more expansive is the concept of "Expanded Opportunity."

How Well OBE Works

The foregoing section of the chapter suggests that operationally OBE's four power principles cannot be addressed and implemented in isolation from each other because each one adds important dimensions and considerations to the others. By working as a congruent system of factors and forces, the four power principles are, in fact, capable of redefining the success conditions that students face in school with results that, in some cases, transcend common patterns in the literature. Here are a few examples that come to mind that I know personally have involved the systematic application of all four principles. Others abound in recent reviews of the literature on Mastery Learning and in books summarizing its historical development and applications (see, e.g., Block, Efthim, & Burns, 1989; Guskey & Gates, 1986; Kulik, Kulik, & Bangert-Drowns, 1990a; Levine, 1985).

One of the largest and most impressive sets of findings concerning what I will call Outcome-based Instruction involves the achievements of over 4,500 students in the Glendale Union High School District in Glendale, Arizona. Although the district's in-house research by Marc Becker has not been formally published, they have impressive data across a vast array of subjects and classrooms showing that the power of OBE on student criterion referenced test performance, geared directly to the district's goals and objectives in all core courses, increases directly with each principle that teachers systematically add to their repertories of skills. The smallest gains over conventional instruction occur in Glendale classrooms in which relatively unsophisticated forms of "Clarity of Focus" and "Expanded Opportunity" are routinely used at the lesson and unit levels. But truly dramatic advantages accrue to those teachers who apply all four principles consistently and systematically and who design their units and lessons down from clearly identified higher-order course outcomes that they expect all students to demonstrate before receiving a grade of credit.

The results are so powerful in these "high implementation" (HI) classrooms that when student socio-economic status

(SES) is taken explicitly into account in the data analysis, the HI students dramatically outperform their SES counterparts taking the same courses out of the same books in conventionally taught classrooms, regardless of subject. The most impressive findings, however, involve the low SES students in these HI classes. As a group, they outperform both the medium and the high SES students in conventional classrooms as well. This, from my twenty-five years of experience in the field as a sociologist, is a rare finding indeed.

A second impressive example occurred in the Oak Park, River-Forest High School in Oak Park, Illinois. In 1989 Richard Deptuck, the head of the school's mathematics division, "consistently, systematically, creatively, and simultaneously" applied OBE's four principles in a section of algebra 1 that lasted only second semester—half the normal time. During first semester, the class had been taking general math (from another teacher), and most of them had failed. Deptuck voluntarily traded assignments with the teacher in order to test the power of OBE for himself in a systematically self-designed-down version of algebra 1. The culminating outcome of this course was that all students could successfully solve quadratic equations using alternative modes of solution by the end of the single semester.

Naturally, all of Deptuck's students passed the course. But the real "power" finding was that his class scored as high as or higher than any of the other twenty-plus sections of algebra 1 in the entire school on the district's standardized algebra test at the end of the year, and the students in those other sections had had twice as long to learn it, with much less of a mathematics deficit when they started.

The third example concerns Alhambra High School in Phoenix, which, in 1987 when they began to entertain the notion of getting into OBE, was a mainly Anglo, solidly middle-class student body that scored in the upper half of the district's achievement tests in all core subject areas at all grade levels. At the time, over a third of all students carried at least one F on their records and only a fifth were headed for college. In 1991 Alhambra is a different school: 45 percent of the students are non-Anglo, with over half of the student body on free or reduced lunch programs, and the Alhambra neighborhood is the focal point of serious gang problems and violence. But Alhambra is now the highest achieving high school in Phoenix in all subject areas at all grade levels, and 90 percent of its 1991 graduating class was headed to some form of higher education. The F rate is below 5 percent, and both the daily attendance and dropout data are dramatically better than they were in 1987.

What accounts for the difference? The three OBE premises and the four principles have transformed the culture of the school and the way the vast majority of teachers do business in their classrooms. These have all been bolstered by the committed OBE leadership of the principal, David Briggs, who has "consistently, systematically, creatively, and simultaneously" done the things necessary to transform the conditions of success for staff as well as for students at Alhambra. Four years ago, the school's motto could have been: "Bell Curves R Us!" Today it is: "All kids can succeed!" and they are all wearing T-shirts that proclaim it.

Many other noteworthy examples of "success for all" abound across U.S. and Canadian schools, manifesting the power of the four principles. Based on what I know about these many cases, I would like to draw a conclusion about OBE implementation: it definitely appears that the power and synergy of using all four principles together give teachers and their students an extraordinary advantage over those using just some of the principles or some other kinds of design and delivery approaches. In fact, these data further suggest that anything less than all four principles is not really OBE but simply an attempt to approximate it.

THE CONTINUING EVOLUTION OF THE OBE PARADIGM

This approximation strategy certainly helps account for some of the dilemma noted at the beginning of the chapter concerning quite imperfect ideas about OBE and its implementation requirements, but not all of it. My personal interpretation of this dilemma is that OBE represents such a deep and far-reaching change in the entire purpose and paradigm of education as most Americans have known it that comprehending this paradigm change, let alone embracing and implementing it, lies beyond their ken.

The paradox of this situation is that the generic nature of OBE is a very old idea that shaped the functioning of the craft guilds of Europe in the Middle Ages and continues today in the form of highly successful personnel development models used by the U.S. military and the corporate community (see, e.g., Bowsher, 1989, for a wonderful example of how major U.S. corporations have created "success for all" instructional designs to continually upgrade their employees using principles that are virtually identical to OBE's. From their perspective, if an employee does not learn successfully, they check the training program for flaws, not the employee!). OBE is also embodied in many forms of applied performance certification, including CPR training, lifesaving certification, pilot licenses, drivers' licenses, and, as noted earlier, scouting merit badges.

In other words, we find examples of OBE everywhere in the real world but almost nowhere in the unique world of schooling. There OBE is anathema because the paradigmatic structures, imperatives, and processes that have governed twentieth-century education in the United States are far more time-based, custodial, and selection-oriented than anything implied in OBE's premises and principles (see Sizer, 1983, 1984; Spady, 1988; Spady & Marshall, 1991). In addition, I see education is a world governed by the four deadly P's: Programs, Processes, Procedures, and (the verb) Provide—all concepts that place a premium on attending to and improving the means of education under the assumption that the means are synonymous with the results. Clearly, until only recently the practitioner pioneers of OBE have had to swim against the tide of institutional inertia and public support.

So, if the two paradigms at issue here are so different from each other and the traditional paradigm is so pervasive and entrenched, why is so much explicit attention being given today to outcome-based approaches to reform? The answer, I believe, lies in the educational reform history of the 1960s. I turn there for a deeper look at the evolution and continuing dilemma of the OBE paradigm.

There are two distinctive tracks in the reform research of the 1960s that account for the great interest in OBE today. The best known in OBE circles is the pioneering observations of John Carroll (1963). Carroll pointed out that the (then and still) current "model" of schooling was essentially intolerant of differences in instructional or learning time for students but extremely tolerant of wide differences in their achievement. His big paradigm "ah-ha" was the notion that these two factors could just as easily be reversed; that "A Model of School Learning"—the title of his now famous paper—could at least theoretically be developed that would set clear (criterion-based) standards for learning that all students would attain but allow for the inevitable variation in the time needed for them to do so.

So, what is now fixed becomes variable, and what is now variable becomes fixed—a novel idea that was met, from my biased perspective, with resounding indifference by most researchers and educators, mainly because it was not "realistic" in lots of ways. In other words, it absolutely did not fit the paradigm thinking and structures of the day, and there was no reason to challenge, let alone revolutionize, that paradigm . . . until 1966, that is.

EXTERNAL PRESSURES TO RESTRUCTURE THE PARADIGM

In 1966 both the educational research and practitioner communities were jarred to their eyeteeth with the publication of the *Equality of Educational Opportunity* study by James Coleman and many others (1966). The bottom-line conclusion of this enormous national study of U.S. schools from coast to coast was that schools do not make a difference in altering the powerful influence of family background on student achievement. In other words, variations in all the means of education they could get their hands on (including per pupil expenditures) did not affect student aspirations and achievement once the socioeconomic and racial backgrounds of the students in a school were taken into account statistically.

These findings, as Chester Finn (1990) perceptively argued in his article "The Biggest Reform of All," cracked the heretofore unquestioned legitimacy of both the paradigm of schooling itself and the paradigm of reform strategies that bolstered it. Previously, investing more in improving the means was assumed to be the solution needed to assure that improvements in the ends would also occur, the ends, in the case of Coleman and his colleagues, being the educational achievements of racial-minority youngsters. Promises to "fix" or improve the means were no longer taken to be a guarantee that student learning would get fixed at the same time, and both state and local policymakers were compelled to focus on achievement in its own right and began using it both as a lever for reform and as the only legitimate evidence that things were, in fact, improving.

That is why in the late 1970s calls for competency testing were rampant in state capitols: legislators and state boards of education insisted on knowing whether students were achieving or not, and basic skills were usually their bottom-line concern. And, in some cases, that is why those calls for improved test scores are no less strident today. They have simply taken on a bit more sophistication about the substance and limitations of certain kinds of tests.

Slowly but surely, then, the word *outcomes* has taken center stage in the policy formulations of state boards of education and state legislatures, whether or not they know anything at all about authentic OBE. During the eighties this orientation grew so strong and pervasive that Finn (1990) declared it an authentic and irreversible "paradigm shift" in relation to educational reform policy. Improved outcomes will, he believes, become *the* standard by which reform legislation will be based in the future, and that will keep local districts focused on outcomes. Without question, this external pressure, expressed through the public's continuing dissatisfaction with the outcomes of schools, has played a huge role in attracting people to the "outcomes" label.

Another major force that has expressed itself externally is what is known as the effective schools movement, whose original research base was established by Wilbur Brookover in the early 1970s (see Brookover, et al., 1978) and later extended into a major force for reform, especially in large districts with significant populations of minority groups, by Ronald Edmonds (1978) and Lawrence Lezotte (see Lezotte, this volume). There are strong parallels between the philosophical orientations of the effective schools approach and the three premises of OBE. The key differences are their explicit focus on questions of equity in achievement across racial, SES, and gender lines and their lack of an operational instructional design and delivery model (as distinct from an improvement strategy) that would directly address the equity/achievement issue. They have gotten congressional support for their work and influenced several state legislatures to direct their reform efforts toward supporting their particular improvement strategy with its emphasis on achieving equality of student outcomes across key population groups.

In addition, the National Business Roundtable (1991) — representing the nation's top 200 corporations—issued its own reform manifesto entitled *Essential Components of a Successful*

Education System. One of those components is that schools be outcome-based, and the Roundtable's leaders, in fact, understand what the concept really means. Their plan is to aggressively lobby every state legislature and statehouse in the country to get their essential components embodied in state policy. They have been joined by the National Alliance for Business, which got behind former president Bush's six goals for U.S. education as a formal force to lobby for outcome-oriented reforms on the national level. Do not bet against them.

And who can ignore the word *choice?* It is now the clarion call of reformers of every stripe who argue vehemently that real improvement will come only when schools have to improve or face the threat of losing their clientele—and with them their public financing guarantees. One aspect of their argument seems solid to me, and that deals with the incapacity of the educational community to transform its own paradigm from within. That may be a virtually impossible idea in its own right, but the history of OBE reform suggests that it is true. Reform did not spontaneously arise out of the system in response to the compelling logic of John Carroll's ideas. The system did what paradigms do: shape and limit the thinking and options for action of those within and even without the system, despite claims of new knowledge and insights.

Yes, OBE's pioneers and leaders have had to deal with this incredible institutional inertia from their earliest days of wanting to put Carroll's ideas into practice, and the obstacles are still everywhere. But the context for responding to reform ideas is now far different than it was in the sixties, and the eventual result will be, too.

THE EDUCATIONAL COMMUNITY'S OBE PARADIGM SHIFT

The history of how the educational community responded to John Carroll's early ideas is a subjective one, but its key players are known and have been unrelenting in their promotion and extension of the original Carroll concept.

The most notable early OBE paradigm pioneers were Benjamin Bloom (1968) and James Block (1971), whose awareness of Carroll's work and commitment to giving it operational form created the seeds from which the larger OBE concept has emerged. From my perspective, Bloom's and Block's work was an attempt to bring what we now recognize as the philosophical premises and operational principles of OBE into the classroom and have teachers, operating under the constraints of self-contained classrooms in calendar-driven schools, use different instructional planning, delivery, and assessment strategies in working with students. Their intention was clear: bring about major improvements in student learning success by changing instructional delivery strategies.

Their work, known internationally as mastery learning (see Guskey, this volume), demonstrated beyond all doubt that changes in intention and strategy could pay off handsomely for both teachers and students. But mastery learning as an instructional strategy could not address or overcome the myriad organizational factors in schools that militated against its widespread and full-blown use. It was very much like putting a large, round peg (mastery) into a small, square hole (the inertia of a time-defined system). The two were inherently incompatible, and the hole represented the stronger force by far.

For example, to this day schools remain time-inflexible

institutions, even though mastery learning asks teachers to use time-flexible/expanded-opportunity strategies with students. In addition, grading and reporting systems continue to reinforce not only the time-based nature of the school but also its comparative/competitive achievement culture, which mastery opposes. Both the content frame and the structure of the curriculum remain unchanged in the face of mastery learning, although teachers can define and prioritize some of their own objectives within the curriculum model that is given. The list could go on, but these examples make the point.

Block (1974) especially recognized early on that there was a host of administrative, sociological, economic, and policy implications tied to the principles and premises that mastery was attempting to implement and that larger system changes would be needed if mastery was to reach its full reform potential. But the model itself inherently stressed change in instructional processes rather than larger organizational redesign, and teachers were viewed as the model's primary consumers and users. Unless exceptional district leadership existed to provide significant understanding and support for the larger implications of the concept—as it did in a few notable places like Johnson City, New York—mastery could easily, but inappropriately, be treated as just another instructional technique (like any number of instructional techniques) that teachers needed to learn and use. In the meantime, the paradigm of schooling would proceed unchanged.

Fortunately, exceptionally enlightened and committed district leadership did exist in the person of John Champlin in Johnson City. Champlin (1983) had the foresight to recognize and begin institutionalizing the political, organizational, and cultural changes needed to set the stage for Mastery's "Success for All" philosophy and principles to be implemented districtwide. He, in continuing consultation with others over a period of years, saw the scope and implications of the Carroll model as having ever-wider organizational boundaries: from the classroom to the department, to the school, to the district, to the state, to the system as a whole.

Over time the notion began to surface among mastery advocates that Carroll's ideas were not just about instructional delivery—although it represented the ultimate bottom line of the approach—but about system change. Over time many of the leaders in what fifteen years ago was a joint mastery learning/OBE movement began to recognize and forcefully articulate that we needed a different paradigm of education into which this Carroll/Bloom/Block instructional paradigm could fit compatibly. The evolution of these ideas proceeded up this hierarchy as people recognized that the real forces of influence and support moved downward:

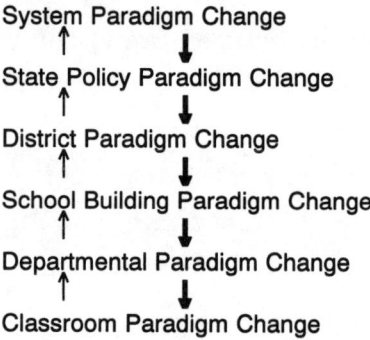

And as this dialogue proceeded and became more complex, another dialogue arose alongside of it related to the concept of outcomes. Were we talking specific objectives or were we talking global competencies? Were outcomes simply discrete skills or pieces of information that students could learn to a high level of proficiency as part of a specific assignment or curriculum (what my colleagues and I [see Spady & Marshall, 1991] have named "Traditional OBE"), or were they more global demonstrations of learning and competence that ultimately had to be taken outside the walls of the classroom and applied in complex role-performance contexts (what we are calling "Transformational OBE")?

As a part of this latter ongoing dialogue, other related questions arose related to the appropriate scope of instructional design, delivery, and documentation. Should OBE's four principles be applied to outcomes at the lesson level, the unit level, the course level, the school building level, the program level, the ultimate end of schooling (i.e., exit) level, or to all of them? What does this mean in relation to the "Design Down" principle? Where should one design down from? And what does it mean in relation to the "Expanded Opportunity" principle? When is it appropriate to close off the opportunity to demonstrate something you want students to learn and retain once they walk out the door into their "real" life roles? And when is it appropriate to think students should be "done" learning something that has life-long implications?

While these discussions continue unabated and reflect the vitality of the concept's continued evolution, some of its most salient features can be summarized in a diagram similar to the previous one. There appears to be a strong correlation between the concept of what a culminating outcome is and should represent and when that culmination should take place. When integrated, this connection can be portrayed as a hierarchy that moves from a more micro perspective at the bottom to a more macro one at the top. Its conceptual evolution has proceeded historically from bottom to top, while its true Outcome-based paradigm implications flow from top to bottom.

```
       Culminating Exit Demonstrations
       ↑               ↓
       Culminating Program Demonstrations
       ↑               ↓
       Culminating Course Demonstrations
       ↑               ↓
       Culminating Unit Demonstrations
       ↑               ↓
       Culminating Lesson Demonstrations
```

In other words, a serious dialogue continues to this very day concerning what the significant culminating demonstrations of learning should be and when and how students should be held accountable for them. Included in this dialogue are viewpoints about different "models" or conceptions of what OBE is or should be all about and what we should be expecting from students not only at the end of specific lessons, units, and courses, but also at the end of their entire schooling experience (see Spady & Marshall, 1991).

THE STATE OF CURRENT OBE ADVANCES

As the foregoing section suggests, the OBE concept has undergone a significant transformation over the past two decades. The best characterization of this evolution is reflected in the subtitle of this paper: *From Instructional Reform to Paradigm Restructuring*. Today's potential implementors are faced with questions far more complex and far-reaching than those their colleagues addressed in the late sixties.

The OBE paradigm pioneers of today are looking at comprehensive models of total organizational transformation and paradigm change that proceed from a strategic analysis of future trends and life conditions that students will inevitably encounter during their lives. These trends are used as the driving force in the conceptualization of exit outcomes that are increasingly being framed as role-performance demonstrations in life-role contexts. These "transformational" exit outcomes are being used, in turn, as the driving force in a complete rethinking of what needs to be in the curriculum, how to frame and organize it, and how to create the learning contexts that enable something other than conventional book learning to occur instructionally for students. The intended goal of all this discussion about curriculum reform and restructuring is: to be certain that the critical enabling outcomes for these ultimate culminating demonstrations will both be in place and be systematically addressed by students and teachers starting on Day 1 of kindergarten.

Along with this attention to the content and structure of the curriculum has come a national debate over something called "Authentic Assessment." From a transformational OBE perspective, "Authentic Assessment" simply means making sure that the content, process elements, role-performance dimensions, and context elements implied in the outcome are explicitly and accurately embodied in the intended culminating demonstration. This attention to the relevance, or validity, of assessments is a central piece of most advanced OBE developments.

In addition, today's Transformational OBE trailblazers are using the Outcome-based paradigm perspective to incorporate many other reform ideas and practices under its eclectic umbrella. These include: Quality Management, School

Restructuring, Strategic Planning, Transformational Leadership, Site-based Management, School Renewal, Effective Schools, Teacher Teaming, Cooperative Learning, Effective Teaching, Curriculum Alignment, Critical Thinking Strategies, Clinical Supervision, Interdisciplinary Curriculum, and, of course, Mastery Learning.

Despite their vision, determination, and all these tools with which to work, the challenge facing these pioneers is formidable: the policies, thinking, organizational structures, funding arrangements, preprofessional training programs, curriculum frameworks, testing programs, credentialing mechanisms, employment contracts, job classifications, and extracurricular sacred cows that currently define and perpetuate the existing paradigm of education will be extremely difficult to overcome. But we should not forget: even the White House is advocating radical change in education. The way things are going, transformational OBE could be it.

18

- ASSESSMENT
- CLIMATE
- LEADERSHIP
- MOTIVATION
- ORGANIZATION/ MANAGEMENT(CLASSROOM)
- ORGANIZATION/ MANAGEMENT (SCHOOL)

The Quality School

William Glasser
Institute for Reality Therapy

As I read books like this, as well as articles in educational journals, I am struck by the soundness of almost all of the ideas. There is no shortage of proven suggestions for improving our schools. Yet I have been going into schools for thirty years, spending time in classes, talking to both students and staff, and what strikes me is the lack of change. It is as if the schools are unaware of the many ideas for improvement. Here and there I see glimmers of innovation, but there are almost no schools where something new and much better is actually in place.

Education will not be improved by schools continuing to do the same things that have never worked and are still not working. As I will explain in this chapter, schools do not change because the way almost all teachers are managed has led them to be fearful of doing anything different from the "safe," but ineffective, things they have always done.

The problem of the schools is simple to describe: regardless of the school they attend, far too few students are working hard to learn. To confirm this, I once asked about forty high school student leaders who were attending a conference in Pittsburgh sponsored by the Fox Chapel (PA) School District to define a "good student," which they did easily. I then asked how many good students there were in their schools. The consensus was between 20 and 45 percent. When I asked them if this number was so low because many students were handicapped or retarded, they said, "No, they don't work because they don't like the schoolwork they are asked to do."

The students to whom I was talking came from schools that were selected for excellence as a prerequisite for attendance at this conference. They were all well funded and populated mostly by students who came from homes where education was strongly supported. This means that in our best schools fewer than half of the students are good students. In the underfunded, overcrowded schools of our big cities, this number drops to less than 10 percent.

Capable students not working in school is the only problem and has been for over a hundred years. To talk about discipline, dropouts, drugs, teenage pregnancies, learning disabilities, dysfunctional homes, poor financial support, or any of the other related problems is to avoid facing the real issue, which is that huge numbers of capable students do not like schoolwork and refuse to make the effort to become good students. Unless we can persuade a larger percentage of capable students to work hard, nothing will change.

If we could run schools where students were willing to make this effort, we would eliminate many if not all the other problems that we complain about. Quality schools, as exemplified by the Johnson City (NY) School system (see Champlin & Mamary, 1982), is my answer to this problem. These schools are managed in the way that I suggest in my book *The Quality School* (Glasser, 1990). The result is that almost all of the students are working hard and doing competent school work.

A quality school is one in which at least 90 percent of the students are working hard and doing competent work in all of their academic classes. Further, all students, even the few who are not doing competent work in all their classes, are doing some work in at least one class that both they and their teachers would judge is quality work. While it is difficult to define quality in any exact sense, it could be said that small as the quantity might be, it would be the very best that the student is capable of doing.

But we will not have quality schools until we face the fact that almost all of the efforts to improve any school do not even address the main issue—calling the adults who direct classrooms "teachers." While they do teach some of the time, teaching is not what most of them do most of the time. *What most people who "teach" in public schools do most of the time is manage.* If we are unwilling to face this fact, we will not implement one good suggestion from this book or anywhere else.

A manager can be accurately defined as a person who has an agenda and whose job it is to persuade the workers (in school the workers are the students) to accept his or her agenda, work hard, and do a good job. Whether the effective manager works in a factory, is a parent, or "teaches" in a school, the task is the same, and it is very difficult. Of those jobs demanding effective managing, "teaching" is without a doubt the most difficult.

This is not to say that teachers who do nothing but teach do not exist. They do, lots of them, but few exist in the academic classes, grades one through twelve, of our public schools. A pure teacher, who does not manage at all, is someone whose students want to learn what she or he teaches and are willing to work hard to learn it. Examples are nonacademic teachers like those who teach driver education or those who coach or teach in purely voluntary academic classes like advanced science or math. Given students who all want to learn, schools would have no problems because almost all "teachers" can teach any student who is willing to work hard.

What our academic "teachers" seem unable to do is teach the vast majority of students who, liking neither what they are asked to learn nor how they are asked to learn it, refuse to put much effort into the learning process. Since even in our "best" schools well over 50 percent of all students *choose* to be in this minimal-learning group, we must face the fact that managing students successfully is a very hard job but still *the* job that we must learn to do much better.

To put the difficulty of managing students in perspective, let us look at how much easier it is to manage in industry. For at least five reasons it is much easier to manage employees than to manage students. First, as much as workers may not like what they are asked to do, they are paid to do it and they need the money. Second, they can almost always see the sense of what they are asked to do and are easily able to judge whether or not they are doing a good job. Third, they are almost never asked to take work home. Fourth, if they do not do a good job, they can be discharged and others are usually both willing and able to take their places. And fifth, unlike schools, industry recognizes that management is the major problem and is willing to spend millions of dollars to try to improve it. Still, even with all these advantages, most industries are not able to persuade their employees to do what they are capable of doing, further proof of how difficult it is to manage effectively.

Parenting is also not easy, but it is easier than "teaching" because in most cases the child loves the parents and wants to please them. Students, though, do not usually love their teachers; they are not paid to do the work; they are asked to do a lot of boring work that neither they nor anyone else can see any sense in doing; and they are asked to do a lot of homework that is usually even less sensible than what they are asked to do in class.

Given this dismal array of nonincentives, most "teachers" do not know how to persuade (manage) students to choose to do the schoolwork that they are capable of doing. In their frustration, the "motivator" that almost all "teachers" choose to use is coercion, usually punishment. If it worked, there would be no problem, but it does not. Our schools are overflowing with threats and punishments, but the more we use coercion to manage, the less our students choose to do. Not only does it not help, but, as I will explain later, coercion of both teachers and students increases the problems that we complain about.

If we agree that better management is the skill that teachers and principals have to learn, the sensible thing to do is look for good management models. In the schools, there are few besides Johnson City. We should look to Japan, where many managers in the world are also looking. It is evident that the Japanese have figured out how to manage their industrial workers so that they work hard and build quality products. In fact, their ability to manage for quality has been a major contributor to their quick ascent from devastation to being the richest country in the world. What we need to do is learn how they have done this and then try to apply this knowledge to the management of students in our schools.

It is intriguing to discover that what the Japanese do is not inherent in their culture. They were taught to manage by an American, W. Edwards Deming (1982), who had taught the same ideas in the United States for many years before he went to Japan. Deming, who died in 1993 in his nineties, was considered the dean of those who teach quality management. During World War II, he was active in training American managers how to manage unskilled workers so that they would do quality work in our war production factories. After the war, when he suggested to the same companies that they continue to emphasize managing for quality when they converted to peacetime products, they scoffed at him. The leaders of the U.S. automobile industry were especially incredulous when he told them (what has now been proved in Japan) that it is less expensive to build a quality car than a shoddy one.

Someone in the MacArthur administration of Japan brought Deming there in 1950, and, unlike the American industrialists, the Japanese listened. Deming told them that if they would learn what he taught, they would become the world's leader in any product that they built. With Deming's help, the Japanese have gone from a prewar reputation for shoddy products to a postwar reputation for quality that is unprecedented in history. And Deming himself has said that there is nothing that he teaches that could not be applied in any country and that would not work as well in the schools as in a factory.

Deming's ideas are divided into two parts; (1) the psychology of how to manage workers and (2) the statistical methods that workers need to use to achieve quality. *The Quality School* is my effort to bring his management psychology to the schools. Deming's statistical work is not applicable and will not be covered. But, as I will shortly explain, my book is much more than an application of Deming's ideas. It also provides what Deming's book does not, namely, an explanation of *why* his ideas should be used.

What is puzzling is that, as much as Deming's management psychology has led the Japanese to riches, it has not been widely adopted in U.S. industry. Many U.S. manufacturers have tried. They have hired Deming and Deming-trained personnel. They have spent millions on training, but, with very few exceptions, as described in detail in a fairly recent book (Gabor, 1990), they been unable to put to work in their factories what has been so successful in Japan. And as much as schools have tried to follow the Johnson City model (which turns out to be close to the Deming model), many schools, both here and in Japan, have been unable to do it.

I believe that what stops both schools and factories from changing to Deming's way is that he asks them to change their basic belief in how people function, and this is too much for most managers to accept. For cultural reasons, U.S. managers, more so than Japanese ones, are unwilling to accept the word of an authority, even one with good evidence, that what he or she recommends works, unless that authority explains clearly why these changes need to be made. Deming does not provide such explanation, and that is why his recommendations have been so difficult to put into practice.

Regardless of culture, however, anyone's best chance of persuading people to change their beliefs is to offer them a new set of beliefs to replace the beliefs we are asking them to give up. What I offer in *The Quality School* is a new theory of how human beings function called "control theory." This theory explains clearly why we should change to the management psychology that Deming recommends.

I am asking managers to replace their traditional belief in stimulus-response psychology, a belief about how we function that has been held by most people for thousands of years, with a new belief, control theory. This is a big request because the knowledge of how to apply control theory to the lives of human beings is less than twenty years old. There is, however, much interest in control theory. Starting with the original work of William Powers (1973), who was the first to apply this theory, I have expanded and clarified his theoretical ideas to the point where it is now easy to learn how to use this theory in both one's life and one's work. I have also trained over a hundred people who teach this theory all over the world, so it is readily available to any school or business that wants to learn it.

I believe that learning control theory is the key to implementing Deming's management concepts in schools or anywhere else. Johnson City was introduced to control theory about ten years ago, and, without input from Deming, the staff has gradually come to realize that this theory is basic to their success in managing both students and teachers. But knowing about Deming has helped them even more, so I think it is fair to say that *a quality school is a combination of Deming's management psychology and the control theory that explains why it works.*

DEMING'S CONTRIBUTION

Deming has summarized his management psychology in what he calls his fourteen points. He also describes what he calls seven deadly sins to avoid. Using both my knowledge of control theory and my long-term understanding of schools, I have reduced Deming's twenty-one basics to three. If we could persuade a school principal and at least three-quarters of the teachers to use these three concepts to manage the teachers and the students respectively, we could transform any school into a quality school in no more than five years with a small amount of staff training.

THREE BASICS

BASIC ONE—MANAGING WITHOUT COERCION. To persuade workers (or students) to do quality work, Deming says that the manager must eliminate all fear in the managerial relationship. The manager must refrain from doing anything that could be construed by the worker as coercive. This means that principals must never coerce teachers and teachers must never coerce students.

It means eliminating all threats, punishments, lowering of grades, and anything else that could be construed as trying to use the threat of pain to force a student or a teacher to do what he or she does not want to do.

Since the purpose of a quality school is to persuade almost all students to work hard and do some quality work, managers and workers cannot be adversaries. The more adversarial the relationship, the poorer the quality of the work. People do not work hard for managers they do not like. Deming teaches that managers and workers must be friends: they must care for each other, and, in school, both students and teachers must believe that a major goal of those who manage them is to treat them well.

In *The Quality School*, this type of noncoercive manager is called a lead-manager. Lead is taken from the term "leader." A leader is a person whom people want to follow because they believe that this person primarily has their benefit in mind. This is in contrast to the usual coercive manager, called a boss-manager, whose way to try to get people to work hard is to coerce them, usually with the threat of punishment. In the boss's mind, it is his or her benefit, not that of the workers, that is paramount.

BASIC TWO—EMPHASIZING QUALITY IN ALL ASSIGNED ACADEMIC WORK. In a quality school, the emphasis would be on quality work, meaning work that both teacher and student could look at and agree that it is work to be proud of. Teachers would choose to do something about quality and explain through the use of class discussions that such choosing is what we all want. The teacher-manager's goal would be to persuade each student in every academic subject to choose to do what that student would judge is quality. But what makes this persuasion much more tangible is that one of the requisites of quality is usefulness. Therefore, in a quality school not only would there be no punishment but also students would never be held responsible for schoolwork that has no use in their lives.

Useful does not necessarily mean practical: it could be any use, enjoyable or aesthetic. But it would be the teacher's job to explain, in a way acceptable to all students, why what is taught is so useful that it pays to make a strenuous effort to learn it. In almost all schools, there is too much taught and tested that has no use for anyone and will soon be forgotten, no matter how well or poorly the students perform. Memorizing U.S. presidents in the order in which they were elected, as my older son had to do for a test, is good example of useless schoolwork.

This criterion of usefulness, however, would not preclude teaching anything that the teacher thought was of value. It would only preclude asking students to remember what they do not deem useful for a test. What would be emphasized and tested for in a quality school would be skills, not the facts, information, and formulas that are readily available in both books and computer software. There is no need to memorize facts that are not in daily use in our lives, and there is no possibility of quality in memorizing anything that has no use. This emphasis on skill teaching and testing would not prevent a teacher from asking a student to memorize a short poem for an aesthetic purpose in the hopes that the student would find the experience valuable. Many students would, but those who do not should not be punished for their unwillingness to agree. Again, it is not the willingness to coerce but the skill to persuade that is the hallmark of a good teacher-manager.

Skills are always useful, and any skill, like writing, speaking, or learning how the Constitution protects our civil rights, has the potential for adding quality to our lives. There is no quality in just learning the Bill of Rights; the quality is in learning how to actually use its protection. It is the skill to use the Constitution, not its words, that would be tested for in a quality school.

There would be no busywork or tedious work like doing problem after problem in long division. As soon as students could demonstrate competence in an arithmetic process such as long division by doing one or two problems by hand, they would be encouraged to use calculators to do further calculations. This would free them from drudgery and allow them to concentrate on learning that what to calculate, not how, is the real reason to study mathematics.

Except for the possibility of practice tests to prepare students for the senseless mass-testing obsession of the real world, there would be no objective tests in a quality school, as nothing that can be measured on an "objective" test could possibly have any inherent quality. All tests would have written or oral answers that call for the student's opinion, evaluation, or ability to use what he or she has learned. There would also be take-home tests in which students would be encouraged to consult with parents or others as one would do to learn or to solve problems in the real world. Group work, even on tests, would be encouraged as it is reflective of life, where people need to learn to work together.

There would be no cheating in a quality school; students would be encouraged to work together and help each other even on tests. It would be the student's ability to use what is learned, not just to know what it is, that would always be tested; no one can cheat on usage. You can or cannot do something. Usage is like throwing a basketball through a hoop: there is no way to cheat. For example, could the students show the teacher how they would use a road map to find a city or that they have received an answer to a letter they wrote? What students "cheat" on now is nonsense knowledge like the height of a mountain, a date in history, or the name of a person. Without nonsense, by emphasizing skills and the use of these skills on tests, there would always be the chance for quality and no reason even to think about cheating.

BASIC THREE—STUDENTS WOULD BE ASKED TO EVALUATE ALL OF THEIR WORK. Deming claims that quality work costs less than shoddy work and that one way to save this money is to ask the worker to evaluate his or her own work instead of paying an inspector. He claims that workers know more about their work than anyone else and that in a noncoercive working environment they want to do quality work and do not need that anyone be paid to inspect what they do. He explains that where quality is concerned, the problems with inspection—whether it is a teacher grading a paper or an inspector checking a ball bearing—are that the worker tends to do only enough to get by, and the inspector sets the level far below what the worker is capable of doing because he is afraid for his job if he rejects too much work.

Inspection, whether in school or in the factory, costs more, mitigates against quality, and emphasizes "good enough." And "it's good enough" is what most students answer when they are questioned about the quality of their work. They do not feel that quality is their responsibility. That belongs to the teacher or inspector. But when students are given the task of inspecting their own work in a noncoercive emphasis on quality atmosphere, they do not want to judge themselves as inferior. So basic to Deming and the quality school is the idea that all students can and should be taught to inspect all of their own work.

In the factory, Deming is correct in assuming that the worker knows more than anyone else about the work because he or she usually does it over and over or, at least, is very familiar with it. In school, however, much of what a student does is new, so the student needs help from the teacher if he or she is to evaluate the work accurately. In a quality school, the evaluation of the work is done by both the student and the teacher, with the emphasis on teaching the student how to do a good job of self-evaluation. Once the teacher is confident that the student knows how to self-evaluate well, the student's evaluation will count more and eventually might be given as much weight as or even more weight than the teacher's.

There would be no sense in asking a student to evaluate his or her work unless he or she also had a chance to improve it. This means that there would be no final grades in a quality school. Grades would reflect where the students were when they wanted to stop trying to improve. Both teachers and students have shown concern that if students knew they had a chance to improve, they would not try hard the first time. This is possible, especially in the beginning, but most students would find that doing something over is more difficult that doing it once. So in time, this would not be a problem.

If a student wanted to improve her grade after inspecting her work, she would know that she always has that chance. This opportunity would encourage her to keep looking over her work with the idea of improving it, a process that is necessary for quality and almost nonexistent in our present "it's good enough" schools. It would also follow that there would be little assigned homework in a quality school. Homework would be self-assigned as students would take home work that they wanted to improve so they could get a better grade. Class would emphasize new work; home would be the place to improve what is done in class, and students would always get credit for increasing the quality of what they do.

I know of no school in the country where all these Deming

basics are in place at this time, but Johnson City is already working on the self-inspection and the elimination of testing for nonsense—both of which are necessary if we are to have quality. I try to keep a little ahead of them, but, with lead-management in place, they always catch up fast. Any school that incorporates these three basics into its program will in a few years become a quality school. But as the Johnson City administrators confirm, unless all who manage know control theory, this will not be possible. In fact, part of the process of becoming a quality school is also teaching control theory to all the students, starting in kindergarten. Materials have been developed to do this (Glasser, 1984).

CONTROL THEORY

Control theory is a biological theory of how we function as living creatures. The main way it differs from the generally accepted S-R (stimulus-response) theory is that control theory has as its basic premise the contention that all of our behavior is an attempt to satisfy needs that are built into the genetic structure of the brain. Simply stated, all our motivation is internal. S-R theory claims that we are externally motivated: all our behavior is our reaction or response to a stimulus that exists outside of ourselves.

For example, S-R theory claims that we answer the phone because it rings, but control theory contends that this is never the case. The ring of the phone does not make us do anything; in fact, what happens outside of us never makes us do anything. What we call a stimulus is actually information, and information itself never makes us do anything. It is always we who decide how to act on the information, and how we act is always in the direction of what at the time will best fulfill one or more of five basic needs: *love and belonging, power, freedom, fun,* and *survival.*

This means that no one can make another person do anything that the other person does not want to do. We answer a phone, not because it rings, but because it satisfies one or more of our needs, such as for love and belonging, better than anything else at this time. If we have something better to do, we will let the phone ring. All of our behavior, then, is our best attempt at the time to choose to do something that will satisfy one or more of these five needs. We do not do anything because of what happens outside of ourselves.

But the whole world believes that you can force, bribe, or coerce someone into doing what they do not want to do. And they point out examples of people doing what they do not want to do when the pressure is applied. For example, people who are threatened with a great deal of pain or promised a great reward often do what is distasteful to them. But the decision to do this came from their careful appraisal of their needs. They then decided that it was better to do what was distasteful than suffer the consequences or fail to reap the reward. The decision always came from inside their own heads. Some people have given up their lives rather than to do something that is against their principles, but remember that our principles, too, come from our needs, not from the world around us.

It is in understanding quality that control theory is most helpful. In general, it is safe to say that control theory explains that it is impossible to force or bribe a person into doing quality work. In school, you can make people do some work to avoid pain, but you cannot make them do quality work. Introspect your own lives and you will see that whenever you did quality work, you did so because it satisfied you to do it, not because someone else forced you. You may have done it because you loved another person, but in doing it for that person you were able to satisfy your need for love.

During our lives we keep careful track of what is satisfying to our needs, and control theory explains that we store this information in a special place in our memory that is called our *Internal* (Glasser, 1984) or quality world (Glasser, 1990). As we live and learn what is satisfying, this hypothetical place becomes an internal representation of an ideal world that we would like to live in if we could. In it are all our loved ones, our prized possessions, our ideals and values, and everything that is most important to us because we have found that these things are most satisfying to our needs.

In order to manage people successfully, it is necessary to develop the skill to persuade them to put what we want, our managerial agenda, into their quality world. Only when they do will they work hard and do a quality job of what we ask them to do. The whole thrust of Deming's three basics, therefore, is to persuade students to put into their quality worlds their schools and teachers, together with the schoolwork they assign. When this is done, students will do quality work, and when all the students and teachers do quality work, their school will become a quality school.

This is why learning control theory is so important. Students will not put a place where they are coerced or a person who coerces them into their quality worlds. And if we ask students who have schoolwork in their quality worlds to evaluate their work, they cannot help trying to improve it if they believe that this is possible.

There is much more to all aspects of a quality school than I can possibly explain here. For further information, I suggest you read *The Quality School.* If after you read this book you want to learn more, contact the Institute for Reality Therapy and ask how your school can become a part of the quality school consortium.

- CLIMATE
- COMMUNITY/PARENT INVOLVEMENT
- CURRICULUM
- LEADERSHIP
- ORGANIZATION/ MANAGEMENT (SCHOOL)

The School Development Program

James P. Comer
Yale University

The School Development Program (SDP) model was established in 1968 in two elementary schools as a collaborative effort between the Yale University Child Study Center and the New Haven School System. The two schools involved were the lowest achieving in the city, had poor attendance, and had serious problems with relationships among and between students, staff, and parents. Staff morale was low. Parents were angry and distrustful of the schools. Hopelessness and despair were pervasive.

Our Yale Child Study Center staff—social worker, psychologist, special education teacher, child psychiatrist—provided the traditional support services from these disciplines. But we focused more on trying to understand the *underlying* problems and how to correct them or to prevent their manifestations than on treating individual children or on finding deficiencies in staff and parents. We eventually identified underlying problems on both sides—family stress and student underdevelopment in areas needed for school success as well as lack of necessary organizational, management, and child development knowledge and skills on the part of school staff.

Because of preschool experiences in families under stress, a disproportionate number of low-income children were perceived by the schools as "bad," undermotivated, and of low academic potential. The behavior, in fact, reflected underdevelopment or simply development that was appropriate on the playground, at home, or other places outside of school but inappropriate in school.

The school staffs lacked knowledge about child development and behavior and understood school achievement as a function of genetically determined intellectual ability and individual motivation only. Thus, the schools were ill-prepared to modify behavior or close their students' developmental gaps. The staff usually responded with punishment and low expectations. While such responses were understandable under the circumstances, they usually led to even more difficult staff-student interactions, and, in turn, difficult staff-parent and community interactions, staff frustration, and a lower level of performance by students, parents, and staff.

Even when there was a desire to work differently, there was no mechanism at the *building level* to allow parents, teachers, and administrators first to understand the needs and then to collaborate with and help each other address them in an integrated, coordinated way. This led to blame-finding, fragmentation, duplication of effort, and frustration. There was no sense of ownership and pride in the school. The kind of synergism that develops when people work together to address problems and opportunities could not exist. This lack of synergism led to frequent and severe behavior problems and a sense of powerlessness on the part of all involved.

The need for an organizational and management system based on the knowledge of child development and relationship issues was clear. It was also clear that a *comprehensive* approach, rather than a piecemeal one that addressed any particular area of need, would be best.

A number of realities about the U.S. educational system became apparent to us during the early years of our program. Many of these realities still hold today. The organization and management of the vast majority of U.S. schools are deeply entrenched in the attitudes, values, and ways of the larger society and maintained by traditional training and practice. Most individuals and systems generally resist change. Thus, research findings, mandates from outsiders, administrators, in-service education, and the like rarely bring about significant or sustained change.

In the early school reform literature much attention was given to the need for greater "time on task." But unless a school can create a climate of relationships that reduces behavior problems and motivates academic learning, simply calling for greater time on task is useless. Simply requiring students to stay in school during a longer day or year is useless. There is no reason to believe that students will learn in two hours what they did not learn in one, unless the learning environment is changed. A safe and orderly environment, higher expectations, and all of the conditions believed to be important for effective schooling must be created where they do not exist ordinarily, and they cannot be mandated.

In order to promote desired change, mechanisms must be created that allow parents and staff to engage in a process in which they gain and apply child-development systems, and individual-behavior knowledge and skills to every aspect of a school program in a way and at a rate that is understandable and nonthreatening. Each successful activity outcome for staff, students, and parents encourages the staff to use these ways of working again, until the new way eventually replaces the old.

How Does SDP Work?

In response to the conditions we found, working collaboratively with parents and staff we gradually developed our present nine-component (three mechanisms, three operations, three guidelines) model: (1) a *governance and management team* that is representative of the parents, teachers, administrators, and support staff; (2) a *mental health* or *support staff team;* and (3) a *parents program.* The governance and management team carries out three critical operations—the development of (4) a *comprehensive school plan* with specific goals in the social climate and academic areas; (5) *staff-development* activities based on building-level goals in these areas; (6) periodic *assessment* that allows the staff to *adjust* the program to meet identified needs and opportunities.

Several important guidelines and agreements are needed. Participants on the governance and management team (7) *cannot paralyze* the leader. On the other hand, the leader cannot use the group as a "rubber stamp." While the principal usually provides leadership to the governance and management group, (8) *decisions are made by consensus* to avoid "winner-loser" feelings and behavior. And (9) a *"no-fault" problem-solving* approach is used by all of the working groups in the school. Eventually these attitudes permeate the thinking of most individuals.

In some cases—often after all involved are comfortable with the process, but sometimes initially—a staff member rather than the principal serves as the leader of the governance and management team. This substitution works when it is a genuine arrangement to promote leadership from within the staff and not an act of disengagement by the principal. With this arrangement, it is important for the principal to be present and fully involved in meetings and in facilitating the process.

The principal has legal and administrative responsibility for everything that goes on in the school. The governance and management team is the key programmatic activity of the school and the responsibility of the principal. And all of the areas of activity in a school outside of the work of the governance and management team are the responsibility of the principal; for example, implementation of school board policies, sensitive legal or personnel issues, operational responsibilities such as emergencies, and others. The team cannot paralyze the principal in these areas, and the principal must facilitate the work of the governance and management team, even when he or she is not its leader.

These nine components, developed in the 1968–69 school year, continue to make up the essential elements of the SDP. The governance and management team is the most important component. Made up of representatives of all the adult stakeholders — parents, teachers, administrators, professional and nonprofessional support staff, and also students in middle and high school — this team contains the "seeds" of a sense of community that flourishes throughout the school when the process is carried out properly. Working collaboratively, the governance and management team gives a school a sense of direction, prioritizes and coordinates activities, provides communication, and most important, allows everybody to experience a sense of ownership and a stake in the outcome of the building program. This ownership motivates desirable behavior among parents, staff, and students, and the components of the program become synergistic rather than antagonistic.

When we began our work, the psychologist, social workers, special education teachers, and others each received student referrals separately, worked without communication, and did not cooperate with each other. This referral system resulted in fragmentation, duplication, inadequate follow-through, and other ineffective practices. We arranged for these support staff persons to be assigned to a school at the same time and to work together as a team. Teachers now refer and make presentations to the team. The child development and behavioral dynamics of a case are discussed, and in some cases suggestions to the teacher are sufficient to address a problem. In other cases a team member observes in the classroom, with a follow-up in a subsequent case conference. Where necessary, a case manager is selected from among the team members, and a variety of approaches developed by the team members are used to try to help a youngster.

While working with individual students, mental health staff members sometimes notice troublesome patterns of behavior that stem from school policies and practices that are harmful to students and often to staff and parents as well. Procedures and practices are adjusted, based on the developmental and relationship needs of children and the relationship climate needs of the school. A support or mental health staff person serving on the governance and management team helps them apply child development and relationship knowledge to all activities, policies, and practices.

For example, on one occasion it was noted that the presence of kindergarten students at an assembly was disruptive. They became restless, teachers were kept busy trying to control their behavior, and other students were annoyed. The mental health person, knowledgeable about child development, pointed out that children this age have difficulty sitting and listening for an extended period of time. With this in mind, programs were arranged so that the kindergarten class could come in last, perform first, listen for a tolerable length of time, and leave during a planned break in the program. On another occasion, it was observed that staff, parents, and students alike had low energy levels during late January and much of February. The annual parent-staff dance was moved to early March and called the "Spring Fling." The exciting activities throughout the school leading up to this major event served to energize everybody.

Many problems stemmed from a high turnover of students, with new students entering a strange new environment. This turnover often led to acting-out behavior of one kind or another. Such behavior was greatly reduced with the introduction of an orientation program for new students. This program eventually led to a transition program for students leaving the school or going to the next grade level, particularly when it is in another school. Observing the discontinuity in the life of one child led to a program of keeping students with the same teacher for two years. Some children who made no academic gains the first year made two years of academic gain in the second.

Eventually the mental health team helped the staff realize the need to support students during all potentially traumatic events—e.g., illness, death, injury—and to orient them for all special occasions—e.g., visits outside of the school, visitors to the school, and new curricular activities. As the mental health and governance and management teams worked together to address student needs, a Crisis Room, a Discovery Room, activity groups, and other facilities and activities were developed to try to help youngsters function adequately in school. Referrals are made for treatment outside of the school where necessary.

In short, the focus on individual children's problems that were caused by life conditions, school conditions, or both led to a focus on *prevention*. Case management and preventive activities are carried out simultaneously, and both help create good relationships among students, staff, and parents.

Parents participate in three major ways or levels: (1) on the governance and management team through representatives they select; (2) as a parent group or team working with the staff to plan and support social and academic activities; and (3) as they attend various school events. With staff, parents sponsor projects designed to create a good social climate in the schools and work as assistants in classrooms, the cafeteria, the library, and at school functions. A teacher or some other staff person serves as a liaison to facilitate parental involvement.

As the governance and management team addresses the problems and opportunities in the school in a systematic way, the functioning of students, staff, and parents improves, and the hope and energy levels of the staff go up. Increased time for planning results, leading to improved curriculum development. Eventually the curriculum — and indeed the entire school experience — begins to promote overall development among students. The staff development program helps the teachers gain the skills necessary to promote personal, social, and academic growth in students.

Our early work led to a program called "The Social Skills Curriculum for Inner-City Children." Through this program we integrated the teaching of basic academic and social skills and arts appreciation in a way that channeled the aggressive energy of the students into the energy of learning, play, and/or work.

Our first social skills unit was created around an upcoming mayoralty election in New Haven, CT. Each student wrote a letter inviting the candidates to make a presentation before the student body, and each wrote a thank-you note after the candidates did so. Parents used money raised through activities they sponsored to create a good climate in the school by renting buses and going on field trips with staff throughout the city. They looked at conditions in the community—roads, signs, buildings—and related them to the responsibilities of government and the mayor.

Back in class, students discussed these issues and wrote papers about them. Again, this unit was a language arts, social science, social skills lesson. Throughout the unit, students worked on a dance drama program that they presented on the day the candidates visited the school. They learned the skills needed to be hosts to their parents, the staff, and the candidates.

The important relationship between basic skills and knowledge needed to be a citizen of the community was apparent through this activity. The students were related emotionally to their own community, and the staff viewed themselves as preparing their students for future participation as citizens. The activity gave the students a variety of ways to demonstrate their abilities and to gain academic skills. It also provided the teachers with a variety of ways to observe and develop the students' potential. All social activities are now designed to promote the social interactive, psycho-emotional, moral, linguistic, and intellectual-cognitive development of the students.

This initial effort has been expanded into a K–12 social development program designed to give students the mainstream skills gained by middle-income children from better-educated families simply by living with their parents. In the upper grades the program is designed to relate the students to the mainstream economy.

How Well Does SDP Work?

Efforts to document the effects of the School Development Program are based on our philosophy that education should promote personal and social as well as academic growth and that they are related. Effects of SDP have been assessed in various ways, on different outcomes, and using diverse strategies and methods. In this section we briefly summarize some of the major evaluative research findings on these effects.

ACADEMIC EFFECTS

A trend analysis of achievement data among fourth graders in the two pioneer SDP schools in New Haven conducted by our research team indicated steady gains in mathematics and reading between 1969 and 1984. The grade-equivalent scores for the two schools increased from about 3.0 in reading and mathematics in 1969 to 6.0 in reading and 5.0 in mathematics in 1984.

Several experimental control-group studies involving randomly selected students in carefully matched schools reported significant differences in academic achievement between students in SDP schools and those in non-SDP control schools. A study by Cauce, Comer, and Schwartz (1987) reported that seventh-grade students in SDP schools had significantly higher averages in mathematics and overall grade point average than students in non-SDP schools. Studies by Haynes, Comer, and Hamilton-Lee (1988a, 1989) reported that elementary school students in SDP schools showed significantly greater one-year positive changes in grade equivalent scores in reading, mathematics, and language on the California Achievement Test compared to students in non-SDP schools. SDP students also had significantly greater positive changes in classroom grades than non-SDP students.

In a retrospective follow-up study (Haynes, Comer, & Hamilton-Lee, 1988b), 102 sixth- and eighth-grade students were studied. Fifty-seven had come from non-SDP elementary school and forty-five had come from an SDP school. The academic achievement of these students was measured by report card grades and by percentile scores on the Metropolitan Achievement Test. Significant differences in favor of the SDP students were found for sixth graders in mathematics, language, and Total Battery on the MAT. SDP students obtain consistently higher scores on all other achievement measures, but these differences did not approach significance. At the eighth-grade level, no difference was significant, but, again, SDP students consistently scored higher than non-SDP students.

School level aggregated data analyses provide evidence of significant SDP effects on achievement. In 1986 an analysis of achievement data in the Benton Harbor (MI) Area Schools showed significant average four-year gains, between 7.5 and 11.0 percentile points, in reading and mathematics, at the second, fourth, fifth, and sixth grades for SDP schools. These gains exceeded those reported for the school district as a whole. Program schools also registered higher gains in mathematics and reading than the district as a whole in the percentage of students obtaining 75 percent and above of the objectives on the Michigan Educational Assessment Program.

An assessment of SDP effects conducted by the research office of the Prince George's County (MD) Public Schools in 1987 revealed that average percentile gains on the California

Achievement Test between 1985 and 1987 were significantly greater for SDP schools than for the district as a whole. At the third-grade level, SDP schools gained about 18 percentile points in mathematics, 9 percentile points in reading, and 17 percentile points in language compared to gains of 11, 4, and 9 percentile points for the district as a whole. At the fifth grade, program schools recorded gains of 21, 7, and 12 percentile points in mathematics, reading, and language respectively compared to gains of 11, 4, and 7 percentile points for the district as a whole. Further analysis also revealed that academic gains were linked to the degree and quality of implementation of the SDP.

BEHAVIOR AND SCHOOL ADJUSTMENT EFFECTS

Measures of attendance, suspensions, classroom behavior, group participation, and attitude toward authority were used to assess students' school adjustment. Aggregated data analysis conducted in Benton Harbor indicated that over a four-year period (1982 to 1985) SDP schools experienced significantly greater declines in suspension days, absent days, and number of corporal punishments recorded, compared to the district as a whole. For example, SDP schools recorded a 19 percent decline in suspension days compared to a 34 percent increase in suspension days for the district as a whole. Similarly, for corporal punishments, SDP schools recorded a 100 percent decline compared to a 36 percent decline for the district as a whole. As a direct result of the SDP, corporal punishment is no longer legal in the Benton Harbor Area Schools.

Experimental, controlled studies conducted by Haynes,et. al. (1988a, 1989) indicated that SDP students experienced significantly greater positive changes in attendance and teacher ratings of classroom behavior, attitude toward authority, and group participation compared to non-SDP students. A study by Cauce, et. al. (1987) found that SDP students reported significantly better-perceived school competence and self-competence compared to a control group of non-SDP students.

SELF-CONCEPT

In a recent study (Haynes & Comer, 1990) SDP students in the fourth and sixth grades were compared to non-SDP students on six self-concept dimensions using the Piers Harris Self-Concept Scale; any pretest differences that existed between SDP and non-SDP students were statistically controlled. Both groups of students were also compared to the national normative sample on total self-concept. On the posttest measures, SDP students scored significantly higher than the non-SDP control group students on all six self-concept dimensions and significantly higher than the normative group on total self-concept. Another study by Haynes, et. al. (1988a) also indicated that SDP students showed significantly greater positive changes in self-concept compared to non-SDP students.

CLASSROOM AND SCHOOL CLIMATE

In a quasi-experimental study involving 288 students (Comer, Haynes, & Hamilton-Lee, 1989), students in SDP schools reported significantly more positive assessments of their classroom climate than students in non-SDP schools. Classroom climate was assessed using the Classroom Environment Scale (Trickett & Moos, 1973). The 155 parents and 147 teachers also completed a school climate questionnaire designed by Haynes, et. al. (1989). Parents and teachers of students in SDP schools reported significantly more positive assessments of their schools' climate compared to parents and teachers of children in non-SDP schools.

WHITHER SDP?

The SDP model is now being utilized in over 150 schools in fourteen school districts in twelve states and the District of Columbia. It is also being utilized in several middle schools and three high schools. Change agents or facilitators are selected and trained to implement the program, under the direction of their local school superintendent, with minimal direct support from the Yale Child Study Center. In addition, small representative groups of parents, teachers, administrators, and district office staff participate in orientation workshops at Yale. This exposure enables the change agent, with others, to implement the process in their home districts.

While many school improvement approaches have emerged in recent years, most differ from our SDP approach in at least three significant ways. First, most give specific attention to one major group within a school setting—either the students, the teachers, or the parents—or to one program area—curriculum, social skills, or artistic expression, and so on. We use a *comprehensive* approach in which all groups work in a collaborative fashion, and resources and programs are coordinated to establish and achieve school objectives and goals.

Second, most programs are not driven by child development and relationship concepts at all or, at best, they utilize such concepts only in regard to the students. All aspects of our work are driven by relationship and child development imperatives, focusing most on institutional arrangements that hinder adequate functioning.

Third, many programs focus exclusively on academic achievement. We attempt first to create a school climate that permits parents and staff to support the overall development of students in a way that makes academic achievement and desirable social behavior at an acceptable level possible and expected. We believe that such an approach has a much greater potential for improving students' chances to achieve school success, for decreasing their likelihood of being involved in problem behaviors, and, as a result, for increasing their chances for life success.

We understood from the beginning that our program simply helps create the social infrastructure that makes improved teaching and learning possible. Our process model is a critical missing link in education reform, but by itself it is not enough. It permits many schools to transform and improve their programs but could permit many more with adequately trained staff and appropriate teaching and curriculum approaches. We are in the process of developing a program to address these needs and to more widely disseminate and expand our process model.

The partnerships we are developing with schools of education, state departments of education, and other institutions and with school districts will eventually enable the former to support the efforts of local and neighboring school districts independent of the Yale Child Study Center and will eventually enable them to work with other school districts of their choosing. We have also developed a consortium in which we are working with the New Haven School System and Southern Connecticut State University to develop a curriculum at the university that will better prepare students to work in urban areas. It is hoped that the curriculum will serve as a model for other preservice schools. We are developing "how-to" videotapes of commercial quality (and related manuals) that will complement our work in school districts where we are directly involved and will enable other school districts to implement the model without our presence.

We are currently exploring a partnership arrangement in which we would participate with over 100 research schools of education involved in promoting community-based professional development schools for training teachers; a national administrators group committed to school reform; and a state consortium of organizations whose goal would be to bring the political, economic, and social welfare communities together in support of education. We believe that such a consortium on a national level would provide a nucleus of commitment to change that would be large enough and powerful enough to overcome deeply entrenched but anachronistic and harmful practices and promote practices that would help most of our children learn at an adequate-to-optimal level.

The School Development Program is not a "quick fix" nor is it an "add-on." It is not just another new activity to be carried out along with all the other experiments and activities being carried out in a school. It is a nine-element process model—three mechanisms, three operations, three guidelines—that takes significant time, commitment, and energy to implement. It is a different way of conceptualizing and working in schools, and it completely replaces traditional organization and management. All of the activities in a school are managed through the SDP process. And most important, the School Development Program produces desirable outcomes only after a cooperative and collaborative spirit exists throughout a school.

PART III

Selecting and Integrating School Improvement Programs

Now, what does one do with the eighteen innovations described in Part II? Each author convincingly presents the value of using his or her ideas in schools. Students will benefit, the school organization will be healthier, parents become more involved, et cetera. We are convinced.

But which innovations and how many are right for which schools? Is one idea more important than another? Does one idea precede another? Where does school improvement begin? And how do schools with existing improvement projects organize and add to their activities? These are the questions we hear most frequently when we work with educators in schools and districts.

In Part III we address those questions. To do that we describe specific frameworks for application. These frameworks are practical and build upon the theoretical base Block introduces in chapter 1. In the next chapter Everson describes analysis and decision-making processes school leaders can use to identify problem areas and to select solutions related to the students' well-being. Guskey takes Everson's framework one step further by addressing the natural complexity of substantive school improvement, where school leaders need to address many issues and innovations simultaneously. In his chapter, Guskey clearly introduces a process to help educators think about integrating innovations and assessing how one innovation enriches another.

Our hope in providing these frameworks is that educational leaders will find enough support and guidance to develop their schools continually, using the best research- and development-based innovations to educate all of the youngsters in their care.

20

Selecting School Improvement Programs

Susan Toft Everson
Mid-continent Regional Educational Laboratory

Seymour Sarason writes, in *The Culture of the School and the Problem of Change* (1971, p. 121), "... man's desire to change is more than matched by his ingenuity in avoiding change, even when the desire to change is powered by strong pain, anxiety, and grief." In this time when the pressure for better schools is stronger than ever, it is important to remember Sarason's words. Even though the place and structure we call "school" has looked the same for a long time, the people inside that structure face changes every day, changes that are coming at breakneck speed. If you ask schoolteachers or administrators to describe a "normal" school day, often they smile or laugh and say, "What do you mean by 'normal'?" These days, every day is different, every class of students has its own personality, every year has new and increasingly difficult challenges.

The demand for educators to face changes and to do a better job is coming from every sector of our society. Avoiding change is impossible, no matter how ingenious we may be. In other words, deciding whether to change or not is not the question before us. What is before us are questions about what to change, what ideas and practices to try, and how to make decisions so that the changes have the best chance for success.

What we want, then, is *planned change.* We want to improve by making reasoned, informed decisions about the actions we will take. This book is about planned change. Each of the chapters in Part II describes "possibilities" for change available to school leaders as they clarify their school's problems and seek appropriate solutions.

This chapter proposes a process for decision making about "possibilities" for improvement—a framework that school leaders can apply when deciding which solution(s) is (are) the best for them. We address three questions: What is the leader's role or "charge" in planned change? What are some general guidelines for managing planned change? Finally, and most importantly, how do leaders decide what to do so that they increase their chances for real improvement?

THE SCHOOL LEADER'S ROLE IN PLANNED CHANGE

The hope of the current improvement and restructuring movements is that school leaders create and manage organizations in which all students succeed, that is, leave school knowing what they should know and doing what they need to do. One popular strategy to produce that result is "site-based management."

Site-based management is a strategy based on evidence suggesting that when people are involved in decisions regarding their work, better results are achieved. Recent published articles and books describe some of these site-based involvement activities. What seems clear in these publications is that it is not site-based management per se that is the key to its effectiveness and to the effectiveness of the programs being managed. Echoing a theme developed in the earlier chapter by Glasser, it is the *quality* of that management.

Ann Lieberman (1988), for example, finds that teachers in an expanded leadership role become involved in a comprehensive series of actions that include: building trust and rapport, making an organizational diagnosis (analyzing the school's current practices), building skills and confidence in others, using resources, dealing with the change process, and managing the work. Inherent in each of these actions, she adds, are strategies to build structures for collaboration—ways to work together, to focus on the school's problems, and to enhance the teachers' repertoire of teaching strategies. In a chapter in this book, James Comer supports these ideas by describing a school-level program based on teamwork and consensus that positively affects the students in the school.

Louis and Miles (1990), to take another example, suggest other qualities that exist when leaders/decision makers succeed in "getting knowledge to action." They include: clarity (knowledge of the action is understood), relevance (knowledge of the action is meaningful and connected to one's normal life and concerns), action images (knowledge is exemplified in specific mental pictures of what to do), will (motivation and interest exist—there is a will to do something with the knowledge), and skill (the behavior and ability to carry out the action exist). Interestingly, Louis and Miles found that many change efforts founder on the qualities of will and skill.

What these findings say about the role of the school leader in planned change is that if we want to implement changes successfully, teachers and administrators must have active roles in which they work together successfully and, in those roles, are responsible for their own work. In short, working together, educators must plan their actions, manage those actions, and be accountable for the consequences/results. Inescapably, these actions require decisions regarding planned changes.

SOME GENERAL GUIDELINES FOR MANAGING PLANNED CHANGE

What, then, do we know about the management of educational change that can help school leaders get the most out of planned change efforts? Fortunately, there is a body of rich information synthesized from years of investigation from which to get helpful ideas.

One expert on educational change, Michael Fullan (1990), provides four points from which we can create some general guidelines for the effective management of educational change:

There must be active initiation of that change. Educators must take action early in their improvement process. Planning to act produces little. It is like learning to swim. On the side of the pool, the learner listens and talks to the instructor about swimming but does not learn to swim. To learn to swim, he or she must get into the water and try out "the talk." This also is true in schools.

Often, actions are avoided in schools because they produce uncertainty. Early in the process particularly, fear of incompetence and failure emerge and anxiety results. So, active initiation of planned changes inevitably creates anxiety. There is a relationship between trying something new and feeling anxious. Certainly, getting into the pool to learn to swim produces anxiety for the learner. No matter how carefully we plan, changing is a lot harder than talking about change; and people are going to be anxious when making changes. *If anxiety is inevitable, support must be available.* The swimming instructor has to soothe the learner's fears of drowning or incompetence. Educators need the same soothing support. They must feel safe and supported as they try out "the talk."

To produce successful results, *both a person's beliefs and practices must change.* Focusing on one over the other is useless. The new swimmer must change behaviors and also believes swimming is worth the effort if he or she is to succeed. When facing educational changes like those described in Part II, it is as easy to imagine an educator saying, "I'll believe it when I see it" as it is to imagine one saying, "I'll do it when I believe it." One teacher approaches change from a practice point of view; one from a belief point of view. But both practice and belief are integral to any planned change process, and both warrant attention in the management of any planned change.

In educational change, *ownership grows over time;* it is not something that occurs at the beginning of the change process. This point makes such good sense, yet school leaders have spent years worrying about complete "buy-in" and "getting everyone on board" before they take action. Using our swimming analogy, we know that the new swimmer's stake in the process will grow as he or she becomes more and more adept. So it is with educators engaged in planned change. Instead of waiting for ownership to occur before we act, we must move ahead, taking action, supporting people as the inevitable anxiety sets in, and acknowledging the changes in people's beliefs and practices that occur along the way.

A second expert on educational change, Larry Cuban (1988), offers these additional insights about planned change:

Change does not necessarily create improvement. Consequently, we should carefully select the changes we implement, monitor their progress, and report the results so that people assess what is happening and come to conclusions about whether improvement is occurring.

First- and second-level educational reform (or change) must be distinguished. First-level reform addresses problems of program quality (e.g., more students are required to take a subject like algebra, or teachers must use a specific instructional model); second-level reform addresses organizational (systemic) problems (e.g., the structural changes associated with programs like alternative high schools). Matching the appropriate level of reform to the right type of problem is a key to reaping the improvements desired; reforms and the problems they are supposed to solve are often mismatched.

Change can occur in the organizational core (mainstream) of the school or on the periphery (satellite programs). Most examples of second-level (systemic) reform occur on the periphery (e.g., alternative high school programs, gifted education programs, and so on); they exist without influencing the "regular" school or the organization's core. Consequently, the kind of substantial organizational changes that are needed get treatment of first-level reform (e.g., "fixing" the climate of the school with a teacher buddy system or an inservice workshop) while real structural changes are kept at a safe distance (e.g., in a separate location or program). The mismatch expends resources and energy while maintaining the status quo. So, what does this tell us? When we manage planned change, we must manage a process of decision making that aligns the level (program or system) of the reform (the change) and its place in the school (core or periphery) to the nature of the problem we are addressing.

In combination, then, Fullan and Cuban provide two different ways of looking at planned change and seven ideas from which to draw some general guidelines about managing change:

- Active initiation is essential.
- Anxiety is inevitable, so support must be given.
- Both practices and beliefs change with any planned change effort.
- Ownership grows over time with successful action.
- Change does not always create improvement; monitoring and assessing allow educators to draw conclusions regarding improvements.
- The type of reform (first or second level) should match the type of problem being addressed (program or system).
- Reform can occur in the core (mainstream) of a school or on the periphery. Reform should occur *where* the need exists.

A Process to Make Decisions About Changes

Certainly, gaining general knowledge of the field of planned change and developing, as appropriate, related general skills (e.g., planning, decision making, facilitation, and so on) are desirable. In fact, the most important guideline to planned change may be to study and learn all that is available to help us manage it.

But general understanding of guidelines for planned change can take school leaders only so far. The educator's role may be clear and everyone may be knowledgeable about and skilled at managing change, but the questions—what to change and what to try or implement—are still unanswered. Answering these questions requires two actions. The first question requires *identification* of problems and the second question requires *selection of solutions*. *Alignment* between the problems and the solutions also must occur.

Since the innovations in Part II offer rich, research-based solutions and every solution has the potential to improve the school and help the students learn, what follows is the description of a process educators can use to *identify*, *select*, and *align* some of these school improvement programs. This process was developed by combining findings from research on educational change, organizational development, planning, school improvement, and other similar areas by the author as she has worked with hundreds of school leaders to implement school improvement. While the process described here focuses specifically on our particular menu of programs from Part II, the process may be applied to other improvement programs as well.

IDENTIFYING PROBLEMS

STEP ONE: DATA COLLECTION ABOUT CURRENT PRACTICES. To gain a clear picture of current practices in a school, the school's professionals must gather information about those practices. Typically, "needs assessment" is the first step in the decision-making process.

But often needs assessment has meant that the school faculty generates a list of possible goals for improvement and votes for favorites, frequently by a questionnaire or survey. Unfortunately, such an assessment has flaws. While perceptions or opinions ("felt needs") are important, they are inadequate as the sole information source for decision making. Perceived needs and real needs often differ.

So other information sources must be tapped and added to the needs-assessment analysis for the purpose of verifying or refuting these perceptions/opinions. Some examples of additional data sources are given in Figure 20.1.

Figure 20.1

EXAMPLES OF DATA SOURCES

- Interviews
- Observations
- Questionnaires
- Focus Groups
- Logs or Diaries
- Tests
- Data Forms
- Demographic Information
- Documentation of Staff
- Development Activities, e.g., attendance, topic, etc.

Minimally, two additional sources are needed beyond the "felt-needs" assessment. When we gather and use these additional sources to verify "felt needs," we call this process *triangulation* of data using three sources to check for common messages—a felt-needs assessment looking at perceptions/opinions and two additional sources to check those perceptions/opinions (Figure 20.2).

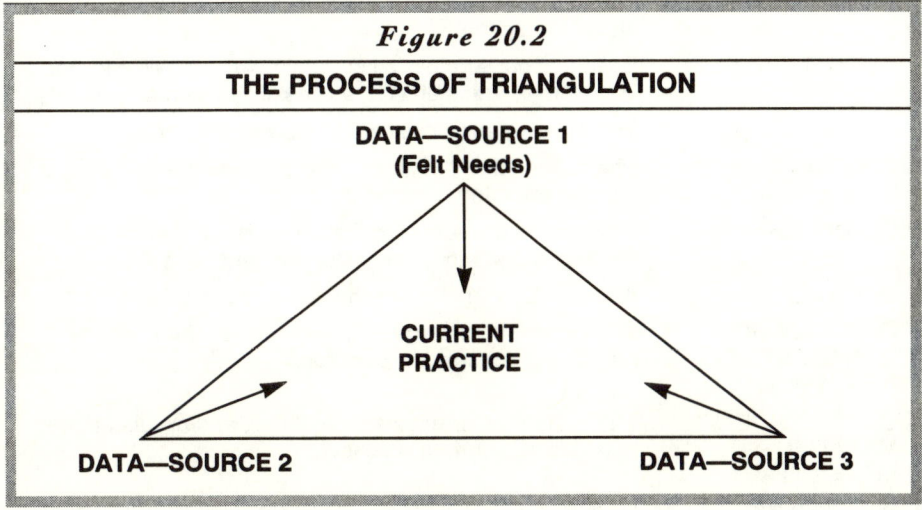

Figure 20.2

THE PROCESS OF TRIANGULATION

One hazard to watch for in identifying needs is getting caught up in analyzing minutiae, for example, how many students turn homework in late? To avoid this hazard, we suggest following the advice of David Berliner (1980), who recommends that we look at "big variables" when planning change. "Big variables" are the *major* attributes that make a school a *school* and not a business, library, hospital, or some other organization.

Again, Everson has developed a strategy to use Berliner's big variable idea to help school leaders plan and implement changes. She, with the help of many school people, submits the following as an example of a list of "big variables" and their definitions:

Figure 20.3
DEFINITIONS OF BIG VARIABLE

ASSESSMENT:	A process to monitor how well a student is progressing toward established outcomes.
CLIMATE:	Order, safety, culture, norms, and social interaction of school or classroom.
COMMUNITY/PARENT INVOLVEMENT:	Community/parental participation and support for learning.
CURRICULUM:	The content (both formal and informal) of what is studied in school.
EXPECTATIONS:	Beliefs about whether all students can and will succeed and whether the staff can successfully teach all students.
FACILITIES:	The building and physical structures of schools.
INSTRUCTION:	The actions and practices used by a teacher to help the student learn the curriculum.
LEADERSHIP:	The person or persons guiding others with vision and strategies that move the group forward.
MOTIVATION:	A person's incentive or stimulation to act.
ORGANIZATION/ MANAGEMENT (CLASSROOM):	The system of strategies, guidelines, and/or rules that provides structure to a classroom.
ORGANIZATION/ MANAGEMENT (SCHOOL):	The system of strategies, guidelines, and/or rules that provides structure to a school.

As school leaders triangulate their data, then, they look for common messages across data sources about the "big variables" in their school. For example, what do the data tell us about our expectations, curriculum, and so on?

To summarize, there are two tasks in Step One:

1. Collect data from at least three data sources including "felt needs," and
2. Look across these data for "common messages" about the "big variables" in the school.

For more details about accomplishing these tasks, we recommend a structure developed in the Georgia Research and Development Utilization Project (Gray, 1978). In this project, teachers developed a model for planning that involved the use of a "felt needs" assessment to determine what a cross section of the school community thought ought to be the highest priority improvements. The felt needs are then verified by objective means such as achievement scores, student products, interviews of students, teachers, administrators, parents, and observations.

STEP TWO: BEST PRACTICES STUDY. While the "current practices" picture is being filled in, we also want to study what research and development (R & D) tells us about "best practices" in the same "big variables." By "best practices," we mean research-based practices that are most effective and equitable in generating student learning outcomes.

There are a number of ways educators can study "best practices." Certainly, school study groups make sense; this book offers a handy resource for such groups. Additionally, workshops, in-service education programs, courses, conferences, and summer institutes provide resources for school faculties to use for study. Educational journals, especially *Educational Leadership* and *Kappan,* also frequently offer articles that include practical syntheses of current research and development findings.

It is important to use a triangulation process to study "best" practices just as it is to study "current" ones. A single source of information can be biased and limited. By studying multiple sources, "common messages" regarding best practices emerge.

Using instruction as our example, we can begin to identify the characteristics of effective instruction by looking for descriptions of similar functions/behaviors across sources. For example, we can make a legitimate argument that effective instructional practice includes stating (a) a clear purpose or meaning for the lesson, one (b) that the students understand. A study group that reads, say, the Carnine et al., Cohen, Guskey, and Hunter chapters in this volume could identify such a "best" effective instruction practice. Again, we look for common messages across multiple data sources.

In summary, then, Figure 20.4 shows what we want to complete in Steps One and Two:

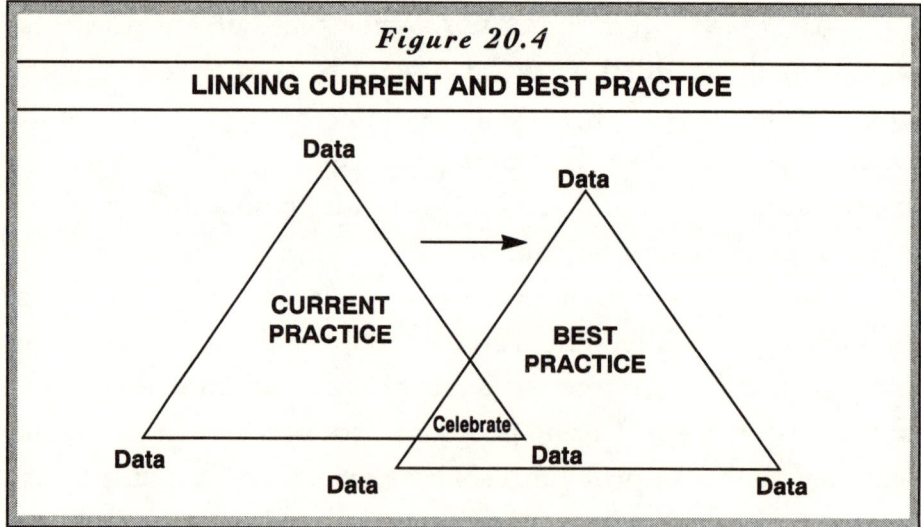

Figure 20.4
LINKING CURRENT AND BEST PRACTICE

STEP THREE: DISCREPANCY ANALYSIS. When we have our current and "best practices" data in hand, we do a discrepancy analysis. That is, we find the "big variable" areas where current and best practices match and those where they differ.

When matches occur, the people involved should *celebrate* their successes! As educators, we do too little celebration of real successes. But what happens when we identify "big variable" areas in which current and best practices do not match? Now, we know we have identified areas for improvement, which we call *targets*. Our task in planned change is to move current practices toward the best practices in targeted areas so that we create as much overlap and, hence, celebration as possible.

Obviously, the work to make that move from current to best practices never ceases. The triangles are fluid and dynamic; new data are being fed into those pictures constantly, so the continuous use of Steps 1, 2, and 3 and the updating of the pictures are necessary for current and accurate analysis.

STEP FOUR: CLARIFICATION OF PROBLEM. Once we have identified "big variable" target areas, the next step is to clarify within each of those targets the real nature of the problem. According to Bob Ewy (1989, p. 1), a school improvement program developer, "One of the greatest barriers to working constructively toward achieving improvement goals is lack of specificity in stating the problem." Writing a *problem statement* helps educators find that specificity.

Ewy (1989, p 1) offers the following guidelines for writing a good problem statement:

1. Who is affected? Consider these possibilities before deciding what you want to say about this. Is it you? Is it one other person? Is it a small group of people? Is it an entire organization? Is it the school district? Is it the community or society at large?

2. What kind of a problem is it? There are many ways to classify kinds of problems. The following considerations may prove helpful:
   - There is lack of clarity or disagreement about goals.
   - There is lack of clarity or disagreement about the means of achieving goals.
   - There is a lack of skills needed to carry out a particular task.
   - There is a lack of material resources.
   - There is inaccurate communication.
   - There is too little or too much communication.
   - People have different understandings of the same thing.
   - There is insufficient time, or schedules don't coincide.
   - Roles are lacking or inappropriate.
   - Norms are restrictive, unclear, or misinterpreted.
   - There are conflicts of ideology.
   - There is a lack of clarity or a conflict about decision making, e.g., power struggles.
   - Expression of feelings is inappropriate or inadequate.
   - There is conflict related to individual differences.
3. What is the goal for improvement? Ideally, this [step] should be stated so clearly that anyone reading your goal statement would know how to determine when the goal is reached. It would tell exactly who would be doing what, where, how, and to what extent. Until you know where you are going, it is very difficult to make and carry out plans to get there. The more clear you are about your intended target at any given time, the more

likely you will be to recognize that it is an incorrect target, should this prove to be the case.

SELECTING SOLUTIONS

In completing problem statements, the goals within each "big variable" target area are stated, and we are ready to select activities to help reach the goals and meet the needs. The same sources (e.g., this book, journals, workshops) that support the study of "best practices" also can support solution selection.

What we want to encourage in solution selection is quality control in the review of these sources. To do that, school leaders can use the following steps.

STEP ONE: CRITERIA DEVELOPMENT. First, generate a list of selection criteria. Many of these criteria have been detailed in the aforementioned Georgia Research and Development Utilization Project (Gray, 1978). For example: What elements are needed and what do they cost? Is technical assistance or training available? Is follow-up support necessary and, if so, available?

STEP TWO: OPTIONS DEVELOPMENT. Second, develop a list of solutions (e.g., programs or changes) that fit the criteria. Suppose, for example, that you want to do something regarding community/parent involvement, but at a low cost. Innovations such as Accelerated Schools or School Development programs described in Part II might fill the bill.

STEP THREE: OPTION INFORMATION GATHERING. Then, gather information about each option. For example, decision makers need to know: What is the predicted impact on programs and students? What are the results from past use? What are the equity consequences (who benefits)? What are strengths and weaknesses?

And what is appropriate application? Newer programs (e.g., Accelerated Schools) might have less information available than established ones (e.g., School Development). So you might have to dig deeper for information in some cases than in others. But program developers are usually anxious to help (for addresses of our developers, see *Contributors*, this volume, p. xix).

STEP FOUR: CHOICE SELECTION. Once the criteria for selection and program information are gathered, study both and, based on your analysis, narrow the field of choices about solutions and their implementation. Both Accelerated Schooling and the School Development program, for example, have had important impacts and results. But the latter program has been around longer than the former and so has demonstrated this impact and results over a longer term. For building, say, community/parent involvement, then, such a successful mature program might be a safer bet than a younger one. On the other hand, accelerated schools might offer local training and a state network to school leaders, as it does in some locations, so that it would be a good choice.

ALIGNING PROBLEMS AND SOLUTIONS

Now that the needs are clearly identified and a list of possible solutions has been generated, the major remaining task is making sure that the solution proposed will address the needs or problem identified. For example, an instructional quality problem must be matched with instructional development innovations. While peer coaching (Robbins), new technology (Bortnick), new leadership/organization (Comer, Glasser, Levin, Lezotte) are marvelous innovations, they do not address instruction *directly*. The options described by, say, Carnine,

Cohen, Guskey, Johnson and Johnson, or Hunter do focus on instruction and would be more appropriate solutions.

The alignment step helps leaders make the appropriate match between needs or problems and solutions. The key to this step is the use of the problem statement. The solutions selected ought to relate directly to the answers to the three questions in the problem statements—who is affected, what kind of problem is it, and what is the goal for improvement.

Figure 20.5 gives an example of a matrix, developed by Everson, to help educational leaders check the alignment between programs and target areas using the programmatic innovations in this book. Everson developed the matrix to help school leaders identify the primary foci of each innovation and match those foci to the "big variables." While each innovation is marked for its primary emphases, it also is true that many of the programs described in this book have secondary emphases also. Those are not identified here, although the reader is encouraged to create a secondary set of markings if it is helpful to the solution selection process. Furthermore, the reader can use the matrix analysis for school improvement programs not described in this book and can add additional "big variables" as well. The important issue is whether the program innovation matches the identified target area.

It is important to note that the solution selection process described here is related directly to the formal program innovations described in this book. In no way does this imply that the informal creation of new practices by teachers and others in schools and districts is less valuable and should not be tried. In fact, the process described here provides a system that can help educators assess the impact of their creative ideas as they implement them so that they institute quality control. The same

Figure 20.5
TARGETING OUR MENU OF INNOVATIONS

	Cooperative Learning	Critical Thinking	Interactive Learning/Hypermedia	Mastery Learning	Assessment as School Improvement	Direct Instruction	Instructional Alignment	Mastery Teaching	Peer Coaching	Teaching for Literacy	Writing Across Curriculum	Accelerated Schooling	Effective Schooling	Early Childhood Education	Invitational Education	Outcome-based Education	Quality School	School Development Program
Assessment				X	X		X						X			X	X	
Climate									X			X	X		X		X	X
Community/Parent Involvement												X	X	X				X
Curriculum	X	X	X		X	X	X		X	X			X		X			X
Expectations				X			X					X	X		X	X		
Facilities			X						X									
Instruction	X	X	X	X		X	X	X		X	X			X				
Leadership												X	X				X	X
Motivation		X							X		X			X		X		
Organization/Management (Classroom)	X			X			X	X							X		X	
Organization/Management (School)	X				X			X					X	X	X	X	X	X

analysis and decision-making steps apply to locally developed interventions and increase the chances of separating those that help students from those that do not.

IMPLEMENTATION. Once the alignment is assured, the solutions are implemented. Data regarding the effectiveness of this implementation and of the solutions themselves are then gathered, and the analysis and decision-making process we described continues cyclically. To recap, the steps to the process are:

Problem Identification
    Step 1—Data Collection on Current Practices
    Step 2—Best Practices Study
    Step 3—Discrepancy Analysis
    Step 4—Clarification of the Problem(s)

Solution Selection
    Step 1—Criteria Development
    Step 2—Options Development
    Step 3—Option Information Gatherin
    Step 4—Choice Selection

Problem/Solution Alignment
    Check for a match between the solutions selected and the problems identified.

CONCLUDING COMMENT

This chapter has proposed that change in schooling is inevitable. What is not inevitable is school leaders' attitudes toward change. We believe that change can be productive if it is planned.

Our framework for planning school change can be summed up as follows: In order to produce the successful results that should come from any planned change effort, educators must be actively involved in those decisions about the changes they are expected to make; educators must have the knowledge and skill to manage planned change processes; and, most important, educators must be informed and wise decision makers so that the changes match the areas that need changing and thus have the best chance to create improvements that increase student learning.

In some of the research on staff development, one of the characteristics of effective programs is that classrooms and schools function like "action laboratories" (Loucks-Horsley, 1987). This means that teachers and administrators investigate new options as part of their regular routines, assess the impact on students, and modify their "actions" according to their assessment. The analysis and decision-making cycle described here assists that process. It seems to us that this approach has a far better chance of fulfilling the demand for "better schools" that educators face. And if we succeed, perhaps the ingenuity Sarason describes in the opening quotation of this chapter can be focused on progress rather than on ways to inhibit it.

21

Integrating School Improvement Programs

Thomas R. Guskey
University of Kentucky

At no other time in the history of education have there been more new ideas and innovations available to educators. Administrators and teachers who are planning school improvement programs today can choose among an exceptionally wide variety of models and strategies. Each of these options promises to improve student learning and enhance the quality of education. At the same time, each represents a somewhat different vehicle to use on the road to educational excellence.

A number of reasons have been offered to explain this proliferation of innovations in education. Some observers suggest that entrepreneurial factors are the principal cause. They argue that public pressure for better results has left educators desperate to find new ways to improve student learning. As a result, many are willing to invest large amounts of money in new programs, especially those that promise quick-fix solutions to sticky educational problems. Opportunistic entrepreneurs have responded by developing scores of educational strategies and materials designed specifically to appeal to pressured educators. Thus, according to this view, it is financial reasons, not educational ones, that are chiefly responsible for the myriad of educational innovations "on the market" today.

While there is little doubt that entrepreneurial factors are at work, we believe a stronger contributing factor behind the growing number of innovations in education is advances in our understanding of teaching, learning, and schooling processes. Researchers are constantly discovering new knowledge about how individuals learn, how learning can be enhanced, and how schools can be structured better to facilitate learning. As this knowledge base expands, new types of expertise, new forms of pedagogical practice, and new approaches to schooling are needed by educators at all levels. These new approaches often take the form of school improvement innovations and frequently include curricular, instructional, and/or assessment materials designed to facilitate implementation. We are convinced, therefore, that the multitude of these modern innovations available to educators is a positive development, stemming primarily from unprecedented growth in the professional knowledge base of education.

A quick analysis of the most popular school improvement innovations in education today shows that they share several characteristics. All seek to provide better learning opportunities for students so that more can meet with learning success. Most innovations also can be adapted for use in various types of districts, in schools of different sizes, at any grade level, and in almost any subject area. What is more, all have numerous advocates eager to testify that a particular strategy does, indeed, improve educational outcomes, although the theoretical and research foundations of each differ greatly in strength.

SELECTING SCHOOL IMPROVEMENT INNOVATIONS

The number and kinds of school improvement innovations that school leaders choose to include in an improvement program vary from district to district and from school to school. Some center their plans on the comprehensive implementation of a single innovative so that their efforts can be well focused and clearly articulated. The vast majority of districts and schools, however, include a combination of innovations in their improvement programs. While the educational leaders in these settings may be aware of the need for coherence among their improvement initiatives, they are sensitive to the political risks of "putting all their eggs in one basket." They also may recognize that no single innovation is likely to solve the wide array of problems schools typically face.

School leaders also vary in the criteria they use to select innovations for an improvement program. Occasionally they employ the decision-making process advocated in the previous chapter. In such cases, a set of innovative strategies is selected after careful consideration of pertinent evidence, such as results from a faculty needs survey, scores from a comprehensive student assessment program, or data gathered through a formal internal evaluation. More often, however, innovations are selected on the basis of personal preferences or impressions of a few key individuals. The style of presentation or the personal appeal of the purveyor of an innovation can sometimes influence decision makers as much as the characteristics of the innovation itself (Abrami, et al., 1982).

PUTTING THE SCHOOL IMPROVEMENT INNOVATIONS TO WORK

Once they have chosen a set of improvement innovations, school leaders generally turn their attention to implementation. To begin, they must allocate substantial funds to purchase the necessary materials and to hire experts to introduce the innovations. In addition to the financial burden, each innovation also requires considerable amounts of time for initial staff development and for essential follow-up activities. Faced with limited resources, districts and schools can seldom implement their selected innovations all at once.

As a result, most school improvement programs are implemented incrementally, one innovation this year, another next year, and so on. Each year an expert is invited to or recruited from the district to introduce staff members to a particular strategy. A small group of teachers and administrators is trained in the strategy's use, and then follow-up sessions are scheduled to support implementation efforts during that school year. This step-by-step approach assumes that teachers and administrators will assimilate each strategy as it comes along, add it to their repertoires of professional skills, and consequently improve their work with students.

Unfortunately, current evidence indicates that improvement programs implemented in this manner rarely bring any sort of lasting improvements (Huberman & Miles, 1984; Latham, 1988; Loucks-Horsley, et al., 1987). One reason for this failure is that practitioners often need more than one year to grow comfortable with any change. For the majority of teachers and administrators, the first year of implementation is a time of trial and experimentation. In particular, if the new strategy requires the use of unfamiliar practices, a great deal of effort goes into *adjusting to the innovation* and *adjusting it to fit* the conditions of particular classrooms and school contexts. Berman and McLaughlin (1976, 1977) refer to this process as "mutual adaptation" and recommend that practitioners have an extended period of time to work through this difficult phase. Thus, if support and follow-up activities are withdrawn after a year in order to devote resources to yet another innovative school improvement strategy, the first strategy's true effects are not likely to be realized by many teachers or administrators, nor will they reach many students.

Practioners, on the other hand, will be acutely aware of the costs of the first strategy in terms of the time and effort its implementation required. A small number may perceive its potential benefits, but without direct evidence of positive effects on students, very few indeed will persevere to refine their use of the strategy (Guskey, 1986). Instead, many will abandon their efforts and return to the old familiar strategies they used in the past.

A second reason the incremental approach fails to yield long-term improvement is that practitioners who experience support and follow-up for a year or less may come to view the innovation as an isolated fad. Most will see no relation between the current focus and programs that came before or those that may come afterward.

For these reasons, experienced teachers and administrators often shun new programs. They have learned that the present innovation will be gone in a year, only to be replaced by yet another bandwagon (Latham, 1988). In fact, it is not unusual to hear practitioners refer to the staff-development program topic of the moment as TYNT, for "This Year's New Thing." And cynics know, of course, that TYNT is bound to be different from LYNT, which was "Last Year's New Thing." Veteran teachers and administrators frequently calm the fears of their less-experienced colleagues who express concern about implementing a new strategy with the advice, "Don't worry; this too shall pass."

Our jack-of-all-strategies-master-of-none pattern not only obscures improvement and provokes cynicism. Sadly, it also imposes a sense of affliction. Too often, practitioners learn to see all innovations as trials they must endure in a futile attempt to cure what uninformed outsiders perceive as the ineptitude of educators. Such failures are further amplified by the mismatch between "real needs" and "proposed solutions," as we discussed in the previous chapter.

INTEGRATING THE SCHOOL IMPROVEMENT INNOVATIONS

What is needed today even more than extended support and follow-up is a precise description of how to integrate a system's collection of school improvement programs into some kind of coherent framework that matches the system's identified improvement needs. It is difficult enough to learn the particular features of the individual programs, let alone figure out how they can be used together. Furthermore, because no one innovation is totally comprehensive, many problems will remain unsolved. It is only when several strategies are carefully and systematically integrated that substantial improvements in learning become possible.

Ideally, the purveyors of the various innovations would lead the way to a judicious, methodical synthesis of the various strategies. In presentations and demonstrations, they could show how the strategies they advocate can be used in conjunction with others, especially those with which a district's or building's staff are already familiar. They could describe how the others complement the ones they favor, then suggest practical, efficient, and manageable ways for teachers and administrators to combine and integrate them.

Although this ideal is realized occasionally (see whole issue of *Educational Leadership*, 47(5); Guskey, 1988a, 1990a; Mevarech, 1985), it seems unlikely to become common practice. One reason is that many of the strongest advocates of singular innovations are so deeply involved in the ongoing development and refinement of their particular ideas. Most work extensively with school districts on program implementation, some participate in efforts to improve and refine their ideas, and a small number are engaged in research studies to determine how effective their strategy is under various conditions. As a result, few have or take the time to develop the deep understanding of other innovations necessary for suggesting how to synthesize them for use in schools or classrooms.

Further, an underlying sense of competition among the proponents of different strategies often hinders efforts to integrate. With limited funds and time for staff development, school leaders may have to choose among innovations. Consequently, some presenters emphasize the strong points of their strategy and what they regard as weaknesses in the others in order to enhance "sales." They are not inclined to concentrate on how different strategies can be combined for fear this might diminish the use of theirs. Unfortunately, this rivalry promotes a separatist view of the innovations and increases the frustration and cynicism of practitioners.

If specific ideas on how the various innovations can be integrated does not come from their most fervent advocates, from whom will it come? We believe it will have to come from the same team of administrators and teachers who develop the district or building improvement program and who choose the set of innovations to be included in that program. This belief, and our absolute confidence in the importance of *integration* for meaningful improvement, led to the development of this book.

CREATING A FRAMEWORK FOR INTEGRATION

To aid school leaders in their efforts to synthesize the different innovations that constitute their school improvement programs, we offer five general guidelines. These guidelines are not a comprehensive formula for improvement. Rather, they should be taken as a frame of reference for addressing issues crucial to the success of integrating any combination of innovations.

1. *All innovations in the improvement program should share common premises and goals.* Every innovative strategy described in this book is specifically designed to increase learning and enhance the well-being of students. Although many are based on different philosophical perspectives and focus on different aspects of teaching, learning, and schooling, all presume that learning can be improved and that educators strongly influence learning. Furthermore, all emphasize that when students experience greater success in learning, they feel better about learning, better about themselves as learners, and are more highly motivated to continue learning in the future. Explicit acknowledgement of these *shared* premises and common goals is a necessary first step in bringing about their systematic integration.

2. *No single innovation can do everything.* Despite the claims of some advocates, no innovation will solve all the complex problems facing educators today. Therefore, a highly effective improvement program must note the different strengths of various innovations and employ a combination of strategies that will positively influence different aspects of teaching, learning, and schooling.

We see the process of educational improvement as similar to that of building a new house. When engaged in the complex process of constructing a new house, one frequently needs to drive a nail. A hammer, of course, is an excellent tool for that task. If the only tool one has is a saw, however, this relatively simple task becomes extremely difficult. A saw is not a very good tool for driving a nail. But in building the house one also needs to cut boards. If the only tool one has is a hammer, again this simple task becomes nearly impossible. A saw is a necessary tool for that task.

Similarly in educational improvement, the complexity of the process requires a variety of tools. One alone will not serve all purposes well. School and classroom contexts differ, as well as the needs within those contexts. To be effective at any level of education, practitioners must develop their skills in using a combination of tools or innovations, each for the purposes for which it is most appropriate. The "Big Variables" matrix described in the previous chapter was specifically designed to offer practitioners guidance in selecting the particular innovations or tools that will best meet their needs in their particular context.

3. *The innovations in the improvement program should complement each other.* The complementary nature of innovations must be emphasized and constantly reinforced if practitioners are to understand how to integrate them and how to translate that synthesis into classroom and schooling practice. Whenever presenters introduce a new program, they should illustrate how it ties in with the ones introduced earlier.

   Of course, differences between programs should be pointed out, particularly points of disagreement. Again, the "Big Variables" matrix may be useful in drawing these distinctions. But attention needs to move beyond simple comparative analyses and toward practical syntheses. The compromises necessary to attain such a synthesis are far more likely to enhance the effectiveness of each program than to detract from any one.

4. *All innovations need to be adapted to individual classroom and building conditions.* Few practitioners can take what they have learned from staff development, move directly into the classroom or school building, and begin employing the new program with success (Crandall, 1983). Educators need time to experiment and work through the process of mutual adaptation.

   Support during this period of adjustment is critically important, and that support must be extended beyond the first year of implementation (Guskey, 1986; Loucks-Horsley, et al., 1987). Teachers and administrators alike need ongoing guidance and direction to adapt the program to their needs while still maintaining its fidelity. Without the necessary guidance and support, the innovation is apt to be implemented poorly or incompletely, and improvements will then be minimal.

5. *The results achieved with a well-conceived combination of innovations are likely to be greater than those attained using any single one.* The various innovations described in Part II are, for the most part, complementary in nature. Using a combination of them, therefore, is likely to prove very powerful. In fact, current research evidence suggests that when a combination of programs is employed, each addressing a different aspect of the teaching, learning, or schooling process, the results can be *additive*. That is, if one innovation is in place and another is added, the benefits of the new program do not duplicate those of the established one but, rather, add to them (Bloom, 1984; Walberg, 1984). For example, when mastery learning and cooperative learning are used together in a positive school culture that supports the implementation of improvement plans, results are most impressive (Guskey, 1990a; Mevarech, 1985).

Of the five guidelines offered, this is probably the most crucial—and the most neglected. If the effects brought about by different programs were not additive, the incentive to use them in combination would be far less compelling. It remains our challenge to determine the optimal combinations for particular contexts and to implement them in ways that give them the greatest chance to produce their best results.

SOME EXAMPLES

Space precludes a full treatment of all the different ways any particular collection of school improvement innovations might be integrated. Besides, several recent journal articles do this well, and we see no need to duplicate those efforts. The February 1990 issue of *Educational Leadership*, for example, was devoted in its entirety to "Making Connections" among such programs as critical thinking and mastery learning (Arredondo & Block, 1990), cooperative learning and mastery teaching (Davidson & O'Leary, 1990), and mastery teaching and writing (Weber, 1990).

We would like to describe, however, two examples of frameworks for integrating innovations that we have found particularly useful in our work. We have yet to use a third example developed by Fullan and Hargreaves (1991), but many of our Canadian colleagues find it to be a useful integrative tool as well.

A LEARNING FRAMEWORK FOR INTEGRATION

The first of these frameworks was developed by Marzano, Pickering, and Brandt (1990). It is based on various dimensions of learning and focuses on the classroom, curriculum, and instruction. As described earlier, an overriding concern among all of the innovations described in this book is that all students attain certain learning outcomes. At the same time, different innovations focus on different dimensions of the teaching, learning, and schooling process. By recognizing the dimensions of learning a particular innovation stresses, school leaders can pull together innovations that collectively stress those dimensions most needed in that setting, as described in the preceding chapter by Everson.

Marzano and his colleagues propose that school improvement innovations can address five different kinds of student thinking. One is the thinking required to *develop positive attitudes and perceptions toward learning,* such as attitudes about self and climate, self and others, and self and tasks. A second is the thinking required to *acquire and integrate knowledge,* specifically the mental process of constructing meaning, organizing content, and storing or practicing that content. To *extend and refine knowledge* requires a third kind of thinking. This involves the mental operations of comparing, classifying, inducing, deducing, analyzing errors, constructing support, abstracting, and analyzing value. The fourth kind is the thinking needed to *make meaningful use of knowledge* through such processes as oral discourse, composing, problem solving, decision making, and scientific inquiry. Finally, there is the kind of thinking needed to *develop desirable habits of mind,* especially critical, creative, and self-regulatory thinking skills.

This "Dimensions of Learning" framework has been used by Marzano and his colleagues to compare a host of school improvement innovations. Included in their comparisons are many of the programs described in this book, such as cooperative learning, mastery learning, mastery teaching, and direct instruction. Others, such as teacher expectations (e.g., TESA), critical thinking (e.g., Tactics for Thinking), and learning and teaching styles (e.g., 4MAT), are also included. Figure 21.1 shows Marzano and his colleagues' comparisons of these programs.

Two observations regarding the comparisons in this figure are in order. First, the ratings of the programs included in this book are probably conservative. Marzano and his colleagues' ratings are based on early writings about each program and, in

Figure 21.1

COMPARISON OF SELECTED PROGRAMS ON THE DIMENSIONS OF LEARNING

Program	A	B	C	D	E	F	G	H	I	J	K	L	M	N	O	P	Q	R	S	T
Dimension #1: Attitudes																				
1. Self and Climate	S	S	S	S	M	–	–	–	–	–	–	–	–	–	–	–	–	M	S	–
2. Self and Others	M	S	S	M	M	–	–	–	–	–	M	M	–	M	–	–	–	M	S	M
3. Self and Task	S	S	M	S	M	S	S	S	S	M	–	–	–	–	–	–	–	S	S	–
Dimension #2: Acquiring and Integrating Knowledge																				
1. Declarative																				
a. Constructing Meaning	S	M	S	S	S	S	S	S	M	–	–	–	–	–	–	S	M	S	S	M
b. Organizing	S	M	S	S	S	S	S	S	M	–	–	–	–	–	–	S	S	S	M	S
c. Storing	S	–	M	M	S	S	S	S	M	–	–	–	–	–	–	M	S	S	S	S
2. Procedural																				
a. Construcitng Meaning	S	M	S	S	M	S	S	S	M	–	–	–	–	–	–	–	–	M	S	–
b. Organizing	S	M	S	S	M	S	S	S	M	–	–	–	–	–	–	S	M	S	M	M
c. Practicing	S	–	M	S	–	S	S	S	S	M	–	–	–	–	–	M	S	S	S	M
Dimension #3: Extending and Refining Knowledge																				
1. Compar ing	–	–	–	–	S	–	–	M	S	M	M	M	S	S	M	M	M	M	S	S
2. Classifying	–	–	–	–	S	–	–	M	S	M	M	S	S	M	S	M	M	M	S	S
3. Inducing	–	–	–	–	M	M	M	M	M	S	M	M	S	M	M	M	M	M	S	M
4. Deducing	–	–	–	–	–	–	–	–	–	M	–	S	S	–	–	–	–	–	–	–
5. Anaylzing Errors	–	–	–	–	S	–	–	–	–	S	M	M	S	M	–	S	–	–	–	–
6. Supporting	–	–	–	–	S	M	M	–	M	S	M	M	S	M	M	M	M	–	–	S
7. Abstracting	–	–	–	–	–	–	–	–	–	M	M	M	S	S	M	S	S	M	S	M
8. Analyzing Value	–	–	–	–	–	–	–	–	–	M	–	–	S	S	S	–	S	–	–	S
Dimension #4: Meaningful Use of Knowledge																				
1. Oral Discourse	–	–	–	–	S	–	–	–	–	–	–	M	–	S	S	–	–	–	–	–
2. Composing	–	–	–	–	–	–	–	–	M	M	M	M	–	–	–	–	M	–	–	–
3. Problem Solving	–	–	–	–	S	–	–	–	S	M	S	S	M	S	–	S	–	–	–	S
4. Decision Making	–	–	–	–	S	–	–	–	–	M	M	S	S	M	S	–	S	–	–	S
5. Scientific Inquiry	–	–	–	–	S	–	–	–	–	M	S	–	–	–	–	–	M	–	–	–
Dimension #5: Habits of the Mind																				
1. Critical	–	M	S	–	M	–	M	–	M	–	S	S	M	S	M	–	–	–	–	M
2. Creative	–	–	M	–	M	–	–	–	–	–	S	S	M	S	–	–	–	–	M	S
3. Self-Regulation	M	–	S	M	M	–	M	M	S	–	S	S	–	M	–	–	S	–	M	–

KEY: S = strong emphasis   M = moderate emphasis   – = relatively little emphasis

PROGRAM KEY

A   ITIP. Hunter 1969, 1976, 1982
B   TESA. Kerman, Kimball, and Martin 1980
C   Cooperative Learning. Johnson and Johnson 1987; Slavin 1983, 1986
D   Mastery Learning. Bloom 1971; Block 1971, 1985; Guskey 1985
E   Models of Teaching. Joyce and Weil 1986.
F   Explicit Teaching. Rosenshine 1986.
G   Active Mathetics Teaching. Good, Grouws and Ebmeier 1983.
H   BTES. Romberg 1980.
I   Strategic Teaching. Jones, Palincsar, Ogle and Carr 1987.
J   Bloom's Taxonomy: Cognitive Domain. Bloom, et al 1956.
K   Olympics of the Mind. Gourley 1981.
L   Future Problem Solving. Crabbe 1982.
M   Project Impact. Winocur 1985.
N   Philosophy for Children. Lipman, Sharp and Oscanyan 1980.
O   CoRT. de Bono 1983, 1985.
P   Strategic Reasoning. Upton 1961, Upton and Samson 1963.
Q   Tactics for Thinking. Marzano and Arredondo 1986.
R   The Skillful Teacher. Saphier and Gower 1986.
S   4MAT. McCarthy 1980.
T   Teaching Styles and Strategies. Hanson, Silver and Strong 1986.

—Figure from *Educational Leadership*, February, 1990

many cases, do not reflect current emphases in the various dimensions of learning that these programs are now trying to address. For example, concern with thinking processes that extend and refine knowledge and that use knowledge meaningfully are more central to cooperative learning, mastery learning, mastery teaching, and direct instruction than was once the case.

A second and more obvious observation is that many of the programs included in this book are not rated by Marzano and his colleagues. We leave these ratings to the reader. Doing so should prove a valuable activity and should make the dimensions of learning set forth in this framework more meaningful.

Though it may be a stretch, we also find the Dimensions of Learning framework to be useful in clarifying how the "schooling-focused" programs in this book directly affect self-climate and self-other issues. Accelerated schooling, early childhood education, effective schools, invitational education, outcome-based education, quality schools, and the school development program all attempt to restructure the social climate within which students learn. These programs seek to have schools become places where no student is "at risk," social justice prevails, the world of school is linked to the world of work, and students routinely question current social, political, and economic paradigms in the search for ways to make them better.

We also find this framework to be helpful in illustrating how some of our more "teaching and learning"-oriented programs address self-climate and self-task issues. Assessment, instructional alignment, interactive learning, mastery learning, mastery teaching, peer coaching, teaching for literacy, and writing across the curriculum all attempt to restructure the work climate in which students learn. They seek to develop schools in which students' intrinsic motivation to learn is piqued by educators who show them that learning can be challenging, curiosity provoking, self-controlled, and fun.

As a result of insights gained through the Dimensions of Learning framework, we are currently exploring how various programs might be combined so that the social and work aspects of school learning support each other rather than interfere. Our recent experiments in Missouri combining the strategies of outcome-based education, curriculum alignment, mastery learning, and cooperative learning begin to show the potential of self-climate/other/task combinations (Guskey & Block, 1991; Guskey, Passaro, & Wheeler, 1991).

A TEACHING FRAMEWORK FOR INTEGRATION

A second framework we have found especially helpful in a variety of contexts uses "teaching" ideas to integrate particular innovations. This framework was developed by Guskey (1990b) and is built around what are considered to be the five major components in the teaching and learning process. These components include a specification of learning objectives or outcomes, instruction, en route or "formative" learning assessment, learning feedback and corrective/enrichment instruction, and final or "summative" learning evaluation. The teaching framework set forth by Guskey uses these components as a basis on which to compare the relative strengths of selected school or instructional innovations. Obviously, school leaders could do likewise for other programs from the book that Guskey did not rate.

A summary of Guskey's interpretations of the major strengths of some of the programs we have considered is shown in Figure 21.2.

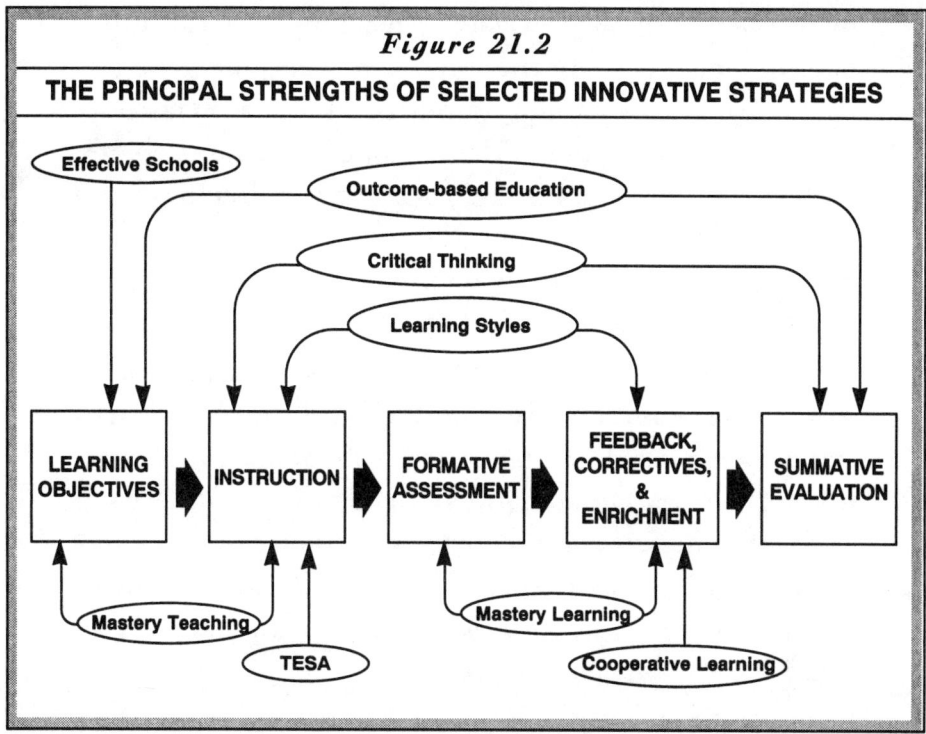

Figure 21.2
THE PRINCIPAL STRENGTHS OF SELECTED INNOVATIVE STRATEGIES

The rationale behind the framework is described as follows:

> For example, as part of an excellent guide for developing a school climate conducive to learning, the effective schools model emphasizes the importance of clearly recognized and accepted learning objectives common to all students. Outcome-based education also stresses the need to state clearly what students are expected to learn but does not relate objectives specifically to school climate. Instead, outcome-based education emphasizes the importance of summative evaluation of performance strictly according to stated objectives.
>
> Neither the effective schools model nor outcome-based education, however, offers much specific guidance on

instructional quality. Mastery teaching, on the other hand, helps to clarify the important decisions teachers must make in planning and conducting classroom instructional activities. TESA, too, concentrates chiefly on instruction, since it helps teachers become more aware of the expectations they communicate to their students. But mastery teaching and TESA say little about assessment of evaluation.

Mastery learning does address (1) formative assessment to give students regular feedback on their learning progress, and (2) pairing that feedback with high-quality corrective activities for students who need additional assistance or enrichment activities for students who have learned very well. But mastery learning is basically neutral with regard to curriculum objectives or instructional format.

Concepts from cooperative learning and learning styles are especially valuable when teachers are planning alternative instructional approaches, especially for corrective or enrichment activities. Though neither cooperative learning nor the learning styles literature offers detailed prescription for evaluation, the data on critical thinking provide several methods for assessing higher level cognitive strategies. (Guskey, 1990b, pp. 13–14).

While some may disagree with these interpretations, we find this analysis and comparisons of programs' strengths to be illustrative of the kind of thinking that innovation integration will require.

BROADENING OUR SCOPE

If school improvement efforts are ever to attain their full potential, educators must broaden their thinking about the way improvement efforts are planned and implemented. To do so, we must first drop the practice of introducing each innovation as an isolated "new idea" without relationship to or regard for other ideas. Throughout all stages of improvement initiatives, we must clearly describe the relationships between existing and new strategies in practical terms. In this way, we can help practitioners at all levels understand that improvement does not necessarily mean *replacement*, but *enhancement*.

Second, we must expect the advocates of a particular program to argue persuasively for the advantages of their approach, but we should press them to be explicit about its limitations, too. Only then can one program's strength compensate for another's weakness.

Third, when new innovations are introduced, we must provide support and follow-up activities for an adequate period of time. After all, improvement means change; and change is a gradual process, taking place not over a period of days, but months and, in some cases, years (Fullan & Stiegelbauer, 1991).

Broadening the scope of planning and implementation will not only encourage the integration of innovations but it will also enhance opportunities for collegial sharing. When different programs are introduced at different times, not everyone will be doing the same thing at the same time. Practitioners are thus likely to be at very different stages of implementation with regard to any one program. This differential experience can be an advantage: experts in one innovation can serve as excellent models, mentors, and peer coaches for those who are just beginning.

When another strategy is considered, the beginner may now become the expert, and so on.

The overarching reason to broaden our thinking about the implementation of new ideas, however, is that a broader view will promote the synthesis of innovative programs. Achieving the optimal integration of innovations will not be easy, but doing so is essential if school improvement efforts are to sustain their momentum, continue to expand, and bring about the kind of results for which the innovations were intended.

The primary task that lies ahead, therefore, is not so much to generate new ideas as to integrate them, not so much to find individual ideas that work as to make a collection of ideas that work together.

COLLECTED REFERENCES

Abrami, P. C., Leventhal, L., & Perry, R. P. (1982). Educational seduction. *Review of Educational Research, 52,* 446–64.

Abt Associates (1977). *Education as experimentation: A planned variation model* (Vol. IV). Cambridge, MA: Abt Associates.

Accelerated Schools Project (1991a). Getting started. *Accelerated Schools, 1*(2).

Accelerated Schools Project (1991b). The inquiry process. *Accelerated Schools, 1*(3).

Afflerbach, P, & Johnston, P. (1984). On the use of verbal reports in reading research. *Journal of Reading Behavior, 16,* 307–22.

Airasian, P. W. (1991). *Classroom assessment.* New York: McGraw-Hill.

Allington, R. (1983). The reading instruction provided readers of different ability. *Elementary School Journal, 83,* 255–65.

American Federation of Teachers (1985, September). Critical thinking: It's a basic. *American Teacher,* 21.

Anderson, L. (1984). The environment of instruction: The function of seat work in a commercially developed curriculum. In G. Duffy, L. Roehler, & J. Mason (Eds.), *Comprehension instruction: Perspectives and suggestions* (pp. 93–115). New York: Longman.

Anderson, L. W., & Burns, R. B. (1987). Values, evidence, and mastery learning. *Review of Educational Research, 57,* 215–23.

Anderson, R. C., Hiebert, E. F., Scott, J. A., & Wilkinson, I. A. (1985). *Becoming a nation of readers.* Washington, DC: The National Institute of Education.

Anderson, R. C., Osborn, J., Tierney, R. (1984). *Learning to read in American schools: Basal readers and content texts.* Hillsdale, NJ: Erlbaum.

Anderson, R. C., Wilson, P., & Fielding, L. (1988). Growth in reading and how children spend their time outside of school. *Reading Research Quarterly, 23,* 285–303.

Applebee, A. (1984). Writing and reasoning. *Review of Educational Research, 54,* 577–96.

Applebee, A. N., Langer, J. A., & Mullis, I. V. A. (1986a). *The reading report card: Progress toward excellence in our schools—Trends in reading over four national assessments, 1971–1984.* Princeton, NJ: Educational Testing Service.

Applebee, A. N., Langer, J. A., & Mullis, I. V. A. (1986b). *The writing report card: Writing achievement in American schools.* Princeton, NJ: Educational Testing Service.

Armbruster, B., Anderson, T., & Osterag, J. (1987). Does text structure/summarization instruction facilitate learning expository text? *Reading Research Quarterly, 21*(3), 331–46.

Armbruster, B., Osborn, J., & Davison, A. (1985). Readability formulas may be dangerous to your textbooks. *Educational Leadership, 42*(7), 18–22.

Aronson, E. (1978). *The jigsaw classroom.* Beverly Hills: Sage.

Arredondo, D. E., & Block, J. H. (1990). Recognizing the connections between thinking skills and mastery learning. *Educational Leadership, 47*(5), 4–10.

Barker, G., & Hunter, M., (1989d). Attribution theory and the middle school. *New England League of Middle Schools Journal, 2*(1), 5–7.

Barnes, D., & Barnes, D. (1990). Reading and writing as social action. In R. Beach & S. Hynds (Eds.), *Developing discourse practices in adolescence and adulthood, 39.* Norwood, NJ: Ablex.

Becker, W. C., & Engelmann, S. (1978). *Analysis of achievement data on six cohorts of low-income children from 20 school districts in the University of Oregon Direct Instruction Follow Through Model* (Technical Report 78–1). Eugene: University of Oregon.

Ben Peretz, M., & Bramme, R. (1990). *The nature of time in schools: Theoretical concepts, practitioner perceptions.* New York: Teachers College Press.

Bereiter, C., & Engelmann, S. (1966). *Teaching disadvantaged children in the preschool.* Engelwood Cliffs, NJ: Prentice-Hall.

Berliner, D. (1980). *Personal communication.* Mid-continent Regional Educational Laboratory, Aurora, CO.

Berman, P., & McLaughlin, M. W. (1976). Implementation of educational innovations. *Educational Forum, 40,* 345–70.

Berrueta-Clement, J. R., Schweinhart, L. J., Barnett, W. S., Epstein, A. S., & Weikart, D. P. (1984). Changed lives: The effects of the Perry Preschool Program on youths through age 19. *Monographs of the High/Scope Educational Research Foundation, 8.* Ypsilanti, MI: High/Scope Press.

Bissett, D. (1969). *The amount and effect of recreational reading in selected fifth grade classes.* Unpublished doctoral dissertation, Syracuse University, Syracuse, NY.

Block, J. (1990). *The Missouri miracle: Local lessons from statewide OBE.* Invited address at the Sixth Annual National Outcome-based Education conference, Phoenix, AZ.

Block, J. H. (Ed.) (1971). *Mastery learning: Theory and practice.* New York: Holt, Rinehart and Winston.

Block, J. H. (Ed.) (1974). *Schools, society and mastery learning.* New York: Holt, Rinehart and Winston.

Block, J. H., & Anderson, L. W. (1975). *Mastery learning in classroom instruction.* New York: Macmillan.

Block, J. H., & Burns, R. B. (1976). Mastery learning. In L. Shulman (Ed.), *Review of research in education, 4* (pp. 3–49). Itasca, IL: Peacock.

Block, J. H., & King, N. R. (Eds.) (1987). *School play: A source book.* New York: Garland.

Block, J. H., Efthim, H. E., & Burns, R. B. (1989). *Building effective mastery learning schools*. White Plains, NY: Longman.

Bloom, B. S. (1968). Learning for mastery. *Evaluation Comment, 1*(2), 1–12.

Bloom, B. S. (1971). Mastery learning. In J. H. Block (Ed.), *Mastery learning: Theory and practice* (pp. 47–63). New York: Holt, Rinehart and Winston.

Bloom, B. S. (1973). *Time and learning*. Thorndike Award Address, 81st annual convention of the American Psychological Association, Montreal.

Bloom, B. S. (1974). An introduction to mastery learning theory. In J. H. Block (Ed.), *Schools, society and mastery learning* (pp. 3–14). New York: Holt, Rinehart and Winston.

Bloom, B. S. (1976). *Human characteristics and school learning*. New York: McGraw-Hill.

Bloom, B. S. (1984). The search for methods of group instruction as effective as one-to-one tutoring. *Educational Leadership, 41*(8), 4–18.

Bloom, B. S. (1987). A response to Slavin's mastery learning reconsidered. *Review of Educational Research, 57*, 507–508.

Bloom, B. S. (1988). Helping all children learn in elementary school and beyond. *Principal, 67*(4), 12–17.

Bortnick, R. M. (1980). Computers and the curriculum. *The School Administrator, 37*(9), 14–15.

Bortnick, R. M. (1987). Problem solving and the computer. *California Public Schools Forum: Microcomputers, 2*, 48–62.

Bowsher, J. (1989). *Educating America: Lessons learned in the nation's corporations*. New York: Wiley.

Boyd, W. L. (1990). The national level: Reagan and the bully pulpit. In S. Bacharach (Ed.), *Educational reform: Making sense of it all*, (pp. 42–51). Boston: Allyn and Bacon.

Brandt, R. (1989). *Effective schools and school improvement: Reading from Educational Leadership*. Alexandria, VA: Association for Supervision and Curriculum Development.

Bredekamp, S. (1987). *Developmentally appropriate practice in early childhood programs serving children from birth through age 8*. Washington, DC: National Association for the Education of Young Children.

Brennan, A., Bridge, C., & Winograd, P. (1986). The effects of structural variations on children's recall of basal reader stories. *Reading Research Quarterly, 21*, 91–104.

Bridge, C. (1986). Predictable books for young readers and writers. In M. Sampson (Ed.), *The pursuit of literacy: Early reading and writing* (pp. 81–96). Dubuque, IA: Kendall/Hunt.

Bridge, C. (1989). Beyond the basal in beginning reading. In P. Winograd, K. Wixson, & M. Lipson (Eds.), *Improving basal reading instruction* (pp. 177–209). New York: Teachers College Press.

Brookover, W. B., Schweitzer, J. H., Scheider, J. M., Beady, C. H., Flood, P. K., & Wisenbaker, J. M. (1978). Elementary school social climate and school achievement. *American Educational Research Journal, 15,* 301–18.

Bruner, J. S. (1960). *The process of education.* New York: Vintage.

Burns, R. B. (1987). *Models of instructional organization: A casebook on mastery learning and outcome-based education.* San Francisco: Far West Laboratory for Educational Research and Development.

Calkins, L. (1986). *The art of teaching writing.* Portsmouth, NH: Heinemann.

Carnine, D. (1991). Curricular interventions for teaching higher-order thinking for all students. Introduction to the special series. *Journal of Learning Disabilities, 24*(5), 261–69.

Carnine, D., & Kameenui, E. (1992). *Teaching higher order thinking to all students.* Austin: Pro Ed. Publishing Company.

Carnine, D., Granzin, A., & Becker, W. (1988). Direct instruction. In J. Graden, J. Zins, & M. Curtis (Eds.), *Alternative educational delivery systems: Enhancing instructional options for all students* (pp. 327–49). Washington, DC: National Association of School Psychologists.

Carroll, J. B. (1963). A model of school learning. *Teachers College Record, 64,* 723–33.

Catton, B. (1952). *The army of the Potomac: Glory Road.* Garden City, NY: Doubleday.

Cauce, A. M., Comer, J. P., & Schwartz, B. A. (1987). Long term effects of a system-oriented school prevention program. *American Journal of Orthopsychiatry, 57*(1), 127–31.

Champlin, J. R. (1983). Four phases in creating and managing an outcome-based program. *Outcomes, 3*(1), 28–41.

Champlin, J., & Mamary, A. (1982). Johnson City's philosophical principles and practices. *Outcomes, 2*(1), 22–23.

Chance, P. (1986). *Thinking in the classroom.* New York: Teacher's College Press.

Cicerelli, V. (1969). *The impact of Head Start: An evaluation of the effects of Head Start experiences on children's cognitive and affective development.* Athens, OH: Westinghouse Learning Conjunctive and Ohio University.

Cleverley, J., & Phillips, D. C. (1986). *Visions of childhood: Influential models from Locke to Spock.* New York: Teachers College Press.

Cochran-Smith, M. (1988). Mediating: An important role for the reading teacher. In C. Hedley & J. Hicks (Eds.), *Reading and the special learner* (pp. 109–39). Norwood, NJ: Ablex.

Cohen, E. (1986). *Designing groupwork.* New York: Teachers College Press.

Cohen, S. A. (1971). The taxonomy of instructional treatments in reading: Its uses and its implications as a classroom analysis scheme. *Journal of the Reading Specialist, 11*(1), 5–23.

Cohen, S. A. (1977). Tests are not all that bad (they're worse!). *Reading World, 16,* 219–22.

Cohen, S. A. (1984a). Implications of instructional psychological research on mastery learning. *Outcomes, 3*(2), 18–25.

Cohen, S. A. (1984b). June, 1984—a researcher's end-of-year reflections. *Outcomes, 4*(1), 7–11.

Cohen, S. A. (1987). Instructional alignment: Searching for a magic bullet. *Educational Researcher, 16*(8), 16–20.

Cohen, S. A., & Hyman, J. S. (1991). Can fantasies become facts? *Educational Measurement: Issues and Practices, 10*(1), 20–23.

Cohen, S. A., Hyman, J. S., Ashcroft, L., & Loveless, D. (1989). *Comparing effects of meta-cognition, learning styles, & human attributes with alignment.* Paper delivered at the annual meeting of the American Educational Research Association, San Francisco.

Cohen, S. A., & Stover, G. (1981). Effects of teaching sixth grade students to modify variables of math word problems. *Reading Research Quarterly, 16,* 175–200.

Coleman, J. S., Campbell, E., Hobson, C., McPartland, J., Mood, A., Weinfeld, F., & York, R. (1966). *Equality of educational opportunity.* Washington, DC: U. S. Government Printing Office.

College Board (1983). *Academic preparation for college: What students need to know and be able to do.* New York: College Entrance Examination Board.

Colvin-Murphy, C. (1986). *Enhancing critical comprehension of literary texts through writing.* Paper presented at the National Reading Conference, Austin, TX.

Combs, A. W. (Ed.) (1962). *Perceiving, behaving, becoming.* Washington, DC: The Association for Supervision and Curriculum Development.

Comer, J. P. (1980). *School power.* New York: Free Press.

Comer, J. P. (1988a). Educating poor minority children. *Scientific American, 259* (f), 42–48.

Comer, J. P. (1988b). *Maggie's American dream.* New York: New American Library.

Comer, J. P., Haynes, N. M., & Hamilton-Lee, M. (1989). School power: A model for improving black student achievement. In W. D. Smith & E. W. Chun (Eds.), *Black education: A quest for equity and excellence* (pp. 187–200). New Brunswick, NJ: Transaction Publishers.

Commission on the Humanities (1980). *The humanities in American life.* Berkeley: University of California Press.

Committee on Economic Development (1985). *Investing in our children. (Business and public schools.)* New York: CED.

Consortium for Longitudinal Studies (1983). *As the twig is bent . . . lasting effects of preschool programs.* Hillsdale, NJ: Erlbaum.

Copeland, K. A. (1987). (*Writing as a means to learn from prose.*) Unpublished doctoral dissertation, University of Texas, Austin.

Crabbe, A. B. (1982). Creating a brighter future: An update on the Future Problem Solving Program. *Journal for the Education of the Gifted, 5*, 2–11.

Crandall, D. P. (1983). The teacher's role in school improvement. *Educational Leadership, 41*(3), 6–9.

Cronin, D. P. (1980). *Implementation study, year 2, instructional staff interviews.* Los Altos, CA: Emrick & Associates.

Csikzentmihalyi, M. (1975). *Beyond boredom and anxiety.* San Francisco: Jossey-Bass.

Cuban, L. (1984). *How they taught.* New York: Longman.

Cuban, L. (1988). Constancy and change in schools. *Noteworthy*, 15–17.

Cuban, L. (1990). Reforming again, again and again. *Educational Researcher, 19*(1), 3–13.

Davidson, M. L., King, P. M., & Kitchener, K. S. (1990). Developing reflective thinking and writing. In R. Beach & S. Hynds (Eds.), *Developing discourse practices in adolescence and adulthood, 39.* Norwood, NJ: Ablex.

Davidson, N., & O'Leary, P. W. (1990). How cooperative learning can enhance mastery teaching. *Educational Leadership, 47*(5), 30–34.

Davis, J. (1991). *Effects of cognitive entry level behaviors on the reading performance of limited, fluent, and native English speaking primary students.* Unpublished doctoral dissertation, University of San Francisco.

Deci, E. (1980). *The psychology of self-determination.* Lexington, KY: Lexington Books.

Delpit, L. D. (1988). The silenced dialogue: Power and pedagogy in educating other people's children. *Harvard Education Review, 58,* 280–98.

Deming, W. E. (1982). *Out of the crisis.* Cambridge: Massachusetts Institute of Technology, Center for Advanced Engineering Study.

Deutsch, M. (1962). Cooperation and trust: Some theoretical notes. In M. R. Jones (Ed.), *Nebraska symposium on motivation* (pp. 275–319). Lincoln: University of Nebraska Press.

DeVries, D., & Edwards, K. (1974). *Cooperation in the classroom: Towards a theory of alternative reward-task classroom structures.* Paper presented at the Annual Meeting of the American Educational Research Association, Chicago.

Dossey, J. A., Mullis, I. V. A., Lindquist, M. M., & Chambers, D. L. (1988). *The mathematics report card.* Princeton, NJ: Educational Testing Service.

Doyle, W. (1983). Academic work. *Review of Educational Research, 53,* 159–99.

Dreeben, R. (1973). The school as a workplace. *Second handbook of research on teaching* (pp. 450–73). Chicago: Rand McNally.

Drewry, H., O'Connor, T., & Freidel, F. (1984). *America is.* Columbus, OH: Merrill.

Duffey, G., Roehler, L., & Hermann, B. (1988). Modeling mental processes helps poor readers become strategic readers. *The Reading Teacher, 41*, 762–67.

Durkin, D. (1978–1979). What classroom observations reveal about reading comprehension instruction. *Reading Research Quarterly, 14*, 481–533.

Durst, R. K., & Newell, G. E. (1989). The uses of function: James Britton's category system and research on writing. *Review of Educational Research, 59*, 375–94.

Edmonds, R. R. (1979). Some schools work, and more can. *Social Policy, 9*(5), 28–32.

Edmonds, R. R. (1978). *A discussion of the literature and issues related to effective schooling.* Paper presented at the National Conference on Urban Education, St. Louis.

Edwards, P. (1990). *Low-income mothers using cooperative small groups: A model for training other low-income parents to share books with their young children.* Paper presented at the National Reading Conference, Miami.

Elia, J. S. I. (1986). *An alignment experiment in vocabulary instruction: Varying instructional practice and test item formats to measure transfer with low SES fifth graders.* Unpublished doctoral dissertation, University of San Francisco.

Elliott, S. N., & Shapiro, E. S. (1990). Intervention techniques and programs for academic performance problems. In T. B. Gutkin & C. R. Reynolds (Eds.), *The handbook of school psychology.* New York: John Wiley.

Emig, J. (1977). Writing as a mode of learning. *College Composition and Communication, 28*(8), 122–128.

Engelmann, S., & Carnine, D. (1991a). *Connecting math concepts.* Chicago: Science Research Associates.

Engelmann, S., & Carnine, D. (1991b). *Theory of instruction: Principles and applications.* Eugene, OR: Association for Direct Instruction.

English, R. A. (October, 1992). *Accelerated school report.* University of Missouri—Columbia, MO: Department of Educational and Counseling Psychology.

Ennis, R. H. (1987a, Summer). A conception of critical thinking—with some curriculum suggestions. *American Philosophical Association Newsletter on the Teaching of Philosophy*, 1–5.

Ennis, R. H. (1987b). A taxonomy of critical thinking dispositions and abilities. In J. B. Baron & R. J. Sternberg (Eds.), *Teaching thinking skills* (pp. 9–26). New York: Freeman.

Ennis, R. H. (1989). Critical thinking and subject specificity: Clarification and needed research. *Educational Researcher, 18*(3), 4–10.

Erikson, E. H. (1950). *Childhood and society.* New York: Norton.

Ewy, R. (1989). *Writing a problem statement.* Aurora, CO: Mid-continent Regional Educational Laboratory.

Fahey, P. A. (1986). *Learning transfer in main ideas instruction: Effects of instructional alignment and aptitude on main idea test scores.* Unpublished doctoral dissertation, University of San Francisco.

Fast, H. (1945). *The selected works of Tom Paine.* New York: Random House.

Feldhusen, J. (1992). *Talent identification and development in education (TIDE).* Sarasota, FL: Center for Creative Learning.

Ferster, C. B., & Skinner, B. F. (1957). *Schedules of reinforcement.* New York: Appleton-Century-Crofts.

Finn, C. E. (1990). The biggest reform of all. *Phi Delta Kappan, 71*(8), 584–92.

Fisher, C .W., & Hiebert, E. F. (1988). *Characteristics of literacy learning in elementary school.* Paper presented at the annual meeting of the National Reading Conference, Tucson.

Fisher, R., & Ury, W. (1981). *Getting to yes.* New York: Penguin.

Flavell, J. H. (1971). Stage-related properties of cognitive development. *Cognitive Psychology, 2,* 421–53.

Flexner, S. B., & Houck, L. C. (Eds.) (1987). *The Random House dictionary of the English language,* 2d Edition, Unabridged. New York: Random House.

Fraatz, J. M. (1987). *The politics of reading: Power, opportunity, and prospects for change in America's public schools.* New York: Teachers College Press.

Franklin, A. J. (1985). The social context and socialization variables as factors in thinking and learning. In S. F. Chipman, J. W. Segal, & R. Glaser (Eds.), *Thinking and learning skills: Vol. 2. Research and open questions* (pp. 81–106). Hillsdale, NJ: Erlbaum.

Friedlander, R. (1988). The Shakespeare project: Experiments in multimedia education. *Academic Computing, 2*(7), 26–29, 66–68.

Fullan, M. G. (1990a). *Management of change: An implementation perspective.* School Year 2020 conference, Oxford, England.

Fullan, M. G. (1990b). Staff development, innovation, and institutional development. In B. Joyce (Ed.), *Changing school culture through staff development,* 1990 yearbook of the Association for Supervision and Curriculum Development. Alexandria, VA: Association for Supervision and Curriculum Development.

Fullan, M. G., & Hargreaves, A. (1991). *What's worth fighting for? Working together for your school.* Ontario: Ontario Teachers' Federation.

Fullan, M. G., & Stiegelbauer S. (1991). *The new meaning of educational change.* New York: Teachers College Press.

Fulwiler, T. (1984). *Teaching with writing.* Montclair, NJ: Boynton/Cook.

Futrell, M. H. (1987). A message long overdue. *Education Week, 7*(14), 9.

Gabor, A. (1990). *The man who discovered quality.* New York: Times Books.

Gelman, R. (1986). Toward an understanding-based theory of mathematics learning and instruction, or in praise of Lampert on teaching multiplication. *Cognition and Instruction, 3,* 349–55.

Gersten, R., Becker, W., Heiry, T., & White, W. A. (1984). Entry I.Q. and yearly academic growth of children in Direct Instruction programs: A longitudinal study of low SES children. *Educational Evaluation and Policy Analysis, 6,* 109–21.

Gersten, R., Darch, C., & Gleason, M. (1988). The effectiveness of academic kindergartens for low-income students: Analysis and discussion. *Elementary School Journal, 89,* 227–40.

Gersten, R., & Keating, T. (1987). Improving high school performance of "at risk" students: A study of long-term benefits of direct instruction. *Educational Leadership, 44*(6), 28–31.

Glaser, E. M. (1941). *An experiment in the development of critical thinking.* New York: Teachers College, Columbia University.

Glasser, W. (1984). *Control theory.* New York: Harper and Collins.

Glasser, W. (1990). *The quality school.* New York: Harper and Collins.

Glickman, C. D. (1990). Pushing school reform to a new edge: The seven ironies of school empowerment. *Phi Delta Kappan, 72*(1), 68–75.

Golden, J. L., Berquist, G. F., & Coleman, W. E. (1976). *The rhetoric of Western thought.* Dubuque, IA: Kendall/Hunt.

Goodlad, J. (1984). *A place called school.* New York: McGraw-Hill.

Goodman, K. (1987). *What's whole in whole language?* New York: Scholastic Inc.

Goodman, Y. M. (1989). Roots of the whole-language movement. *Elementary School Journal, 90,* 113–27.

Gourley, T. J. (1981). Adapting the varsity sports model to nonpsychomotor gifted students. *Gifted Child Quarterly, 25,* 164–66.

Graby, R. P. (1987). *The effect of varying stimulus conditions on cognitive structure: A study in instructional alignment.* Unpublished doctoral dissertation, University of San Francisco.

Graves, D. (1983). *Writing: Teachers and children at work.* Exeter, NH: Heinemann.

Gray, W. (Ed.), (1978). *Project outlines and planning resources: A catalog.* Atlanta: Research & Development Utilization Project, Georgia Department of Education.

Greenberger, Martin. (Ed.), (1990). *Technologies for the 21st century on multimedia.* Santa Monica, CA: The Voyager Company.

Griffin, C. W. (1989). Teaching Shakespeare on video. *The English Journal, 78*(7), 40–43.

Gullickson, A. R., & Hopkins, D. K. (1987). Perspectives on educational measurement instruction for preservice teachers. *Educational Measurement: Issues and Practice, 6*(3), 12–16.

Collected References

Guskey, T. R., & Kifer, E. (1989). *Ranking school districts on the basis of statewide test results: Is it meaningful or misleading?* Paper presented at the annual meeting of the American Educational Research Association, San Francisco.

Guskey, T. R. (1980). What is mastery learning? *Instructor, 90*(3), 80–86.

Guskey, T. R. (1985). *Implementing mastery learning.* Belmont, CA: Wadsworth.

Guskey, T. R. (1986). Staff development and the process of teacher change. *Educational Researcher, 15*(5), 5–12.

Guskey, T. R. (1987a). The essential elements of mastery learning. *Journal of Classroom Interaction, 22*(2), 19–22.

Guskey, T. R. (1987b). Rethinking mastery learning reconsidered. *Review of Educational Research, 57*, 225–29.

Guskey, T. R. (1988a). Mastery learning and mastery teaching: How they complement each other. *Principal, 68*(1), 6–8.

Guskey, T. R. (1988b). Response to Slavin: Who defines best? *Educational Leadership, 46*(2), 26–27.

Guskey, T. R. (1990a). Cooperative mastery learning strategies. *Elementary School Journal, 91*, 33–42.

Guskey, T. R. (1990b). Integrating innovations. *Educational Leadership, 47*(5), 11–15.

Guskey, T. R. (1992). What does it mean to be "research based"? *The Developer, 5.*

Guskey, T. R., Barshis, D., & Easton, J. Q. (1982). The multiplier effect: Exploring new directions in community college research. *Community and Junior College Journal, 52*(8), 22–25.

Guskey, T. R., & Block, J. H. (1991). The Missouri miracle: A success story about statewide collaboration to improve students' learning. *Outcomes, 10*(2), 28–43.

Guskey, T. R., & Gates, S. L. (1986). Synthesis of research on the effects of mastery learning in elementary and secondary classrooms. *Educational Leadership, 33*(8), 73–80.

Guskey, T. R., Passaro, P. D., & Wheeler, W. (1991). Missouri's Thorpe Gordon School: A model for school improvement. *Principal, 71*(1), 36–38.

Guskey, T. R., & Pigott, T. D. (1988). Research on group-based mastery learning programs: A meta-analysis. *Journal of Educational Research, 81*, 197–216.

Haney, W. (1977). *Reanalysis of follow through parent and teacher data.* Boston: Huron Institute.

Hansen, J. (1987). *When writers read.* Portsmouth, NH: Heinemann.

Hargreaves, A. (1989). *Teacher development and teachers' work: Issues of time and control.* Paper presented at the International Conference on Teacher Development, Toronto.

Hargreaves, A., & Dawe, R. (1989). *Coaching as unreflective practice.* Paper presented at the annual meeting of the American Educational Research Association, San Francisco.

Hartke, J. P. (1980, July). Ego-development, cognitive style and transformation. *Dissertation Abstracts International, 41*(1-B), 353.

Haveman, R. (1987). Policy analysis and evaluation research after twenty years. *Policy Studies Journal, 16,* 191–218.

Hayes, D. A. (1987). The potential for directing study in combined reading and writing activity. *Journal of Reading Behavior, 19*(4), 333–52.

Haynes, N. M., & Comer, J. P. (1990). The effects of a school development program on self-concept. *The Yale Journal of Biology and Medicine, 63,* 275–83.

Haynes, N. M., Comer, J. P., & Hamilton-Lee, M. (1988a). The effects of parental involvement on student performance. *Educational and Psychological Research, 8(4),* 291–99.

Haynes, N. M., Comer, J. P., & Hamilton-Lee, M. (1988b). The school development program: A model for school improvement. *Journal of Negro Education, 57*(1), 11–21.

Haynes, N. M., Comer, J. P., & Hamilton-Lee, M. (1989). School climate enhancement through parental involvement. *Journal of School Psychology, 27,* 87–90.

Heibert, E. H. (1987). The context of instruction and student learning: An examination of Slavin's assumptions. *Review of Educational Research, 57,* 337–40.

Henderson, R. W. (1989). Interactive videodisc instruction in pre-calculus. *The Journal of Educational Technology Systems, 17*(2), 91–101.

Herman J., & Dorr-Bremme, D. W. (1982). *Assessing students: Teachers' routine practices and reasons.* A paper presented at the Annual Meeting of the American Educational Research Association, New York.

Hofmeister, A., Lubke, M., & Peterson, L. (1988). A videodisc approach to instructional productivity. *Educational Technology, 16*(22), 16–22.

Hohmann, M., Banet, B., & Weikart, D. P. (1979). *Young children in action: A manual for preschool educators.* Ypsilanti, MI: High/Scope Press.

Hohmann, M., & Weikart, D. P. (in press). *Young children in action: A manual for preschool educators* (Rev. ed.). Ypsilanti, MI: High/Scope Press.

Honig, B. (1990). The state level: The view from California. In S. Bacharach (Ed.), *Educational reform: Making sense of it all* (pp. 52–66). Boston: Allyn and Bacon.

Hopfenberg, W., and Associates (1993). *Resource guide on the accelerated school.* San Francisco: Jossey-Bass.

Huberman, M., & Miles, M. B. (1984). *Innovation up close: How school improvement works.* New York: Plenum.

Hughes, H. (1989, May). Conversion of a teacher-delivered course into an interactive videodisc-delivered program. *Foreign Language Annals, 22*(3), 283–94.

Hunter, M. (1984). Knowing, teaching and supervising. In P. Hosford (Ed.), *Using what we know about teaching* (pp. 169–92). Alexandria, VA: The Association of Supervision and Curriculum Development.

Hunter, M. (1986a). Comments on the Napa County, California, Follow-Through Project. *Elementary School Journal, 87*, 173–79.

Hunter, M. (1986b). To be or not to be—Hunterized? *Tennessee Educational Leadership, 13*(2), 70–73.

Hunter, M. (1987a). Beyond re-reading Dewey . . . What's next? A response to Gibboney. *Educational Leadership, 44*(5), 51–53.

Hunter, M. (1987b). Madeline Hunter responds to Bob Slavin. *Instructor, 96*(8), 60.

Hunter, M. (1987c). If at first . . . Attribution theory in the classroom. *Educational Leadership, 45*(2), 50–53.

Hunter, M. (1988a). Staff meetings that produce staff development. *Principal, 67*(3), 44–45.

Hunter, M. (1988b). Response to Slavin. *Educational Leadership, 48*(2), 29.

Hunter, M. (1988c). Well acquainted is not enough: A response to Mandeville and Rivers. *Educational Leadership, 46*(4), 67–68

Hunter, M. (1989a). What's wrong with Madeline Hunter? *Educational Leadership, 42*(5), 57–60.

Hunter, M. (1989b). Madeline Hunter in the English classroom. *English Journal, 78*(5), 16–18.

Hunter, M. (1989c). Working with the exceptional student. *British Columbia Journal of Special Education, 13*(2), 147–50.

Hunter, M. (1990). Thoughts on staff development. In B. Joyce (Ed.), *Changing school culture through staff development* (pp. 9–14). Alexandria, VA: The Association of Supervision and Curriculum Development.

Hunter, M. (1991). Hunter lesson design helps achieve the goals of science instruction. *Educational Leadership, 48*(4), 79–81.

Hunter, M. (1994). *Enhancing teaching.* New York: Maxwell-Macmillain International.

Hunter M. & Gee, K. (1988). Art Education: Escalate your teaching skills. *NAEA Advisory Bulletin, Part I*. Reston, VA: The National Art Education Association.

Hunter, M., & Russell, D. (1977). Planning for effective instruction. *Instructor, 87*(2), 74–75, 88.

Hutchins, R. (1953). *The conflict in education in a democratic society.* New York: Harper.

Jaques, E. (1985). Development of intellectual capability. In F. R. Link (Ed.), *Essays on the intellect* (pp. 107–42). Alexandria, VA: Association for Supervision and Curriculum Development.

Jenkinson, E. (1988a). How an imaginary movement is being used to attack courses and books. *Educational Leadership, 46*(2), 74–77.

Jenkinson, E. (1988b). The new age of schoolbook protest. *Phi Delta Kappan, 70*(1), 66–69.

Johnson, D. W. (1993). *Reaching out: Interpersonal effectiveness and self-actualization* (5th ed.). Englewood Cliffs, NJ: Prentice-Hall.

Johnson, D. W. (1991). *Human relations and your career* (3d ed.). Englewood Cliffs, NJ: Prentice-Hall.

Johnson, D. W., & Johnson, R. (1984). *Circles of Learning*. Edina, MN: Interaction Book Company.

Johnson, D. W., & Johnson, F. (1994). *Joining together: Group theory and group skills* (5th ed.). Boston: Allyn and Bacon.

Johnson, D. W., & Johnson, R. (1989). *Cooperation and competition: Theory and research*. Edina, MN: Interaction Book Company.

Johnson, D. W., & Johnson, R. (1994). *Leading the cooperative school* (2nd ed.). Edina, MN: Interaction Book Company.

Johnson, D. W., Johnson, R., & Holubec, E. (1993). *Cooperation in the classroom* (5th ed.). Edina, MN: Interaction Book Company.

Johnson, R. (1990, Spring). The videobased setting as a context for learning story information. *Childhood Education, 66*(3), 168–71.

Johnston, P. (1984). Assessment in reading: The emperor has no clothes. In P. D. Pearson (Ed.), *Handbook of reading research* (pp. 147–82). New York: Longman.

Johnston, P. H., & Winograd, P. N. (1985). Passive failure in reading. *Journal of Reading Behavior, 4*, 279–301.

Jones, B., & Idol, L. (1990). *Dimensions of thinking and cognitive instruction*. Hillsdale, NJ: Erlbaum.

Jourard, S. M. (1968). *Disclosing man to himself*. Princeton, NJ: Van Nostrand.

Joyce, B. (1987). A rigorous yet delicate touch: A response to Slavin's proposal for "best-evidence" reviews. *Educational Researcher, 16*(4), 12–14.

Joyce, B., & Showers, B. (1980). Improving inservice training: The messages of research. *Educational Leadership, 37*(5), 379–85.

Joyce, B., Weil, M., & Showers, B. (1992). *Models of teaching* (4th Edition). Boston: Allyn and Bacon.

Kagan, S. (1988). *Cooperative learning*. San Juan Capistrano, CA: Resources for Teachers.

Karnes, M. B., Schwedel, A. M., & Williams, M. B. (1983). A comparison of five approaches for educating young children from low-income homes. In Consortium for Longitudinal Studies, *As the twig is bent... lasting effects of preschool programs* (pp. 133–70). Hillsdale, NJ: Erlbaum.

Katz, L. (1985). Dispositions in early childhood education. *EAC/EECE Bulletin, 18*(2), 1,3.

Keene, S. (1986). *Faces of the enemy.* San Francisco: Harper & Row.

Kennedy, M., Fisher, M. B., & Ennis, R. H. (1991). Critical thinking: Literature review and needed research. In L. Idol & B. F. Jones (Eds.), *Educational values and cognitive instruction: Implications for reform.* Hillsdale, NJ: Erlbaum.

Kinder, D., & Bursuck, W. (1991). The search for a unified social studies curriculum: Does history really repeat itself? *Journal of Learning Disabilities, 24*(5), 270–75.

Kirchner, G. (1988, Jan). Simon Fraser University's New Interactive Learning System to Teach French as a Second Language. *Optical Information Systems,* 38–43.

Knapp, M. S., Shield, P. M., & Turnbull, B. J. (1992). *Academic challenge for the children of poverty, Vols. 1 and 2.* Washington, DC: U. S. Department of Education, Office of Policy and Planning.

Knight, M. B. (1983, Oct). Shifts in the countertransference perceptions of selected psychotherapists undergoing EST self-awareness training. *Dissertation Abstracts International, 44*(4-A), 1031.

Knight, S., & Stallings, J. A. (1992). *Examining the effects of the accelerated school model on teacher and student perceptions and behaviors.* Paper presented at Annual Meetings of the American Educational Research Association, San Francisco.

Koczor, M. L. (1984). *Effects of varying degrees of instructional alignment in post treatment tests on mastery tasks of fourth grade children.* Unpublished doctoral dissertation, University of San Francisco.

Kuhn, T. (1962). *The structure of scientific revolutions.* Chicago: University of Chicago Press.

Kulik, C. C., Kulik, J. A., & Bangert-Drowns, R. L. (1990a). Effectiveness of mastery learning programs: A meta-analysis. *Review of Educational Research, 60,* 265–99.

Kulik, J. A., Kulik, C. C., & Bangert-Drowns, R. L. (1990b). Is there better evidence on mastery learning? A response to Slavin. *Review of Educational Research, 60,* 303–307.

Langer, J. (1986). Learning through writing: Study skills in the content areas. *Journal of Reading, 29,* 400–406.

Langer, J., & Applebee, A. (1987). *How writing shapes thinking: A study of teaching and learning.* Urbana, IL: National Council of Teachers of English.

Latham, G. (1988). The birth and death cycles of educational innovations. *Principal, 68*(1), 41–43.

Leonard, W. H. (1989). A comparison of student reactions to biology instruction by interactive videodisc or conventional laboratory. *The Journal of Research in Science Teaching, 26*(2), 95–104.

Levin, H. M. (1986). *Educational reform for disadvantaged students: An emerging crisis.* West Haven, CT: National Education Association Professional Library.

Levin, H. M. (1988). *Accelerated schools for at-risk students.* New Brunswick, NJ: Center for Policy Research in Education, Rutgers University.

Levin, H. M. (1989). Financing the education of at-risk students. *Educational Evaluation and Policy Analysis, 11,* 47–60.

Levin, H. M. (1991). *Building school capacity for effective teacher empowerment: Applications to elementary schools with at-risk students* (No. RR-019). New Brunswick, NJ: Center for Policy Research in Education, Rutgers University.

Levine, D. (1982). Successful approaches for improving academic achievement in inner-city schools. *Phi Delta Kappan, 63,* 523–26.

Levine, D. U. (Ed.). (1985). *Improving student achievement through mastery learning programs.* San Francisco: Jossey-Bass.

Lieberman, A. (1988). Expanding the leadership team. *Educational Leadership, 45*(5), 4–8.

Lincoln, Y. S., & Guba, E. G. (1985). *Naturalistic inquiry.* Beverly Hills: Sage.

Lipman, M. (1974). *Harry.* Upper Montclair, NJ: Institute for the Advancement of Philosophy for Children.

Lipman, M. (1978). *Suki.* Upper Montclair, NJ: Institute for the Advancement of Philosophy for Children.

Lipman, M. (1980). *Mark.* Upper Montclair, NJ: Institute for the Advancement of Philosophy for Children.

Lipman, M. (1985). Thinking skills fostered by philosophy for children. In J. W. Segal, S. F. Chipman, & R. Glaser (Eds.), *Thinking and learning skills: Vol. 1. Relating instruction to research* (pp. 83–108). Hillsdale, NJ: Erlbaum.

Little, J. (1982). Norms of collegiality and experimentation: Workplace conditions of school success. *American Educational Research Journal, 5,* 325–40.

Little, J. (1990). The "mentor" phenomenon and the social organization of teaching. In C. B. Cazden (Ed.), *Review of Research in Education, 16* (pp. 297–351). Itasca, IL: Peacock.

Loucks-Horsley, S., Harding, C. K., Arbuckle, M. G., Murray, L. B., Dubea, C., & Williams, M. K. (1987). *Continuing to learn: A guidebook for teacher development.* Andover, MA: Regional Laboratory for Educational Improvement of the Northeast and Islands and National Staff Development Council.

Louis, K. S., & Miles, M. B. (1990). *Improving the urban high school: What works and why.* New York: Teachers College Press.

Lysakowski, R., & Walberg, H. (1982). Instructional effects of cues, participation, and corrective feedback: A quantitative synthesis. *American Educational Research Journal, 19,* 559–78.

Lytle, S., & Botel, M. (1988). *PCRP II: Reading, writing, and talking across the curriculum*. Philadelphia: Pennsylvania Department of Education.

Malone, T., & Lepper, M. (1986). Making learning fun: A taxonomy of intrinsic motivations for learning. In R. Snow & M. Farr (Eds.), *Aptitude, learning, and instruction, 3. conative and affective process analysis*. Hillsdale, NJ: Erlbaum.

Mandeville, G., & Rivers, J. (1989). Is the Hunter model a recipe for supervision? *Educational Leadership, 46*(8), 39–43.

Marshall, J. D. (1990). Writing and reasoning about literature. In R. Beach & S. Hynds (Eds.), *Developing discourse practices in adolescence and adulthood, 39*. Norwood, NJ: Ablex.

Marzano, R. J. (1991a). Fostering thinking across the curriculum. *Journal of Reading, 34*(7), 518–25.

Marzano, R. J. (1991b). Language, the language arts, and thinking. In J. Flood, J. Jensen, D. Lapp, & J. Squire (Eds.), *Handbook of research on teaching the English language arts* (pp. 559–86). New York: Macmillan.

Marzano, R. J., Pickering, D., Arredondo, D., Brandt, R., & Blackburn, G. (1992). *Dimensions of learning: Teacher's guide*. Alexandria, VA: Association for Supervision and Curriculum Development.

Marzano, R. J., Pickering, D. J., & Brandt, R. S. (1990). Integrating instructional programs through dimensions of learning. *Educational Leadership, 47*(5), 17–24.

McCarthy, J., & Still, S. (1993). Hollibrook accelerated elementary school. In J. Murphy & P. Hallinger (Eds.) *Restructuring schools*. Monterey Park, CA: Corwin Press.

McCracken, H. A., & McCracken, M. J. (1986). *Stories, songs, and poetry to teach reading and writing*. Chicago: American Library Association.

McDaniel, M. A., & Schlager, M. S. (1990). Discovery learning and transfer of problem solving. *Cognition and Instruction, 7*, 129–59.

McGinley, W. (1988). *The role of reading and writing in the acquisition of knowledge: A study of college students' reading and writing engagements in the development of a persuasive argument*. Unpublished doctoral thesis, University of Illinois at Urbana-Champaign.

McKey, R. H., Condelli, L., Ganson, H., Barrett, B., McConkey, C., & Plantz, M. (1985). *The impact of Head Start on children, families and communities*. Final report of the Head Start Evaluation, Synthesis and Utilization Project. Washington, DC: CSR.

McLaughlin, M. (1976). Implementation as mutual adaptation. *Teachers College Record, 77*, 339–51.

Mehrens, W., & Kaminski, J. (1989). Methods for improving standardized test scores: Fruitful, fruitless or fraudulent? *Educational Measurement: Issues and Practices, 8*(1),14–22.

Meichenbaum, D. (1977). *Cognitive behavior modification*. New York: Plenum Press.

Mevarech, Z. R. (1985). The effects of cooperative mastery learning strategies on mathematical achievement. *Journal of Educational Research, 78,* 372–77.

Mevarech, Z. R. (1989). *Learning mathematics in different "mastery" environments.* Paper presented at the annual meeting of the American Educational Research Association, San Francisco.

Miles, M. (1983). Unraveling the myth of institutionalization. *Educational Leadership, 41*(3), 14–19.

Miles, M. B., & Louis, K. S. (1990). Mustering the will and skill for change. *Educational Leadership, 47*(8), 57–61.

Miller, L. B., & Bizzell, R. P. (1983). The Louisville Experiment: A comparison of four programs. In Consortium for Longitudinal Studies, *As the twig is bent ... lasting effects of preschool programs* (pp. 171–200). Hillsdale, NJ: Erlbaum.

Mizer, J. E. (1964). Cipher in the snow. *NEA Journal, 53,* 8–10.

Morrow, L. (1989). Creating a bridge to children's literature. In P. Winograd, K. Wixson, & M. Lipson (Eds.), *Improving basal reading instruction* (pp. 210–30). New York: Teachers College Press.

Morrow, L., & Weinstein, C. (1986). Encouraging voluntary reading. The impact of a literature program on childrens use of library centers. *Reading Research Quarterly, 21,* 330–46.

Murphy, J. (1990). The educational reform movement of the 1980s: A comprehensive analysis. In J. Murphy (Ed.), *The educational reform movement of the 1980s* (pp. 3–55). Berkeley, CA: McCutchan Publishing Corporation.

National Business Roundtable (1991). *Essential components of a successful education system.* Washington, DC: National Business Roundtable.

National Commission on Excellence in Education (1983). *A nation at risk: The imperative for educational reform.* Washington, DC: U. S. Government Printing Office.

National Council of Teachers of Mathematics Teaching (1991). *Professional standards for mathematics.* Reston, VA: NCTMT.

National School Boards Association (1986). *Should schools use videodiscs?* Alexandria, VA: National School Boards Association.

National Science Board Commission on Precollege Education in Mathematics, Science and Technology (1983). *Educating Americans for the 21st century.* Washington, DC: National Science Board Commission.

Neill, D., & Medina, N. (1989). Standardized testing: Harmful to educational health. *Phi Delta Kappan, 70,* 688–97.

Nicholls, J. (1989). *The competitive ethos and democratic education.* Cambridge: Harvard University Press.

Nickerson, R. S., Perkins, D. N., & Smith, E. E. (1985). *The teaching of thinking.* Hillsdale, NJ: Erlbaum.

Niedermeyer, F. C. (1979). *Curriculum alignment—A way to make schooling more understandable* (SWRL Professional Paper no. 41). Los Alamitos, CA: SWRL Educational Research and Development.

Niedermeyer, F. C., & Yelon, S. (1981). L.A. aligns instruction with essential skills. *Educational Leadership, 38*(8), 618–20.

Nistler, R. J. (1990). A descriptive analysis of good readers' and writers' concepts of authorship at grades one, three and five. In J. Zutell, S. McCormick, M. Connolly, & P. O'Keefe (Eds.), *Literacy theory and research: Analyses from multiple paradigms*, 39th Yearbook. Chicago: National Reading Conference.

Nolen, L. (1991). *Cognitive stretching: Teaching college students a set for transfer using an instructional alignment model.* Unpublished doctoral dissertation, University of San Francisco.

Norris, S. P., & Ennis, R. H. (1989). *Evaluating critical thinking.* Pacific Grove, CA: Midwest Publications.

Olmsted, P. P., & Weikart, D. P. (1989). *How nations serve young children: Profiles of child care and education in 14 countries.* Ypsilanti, MI: High/Scope Press.

Oregon Department of Education (1986). *Correlation of essential learning skills and published tests used in Oregon.* Salem, OR: ODE.

Osborn, D. K. (1991). *Early childhood education in historical perspective.* Athens, GA: Daye Press.

Palinscar, A., Ransom, K., & Derber, S. (1989). Collaborative research and development of reciprocal teaching. *Educational Leadership, 46*(4), 37–41.

Pallas, A. M., Natriello, G., & McDill, E. L. (1989). The changing nature of the disadvantaged population: Current dimensions and future trends. *Educational Researcher, 18*(5), 16–22.

Panel on the General Professional Education of the Physician and College Preparation for Medicine (1984). *Physicians for the twenty-first century: The GPEP report.* Washington, DC: Association for American Medical Colleges.

Pappas, C., Kiefer, B., & Levstik, L. (1990). *An integrated language perspective in the elementary schools.* New York: Longman.

Paris, S. G., Cross, D., & Lipson, M. (1984). Informed strategies for learning: A program to improve children's reading awareness and comprehension. *Journal of Educational Psychology, 76*, 1239–252.

Paris, S. G., Lawton, T. A., Turner, J. C., & Roth, J. L. (1991). A developmental perspective on standardized achievement testing. *Educational Researcher, 20*, 12–20.

Paris, S. G., Lipson, M. Y., & Wixson, K. K. (1983). Becoming a strategic reader. *Contemporary Educational Psychology, 8*, 293–316.

Paris, S. G., & Winograd, P. (1990). How meta-cognition can promote academic learning and instruction. In B. Jones & L. Idol (Eds.), *Dimensions of thinking and cognitive instruction* (pp. 15–52). Hillsdale, NJ: Erlbaum.

Passow, A. H. (1990). How it happened, wave by wave. In S. Bacharach (Ed.), *Educational reform: Making sense of it all,* (pp. 10–19). Boston: Allyn and Bacon.

Patton, M. Q. (1980). *Utilization-focused evaluation.* Beverly Hills: Sage.

Paul, R. (1990). *Critical thinking: What every person needs to survive in a rapidly changing world.* Rohnert Park, CA: Center for Critical Thinking and Moral Critique.

Paul, R., Binker, A. J. A., Martin, D., Vetrano, C., & Kreklau, H. (1989). *Critical thinking handbook: Grades 6–9.* Rohnert Park, CA: Center for Critical Thinking and Moral Critique.

Paulson, F., Paulson, P., & Meyer, C. (1991). What makes a portfolio a portfolio? *Educational Leadership, 48*(5), 60–64.

Pearson, P. D. (1984). Direct explicit teaching of reading comprehension. In G. Duffy, L. Roehler, & J. Mason (Eds.), *Comprehension Instruction: Perspectives and Suggestions* (pp. 222–33). New York: Longman.

Penrose, A. M. (1988). *Examining the role of writing in learning factual versus abstract material.* Paper presented at the American Educational Research Association, New Orleans.

Perkins, D. N., & Salomon, G. (1988). Teaching for transfer. *Educational Leadership, 45*(1), 22–32.

Peter Li, Inc. (1990). *Technology and Learning.* Dayton, OH: Peter Li, Inc.

Peterson, J. M. (1989). Remediation is no remedy. *Educational Leadership, 46*(6), 24–25.

Peterson, K. (1981). *Making sense of principals' work.* Paper presented at the annual meeting of the American Educational Research Association, Los Angeles.

Piaget, J. (1976). *Judgment and reasoning in the child.* Totowa, NJ: Littlefield & Adams.

Pollak, E. (1990, Jan/Feb). The state of videodiscs in education and training. *Instruction Delivery Systems, 4,* 12–14.

Pollak, R. A., & Pollak, R. R. (1990). Laserdisc technology emerges into the 1990's. *Media Methods, 27*(2), 18–19.

Polya, G. (1973). *How to solve it.* Princeton, NJ: Princeton University Press.

Powers, W. T. (1973). *Behavior: The control of perception.* Chicago: Aldine.

Prawat, R. S. (1989). Promoting access to knowledge, strategy, and disposition in students: A research synthesis. *Review of Educational Research, 59,* 1–42.

Pressley, M., Burkell, J., Cariglia-Bull, T., Lysynchuk, L., McGoldrick, J., Schneider, B., Snyder, B., Symon, S., & Woloshyn, V. (1990). *Cognitive instructional strategies that really work.* Cambridge, MA: Brookline Books.

Price, R. H., Cowen, E. L., Lorion, R. P., & Ramos-McKay, J. R. (1988). *14 ounces of prevention: A casebook for practitioners.* Washington, DC: American Psychological Association.

Purkey, W. W. (1970). *Self concept and school achievement.* Englewood Cliffs, NJ: Prentice-Hall.

Purkey, W. W., & Novak, J. (1988). *Education: By invitation only.* Bloomington, IN: Phi Delta Kappa.

Purkey, W. W., & Schmidt, J. (1987). *The inviting relationship: An expanded perspective for professional helping.* Englewood Cliffs, NJ: Prentice-Hall.

Purkey, W. W., & Schmidt, J. (1990). *Invitational learning for counseling and development.* Ann Arbor, MI: University of Michigan ERIC Clearinghouse.

Purkey, W. W., & Stanley, P. H. (1991). *Invitational teaching, learning and living.* Washington, DC: National Education Association.

Raney, P., & Robbins, P. (1989). Professional growth and support through peer coaching. *Educational Leadership, 46*(8), 35–38.

Resnick, L. B. (1987). *Education and learning to think.* Washington, DC: National Academy Press.

Reyes, M. L. (1991). *The "one size fits all" approach to literacy.* Paper presented at the annual meeting of the American Educational Research Association, Chicago.

Rhodes, J. (1989). *A report on the correlation of essential learning skills and standardized tests.* A report to Linn-Benton Education Service District, Albany, Oregon.

Rich, H. L., & Ross, S. M. (1989). Students' time on learning tasks in special education. *Exceptional Children, 55,* 508–15.

Robbins, P. (1984). *The Napa-Vacaville follow through research project.* Final report presented to the National Institute of Education, Washington, DC.

Robbins, P. (1991). *How to plan and implement a peer coaching program.* Alexandria, VA: ASCD.

Rogers, C. R. (1969). *Freedom to learn.* Columbus, OH: Charles E. Merrill.

Rosenholtz, S. (1989). *Teachers' workplace.* White Plains, NY: Longman.

Russell, A. (1990, Winter/Spring). Exploring the territory west of childhood: The early teens. *Carnegie Quarterly, 35,* 9.

Sarason, S. B. (1971). *The culture of the school and the problem of change.* Boston: Allyn and Bacon.

Sathe, V. C. (1983). Implications of corporate culture: A manager's guide to action. *Organizational Dynamics, 5,* 73–84.

Schafer, W. D, & Lissitz, R. W. (1987). Measurement training for school personnel: Recommendations and reality. *Journal of Teacher Education, 38*(3), 57–63.

Schlechty, P. (1976). *Teaching and social behavior: Toward an organizational theory of instruction.* Boston: Allyn and Bacon.

Scholastic Inc. (1990). *Point of view: A scholastic history processor.* New York: Scholastic Inc.

Schwartz, P., & Ogilvy, J. (1979). *The emergent paradigm: Changing patterns of thought and belief.* Menlo Park, CA: Values and Lifestyles Program.

Schweinhart, L. J., Weikart, D. P., & Larner, M. B. (1986). Consequences of three preschool curriculum models through age 15. *Early Childhood Research Quarterly, 1,* 15–45.

Sergiovanni, T. (1992). *Moral leadership: Getting to the heart of school improvement.* San Francisco: Jossey-Bass.

Shanahan, T., & Tierney, R. J. (1990). Reading-writing connections: The relations among three perspectives. In J. Zutell, S. McCormick, M. Connolly, & P. O'Keefe (Eds.), *Literacy theory and research: Analyses from multiple paradigms,* 39th Yearbook. Chicago: National Reading Conference.

Sharan, S., & Sharan, Y. (1976). *Small group teaching.* Englewood Cliffs, NJ: Educational Technology Publications.

Shavelson, R. (1988). Contributions of educational research to policy and practice: Constructing, challenging, changing cognition. *Educational Researcher, 17*(7), 4–11, 22.

Shavelson, R. J., & Stern, P. (1981). Research on teachers' pedagogical thoughts, judgments, decisions and behavior. *Review of Educational Research, 41,* 455–98.

Shepard, L. (1989). Why we need better assessments. *Educational Leadership, 46*(7), 4–9.

Simonds, R. L. (1985). *How to elect Christians to public office.* Costa Mesa, CA: National Association of Christian Educators/Citizens for Excellence in Education.

Sinatra, R. (1986). *Visual literacy connections to thinking, reading and writing.* Springfield, IL: Thomas Books.

Sirotnik, K. (1985). *Responsibility versus accountability.* Paper presented at the annual meeting of the American Educational Research Association.

Sizer, T. (1983). High school reform: The need for engineering. *Phi Delta Kappan, 64*(10), 679–83.

Sizer, T. (1984). *Horace's compromise: The dilemma of the American high school.* Boston: Houghton Mifflin.

Skinner, B. F. (1951). How to teach animals. *Scientific American, 185*(2), 26–29.

Skinner, B. F. (1953). *Science and human behavior.* New York: Macmillan.

Skinner, B. F. (1957). *Contingencies of reinforcement.* New York: Appleton-Century-Crofts.

Slavin, R. (1987). Mastery Learning Reconsidered, *Review of Educational Research, 57,* 175–213.

Slavin, R. (1980). *Using cooperative team learning.* Baltimore: Johns Hopkins University, Center for Social Organization of Schools.

Slavin, R., Leavey, M., & Madden, N. (1982). *Team-assisted individualization: Mathematics teacher's manual.* Baltimore: Johns Hopkins University, Center for Social Organization of Schools.

Smith, F. (1982). *Understanding reading.* New York: Holt, Rinehart and Winston.

Smith, F. (1985). A metaphor for literacy: Creating worlds or shunting information. In D. Olson, N. Torrance, & A. Hildyard (Eds.), *Literacy, language, and learning* (pp. 195–216). Cambridge: Cambridge University Press.

Smith, F. (1986). *Insult to intelligence.* New York: Arbor House.

Smith, L., Dwyer, D., Prunty, J., & Kleine, P. (1987). Images of schooling: The classroom in the school context. *Theory into Practice, 26,* 72–77.

Soled, S. W. (1987, April). *Teaching processes to improve both higher and lower mental process achievement.* Paper presented at the annual meeting of the American Educational Research Association, Washington, DC.

Sousa, D., & Donovan, J. (1990). Four year study of Hunter Model show student achievement gains in some areas. *The Developer, 1*(4), 6.

Spady, W. G. (1981). *Outcome-based instructional management: A sociological perspective.* N/E–P–80–0194. Washington, DC: National Institute of Education.

Spady, W. G. (1988). Organizing for results: The basis of authentic restructuring and reform. *Educational Leadership, 46*(2), 4–10.

Spady, W. G., & Marshall, K. (1991). Beyond traditional outcome-based education. *Educational Leadership, 49*(2), 67–72.

Spandel, V., & Stiggins, R. J. (1990). *Creating writers: Linking assessment and writing instruction.* New York: Longman.

Stafford, W. (1990). *Invitational Education Forum, 10*(4), 5.

Stahl, S. A., & Miller, P. D. (1989). Whole language and language approaches for beginning reading: A quantitative synthesis. *Review of Educational Research, 59,* 87–116.

Stebbins, L. (1976). *Education as experimentation: A planned variation model. Vol. III, A. Findings: Cohort II, Interim Findings: Cohort III.* Cambridge, MA: Abt Associates.

Stebbins, L., St. Pierre, R., Proper, E., Anderson, R., & Cerva, T. (1977). *Education as experimentation: A planned variation model. Vol. IV, A-D. An Evaluation of Follow Through.* Cambridge, MA: Abt Associates.

Stiggins, R. J. (1987). Designing performance assessments. *Educational Measurements: Issues and Practice, 6*(3), 33–42.

Stiggins, R. J., Conklin, N. F., & Associates (1992). *In teachers' hands: Investigating the practice of classroom assessment.* Albany: SUNY Press.

Stone, R. (1984). *A comparison of learning rate of low and high-achievers under mastery learning: A test of Bloom's proposition.* Unpublished doctoral dissertation, University of San Francisco.

Straker, N. (1988). Interactive video: A cost-effective model for mathematics and science classrooms. *The British Journal of Educational Technology, 19*(3), 202.

Tallarico, I. (1984). *Effects of ecological factors on elementary school student performance on norm-referenced standardized tests: Non-reading behaviors.* Unpublished doctoral dissertation, University of San Francisco.

Teale, W. H., & Sulzby, E. (1986). *Emergent literacy: Writing and reading.* Norwood, NJ: Ablex.

Thompson, J. (1967). *Organizations in action.* New York: McGraw-Hill.

Tierney, R. J., Carter, M. A., & Desai, L. E. (1991). *Portfolio assessment in the reading-writing classroom.* Norwood, MA: Christopher-Gordon Publishers, Inc.

Tierney, R. J., & Shanahan, T. (1991). Research on the reading-writing relationship: Interactions, transactions, and outcomes. In R. Barr, M. L. Kamil, P. B. Mosenthal, & P. D. Pearson (Eds.), *Handbook of reading research,* Vol. 2. White Plains, NY: Longman.

Tonjes, M. J. (1991). *Secondary reading, writing, and learning.* Boston: Allyn & Bacon.

Torrance, E. P. (1986). Teaching creative and gifted learners. In M. C. Wittrock (Ed.), *Handbook of research on teaching,* Third edition (pp. 630–47). New York: Macmillan.

Trelease, J. (1985). *The read-aloud handbook.* New York: Penguin.

Trickett, E. J., & Moos, R. H. (1973). The social environment of junior high and high school classrooms. *Journal of Educational Psychology, 65,* 93–102.

Tyson, H., & Woodward, A. (1989). Why students aren't learning very much from textbooks. *Educational Leadership, 47*(3), 14–17.

Valencia, S. (1990). A portfolio approach to classroom reading assessment. *The Reading Teacher, 43,* 338–40.

Valencia, S. W., & Pearson, P. D. (1988). Principles for classroom comprehension assessment. *Remedial and Special Education, 9*(1), 26–35.

Van Nostrand (1979, March). Writing and the generation of knowledge. *Social Education,* 178–80.

Voyager Company (1990). *Ludwig von Beethoven symphony no. 9.* Santa Monica, CA: Voyager.

Vygotsky, L. S. (1978). *Mind in society.* Cambridge: Harvard University Press.

Walberg, H. J. (1984). Improving the productivity of America's schools. *Educational Leadership, 41*(8), 19–27.

Walberg, H. J. (1988). Response to Slavin: What's the best evidence? *Educational Leadership, 46*(2), 28.

Walberg, H. J. (1990). Productive teaching and instruction: Assessing the knowledge base. *Phi Delta Kappan, 71,* 470–78.

Wales, C. E. (1979). Does how you teach make a difference? *Engineering Education, 69,* 394–398.

Wales, C. E., & Stager, R. A. (1977). *Guided design.* Morgantown, WV: University Center for Guided Design.

Warren, D. (1990). Passage of rites: On the history of educational reform in the United States. In J. Murphy (Ed.), *The educational reform movement of the 1980s* (pp. 57–81). Berkeley, CA: McCutchan Publishing Corporation.

Watzlawick, P., Weakland, J., & Fisch, R. (1974). *Change: Principles of problem formation and problem resolution.* New York: W. W. Norton and Company.

Webb, N. (1982). Student interaction and learning in small groups. *Review of Educational Research, 52,* 421–45.

Weber, A. (1990). Linking ITIP and the writing process. *Educational Leadership, 47*(5), 35–39.

Weikart, D. P., Rogers, L., Adcock, C., & McClelland, D. (1971). *The cognitively oriented curriculum: A framework for teachers.* Urbana, IL: National Association for the Education of Young Children.

White, M. A. (1987). *What curriculum for the information age?* Hillsdale, NJ: Erlbaum.

Wiggins, G. (1989). A true test: Toward authentic and equitable forms of assessment. *Phi Delta Kappan, 70,* 703–13.

Winograd, P., & Hare, V. C. (1988). Direct instruction of reading comprehension strategies: The nature of teacher explanation. In C. Weinstein, E. T. Goetz, & P. Alexander (Eds.), *Learning and study strategies: Assessment, instruction, and evaluation* (pp.121–40). New York: Academic Press.

Winograd, P., & Paris, S. (1988). A cognitive and motivational agenda for reading instruction. *Educational Leadership, 46*(4), 30–36.

Winograd, P., Paris, S., & Bridge, C. (1991). Improving the assessment of literacy. *The Reading Teacher, 45,* 108–16.

Wishnick, K. (1989). *Using measures of instructional alignment to predict standardized test scores among fourth grade mastery learning students.* Unpublished doctoral dissertation, University of San Francisco.

Wittrock, M. C. (Ed.) (1986). *Handbook of Research on Teaching,* Third Edition. New York: Macmillan Publishing Company and the American Educational Research Association.

Wixson, K., & Peters. C. (1987). Comprehension assessment: Implementing an interactive view of reading. *Educational Psychologist, 22,* 333–56.

Wolmut, P. (1988). *On the matter of testing misinformation.* Paper presented at the Science Research Associates, Inc. International Conference, Phoenix.

Zeig, J. K., & Munion, W. M. (1990). *What is psychotherapy?* San Francisco: Jossey-Bass.

AUTHOR INDEX

Abrami, P. C., Leventhal, L. and Perry, R. P., 455
Abt Associates, 75, 134, 144
Afflerbach, P. and Johnston, P., 1984, 238
Airasian, P. W., 115, 120, 245
Allington, R., 235
American Federation of Teachers, 57
Anderson, L., 235
Anderson, L. W., and Burns, R.B., 107
Anderson, R. C., Hiebert, E. F., Scott, J. A., and Wilkinson, I. A., 230
Anderson, R. C., Osborn, J., and Tierney, R., 234
Anderson, R. C., Wilson, J., and Fielding, L., 233
Applebee, A., 250
Applebee, A. N., Langer, J. A., and Mullis, I. V. A., 57
Armbruster, B., Anderson, T., and Osterag, J., 87
Armbruster, B., Osborn, J., and Davison, A., 234
Aronson, E., 37, 46
Arredondo, D. E., and Block, J. H., 464

Barnes, D., and Barnes, D., 249, 264
Becker, W. C., and Engelmann, S., 148
Ben Peretz, M., and Bramme, R., 177
Bereiter, C., and Engelmann, S., 130
Berliner, D., 442
Berman, P., and McLaughlin, M. W., 7
Berruetta-Clement, J. R., Schweinhart, L. J., Barnett, W. S., Epstein, A. S., and Weikart, D. P., 292, 303
Bissett, D., 233
Block, J. H., 13, 176, 392
Block, J. H., and Anderson, L. W., 97, 154, 177
Block, J. H., and Burns, R. B., 91
Block, J. H., Efthim, H. E., and Burns, R. B., 91, 97, 106, 177, 383

Block, J. H., and King, N. R., 87
Bloom, B. S., 95, 96, 176, 392, 108, 154,
Bortnick, R. M., 90
Bowsher, J., 386
Boyd, W. L., 8
Brandt, R., 317
Bredekamp, S., 304
Brennan, A., Bridge, C., and Winograd, P., 234
Bridge, C., 233, 234
Brookover, W. B., Schweitzer, J. H., Scheider, J. M., Beady, C. H., Flood, P. K., and Wisenbaker, J. M., 390
Bruner, J. S. 135
Burns, R. B., 97

Calkins, L., 237
Carnine, D., Granzin, A., and Becker, W., 131.
Carnine, D., and Kameenui, E., 135, 143
Carroll, J. B., 176, 387-388, 391, 392, 394
Catton, B., 252
Cauce, A. M., Comer, J. P., and Schwartz, B. A., 424, 427
Champlin, J. R., 393-94
Champlin, J. R., and Mamary, A., 400
Chance, P., 69
Cicerelli, 303
Cleverley, J., and Phillips, D. C., 289
Cochran-Smith, M., 234
Cohen, S. A., 38, 154, 171, 173, 176, 180
Cohen, S. A., and Hyman, J. S., 172
Cohen, S. A., and Stover, G., 169
Coleman, J. S., Campbell, E., Hobson, C., McPartland, J., Mood, A., Weinfeld, F., and York, R., 315-19, 388-89
College Board, 57
Colvin-Murphy, C., 263
Commission on the Humanities, 57
Committee on Economic Development, 294

Author Index

Consortium for Longitudinal Studies, 290
Copeland, K. A., 263
Crabbe, A. B., 69
Crandall, D. P., 462
Cronin, D. P., 133, 152
Csikzentmihalyi, M., 90
Cuban, L., 3, 286, 437
Davidson, M. L., and O'Leary, P.W., 464
Deci, E., 12
Delpit, L. D., 152
Deming, W. E., 403
Deutsch, M., 27,28
DeVries, D., and Edwards, K., 46
Dossey, J. A., Mullis, I. V. A., Lindquist, M. M., Chambers, D. L., 57
Doyle, W., 69
Dreeben, R., 224
Drewry, H., O'Connor, T., and Freidel, F., 251
Duffy, G., Roehler, L., and Hermann, B., 238
Durkin, D., 236, 238
Durst, R. K., and Newell, G. E., 66

Edmonds, R. R., 317, 319–320, 322, 331, 390
Edwards, P., 232
Elia, J. S. I., 172, 177
Elliott, S. N., and Shapiro, E. S., 152
Emig, J., 250
Engelmann, S., and Carnine, D., 138
English, R. A., 276
Ennis, R. H., 58
Erikson, E. H., 304
Ewy, R., 445

Fahey, P. A., 172–173, 177
Fast, H., 259
Feldhusen, J., 271
Ferstar, C. B., and Skinner, B. F., 168
Finn, C. E., 389, 390
Fisher, C. W., and Hiebert, E. F., 69

Flavell, J. H., 135
Flexner, S. B., and Houck, L. C., 60
Fraatz, J. M., 229
Friedlander, R., 81
Fullan, M. G., 218, 436
Fullan, M. G., and Hargreaves, A., 464
Fullan, M. G., and Stiegelbauer, S., xiii, 471
Futrell, M. H., 57

Gabor, A., 404
Gersten, R., Becker, W., Heiry, T., and White, W. A., 149
Gersten, R., Darch, C., and Gleason, M., 148
Gersten, R., and Keating, T., 149
Glasser, W., 1990, 400, 412, 414
Glickman, C. D., 218, 224
Golden, J. L., Berquist, G. F., and Colemen, W. E., 58
Goodlad, J., xiii
Goodman, K., 154,
Goodman, Y. M., 161
Gourley, T. J., 69
Graby, R. P., 173–174, 174–175
Graves, D., 233, 242
Gray, W., 443, 447
Gullickson, A. R., and Hopkins, D. K., 113
Guskey, T. R., 4, 98, 100, 107, 108, 463, 468, 470
Guskey, T. R., and Block, J. H., 8, 468
Guskey, T. R., and Gates, S. L., 1986, 106, 383
Guskey, T. R., and Kiefer, E., 1989, 242, 244
Guskey, T. R., and Pigott, T. D., 1988, 91, 106, 107
Guskey, T. R., Barshis, D., and Easton, J. Q., 1982, 106
Guskey, T. R., Passaro, P. D., and Wheeler, W., 1991, 468

Author Index

Haney, W., 134, 146
Hansen, J., 244
Hargreaves, A., 214, 215
Hartke, J. P., 72
Havemen, R., 7
Hayes, D. A., 263
Haynes, N. M., Comer, J. P., and Hamilton-Lee, M., 424, 425, 426, 427
Haynes, N. M., and Comer, J. P., 427
Hiebert, E. H., 107
Henderson, R. W., 86
Herman, J., and Dorr-Bremme, D. W., 116
Hofmeister, A., Lubke, M., and Peterson, L., 86
Hohmann, M., Banet, B., and Weikart, D. P., 294
Hohmann, M., and Weikart, D. P., in press, 294
Honig, B., 8
Hopfenberg, W., Levin, H. M., and Associates, 281
Huberman, M., and Miles, M. B., 460
Hughes, H., 86
Hunter, M., 190, 203, 204
Hunter, M., and Barker, G., 190
Hunter, M., and Russell, D., 194
Hutchins, R., 313

Ideal Learning, 84

Jaques, E., 67
Jenkinson, E., 76
Johnson, D. W., 1991, 33
Johnson, D. W., 1993, 33
Johnson, D. W., and Johnson, F., 33, 50
Johnson, D. W., Johnson, R., and Holubec, E., 25, 28, 31, 33, 38
Johnson, D. W., and Johnson, R. T., 30, 36, 42, 43, 44, 46, 47, 48, 239, 260
Johnson, R., 86
Johnston, P., 241

Johnston, P. H., and Winograd, P. N., 242
Jones, B., and Idol, L., 236
Jourard, S. M., 346
Joyce, B., 107
Joyce, B., Weil, M., and Showers, B., 12
Joyce, B., and Showers, B., 214, 218

Kagan, S., 39
Karnes, M. B., Schwedel, A. M., and Williams, M. B., 302
Katz, L., 304
Kennedy, M., Fisher, M. B., and Ennis, R. H., 60
Kinder, D., and Bursuck, W., 137
Kirchner, G., 86
Knapp, M. S., Shield, P. M., and Turnbull, B. J., 269
Knight, M. B., 72
Knight, S., and Stallings, J. A., 276
Koczor, M. L., 170-171
Kuhn, T., 72
Kulik, C. C., Kulik, J.A., and Bangert-Drowns, R. L., 91, 106, 107, 383
Kulik, J. A., Kulik, C. C., and Bangert-Drowns, R. L., 107

Langer, J. A., 250
Langer, J. A. and Applebee, A. N., 118, 250
Latham, G., 456, 457
Leonard, W. H., 86
Levin, H. M., 272, 276, 281, 284
Levine, D. U., 168, 371, 383
Lezotte, L. W., 322, 390
Lieberman, A., 435
Lincoln, E. G. and Guba, Y. S., 72
Lipman, M., 69
Little, J., 1990, 221
Loucks-Horsley, S., Harding, C. K., Arbuckle, M. G., Murray, L. B., Dubea, C., and Williams, M. K., 452, 456, 462

Author Index

Louis, K. S., and Miles, M. B., 435
Lysakowski R., and Walberg, H., 154, 177
Lytle S., and Botel, M., 235

Malone, T., and Lepper, M., 1986, 12, 87
Mandeville, G., and Rivers, J., 203, 204
Marshall, J. D., 250, 262
Marzano, R. J., 63, 69
Marzano, R. J., Pickering, D. J., Arredondo, D., Brandt, R., and Blackburn, G., 63
Marzano, R. J., Pickering, D. J., and Brandt, R. S., 464–467
McCarthy, J., and Still, S., 267, 276
McCracken, H. A., and McCracken, M. J., 232
McDaniel, M. A., and Schlager, M. S., 134
McGinley, W., 273
McKey, R.H., Condelli, L., Ganson, H., Barrett, B., McConkey, C., and Plantz, M., 303
McLaughlin, M., 10, 457
Mehrens, W., and Kaminski, J., 172, 181
Meichenbaum, D., 72
Mevarech, Z. R., 104, 459, 463
Miller, L. B., and Bizzell, R. P., 302
Mizer, J. E., 354
Morrow, L., 233
Morrow, L., and Weinstein, C., 233
Murphy, J., 5

National Business Roundtable, 390–391
National Council of Teachers of Mathematics, 129
National Education Association, 57
National School Boards Association, 86
National Science Board Commission on Precollege Education in Mathematice, Science, and Technology, 57
Neill, D., and Medina, N., 242
Nicholls, J., 242

Nickerson, R. S., Perkins, D. N., and Smith, E. E., 69
Niedermeyer, F. C., 168
Niedermeyer, F. C., and Yelon, S., 168
Nistler, R. J., 248
Nolen, L., 175
Norris, S. P., and Ennis, R. H., 118

Olmstead, P. P., and Weikart, D. P., 290
Osborn, D. K., 289

Palincsar, A., Ransom, K., and Derber, S., 238
Panel on the General Professional Education of the Physician and College Preparation for Medicine, 57
Pappas, C., Kiefer, B., and Levstik, L., 235
Paris, S. G., Cross,D., and Lipson, M. Y., 239
Paris, S. G., Lawton, T. A., Turner, J. C., and Roth, J. L., 242
Paris, S. G., Lipson, M. Y., Wixson, K. K., 238, 239
Paris, S. G., and Winograd, P., 237
Passow, A. H., 5
Patton, M. Q., 73
Paul, R., 58, 59, 70
Paul, R., Binker, A. J. A., Martin, D., Vetrano, C., and Kreklau, H., 61
Pearson, P. D., 238
Penrose, A. M., 263
Perkins, D. N., and Salomon, G., 174
Peterson, J. M., 271
Peterson, K., 227
Piaget, J., 59
Pollak, R. A., and Pollak, R. R., 86
Polya, G., 135
Powers, W., 405
Prawat, R. S., 135
Pressley, M., Burkell, J., Cariglia-Bull, T., Lysynchuk, L., McGoldrick, J., Schneider, B., Snyer, B., Symon, S., and Woloshyn, V., 237

Price, R. H., Cowen, E. L., Lorion, R. P., and Ramos–McKay, J. R., 293
Purkey, W. W., 346
Purkey, W. W., and Novak, J., 343, 362
Purkey, W. W., and Schmidt, J., 359, 365
Purkey, W. W., and Stanley, P. H., 343

Raney, P., and Robbins, P., 228
Resnick, L., 69
Reyes, M. L., 151
Rich, H. L., and Ross, S. M., 130
Robbins, P., 214, 216, 221
Rogers, C. R., 346
Rosenholtz, S., 213
Russell, D., 194
Russell, A., 264
Sarason, S. B., 433
Sathe, V. C., 73, 74
Schafer, W. D., and Lassitz, R. W., 113
Schlechty, P., 10
Scholastic Inc., 82
Schweinhart, L. J., Weikart, D. P., and Larner, M.B., 301, 303
Sergiovanni, T., 6
Shanahan, T. and Tierney, R. J., 250
Shavelson, R. J., 13
Shavelson, R. J., and Stern, P., 116
Shepard, L., 240
Simonds, R. L., 76
Sinatra, R., 87
Sirotnik, K., 10
Sizer, T. R., 387
Skinner, B. F., 166
Slavin, R., 4, 106
Slavin, R., Leavey, M., and Madden, N., 39, 46
Smith, F., 151, 230, 72
Smith, L., Dwyer, D., Prunty, J., and Kleine, P., 10
Soled, S. W., 104

Sousa, D., and Donovan, J., 204
Spady, W. G., 371, 387
Spady, W. G., and Marshall, K., 387, 395, 396
Spandel, V., and Stiggins, R. J., 120
Stafford, W., 342
Stahl, S. A., and Miller, P. D., 162
Stebbins, L., 144
Stebbins, L., St. Pierre, R., Proper, E., Anderson, R., and Cerva, T., 144, 146
Stiggins, R. J., 122, 245
Stiggins, R. J. and Conklin, N. F., 113, 116
Stone, R., 178, 179
Stover, G., 171–172
Straker, N., 86

Tallarico, I., 171–172
Teale W. H., and Sulzby, E., 232, 233
Thompson, J., 3
Tierney, R. J., Carter, M., and Desai, L., 242
Tierney, R. J., and Shanahan, T., 263, 264
Tonjes, M. J., 264
Torrance, E. P., 69
Trelease, J., 230
Trickett E. J., and Moos, R. H., 427
Tyson, H., and Woodward, A., 130

Valencia, S., 242
Valencia, S., and Pearson, P. D., 118
Vygotsky, L. S., 230

Walberg, H. J., 106, 107, 108
Wales, C. E., 69
Wales C. E., and Stager, R. A., 69
Warren, D., 3
Watzlawick, P., Weakland, J., and Fisch, R., 72
Webb, N., 239

Author Index

Weber, A., 464
Weikart, D. P., Rogers, L., Adcock, C., and McClelland, D., 294
White, M. A., 86
Wiggins, G., 245
Winograd, P., and Hare, V. C., 239
Winograd, P., and Paris, S., 240
Winograd, P., Paris, S., and Bridge, C., 241
Wishnick, K., 162
Wixson, K., and Peters, C., 241
Wolmut, P., 113

Zeig, J. K., and Munion, W. M., 72

SUBJECT INDEX

Note: Underlining represents the pages on which tables may be found.

Accelerated Schools Project, 269
accelerated schools: and
at–risk students, 269–71; definition of, 275; district support of, 284–85; high expectations, need for, 288; improvements to, 277; initiating, 277–80; and parents, 272, 274, 276, 278, 279, 283–84; principal, role in, 282; school–site empowerment, 273; and student achievement, 267–69, 276; time needed to create, 276, 281; unity of purpose, 272–73, 278; workshop in, 287–88;
accountability, 9, 164; of school staff for learning, 336–37; of student, 155, 188
achievement, measuring, 111; decline of, 179; distribution, *93*; distribution in mastery learning classroom, 97; of students using direct instruction, 144, 146
achievement, student: impact of schools on, 315–16, 317; and reading aloud, 234; and role of aptitude, 173; views of, 153;
active learning, 295, 304
administrators: and cooperative learning groups, 51–52; and role in peer coaching, 219–20, 225–26, 227; and role in accelerated schools, 282, 284–85; and role in effective schools, 326; need for constant investigation of options, 452
aptitude, 172–73, 177
assessment in schools, 111–128; definition of, 111, 115; and failure to develop proper tools, 114; good, 126; of literacy, 240–45; need for change, 127–128; people who use, 115; quality of, 124–26; teacher training in, 113, 169; and technology, 339. *See also* standardized tests
assessment methods, 121–24; performance, *122–23*, 156; personal communication, 123–24; *125;* portfolios, 242–45. *See also* standardized tests, portfolios, outcomes
assessment purposes, 114–17, 124–26; as "moment of truth," 156

at–risk students: accelerated instruction and, 134, 171, 172, 203, 293; and early childhood intervention, 292; high expectations, need for, 131, 133, 270–71, 288, 293, 374, 379–81; history of awareness of, 290, 315–16, 337; and impact of OBE on, 383–84; as needing more time, 339; and questions of equality of access, 314; schooling of, 129–30, 269–70, 285, 291, 330, 366; strengths of, 274
attribution theory, 191
authentic assessment, 397
authentic tasks, 231–42, 249, 407–409
authentic texts, 231, 232

Bay Area Writing Project, 263
Bloom, Benjamin S., 92, 93–94, 95, 96, 97
Brown vs. the Board of Education of Topeka, Kansas, 314

California Mentor Teacher Program, 221
child development and school reform, 416, 417. *See also* School Development Program
Citizens for Excellence in Education (CEE), 75–76
coercion: avoiding, 406–407; in learning, 403
cognitive stretching, 175
Comenius, John Amos, 25, 92
communication as assessment, 123–4; goals of, 150–51
competency testing, 389
competition, negative results of, 27–28, 242
computer–assisted instruction, 187
concept attainment, 187
content. *See* curriculum content.
contingent stimuli, 155
control theory, 405–406, 412–14
cooperation, definition of, 28
cooperative learning, 25–56; approaches to, 38–41; and critical thinking, 261; definition of, 28, 54–55; and direct instruction, 132; effects on students,

503

29, 34, 36, 38, 44, 45–47, 260; elements of, 30–33, *43*, 44, 55; history of, 25–26, 187; and impact on school structure, 27, 49–52; and individual accountability in, 32, 36; and literacy instruction, 239; necessity for, 52–55; obstacles to acceptance, 54, 56; as preparation for the workplace, 53–54; and teacher use of, 29, 50; and writing across the curriculum, 260–62

cooperative learning groups, types of, 36, 55–56; base, 34, 36, 56; formal, 34, 35, 55; informal, 34, 36, 55; and teacher tasks, 35, 36, 37–38, 56

core programs: definition of, 3, 135; and impact on schools, 13–15; and policy makers, 13

collaborative environments, creating, 334

critical thinking (higher order thinking): artifacts, development of, 66; banning of in schools, 76; call for, 57, 117, 134, 337; and direct instruction, 135; longevity of tasks, 66–67; and mastery learning, 104; tasks, *65*, *68*; multidimensionality of tasks, 63, 67, *65*; obstacles to implementation, 69, 70, 71; partial specification of tasks, 62, 63, 67; research on, 69; skills necessary for, 62, 185–186; strong sense, 59, 60, 70, 76; student control of tasks, 64–66, 67; teacher's role, 60, 67, 69; views of, 58, 129; virtues of, 70–71; weak sense, 60–61, 60, 69

culture: as barrier to critical thinking, 74; as paradigm, 73; student's, and accelerated schools, 275

curriculum, preschool. *See* High/Scope curriculum

curriculum alignment, 168–169

curriculum content: current, problems with, 331; issues in deciding on, 156, 164, 178, 184–186, 317, 331, 340

curriculum design, 134

decisions, types made, 183–193,

Deming, W. Edwards, 403–405, 406, 410; beliefs, 406–407,

Deutsch, Morton, 42

Dewey, John, 26

dimensions of learning, 464–68, 466

direct instruction: and at–risk students, 129–30, 131, 133, 134, 135, 144, 146; components of, 131–33; and critical thinking, 135; definition of, 130, 131, 136; examples of, 136–43; as exemplary, 149–50; and failure in early childhood education, 301–302; goals of, 131; and impact on students, 131, 133, 144–46, 148–49, 152; outcomes, 145, research on, 143–150; sample problems, *141*; teacher's role, 131, 132–133, 151–53; test scores, 147

discovery learning, 187

early childhood education: assumptions about, 308–309; as business investment, 294, 297–98; comparison of programs, 301–302; description of model program, 309–10; developing personal traits, 303–304; history of, 289–91; Perry Preschool Project, 292–99; plan–do–review sequence, 294–95; qualities of successful programs, 305–307; research on, 291–99; successful preschool programs, 301–302;

economically disadvantaged. *See at* risk

education: as a cooperative activity, 346; for all, 313, 342

effective schools: assumptions of, 326–27, 469; characteristics of, 319–20, 322–23; definition of, 317–18; early problems with creating, 321–22; first and second generation standards, 334–41; high expectations for all, 334–35; history of, 314–26, 330; and outcome–based education, 390; and parents, 341; prerequisites to, 328–29; research methods, 319; second–generation correlates, 333; and their districts, 324–26;

egocentric thinking 59–60

empowerment of teachers. *See* teachers.

Equality of Educational Opportunity, Coleman, Campbell, Hobson, McPartland, Mood, Weinfeld and York, 315–18, 388–89

ethnocentric thinking, 59–60, 72, 74–76
family. *See* parents.
federal intervention in schools, 6–7, 16, 273; and impact on teaching, 10, 273
formative assessment. *See* tests.

gifted children, 271

hands–on, 187
Head Start, 290, 307
Hegel, 73
heterogeneous grouping. *See* cooperative learning groups
High/Scope Curriculum, 294, 298, 302–307, *305*, 308, 310
higher–order thinking. *See* critical thinking.
hypermedia learning environment, as demanding interaction, 78; power of, 78, 80–81; examples of, 83–85; and writing, 83, 84–85; and impact on student learning, 86–87; and making learning fun, 88–89
hypermedia technology, 79–80: CD–ROM, 79–80; videodisc, 79–80; random access searching, 80; CDI (Compact Disc Interactive), 80; and preparing students for the future, 89–90; research on hypermedia and interactive learning, 85–87;

imaging, 186
independent goals. *See* individualized learning.
individual interests, 78, 100 (as guiding educational exploration);
individualized learning, student, 95, 100: effect on students, 28; as outcome of technology in classroom, 86;
information, increase of, 89, 247
instruction, direct. *See* direct instruction.
instructional alignment: aligning outcomes and instruction, 158–67; assessment in, 154, 156–57, 159; assumptions of, 154–56; background of, 165–69; and "cheating" on standardized tests, 172; components of, 154; definition of, 154, 165–66; instructional outcomes, 157–58; matching instruction with the test, 162–64; misaligned outcomes, examples of, 160–61, 162–63, 174; misalignment, 162, 196; misalignment and test scores, 170; performance indicators, 159–62; reasons for not promoting, 177–82; student learning, impact of on, 154, 169–76; teacher's task, 154, 156
instructional content. *See* curriculum content.
intentionality, as a component of good teaching, 353–54
interactive learning, 77–86; as key to school reform, 77;
International Alliance for Invitational Education, 359
invitational education: assumptions of, 346–48; characteristics of, *345*; definition, 343; Douglas Byrd Junior High School (example), 359–65; and dropout rate, 365; focus areas, 348, 350, *349*; goal of, 356–58; impact of invitational education, 364; invitation, levels of, 350–56
IQ, 191, 303

Japan, as management model, 403

learning. *See* student learning
learning logs, 255–57
learning retention, 192
learning strategies in reading and writing, 236–40
learning styles, 186–87
lesson as "learning opportunity," 193
lesson design, elements of 194–202
life patterns, factors contributing to, 299–301
literacy: assessment of, 240–45; definition of, 230, 246; as skills acquisition, 230, 234; social nature of, 230, 232
literacy instruction, 236–40: literate environments, 231–35; predictable books, 234–35; purpose of, 231; teaching strategies, 236–40; thematic units, 235
literature: reader–response teaching, 252–53; traditional teaching of, 252, 257

literature across the curriculum, 251–52, 253
mastery learning, 91–108, 470; correctives, 94, 95, 96, 98–100, 105; elements of, 97–103; enrichment activities, 99; feedback, 94, 95, 98, 105; history of, 92–94; inability to overcome ineffective school structure, 392–93; instructional components, congruence among, 101–103, *101;* methods, 94–96, 98; outcome–based education, 383; research on, 91, 106–107, 108; student writing, 102–103; teachers tasks in, 98, 99, 102–103, 104, 105, 106, *100*
mastery teaching: history of, 181–83; lesson design, 194–202; misconceptions about, 194, 204; student achievement, 203–204; teacher's tasks, 186, 470, 189–190, 192, 194–202
measurement, issues in, 317
modeling, 197–208; 210; 227–28
motivation: external, 191, 412; extrinsic, 190–91; internal motivation, 191; intrinsic motivation, 190; in learning, 87, 146
multimedia, 77, 78
Multimedia Resource Guide, 80

Napa Project, 203
National Assessment of Educational Progress holistic scoring rubric, 84–85
National Association for the Education of Young Children, 304
needs, basic, 412
needs assessment, 440–443, *441;* "big variables," 442–43, *442*
Next Century Schools, 360

observational learning, 187
operant theory, 166–68
outcome–based education (OBE): and at–risk students, 383–84; characteristics of, 368–71; definition, 368; design from the outcomes, 381–82; and effective schools, 390; impact of OBE on schools, 382–86; and need for high expectations, 379–81; as paradigm shift, 390, 392–97; premises of, 373–75, 469; principles of, 375–82; restructuring school schedule, 377–9; significant outcomes, 376–77
outcomes: assessment, 117–21; examples of, 118–19; of instructional alignment, 154–56; lack of definition, 180–81; learning, 188

paradigms in thinking, 72–74
parents: and accelerated schools, 272, 274, 276, 278, 279, 283–84; and effective schools, 341; involvement with direct instruction, 146, 148; and peer coaching, 218; and reading aloud, 232; and the School development Program, 422; and stress, and impact on students, 416; and successful children, 299–312; as users of assessment results, 116, 242
Parker, Francis, Colonel, 26
peer coaching: and avoidance of judgment, 209; and barriers to, 213; call for, 218; characteristics of, 211–212; benefits of, 216–17; constraints of, 217–28; definition of, 206; formal (in–class), 206–14; forms of, *207;* informal (out of class), 214–15; observation, 209–10; postconference, 211–13; preconference, 208–209; training for, 220–21, *222*
perceptual tradition, 344–45
performance assessment, 122–23, 155
performance indicators (PIs), 155–56, 159, 165
performance validation, 371
Perry Preschool Project, 292–99
Piaget, 74–75, 294, 295, 301
Plato, 58
Point of View interactive media program, 84–86
portfolios, 242–45, 340
predictable texts, 234–35
preschool programs. *See* early childhood education
principal: and impact on school effectiveness, 319; role of: 282, 322, 336; role of in accelerated schools, 282; and the School Development Program, 419–20
public schools: function of, 3; inability to